Habeas Corpus in America

CONSTITUTIONAL THINKING

Jeffrey K. Tulis and Sanford Levinson, *Editors*

Habeas Corpus in America

THE POLITICS OF INDIVIDUAL RIGHTS

Justin J. Wert

 University Press of Kansas

© 2011 by the University Press of Kansas

All rights reserved
Published by the University Press of Kansas (Lawrence, Kansas 66045), which was organized by the Kansas Board of Regents and is operated and funded by Emporia State University, Fort Hays State University, Kansas State University, Pittsburg State University, the University of Kansas, and Wichita State University

Library of Congress Cataloging-in-Publication Data

Wert, Justin J.

Habeas corpus in America : the politics of individual rights / Justin J. Wert.

p. cm. — (Constitutional thinking)

Includes bibliographical references and index.

ISBN 978-0-7006-1763-0 (cloth : alk. paper)

1. Habeas corpus—United States—History. I. Title.

KF9011.W47 2011

347.73'5—dc22

2010037275

British Library Cataloguing-in-Publication Data is available.

Printed in the United States of America

10 9 8 7 6 5 4 3 2 1

Contents

Foreword

I start with a confession. Like, I suspect, many liberal law professors, I have often taught cases involving habeas corpus—that is, the right to demand that the state justify its detention of prisoners—as if they all exemplified a basically timeless set of values reaching back to Magna Carta in 1215. I have done this especially when teaching about Abraham Lincoln's unilateral suspension of the right to habeas corpus. But, of course, these same debates have resurfaced with the Bush and Obama administrations' treatment of detainees who were captured around the world as part of the so-called Global War on Terrorism. Yet, notwithstanding my conviction that change is integral to the American constitutional tradition, I have tended to forget such realities when confronting something as basic to our notions of civil liberty as habeas corpus.

There are many reasons why I am delighted that Justin Wert's *Habeas Corpus in America: The Politics of Individual Rights,* is the first book in a new series, Constitutional Thinking, that Jeffrey K. Tulis and I are co-editing for the University Press of Kansas. His book is a remarkably readable and thorough history of an absolutely key notion that should lead readers, just as I have, to rethink basic propositions that they might well hold about habeas corpus. But an overriding reason for pleasure is how successfully Wert has integrated such a basic principle of liberal constitutionalism as habeas corpus into what has come to be called "American political development" or "American constitutional development," more particularly. As used here, the word *development* signals the belief that one cannot understand *any* American institution simply by looking back to a pristine moment in history or by engaging in philosophical analysis of what, say, the "best" notion of "equal protection" might be.

Professor Wert admirably summarizes his own book in the first sentence of his conclusion, provocatively titled "The Not-So-Great Writ of Liberty": "The account of habeas corpus in American political development offered in this book is predicated on the assumption that while habeas is often understood to be a purely legal mechanism, there have been as many if not more political determinants that have shaped the Great Writ of Liberty." Once one pays full attention to these "political determinants," especially if one believes that the United States is a reasonably "democratic" political order, then it is not surprising to discover the extent to which changes in conceptions (and the administration) of habeas corpus have as often served "the priorities of majoritarian politics" rather than as a "countermajoritarian check against executives or political majorities."

Perhaps most disturbing to many will be the demonstration that one central priority of *national* politics in the 1850s was to assure slave owners that their rights to recover runaway slaves would be respected, which meant, among other things, that state courts would not be allowed to grant a writ of habeas corpus to those arrested by the national government for aiding fugitive slaves. Today we may regard the supremacy of national over state courts as glaringly obvious, but this was not the case during the first seventy years of our post-constitutional polity when the question of federalism—the uncertain relationship of state and national governments—was the most pressing constitutional controversy, one that would, of course, ultimately tear the Union apart. To suppress Wisconsin's right to grant habeas to one of its citizens arrested by the United States, as the Supreme Court did in an eloquent nationalist opinion by Chief Justice Taney, was, among other things, to underscore the subordination of antislavery states to the existing national majority belief that preservation of the Union required full recognition of the rights of slave owners, even to including the detention of those who cast their lot with the slaves themselves.

Things did change somewhat after the Civil War when a temporary majority of Congress, plus President Grant, believed that national power, including the power to grant habeas corpus, should indeed be used to protect newly freed African Americans from those who wished to keep them "in their place" through unwarranted detentions. But, as we all know, this "reconstructive," regime-change-oriented commitment lasted but a few years to be followed by the Compromise of 1877 and a return to white-dominated governments and the subordination of racial minorities. Thus, Wert writes, "By the 1890s, then, habeas's role as a potent tool of regime enforcement for recalcitrant Southern states receded into the background as Congress and the federal judiciary deliberately chose to redirect federal judicial power—and habeas power in particular—away from Reconstruction's initial goals. . . ."

To be sure, Wert presents some counterexamples, perhaps the most important being the so-called habeas corpus revolution led by Justice William J. Brennan during the heyday of the Warren Court. An important contribution of Wert's study is his demonstration of exactly how much this development required an almost willful reinterpretation of the past history of habeas corpus and, more to the point, how much the Brennan-led revolution—by putting state court convictions at risk if they did not accord criminal defendants sufficient protection of their rights, including the suppression of illegally seized evidence and confessions given without adequate notice by the police of the right to remain silent—generated genuine problems for the American system of criminal justice. Unsurprisingly, this radical change in habeas corpus law—

fostered by judges allied with a liberal political coalition—met with stiff resistance, beginning with Richard Nixon's 1968 campaign, from conservatives who increasingly occupied seats of power in Washington, including the Supreme Court, to which the Democrats made no appointments from 1967 to 1993. As a result, the expansion of habeas corpus rights receded, thus attesting, as Wert demonstrates so well, the degree to which the actualities of habeas corpus, at any particular moment in our history, are embedded in the actualities of our polities. Indeed, democratic President Clinton signed without protest legislation passed in 1996 by a Republican Congress designed to cut back access to federal courts by state prisoners.

There are, obviously, many productive ways of engaging in "constitutional thinking." But one of them, surely, is careful attention to the historical development—and therefore changes—in basic legal doctrines and the support given them by varying political parties and institutions particularly at key moments of social transformation. Wert's book should lead all of its readers to rethink central assumptions about the role played by habeas corpus—and courts interpreting its meaning—in American constitutional history.

Sanford Levinson
W. St. John Garwood and W. St. John Garwood Jr.
Centennial Chair in Law, University of Texas Law School,
Professor of Government, University of Texas at Austin

Preface

During the summer of 2001 I set out to research and write about habeas corpus, the purported Great Writ of Liberty. Like many others before me—and, I hope, many after me—I was first intrigued with Abraham Lincoln's use (or nonuse) of the writ during the first months of his fateful presidency. Speaking before a Congress that he called into special session on 4 July 1861, Lincoln asked those representatives who still remained with Union a question that we today still have not answered adequately: "Are all the laws but one to go unexecuted and the government itself go to pieces, lest that one be violated?" Few questions, I thought, were as important as this one, not only from the perspective of political science, but also from the perspective of all citizens who take seriously a necessary sense of duty to country. I would now go forth and attempt to chart the contours of Lincoln's question, taking as my case study his controversial suspension of habeas during the Civil War years. I was confident that a sustained look at habeas's suspension could yield new perspectives and new ways of understanding this immensely important question.

The September 11, 2001, terrorist attack on the World Trade Center did not change my substantive focus—Lincoln's suspension was still worthy of fresh eyes—but it did change the breadth and scope of my analysis. I now thought that the scope of my work not only had to expand to the use of the writ during the first year or two after 9/11, but also had to account for and compare previous uses of the writ during times of war or crisis in American political history.

But as I began to read and think about the use of the writ during times of war, I quickly realized that habeas corpus played just as important a role in times of peace as it did during times of war or crisis. In fact, the use of habeas during war—a thankfully rare occurrence—was largely determined by the use of the writ immediately before the crisis. With this small (and admittedly commonsensical) discovery, I then set out to examine the development of the Great Writ in peacetime as well as during wartime.

The three most recent cases brought before the Supreme Court challenging various issues relating to the war on terror seem to bear out this point. In *Hamdi v. Rumsfeld,* the Court ruled that while the president was authorized to hold individuals as enemy combatants, they were nevertheless allowed to challenge this designated status.[1] In *Rasul v. Bush,* Justice Anthony Kennedy led a majority that allowed noncitizen detainees held at Guantánamo Naval base also to challenge their status through the writ of habeas corpus, severely undercutting the Bush administration's understanding of the jurisdictional reach of the federal courts.[2] And in *Boumediene v. Bush,* the Court—again led by Justice Kennedy—undercut the Bush administration—and Congress—in arguing that the Military Commissions Act (MCA) unconstitutionally suspended habeas rights.[3] While each of these cases dealt with issues directly related to wartime exigencies, we lose a critical perspective by viewing them solely from the perspective of our post-9/11 world. In important ways, the arguments advanced in these cases by the Bush administration—as well as by most of the justices who had been appointed by Republican presidents—were simply extensions of arguments over the constitutionality of peacetime law and order issues advanced by the larger conservative regime over the preceding decades. From this perspective, then, the war on terror habeas cases were inflected with a familiar set of political predilections.

This wider lens soon led me to the book's overarching argument that habeas corpus is a tool of politics and politicians as much as it is a tool of the law and of judges. Understandably, we want the law to be objective, and we want the courts that interpret the law and mete out its judgments to do so without regard to anything other than fidelity to our Constitution and the dictates of justice. Often enough, though, we see this process play out in the opposite direction, and the account of habeas in this book bears this out. But for two important reasons, we should not abandon our normative hope in the rule of law and the ideals of limited government that our Constitution and laws create, especially in the case of habeas corpus. For one, discrete uses and abuses of habeas corpus that are often initiated by politicians, and then carried out by courts, have a life of their own, independent from those who wield power. Uses of the Great Writ of Liberty by antebellum political regimes to vindicate the "rights" of slave catchers are certainly ugly examples of habeas's less than perfect history, but the changes to habeas that provided for these ignoble uses of the writ remained intact long enough for others, such as Reconstruction Republicans, to use them for far nobler purposes. And lest we imagine that courts—especially the Supreme Court—are simply bit players in larger political machinations involving the use and abuse of habeas, we see in the pages that follow a degree of judicial independence from politics that should lead us to reject arguments that simply equate law to politics. Like any institution, courts face pressures from outside of their four walled confines, and they are made up of individuals who understandably try to get their way, but as my account of the development of habeas corpus demonstrates, courts will always fight to maintain at least some degree of independence when politics threatens core features of their institution and the rule of law more generally.

As with so many other fortuitous events in my professional life, this book is the result of the mentorship of Rogers M. Smith. Walking on Locust Walk at the University of Pennsylvania one fateful afternoon in fall 2001, after a less than impressive attempt to convince him that a new study of Lincoln's suspension of habeas corpus was badly needed, Rogers wisely asked me about the use of habeas more generally. When I could not provide an answer, he then gently suggested that it would be interesting to know a little more about the writ. As always, his was a good suggestion. There has been no better mentor, both professionally and personally.

The two other members of my dissertation committee, Marie Gottschalk and John DiIulio, were painstaking readers who never hesitated to challenge me to make better arguments. My first seminar at Penn, "American Political Development," was led by Marie. I have been convinced ever since. John DiIulio always made me feel that what I was doing was important work even when I could not be convinced otherwise. And Mark Graber, who has read almost every iteration of this project, served as an unofficial mentor from the very beginning. I consider it an honor that he continues to show interest in my work.

At the University of Pennsylvania I was lucky enough to have been surrounded with a terrific graduate cohort: Amel Ahmed, Graham and Amy Dodds, Todor Enev, Michael Janson, Marton Markovitz, Joe Mink, Lilach Nir, Andreas Ringstadt, Rob Watkins and Smita Rahman, Stacey Philbrick-Yadav, and Vikash Yadav. There is no one with whom I remain as close today as when we first started graduate school, though, than Dani Miodownik. His wisdom, encouragement, and friendship made all of the difference.

The faculty at Penn was, and still is, second to none. Will Harris, Ian Lustick, Brendan O'Leary, Jack Nagel, Rudy Sil, and Henry Teune, each in his own way, shaped my intellectual development in profound ways. And whether they know it or not, Anne Norton and Ellen Kennedy are still teaching me how to read.

The Miller Center of Public Affairs at the University of Virginia provided me with a final year of funding and introduced me to a wider world of interdisciplinary scholarship and scholars. Brian Balogh and Sid Milkis remain two of the best mentors and scholars in history and political science.

At the University of Oklahoma I was fortunate enough to be part of a terrific group of junior faculty who were similarly toiling away day and night. Paul Goode, Jonathan Havercroft, Greg Miller, Alyssa Hicklin, Eric Heinze, Ariel Ahram, and Kyle Harper each proved helpful. Their continued friendship makes academia a little more bearable. The chair of the political science department, Greg Russell, always believed in my work, even when evidence suggested otherwise. And among the senior faculty at Oklahoma, David Chappell, Glenn Krutz, and Ron Peters were always willing to listen. But no other senior faculty colleague provided more help and encouragement, both personally and professionally, than Keith Gaddie.

At the University Press of Kansas, Fred Woodward proved to be as much of a friend and mentor as he did a superb editor. He believed in this book from the very beginning. I would also like to thank Susan Schott, Larisa Martin, and Karen Hellekson for their skillful marketing and editorial advice.

Although many people have provided support and encouragement along the way, my family has been there for me from the beginning. I am sure my parents think I am more than a little crazy to do what I do, but they never doubted me. They are the only critics who matter. Others, including Tiffany and Jeff Olszewski; Matt and Sherryann Wert; Sue and Steve Kiesel; Jeff Kiesel; Megan Kiesel; and my in-laws, Jim and Laura Strong, all provided encouragement and help when it mattered most.

But it is my wife, Gwyndolynn, who has done more for me than I could ever acknowledge. She has made as many, if not more, sacrifices than I have. And our children, Mitchell and Chloe, continue to make writing harder but everything else in my world more enjoyable. Gwyn, Mitchell, and Chloe can attest to the fact that the errors herein are not theirs but mine alone.

Habeas Corpus in America

CHAPTER 1

Habeas Corpus and History

In the years since September 11, 2001, the writ of habeas corpus once again emerged from legal obscurity, and, as during periods of war and crisis before, it occupied center stage in an unfortunately all too familiar battle over the constitutional limits of governmental power and individual rights during war. Proponents and critics of the so-called war on terror argue that this ancient writ serves either as a dangerous hindrance or as an indispensable protection in the fight to ensure the survival of the Constitution—and our nation— during war. Precisely because the writ's simple but potentially powerful command to bring before a court of law any individual detained by the government to inquire into his confinement could theoretically free those who might harm us, the stakes have never seemed higher. Indeed, in a pointed dissent to the Supreme Court's 5–4 decision striking down Congress' Military Commissions Act, Justice Antonin Scalia warned that "today's opinion . . . will almost certainly cause more Americans to be killed."[1]

But like previous battles over habeas corpus during other periods of war or crisis in American constitutional history—the Civil War and World War II, to name just two—our collective understanding of the meaning, history, and function of habeas corpus remains just as opaque and contentious in the years since 9/11 as it was in 1789, 1865, or 1944. Scholars, legal practitioners, politicians, and citizens alike still hold deeply divergent views about the writ's historical development and normative function; about its scope and limitations; about the conditions under which it can be suspended, limited, and enlarged; about its proper use within our constitutional system of separation of powers, checks and balances, and federalism; and certainly about which rights habeas should protect and who should receive its protection. One of the leading legal authorities of habeas jurisprudence has described our current understanding of the writ as a "bewildering morass that defies explanation at any deep conceptual level."[2] To further complicate matters, almost all existing studies of habeas divide their analysis of the Great Writ of Liberty into extraordinary periods (such as war and crisis) and ordinary periods (such as its evolving use as a remedy for challenging criminal convictions in the United States), making it even more difficult to imagine a systemic and coherent account of the writ's role in American political development.[3] As a result, we still tend to ask very different questions—and therefore always produce very different answers—about habeas's function in American constitutional law, theory, and history.

Some new answers to these problems are the subject of this book. These new answers, however, are derived from a very different perspective than has so far been dominant in studies of habeas corpus. Many *historical* works painstakingly detail much of habeas's early British and American colonial origins, and law reviews blossom with articles that advocate various *legal* approaches and preferred interpretations of the writ's scope and use by courts.[4] This book, however, accounts for the *political* origins and development of habeas corpus in the United States.[5]

Aside from the persistent, but mistaken, distinction in habeas studies between wartime and peacetime uses of the writ, most habeas corpus scholarship continues to proceed from the perspective that habeas is primarily—and sometimes solely—a legal concept. As a result, these perspectives naturally presume that courts are the only institutions in the United States that determine habeas's meaning over time.[6] These overly legal perspectives further suggest that courts—and the justices that comprise them—are the only agents of habeas corpus change and development. These assumptions, which are indicative of much legal scholarship in general that treats courts and the law as distinct from the world of politics in which they exist, consistently produce divergent and unsettled accounts of habeas's important role in American political development.[7]

This book moves beyond these legal and court-centered analyses and attempts to make better sense of the important role that habeas has played in American constitutional, political, and legal development by detailing habeas's consistently and overwhelmingly political role in American constitutional development. I show how habeas has serves as a potent tool of political regime change, enforcement, and dissolution in American politics. Habeas corpus is indeed a deeply legal concept, with a rich pedigree of doctrinal case law in British and American history that has yielded an intricate set of precedential developments that appropriately foreground the role of courts. But when we look at important periods of habeas development outside of their immediate judicial contexts in the United States, a different and more robust picture quickly emerges. Often the most significant changes to habeas corpus have not come exclusively from the oracular pronouncements of judges. Instead, change and development—both positive and negative from the normative perspective of rights protection—are often initiated and led by a coalition of other institutions in American government, including Congress, the president, political parties, state governments, legal academics and jurists, and interest groups. These coalitions, or political regimes, sought to undo the political and legal legacies of the past through strategic changes to habeas corpus in order to establish and then enforce their own vision of constitutional governance in the United States. These regimes certainly understood and took seriously the legal foundations of the writ, but frequently they looked past existing legal precedents and constraints and, often with the aid of courts that were sympathetic to these regimes, fashioned habeas's legal structure—its normative goals, its jurisdiction or reach, and the rights it protects—to reflect the ideals of their regime's governing principles. Habeas corpus thus serves as a vehicle through which political regimes attempt to reorder American governing institutions.

Throughout American history, political regimes refashioned habeas because the writ implicates elements of governmental authority, legitimacy, and individual rights that every political regime seeks to reformulate and then enforce, both politically and legally. Just as important, habeas's location and wording in the text of the Constitution itself further make it a powerful tool in regime enforcement and maintenance. The Constitution only mentions habeas in the form of a negative in the so-called suspension clause in Article I, section 9.[8] The lack of an affirmative, enumerated constitutional grant of power to issue the writ, combined with the lack of an agreed-on definition of habeas, allows Congress and the president to play a significant role in habeas's development apart from courts.[9] Habeas's potential power to reach across the jurisdictional lines of state and national power by removing state criminal cases to federal courts further makes it an important tool in the hands of political regimes, as these regimes have often sought to reorient federalism concerns to advance their vision of constitutional governance.[10] And of course the persistent debates about habeas's suspension further bring forth the writ's force during times of war or crisis. Even during these times of crisis, the use (or nonuse) of habeas corpus has been as much about advocating a regime's particular conception of constitutional governance as it has about ensuring the physical protection of the United States.

But there is yet another crucial reason why political regimes have utilized habeas to give meaning to and enforce their preferred visions of constitutional governance in the United States. Often portrayed as a right itself, habeas is instead best understood as what I term an umbrella right. Although habeas is a right that cannot be suspended except "when in cases of rebellion or invasion the public safety may require it," the real power of habeas—and the persistent point of controversy—is instead centered on the various types of rights that habeas has been used to protect and enforce throughout American political development. Habeas only invokes a procedural right to have a court inquire into an individual's detention by the state, and not any particular substantive right by itself. Defining the substantive content of habeas's procedural reach, then, is a project that has as many, if not more, political determinants as it does legal ones. When regimes sought to enforce various and changing substantive rights in American history—from the property rights of slaveholders in the 1850s to the rights of criminal defendants in the 1960s—they often did so through changes to the procedural aspects of habeas (for example, questions concerning the jurisdiction of federal courts to issue the writ), in order to widen or narrow the ability of courts to enforce and protect changing sets of substantive rights. When political regimes sought to emphasize new enumerated rights (such as those of newly freed slaves during Reconstruction), or when they sought to give more emphasis to some substantive rights as opposed to others (such as the incorporation of some among the Bill of Rights against the states and not others), or when they attempted to give more capacious definitions to enumerated rights (such as the Fourth Amendment's exclusionary rule), habeas corpus was the procedural vehicle through which these substantive rights were announced and enforced. In this way, regimes graft changing conceptions of substantive rights that they seek to recognize and enforce onto the procedural right of habeas corpus. Simple assertions that habeas seeks to protect fundamental constitutional rights thus beg the question of what those rights are—and, just as importantly, who has the authority to define and enforce them.

Conceiving habeas corpus as an umbrella right further allows us to see how the writ shapes and has been shaped by cases and political developments beyond significant cases in American constitutional history that have dealt directly with the nature of the writ and the widening or narrowing of its application. Although some cases, such as *Ex parte Bollman* (1803), *Ex parte Royall* (1886), *Frank v. Mangum* (1915), and *Brown v. Allen* (1953), define the nature of the writ or set more or less accessible procedural hurdles for access to habeas, others, such as *Mapp v. Ohio* (1961), which applied the exclusionary rule to states, are just as important to the development of the writ. As a result of *Mapp,* for example, habeas was soon used to adjudicate a new substantive right—the exclusionary rule—through its procedural reach. Just as important, however, the politics surrounding cases such as *Mapp* spurred enough controversy to elicit new arguments that the reach of habeas should be reduced to counter the seeming errors of the decision. Procedural changes over time to habeas access are important not only for a proper understanding of the development of the writ itself, then, but also for understanding how larger political struggles are often fought through the legal language and procedural rules of habeas corpus.

The major developmental turning points in habeas's history in the United States were thus products of presidential, congressional, and judicial politics. The Supreme Court has certainly served as the venue for habeas adjudication, and at crucial times the Court has also announced new changes to habeas itself, but even then, these court-centered doctrinal changes were very rarely in tension with the goals of the dominant political regime of which they were a part. This does not mean, however, that throughout its history courts simply translated political preferences into judicial outcomes, for the Court's habeas jurisprudence reveals a consistent attempt to maintain its own ability to issue the writ independent of the dominant regime.

The distinction between the procedural and substantive sides of habeas suggests that we need a better account of the politics that contract and expand the Court's ability to hear habeas cases, as well as an account that explains the Court's unique institutional role in those political battles. From our twenty-first-century perspective, which places ever greater weight on an ever-increasing set of discrete rights and liberties, we tend to see it as the job of courts to define as well as adjudicate these rights. Habeas's role in our modern stage of rights development has been momentous, as it has served as the preferred legal mechanism of enforcement of these rights at least since the Warren Court. What this book's account allows us to see, almost in the style of a cautionary tale, are the limits to our court-centered search for ever-increasing rights.[11] Although I do not suggest that politics ever completely overtakes the potential positive qualities of law as a constraining mechanism against recalcitrant majorities, the patterns of habeas development presented here nevertheless show the extent to which political—as opposed to purely legal—variables shape the writ's ability to enforce important substantive rights, as well as the institutional concerns of courts that ultimately limit the writ's complete evisceration. The account of habeas detailed in this book thus shows how the Great Writ of Liberty has almost always been the product of politics, both good and bad.

THE POLITICS OF HABEAS DEVELOPMENT

The political regimes that shaped the development of habeas corpus in American history have waxed and waned over time, but they have common characteristics that we can identify with some precision, especially as they relate to significant changes in habeas corpus doctrine. The most important statutory and court-induced doctrinal changes to habeas have closely tracked the emergence and dissolution of the three classic eras of American constitutional development: the Founding to the eve of the Civil War (1789–1865), the Civil War and Reconstruction to the momentous court-packing plan of 1937 (1865–1937), and our current post-1937 constitutional order or era.[12] These constitutional eras gave rise to various political regimes that sought to change American governmental institutions in the service of larger ideas about constitutional meaning and governance, from the attempts of balancing nationalization with states' rights during the antebellum period, to the short-lived consolidation of national power in the service of racial egalitarianism of the Civil War and Reconstruction, to the rise of the New Deal's economic and administrative state.[13]

During these eras, political regimes sought to achieve what Karen Orren and Stephen Skowronek describe as "political development," or a "durable shift in governing authority" within and through political institutions in the United States.[14] Habeas serves regimes in part by giving legal and constitutional legitimacy to the authority that they need in order to govern. Because political regimes use habeas as a legal mechanism for political change, we also see important habeas change associated with the emergence and dissolution of partisan and party regimes in the United States.[15] And as we will see in the chapters that follow, because periods of American party system development are partly sustained by judicial policy making by regime-affiliated courts, habeas changes are a significant part of this larger process as well.[16]

Not surprisingly, then, presidents often initially lead these new regimes and use their election to repudiate a previous political regime's constitutional visions.[17] These reconstructive presidents are "called upon to reconsider basic substantive political values and reconfigure existing institutional arrangements."[18] As we will see, reconstructive presidents played a large role in shaping new constitutional visions of governance that featured simultaneous redefinitions of habeas in order to realize their agendas, from Andrew Jackson to Abraham Lincoln to Ronald Reagan. In practice and over time, the bulk of the work of these regimes takes place through political coalitions that work across all of the institutions of American politics. Regimes attempt to reshape political institutions to create a logic of political, legal, and constitutional governance that legitimates and enforces the regime's preferred vision of the new constitutional era, and one of the most important ways that these political regimes sought to achieve their larger goals was through procedural and substantive changes to habeas corpus. These changes and developments, whether in the form of direct statutory changes by Congress, self-imposed limitations

or enlargements by regime-affiliated courts, or even suspensions and modifications of habeas access by presidents during war, were carried out in order to
institutionalize and enforce contending visions of constitutional governance
by dominant political regimes.

In the context of Orren and Skowronek's definition of political development (a durable shift in governing authority), we can begin to see why habeas
is important in regime-building projects that seek to achieve significant change
in American politics. Orren and Skowronek argue that a shift in governing authority represents a "*rea*rrangement, *re*direction, *re*construction" in relations
among political institutions.[19] Moreover, because these shifts are often starkly
willful changes in power, they are often contentious and require a fundamental reorientation of the objectives of political institutions in service of new
constitutional ideals. Just as important, these shifts also need to be enforceable.[20] As new regimes attempt to usher in fundamental changes in American
political institutions, it is understandable why they would look to the writ of
habeas corpus to achieve and enforce these changes, because habeas can give
legal and constitutional legitimacy to the often difficult and controversial attempts at announcing and enforcing new regime principles.[21]

But habeas has also played an important role in the dissolution of each
political regime. Just as newly ascendant political regimes have attempted to
refashion habeas to help enforce core components of constitutional governance, contending or competing regimes have zeroed in on the goals of the
dominant regime that originally enforced these principles through habeas to
foster their own regime-building projects. Thus each use of habeas creates a
ready-made target for contending regimes. The authority that regimes need to
enforce their visions of constitutional governance across political institutions
(that is, to achieve political development) is difficult to achieve completely,
and the strategic changes to habeas that these regimes carry out often become
difficult to maintain over time.[22]

To some degree, political institutions also have a life of their own, with id-
iosyncrasies and histories that seem to operate at a tempo that is never quite
in step with the changes that regimes attempt through and within them. Fundamental changes to habeas through political institutions are no exception.
These institutional constraints to large-scale political change not only operate
within institutions but also between institutions. Ascendant political regimes
can never start with a blank institutional slate, where changes to and through
these institutions can immediately hold sway and translate into governance.[23]
The executive, Congress, and the judiciary each have idiosyncratic developmental histories as well as internally developed sets of rules and duties that

naturally resist large-scale change. Even when regimes are able to make strategic changes to habeas, these changes have to be filtered through a variety of distinct political institutions. Congressional statutory changes to federal courts' habeas jurisdiction, self-imposed judicial rules on habeas procedure that may be more or less deferential to state courts, and even presidential suspensions of habeas all have to be mediated through the appropriate political institutions.

The political regimes identified in this book were largely successful in their attempts to refashion constitutional governance in the United States through changes to habeas corpus. For important reasons, however, these changes have generally been partial and temporary, in part because of the inability of any one regime to perfectly align America's political institutions with its preferred vision of constitutional governance. Critical or realigning elections, or exogenous shocks to the polity in the form of war or crises, may usher in new constitutional eras with their succession of associated political regimes, but constitutional change and governance in general are still constrained by the dynamics of political institutions themselves.[24] Even dominant regime leaders such as Franklin Roosevelt faced great difficulty in fully aligning even sympathetic institutions with his vision of constitutional governance.[25] Similarly, for Abraham Lincoln and the Republican coalition during Reconstruction, political institutions seemed to diverge with the new regime's goals as often as they aligned.[26] Regimes are often constructed through compromise, and they are held together by multiple and sometimes diametrically opposed coalitions with identifiably different agendas. Thus when each major regime, whether Federalist, Jacksonian, Republican, New Deal, or conservative, attempted to fashion changes to habeas corpus in ways that facilitated judicial enforcement of some of their key constitutional principles, they were only partially successful.

As an example of this process, consider the momentous changes to habeas during Reconstruction. The newly victorious Republican Party came to power in the wake of the critical or realigning election of 1860 with a strikingly different vision of constitutional governance than that of its rivals.[27] This regime was initially led by Abraham Lincoln, who first put forth his program of Reconstruction four nights before his assassination. After Lincoln's assassination, however, his successor, Andrew Johnson, tried unsuccessfully to lead the regime on the basis of a specifically states' rights and racially backward conception of the Republicans' larger regime-building efforts.[28] Opposing Johnson with a clear electoral mandate after the 1866 elections, radical congressional Republicans put forth a sharply opposed constitutional vision for Reconstruction. They significantly transformed federal habeas corpus for state prisoners in order to give legal support to the enforcement of their regime-building principles, particularly the Thirteenth Amendment, the Civil Rights Act of 1866, and other congressional plans for Reconstruction. As detailed in Chapter 3, the Habeas Corpus Act of 1867 was passed by Republican congressional majorities over and against the veto of Andrew Johnson in order to give legal enforcement to these regime principles. The 1867 act significantly transformed the antebellum role of habeas corpus in the United States, as it provided for the first time ever for postconviction review of state court judgments by federal courts.[29] Habeas was thus used to enforce the Republican regimes' governing principles. Throughout this period, and with only minor exceptions, the Republican regime crafted its vision of constitutional governance with the aid of the federal judiciary. But as the Republican regime began to lose political power and popular support over the next few years, these habeas changes, and the regime principles they were designed to enforce, came under increasingly intense criticism from the Democratic Party, as well as from some Republicans who, for various reasons, had either abandoned their commitments to Reconstruction or had always been doubtful of them.[30]

As the Republican regime waned and Democrats rose to power, they were able to use the changes made to habeas by Republicans as examples of what they believed were the excesses and constitutional mistakes of Reconstruction. Congressional Democrats were then able to refashion habeas by ceding more judicial oversight over habeas cases under the 1867 act back to a Supreme Court that had also become resistant not only to these habeas changes, but also to most other Reconstruction-era constitutional changes. With congressional support, the Supreme Court announced the famous "exhaustion" rule for habeas in *Ex parte Royall* in 1886, which required state defendants seeking to challenge their confinement through federal habeas corpus to first exhaust all state-level appellate processes before their habeas petitions could be considered, thus effectively returning a significant amount of power over criminal cases back to the states.[31] As the Republican Reconstruction regime that had ushered in momentous constitutional changes to the American political order fell from power in the last third of the nineteenth century, habeas changes tracked these larger regime developments. They became tools of a new regime (and liabilities to the old one) that sought to undo congressional Reconstruction by returning constitutional power to the states as part of its more general abandonment of the Reconstruction Republican regime's constitutional principles.

Thus within distinct periods of American history, habeas development and change have been the means by which political regimes have sought to legalize their new constitutional visions. These regimes would fashion and refine the legal procedures of habeas in order to fulfill and enforce their regime's particular political and constitutional visions of rights, liberties, and governmental power. Competing regimes then often found that they too could begin to advocate for new regime principles through proposed habeas reforms and changes when they were able to regain political or judicial power. Thus the legal and political legacies of habeas jurisprudence both enabled and constrained any regime's use of habeas.[32] As regimes dissolved, habeas would play a dual role, serving to jeopardize the old regime and setting the stage for the enforcement of the new one.[33]

These institutional limitations are important for understanding change in habeas, not only because they limit the extent of habeas change that any one regime can expect to achieve, but also because they structure the political space in which contending regimes begin their own regime-building projects that use habeas changes to institutionalize their own visions of constitutional governance. These institutional limitations make habeas change stunted, partial, and impermanent. All of this suggests that we should also not expect that habeas will continue to operate in the way many optimistically say it does today, in which the procedural availability of the writ increases while its substantive content—individual rights and liberties—increases as well. Nevertheless, by accounting for habeas's role in larger regime-building projects in American history, we can identify the patterns of politics that do produce the conditions in which more normatively appealing accounts do and do not occur.

HABEAS AND HISTORY

The interaction between habeas development and the larger landscape of American politics detailed in this book belies some of the most time-honored accounts of habeas's history and function. This is partly because most legal accounts of habeas are either written to give legitimacy to contemporary regime constructions of habeas changes or designed to advocate alternative conceptions of habeas that are critical of the use of the writ by contemporary regimes.[34] Part and parcel of the use of habeas by any political regime, then, is the simultaneous project of redefining and reinterpreting the meaning and history of the writ.

Existing accounts of habeas's role in American constitutional law are crafted with many different goals in mind, but they are almost always advanced within larger normative debates about contemporary constitutional governance. Some argue that habeas's historical function has been fundamentally misunderstood and that the habeas doctrines produced by modern courts have strained the writ's reach, jeopardizing its effective use, not to mention the original intent of those who framed the Constitution, which was only to correct the most egregious cases of rights deprivations by executives before trials began.[35] These accounts were largely put forward during and after the Warren Court's habeas revolution of the 1960s. These Warren Court habeas changes significantly expanded the class of cognizable rights that state defendants could now claim as substantive "constitutional" rights as the Court— and the larger New Deal and Great Society coalitions—used habeas to enforce the project of selective incorporation of the Bill of Rights against states.[36] Others argue that we can find an ideal role for habeas in American constitutionalism if we only theorize a more proper role for the tremendous oversight power that habeas gives to federal courts in supervising and correcting judgments of state courts, considering the fact that these courts have been asked to enforce an ever-increasing set of substantive rights in the twentieth century.[37] These accounts of habeas defend both its increased procedural and its substantive scope. Still others suggest that nothing has really changed. They paint a picture of habeas's development that suggests that the writ has always been used to protect substantive individual rights throughout its history, and that habeas has always been envisioned, at least since the Founding, to serve as a mechanism through which federal—as opposed to state—courts should enforce these rights.[38] These readings of habeas, which are largely a defense of expanded habeas jurisdiction in the twentieth century, try to maintain the legitimacy of federal habeas corpus review of state courts in the face of the modern conservative coalition's habeas critics.[39] Further, there are approaches to the study of habeas's use (or nonuse) during times of war or crisis that argue for either a more efficacious use of the writ during war or a severely diminished one.[40] Both on and off the bench, these interpretations of habeas's development and normative purpose are almost always devoid of political context, as they feature purely legalistic and doctrinal arguments that envision either a broad or narrow role for federal court habeas power.[41]

Although there are certainly diverse approaches to understanding habeas, there are nevertheless important similarities in the core assumptions shared by most studies. First, most of these approaches foreground the role of courts at the expense of other political institutions in shaping habeas doctrine. For example, both opponents and critics of an increased role for federal habeas courts frame the debate as a choice that federal courts can make on their own between judicial activism and judicial restraint in granting habeas review.[42]

Aside from a general neglect of the role of other institutions, such as Congress or the presidency, that have played a significant role in both enlarging and reducing federal courts' habeas powers, there is present in these accounts a larger assumption that any amount of judicial activism or restraint more generally is not partly or even completely determined by extrajudicial political coalitions and their preferred conceptions of judicial power.

Most of these approaches also fall prey to one of the most levied critiques of legal-academic work in that they attribute a Whiggishly developmental trajectory to habeas's history.[43] Because these accounts are often normative defenses of existing habeas jurisprudence, or quasilegal briefs that critique habeas case law, they have a tendency to exhibit the qualities of what Alfred Kelly famously called "law office history."[44] Many legal accounts of the history of habeas weave them together as a seamless, progressive whole. Almost in the style of a lawyer's brief, which is only concerned with presenting facts in a way that are most beneficial to the client, these studies put forward a defense of particular normative conceptions of the use of habeas by picking and choosing historical developments and uses of the writ that are most sympathetic to their arguments.[45] These accounts cannot—and in many studies simply do not—acknowledge the fact that habeas was used in the nineteenth century by slaveholders to recover their fugitive slaves, or that habeas was used to "have the body" of a slave brought before a court to determine its rightful owner when it was stolen or when it was part of a contested will. Law office history simply ignores these and other examples that do not fit nicely into their more normative accounts of habeas's historical development.

These Whiggish histories have nevertheless served as an important component of habeas development. Starting with Coke and then Blackstone, the purported core function of habeas as a legal mechanism for vindicating due process rights has its roots in Whiggish interpretations.[46] From the seventeenth and eighteenth centuries onward, these and other English jurists consistently, if inaccurately, portrayed habeas as linked to Magna Carta's famous due process provisions. Even though the records of habeas's earliest use (which were unquestionably lackluster) predate the Magna Carta by fifteen years, Coke, Blackstone, and others were successful in grafting notions of due process onto habeas. Blackstone's grand rhetorical account of habeas as "another Magna Carta" was as much contrived as it was sincere in trying to give substantive content to the procedural operation of the writ.[47] Both for English and American colonial understandings of habeas, these Whiggish readings had important political effects, especially because most of the founding generation relied on Blackstone's *Commentaries* in their own legal training generally and for their understanding of habeas in particular.[48] Consistently throughout the subsequent development of the writ, courts, legislatures, executives, political parties, and state governments would continue to be strategically selective in their accounts of habeas's development in service of their regime-building goals. Although Whiggish histories might not make good social science, they are nevertheless an important component of every regime's attempts at reordering American political institutions.[49]

HABEAS, THE COUNTERMAJORITARIAN PROBLEM, AND JUDICIAL (IN)DEPENDENCE

Although these approaches are often very different—and controversial—there is yet another unquestioned assumption in most accounts of habeas that leads them to concentrate solely on courts. Especially since the 1950s, legal scholars have been, in the words of Barry Friedman, "obsessed" with the purported "counter-majoritarian" function of the Supreme Court.[50] From this perspective, judicial review is a potentially deviant function because it "thwarts the will of representatives of the actual people of the here and now" and "exercises control, not on behalf of the prevailing majority, but against it."[51] The assumption, of course, is that courts act independently from other institutions, so if and when they exercise judicial review over and against Congress, the president, or even state governments, they are automatically, and by definition, thwarting majoritarian will. The heavy lifting of twentieth-century constitutional theory was thus devoted to offering alternative theories of the proper use of judicial review by courts that would help legitimize this function. Sometimes the countermajoritarian powers of the Court could be used legitimately to open the channels of the political process to "discrete and insular minorities,"[52] or to vindicate substantive individual rights,[53] or to enforce original conceptions of the Constitution's enumerated rights, structures, and duties.[54] Whatever the model for judicial review, there was present in all of these theories the assumption that when the Supreme Court exercises judicial review, it is always inimical to the wishes of the majority.

Habeas only compounds the problem of the countermajoritarian difficulty because, in many ways, it represents the embodiment of countermajoritarianism itself. Consider, for example, Eric Freedman's account of habeas change and development: "Attempts to extend the range and efficacy of the writ have accordingly been inseparably connected for centuries with attempts to secure justice for those who at any particular moment find themselves execrated by the dominant forces in society."[55] Not only are habeas change and development often portrayed as one unbroken, progressive line, but this supposed development is also linked to the ever-increasing protection of minority rights by courts against "the dominant forces in society."

These sorts of Whiggish and countermajoritarian accounts are not of recent vintage. For centuries, the Western legal tradition has imputed an almost mystical status to the writ of habeas. Zechariah Chafee referred to habeas as the "most fundamental human right in the Constitution."[56] Blackstone called it another "Magna Carta," a "stable bulwark of our liberties," and the "great and efficacious writ."[57] For Alexander Hamilton, the protection of fundamental rights was already fully secured in the Constitution without a Bill of Rights because, along with the prohibitions against ex post facto laws, bills of attainder, and grants of nobility, the habeas corpus clause in Article I would serve as the defense against arbitrary arrests and imprisonments that, in his words, were the "favorite and most formidable instruments of tyranny."[58] In cases as diverse in kind as they are diverse through time, federal courts throughout American constitutional history have similarly lauded the writ's countermajoritarian function. For Chief Justice John Marshall, habeas was a "great constitutional privilege," and courts in each century continued to assert that "there was no higher duty than to maintain it unimpaired."[59] In *Ex parte Yerger* in 1868, Chief Justice Chase proclaimed, "The great writ of habeas corpus has been for centuries esteemed the best and only sufficient defense of personal freedom."[60] In *Fay v. Noia* in 1963, Justice William Brennan described the grand rhetoric of habeas on and off the Court: "These are not extravagant expressions," because "behind them may be discerned the unceasing contest between personal liberty and government oppression."[61]

It is true that at times throughout history, habeas has, in the words of Justice Oliver Wendell Holmes, "cut through all forms . . . to the tissue of the structure" of unconstitutional and rights-depriving incarcerations and detainments in the United States.[62] And when it has, courts boldly announced that their use of habeas was in the service of the vindication of individual rights as diverse as the Sixth Amendment's right to counsel for indigent defendants and the Fifth Amendment's due process clause for alien detainees at Guantánamo Bay.[63] But it is also true that habeas has been used to return slaves to their masters and to free slave catchers. Presidents have ignored writs of habeas corpus issued by courts, suspended habeas, and used their executive powers more generally to skirt the writ's reach.[64] Congress has sought at times to increase and decrease the writ's jurisdiction for both noble and ignoble reasons. These historical realities chip away at the supposed countermajoritarian and linearly progressive foundations of habeas that most legal scholars take for granted.

Some important questions thus emerge. To what extent have habeas decisions—whether they have vindicated rights of indigent defendants or slaveholders—actually been inimical to the wishes of majorities? To what extent were these decisions made by courts independently of the larger political regime? When changes to habeas were made, either by the Court itself or by other institutions, were they in fact made to "provide a prompt and efficacious remedy for whatever society deems to be intolerable"?[65]

An increasing number of political scientists, legal historians, and legal academics have questioned the utility and historical accuracy of the purported countermajoritarian problem, and they have begun to construct theories of judicial decision making that allow us to see this process through a larger political lens. Their work informs the analysis of habeas's development that I advance in important ways because I treat habeas as both a political and legal determinant of change in regime building throughout American constitutional history.

The Whiggish assertions of habeas as a bulwark of liberty, or as another Magna Carta, simply do not match the real historical and political development of the writ, and the use of habeas by political regimes to enforce their preferred conceptions of constitutional governance calls into question the utility and accuracy of purely legal or doctrinal explanations of habeas corpus more generally. Nevertheless, the judicial branch has shaped the contours of habeas in important ways, and when it has, its notions of what habeas corpus is, what it should do, and how it should be adjudicated need to be understood better. We thus need a broader lens through which to account for the double-edged sword of habeas's history to explain how and why it was used both to deprive and protect individual rights.[66] We also need to look beyond purely legal and doctrinal models in order to account for its use not only by courts, but also by other political institutions, especially when courts sympathetic to or affiliated with the dominant political regime seem to demand a great deal of institutional independence in habeas cases that is often at odds with the larger regime's preferences.

Inspired by Robert Dahl's analysis of judicial decision making at the height of the behavioral revolution in the 1950s that questioned the assumptions of the Supreme Court as a Galahad that serves to vindicate minority rights in the face of majority deprivations, the regime politics approach has, in the words of Howard Gillman, sought to "incorporate legal studies into a more general set of hypotheses about how political regimes organize, exercise, and protect their power."[67] According to Dahl, the Court has very rarely struck down national legislation through its power of judicial review. Instead, its use of that power has generally been consistent with and supportive of the contemporary dominant national coalition.[68] Contrary to more legally normative conceptions of the judicial role, the Court is not simply "a legal institution," but "also a political institution . . . for arriving at decisions on controversial questions of national policy." The relationship of the Court to other political institutions is structured by "relatively cohesive alliances that endure for long periods of time" in American politics.[69] The result of these alliances is that except for key transitional periods, Court majorities will have been appointed by, and hence supportive of, those alliances. When the Court advances purportedly legal, as opposed to overtly political, reasoning, this is simply window dressing designed to ensure the legitimacy of the judicial function as it conforms its decisions to the dominant political coalition. Others, including Robert McCloskey and Martin Shapiro, continued the emphasis on the political foundations of the judicial function as each in his own way showed how political science could easily peel away the legal veneer of older analyses of constitutional law and demonstrate a pervasive role for politics in the judicial function.[70]

Variations and advances on the Dahlian theme of the Court's relationship to the national policy-making process have made important contributions to our understanding of Supreme Court decision making that move past the strictures of the legally centered assumptions of the countermajoritarian difficulty. Mark Graber and others have shown, for example, how legislatures often find that deferring difficult issues to sympathetic or regime-affiliated courts can be effective in securing policy goals that would otherwise remain dead on arrival.[71] Judicial review is thus best understood as nonmajoritarian rather than countermajoritarian, and resolution of these legislative issues by the Court often indicates that its powers are being used in the service of larger majoritarian goals rather than in the service of the rights or interests of minorities. Not only do courts seldom overturn the political preferences of the dominant national coalition, but they also sometimes act as "a forum for the resolution of disputes that present political problems for party leaders."[72] More broadly, others have shown how the Court's decisions in such diverse areas as criminal procedure rights, school desegregation, federalism concerns, voting rights, executive power, and abortion, to name just a few, are best understood as complements, rather than impediments, to the larger political regime's visions of constitutional governance.[73] As a result, we should expect that justices, appointed by presidents and confirmed by the Senate, will reflect the goals of the regimes in which they were appointed.[74]

The most systematic advocates of the regime approach put forward a more developed and nuanced theory of the political dynamics of judicial decisions that moves beyond the rather prosaic assumption that the Court simply follows the election returns. The political regimes approach, which is deeply indebted to the work of Dahl, Shapiro, and McCloskey, nevertheless brings the role of law back into the study of courts even as it admits of a significant relationship between the Court and the larger governing regime. Leading this charge, Cornell Clayton and David May argue that "legal principles" do indeed shape judicial outcomes, but the law in this sense is the product of larger social and political forces. As they describe this dynamic, "judges reach the decisions they do for a variety of reasons, some undoubtedly having to do with immediate policy preferences and perceived institutional constraints, but most having to do with a desire to give a professionally principled interpretation of law or an authentically held view about the appropriate mission of courts."[75] Thus building on the Dahlian insight, but contrary to judicial behavioralists of the attitudinal variety, they put forward a model of judicial decision making that attends to the legal factors involved in this process as much as the political ones.[76] "Patterns of party politics, group coalition building, critical elections, the policy agenda of governing elites, and other features of the political regime" reveal political influences on the judiciary's construction and institutional understanding of how the law constrains their own decisions.[77]

This is an important aspect of the regime politics approach that my account of habeas's development can help clarify, particularly because some of this scholarship tends to swing the pendulum of judicial decision making too far in one direction, often sacrificing judicial independence and conceptions of the law at the altar of politics and political regimes.[78] The most prominent criticism levied against the regime politics approach is that it too often portrays the Court's relationship to the dominant national coalition in a way that would seem to load all judicial decisions in the direction of always supporting (or at least sympathizing with) some political majorities in some political institutions all of the time. As long as there are political majorities that would seem to benefit from a decision (and there almost invariably are), then these scholars are in danger of committing the cardinal sin of social science by "selecting on the dependent variable" because we can always identify a relationship between the Court and the dominant national coalition.[79] Thus a complete reliance on "external sources of the Court's decisions" suggests that "someone else [other than the Justices] is behind the wheel."[80] As a result, the relative independence of the judiciary and its unique institutional role are relegated to nothing more than a forum for the judicialized policy preferences of any number of political coalitions. As Thomas Keck suggests, scholars who use the perspective of regime analyses should simply recognize that there is almost always a relationship between the Court and the large political regime, but that this relationship is never a simple one. Instead, Keck and others argue that the real questions scholars should ask of this relationship "is whether—or to what degree, or under what conditions—judges are likely to act independently of the wishes of other power holders."[81]

The dominant forces of the political regime may indeed exert a measurable influence on institutions such as the Supreme Court, but the unique institutional role of the judiciary—and of the justices themselves—mitigates any claim that this influence is complete. The development of habeas shows this to be the case in important ways. Despite statutory restrictions to habeas jurisdiction for state prisoners over the years that were supported by various political regimes, the institutional power of the Court to issue the writ has increased in the aggregate. Habeas now serves to test the legality—or constitutionality—of a host of constitutional rights both before and after conviction. This increase, however, is better understood as an increase in the procedural ability of the Court to issue the writ as a general rule and not necessarily in terms of the writ's substantive content. The Court has thus sought to enlarge and protect its ability to hear habeas cases as an institution even when it has decided to work with other political institutions to determine which substantive rights fall under habeas's protection.[82]

According to many commentators, for example, the end of the Warren Court and the ascendance of the Burger Court portended a revolution in constitutional law, as the Court that was partly engineered by Richard Nixon was supposedly poised to undo the seismic changes created during the 1960s. Instead, the Burger Court has been aptly termed a counterrevolution that wasn't.[83] If the Court really did follow the election returns with respect to habeas, then we would expect that Burger Court majorities would have dismantled the expanded procedural and substantive changes to habeas that had been created during the Warren Court. Instead, only some of the substantive rights that the Warren Court had announced were jettisoned through habeas.

For example, without denying itself the procedural power to entertain habeas positions from state defendants in general, a conservative majority of the Burger Court held in *Stone v. Powell* that the exclusionary rule announced in

Mapp v. Ohio could not automatically trigger a habeas hearing.[84] Because the exclusionary rule was only a judicially created prophylactic device and not a constitutional right per se, the Court argued that "our decision today is not concerned with the scope of the habeas corpus statute as authority for litigating constitutional claims."[85] Thus while the Burger Court might have been willing to jettison some of the substantive rights that were grafted onto habeas during the 1960s, it was not willing to divest itself—and the judicial institution—of the procedural ability to entertain habeas claims more generally. As Rogers M. Smith has argued, institutions influence the self-conception of those who occupy roles defined by them in ways that can give those persons distinctly institutional perspectives, and the Court's solicitous posture toward its own procedural ability to issue the writ, regardless of the changing sets of substantive rights that are adjudicated through habeas, can help us understand the extent to which judicial independence can crosscut larger regime conceptions of the writ at any one point in time.[86] It is not surprising, for example, that even with a largely sympathetic majority on the Court, the Bush administration was ultimately frustrated with the Court's trio of habeas decisions since 9/11 that consistently carved out a judicial role through habeas for the supervision of enemy combatants.[87] Although a Republican-appointed majority bent over backward to argue that hearsay, for example, could be used in military tribunals, they were nevertheless unwilling to budge when it came to the threshold question of the availability of the writ in general.[88]

Liberal or conservative, activist or deferential, it appears that the Court is first concerned with its own institutional power to issue the writ and only secondarily concerned with changing conceptions of which rights make up habeas's substantive content. This first concern suggests that the Court will not bow to or work in concert with political regimes or dominant national coalitions when its conceptions of habeas would ultimately seek to divest the Court of habeas power completely. The Supreme Court will, however, largely serve political regimes when they seek to enlarge or decrease the substantive rights that are enforced through habeas.[89]

The regime perspective of habeas development put forth in this book, which is sensitive to judicial independence and to the judiciary's relationship to the larger political regime, further allows us to account for habeas change not only during peacetime but also during war. Although Lincoln's suspension of habeas in 1861 (and the subsequent suspensions that were authorized by Congress up to the end of the Civil War in 1865) is of course important with respect to larger questions of executive war power, because it implicates critical questions of the proper allocation and use of constitutional power during war or crisis, it cannot be completely separated from the larger orbit of constitutional politics that preceded it. For Lincoln, as for the congressional Republican regime that would arise after his death, traditional limits on the scope and use of habeas during war did not stand in the way of preserving and defending the Union (perhaps the supreme regime commitment), especially when landslide electoral victories, such as those in 1866, appeared to welcome large-scale political and constitutional change. Lincoln's famous rebuttal to those who claimed that his suspension of habeas without congressional approval was unconstitutional—"Are all the laws but one to go unexecuted and the Government itself go to pieces lest that one be violated?"—is indicative of habeas's use by regime leaders, regardless of whether it occurred within the crucible of war. In the face of previous legal interpretations of habeas that directly contradicted executive suspension, Lincoln was willing to reinterpret any constitutional provision, including habeas, in ways that he thought would allow him to save the Union. Similarly, the legislative approvals of further executive suspensions of the writ by the Reconstruction Republican Congress, and certainly the congressional changes to habeas in the Habeas Act of 1867 that significantly changed its procedural and substantive reach, show how the Republican regime reinterpreted previous procedural limitations to habeas in drastically new ways in order to enforce Reconstruction programs. These habeas changes were, as I show in the chapters that follow, crafted by the regime and countenanced by the Court, but the judiciary did not completely bow to the regime, even during war. When, for example, the Court was forced to back down from hearing the first habeas case stemming from the 1867 act when Congress summarily revoked its habeas jurisdiction, the Court nevertheless went to great lengths in that very same case to argue that it still had broad habeas powers under the Judiciary Act of 1789. These regime linkages are too often ignored in most accounts of wartime uses of habeas. What a regimes approach shows us is that more often than not, the politics of habeas during war mirrors the already developing peacetime goals of the extant regime. As a result, the distinction between the role of habeas litigation in times of war and that peace is often overdrawn. Just as important, moreover, is the fact that the judiciary will always fight to preserve some measure of its habeas power during war as it does during peacetime.

The use of habeas by political regimes has largely mirrored larger political and constitutional eras in American political development. Writing for the majority in one of the most important habeas cases of the Warren Court, Justice

William Brennan proclaimed that "all significant statutory changes in the federal writ have been prompted by grave political crises."[90] Although Brennan's description is undoubtedly an overstatement, the most salient habeas developments have nevertheless been forged on the cusp of larger political, social, and legal developments in the United States. In order to account for these developments both on and off the Court, the book's chapters proceed chronologically. A linear, historical account of habeas development is also important because most studies of habeas are mistakenly divided between the writ's "ordinary" and "extraordinary" uses. It is therefore especially important to present various wartime applications of habeas development as part of habeas's overall ordinary historical development instead of treating them separately. Thus the salient wartime habeas cases during the Civil War and World War II are treated in the same chapters that discuss, for example, habeas during Reconstruction and habeas during the New Deal.

Chapter 2 traces habeas development and change from the Founding to the eve of the Civil War. Federalism concerns pervaded the antebellum republic on almost every substantive issue, and habeas played an important role in these developments. Both the construction of the suspension clause during the debates in Philadelphia and that in the Judiciary Act of 1789, which set forth federal court jurisdiction for habeas during the first Congress, evidenced an attempt to balance habeas between the political concerns of the state governments and the national government. The antebellum order's inability to forge a permanent settlement on habeas and other issues that implicated both state and federal governmental powers set the stage for both political and regional disagreements. Debates concerning economic policy were particularly acute in the antebellum era, as were the related but distinct challenges of territorial expansion, Indian removal, and foreign policy. Bound up within all of these challenges, however, was the persistent, though often muted, issue of slavery. No other issue so divided the antebellum order. And in the decade leading up to the Civil War, habeas corpus played a critical role in the sectional and ideological battles over slavery that ultimately led to the Civil War. Habeas's role in this larger struggle is often overlooked in contemporary analyses of habeas's history and development, especially among legal-liberal academics who support broad national habeas power. What is so striking about antebellum habeas is the fact that the Great Writ was used in both noble and ignoble ways by proslavery and antislavery proponents in the larger sectional and ideological battles over slavery and its expansion. Our modern paradigm of habeas corpus was thus inverted before 1860, with some states asserting their sovereignty in ways that were solicitous of individual rights. They were able to secure broad, substantive protections for fugitive slaves that challenged national proslavery policies through the writ. At the same time, Southern states were using habeas to adjudicate slave cases in ways that were protective of the rights of slave owners and their property.

This matrix of state habeas power, which was almost evenly divided between its ugliness and its humanity, would ultimately be resolved in favor of strong national enforcement of slavery through habeas corpus during the twilight of the antebellum order. On both the state and national levels, habeas development during the first half of the nineteenth century was spurred by political forces that worked to establish two very different conceptions of constitutional governance. To understand these developments, this chapter traces habeas development from the Founding era to its two major statutory changes in 1833 and 1844 as well as its role in the increasingly divisive arena of slavery. The major statutory changes to federal court habeas jurisdiction before 1850 were not directly linked to slavery question, but state-level habeas changes most certainly were. These two independent tracks of habeas development would eventually come to a head as the issues of the extension of slavery and the extraterritorial application of its attendant enforcement through law engulfed the nation. In the antebellum constitutional world, we thus see how habeas was used to enforce multiple conceptions of constitutional governance as regimes used the writ to help create and enforce their regime's core principles. Controversies over the various uses of the writ during this period also led to the demise of each regime as state-level enforcement of fundamental rights for both slaves and slave owners through habeas gave way to national enforcement of the rights of freedmen. The Supreme Court nevertheless sought to maintain its own institutional power to issue the writ independently of any of the particular substantive conceptions of rights that contending regimes attempted to protect through the writ.

Chapter 3 accounts for the momentous changes to habeas during and after the Civil War. No other period of American constitutional history was as significant in terms of habeas's development. One major goal of this chapter is to show how habeas's suspension during the Civil War, and its subsequent expansion by Congress at the beginning of congressional Reconstruction, were not separate developments but were instead of a piece with the Republican regime's larger goals of constitutional governance during and after the Civil War. Although Congress certainly towered over both Andrew Johnson and the Supreme Court during the height of Reconstruction, the unprecedented habeas changes during this period were forged by a partnership between Congress and the Supreme Court. The precedents for these large-scale habeas revisions by Radical Republicans were found in the antebellum order's national enforcement of the fugitive slave law. Just as politically determined as the antebellum regimes, the congressional Reconstruction regime found that habeas could also be manipulated to suit their enforcement needs, especially when they had the luxury of a largely sympathetic Supreme Court to support them. But as Radical Reconstruction waned, so did political support for increased habeas power by federal courts. With the ascendancy of a resurgent Democratic Party and a general waning national commitment to the goals of Reconstruction, Congress and the Court worked together in the 1880s to recalibrate habeas to the new visions of constitutional governance of the ascending Democratic Party. During habeas's post–Civil War contractions, however, the Supreme Court was able to maintain a large degree of control over the procedural aspects of federal habeas, even as the larger political regime became less and less committed to broad, substantive interpretations of the reach of habeas.

Chapter 4 highlights the habeas changes by the Supreme Court from the height of Jim Crow at the turn of the twentieth century to the end of the Warren Court. These more Court-centered changes and developments were still linked to larger political concerns that racked the nation in the first four decades of the twentieth century. Racial politics form the backdrop for these habeas developments in three contexts: the persistent problem of lynchings and mob-dominated courtrooms in the Jim Crow South, the internment of Japanese Americans during World War II, and the beginning of a more racially tolerant society after the war. The Supreme Court increasingly served as the venue for change in habeas doctrine during this period, as it was clear to the congressional and presidential wings of the New Deal regime that some of their core governing principles needed further legal enforcement to buttress attempts to end lynching and establish even the most basic civil rights protections for minorities. These larger regime concerns motivated two of the most important habeas cases during this period, *Frank v. Mangum* and *Moore v. Dempsey*.[91] The Court's link to the larger political regime during this period again shows how habeas development was affected as much by political as by legal considerations, as the Court slightly broadened habeas access for state prisoners, but only in the most egregious cases of due process violations. We see this pattern play out in the Court's decisions concerning Japanese internment during World War II, but again, the Court's support for the larger regime went only so far. No Court majority was willing to go so far as to deny itself the power to issue the writ, even if it chose not to grant habeas relief in specific cases.

Chapter 4 then highlights the transformations in the American political landscape ushered in by the New Deal and Great Society. As it did in other areas of constitutional law during the 1950s and 1960s, the Court revised and redefined habeas to enforce the dominant regime's particular vision of constitutional governance through a reinterpretation of the criminal process provisions of the Bill of Rights and the Fourteenth Amendment. These habeas changes soon led to political and legal backlash from an emerging conservative coalition that increasingly channeled its criticism of the New Deal–Great Society coalition through a sustained challenge to what it perceived as a perversion of the Great Writ's original meaning and purpose. During Richard Nixon's 1968 presidential bid, the ascendant Republican coalition was able to gain traction by criticizing the Warren Court's transformation of the writ from an extraordinary to an ordinary remedy for any and all seemingly constitutional violations.

Chapter 5 traces the initial attacks on the Warren Court's habeas changes by the Nixon and Reagan coalitions and their subsequent attempts to refashion habeas in the service of larger conservative Republican visions of states rights federalism and race neutrality. Between 1968 and 2008, Republicans occupied the presidency for twenty-eight years. They appointed twelve new members to the Supreme Court, including three chief justices. On and off the Court, conservatives worked diligently to roll back, but not completely undo, the habeas changes made during the 1960s, choosing to maintain some of the increased procedural changes to habeas that provided for increased federal court supervision of state courts so an increasingly conservative-leaning Supreme Court could give the regime's preferred substantive content to constitutional rights through the writ. The failed attempts by the Reagan administration to refashion habeas during the 1980s were successfully received a decade later when the Republican Party wrested control of both houses of Congress in 1994. In 1996, Congress passed the Antiterrorism and Effective Death Penalty Act (AEDPA), which, among other things, implemented many of the conservative regime's failed habeas changes during the previous decade. But importantly, these changes, and the Court's subsequent habeas cases, further show how even a regime-affiliated Court was able to maintain a large degree of institutional independence.

The concluding chapter weaves together the book's overall themes concerning habeas's political linkage to governing coalitions to provide an account of habeas's role since 9/11. Like previous uses of the writ during the Civil War and World War II, habeas since 9/11 is best understood as the continuation of the Republican Party's larger regime commitments to unilateral executive war power and decreased procedural rights for criminal defendants. Nevertheless, a regime-affiliated Supreme Court, with a majority of Republican-appointed justices, halted the attempts of President George W. Bush and many congressional Republicans to preclude enemy combatants from enjoying habeas rights. The war on terror's habeas cases confirm that no matter how reliably linked the Court is to the larger political regime, its institutional conceptions of even minimal habeas access, as well as its conception of its own role in the American constitutional system, precludes its full cooperation in giving legal imprimatur to any regime's constitutional vision of governance that threatens to eviscerate basic judicial functions.

CHAPTER 2

Antebellum Habeas

On 16 October 1847, a large crowd filled the tiny courthouse in Charleston, Illinois. They came that night to see Chief Justice Wilson of the Illinois supreme court and Judge Treat from the eighth circuit of Illinois rule in a habeas corpus proceeding. Earlier that year, Anthony Bryant, a former slave to Robert Matson, and Bryant's wife, Jane, who, along with her children, still belonged to Matson, fled Matson's Coles County estate in fear that Matson's mistress would make good on her threat to ship Jane and her children off to plantations further south. Local antislavery activists in Charleston spirited the Bryant family away to safety. Unable to convince them to return, Matson hired Charleston attorney Usher F. Linder in an effort to secure the return of the slaves—his property—in a court of law. Linder first secured a writ of habeas corpus to remove the absconded slaves from antislavery confines and bring them before the local justice of the peace. The slaves were compelled to return, and because they did not have certificates of freedom, which were required under Illinois's black codes, they were remanded to the local jail to await further legal resolution. Two local antislavery activists, Gideon Ashmore and Hiram Rutherford, then sought another writ of habeas corpus to have the slave family brought before Justices Wilson and Treat that fateful Saturday in October.[1]

The impending case drew widespread interest, and in the days leading up to the trial, people traveled from far across the state to see the resolution of the case firsthand. Among those who came to Charleston a few days before the Matson slave trial was a prominent Illinois attorney who, aside from having two other cases to argue at the courthouse in Coles County before he went to Washington to take his newly won seat in the House of Representatives, probably surmised that his services could be of use to the parties involved in this high-profile habeas case. Not long after he arrived, his strategy paid off: Matson's attorney, Orlando Ficklin, secured him as cocounsel in the case.

Abraham Lincoln was no stranger to fugitive slave cases or habeas corpus, even in 1847. A few years earlier, antislavery activists secured his legal services in a similar fugitive slave case involving habeas, although in that case he successfully represented the slave and secured her freedom.[2] But this time, he would represent the ugly side of American slave law. With his cocounsel secured, Linder and Lincoln made a persuasive case that evening before Justices Wilson and Treat, arguing that Matson, who was a citizen of Kentucky, only brought his slaves to Coles County for short periods of time to work his plantation. Because he never intended to become a citizen of Illinois and he never verbalized any intention to keep his slaves there permanently, they should not be freed. According to Ficklin's account, Lincoln's argument before the court that evening proceeded with "trenchant blows and cold logic and subtle knitting together of presentation of facts favorable to his side."[3] The Bryants' attorneys argued that the provisions of both the Northwest Ordinance of 1787 and the Illinois constitution served to confer freedom upon the Bryant family. Interestingly, the slaves' attorneys neglected to cite as precedent Lincoln's slave case years before, which certainly would have cast his position in this case in an uncomfortable light because Lincoln made the exact same argument.[4]

Justices Wilson and Treat ultimately ruled in favor of freedom that evening in the habeas case, and the Bryant family was liberated from bondage. Lincoln lost the case for Matson. The Bryant family eventually relocated to Liberia, where by all accounts they lived the rest of their lives in utter poverty.

From our twenty-first-century perspective, the Matson slave case, like habeas corpus in the antebellum United States, is replete with irony. Aside from Lincoln's seeming about-face from his position on the side of freedom in the *Bailey* case, the Bryants' attorneys were both committed proslavery men. In fact, Lincoln's cocounsel, Orlando Ficklin, was the only attorney who represented the party with which he was personally allied. Before the momentous changes to habeas that would follow from Reconstruction and the Civil War, habeas played a protean role in antebellum political development, serving the interests of diametrically opposed political interests in the United States. The political influences upon habeas development far exceeded any consistent or logical development from the perspective of neutral legal principles, logically reasoned legal exegesis, or the purported countermajoritarian functions of courts. And as in the Matson slave case, supposed victories for individual rights through habeas were all too often belied by the writ's varied uses before the Civil War.

As Lincoln's involvement in fugitive slave cases shows, our modern notions of habeas as a progressively developing right that serves to free those detained in violation of the Constitution are belied by the fact that antebellum habeas was used both to free slaves and to return them to slavery. Our modern conceptions of habeas are also challenged by the fact that when habeas was used in efforts to secure freedom for fugitive slaves, it was through state, not federal, courts that this most fundamental of all human rights was secured. This inverted institutional role of state habeas protection before the Civil War is difficult for modern habeas advocates to acknowledge. One of the most important contemporary arguments for broad federal habeas review of state court decisions premises its position on an assertion that "federal habeas review is justified not by an *ideal* model of federal and state relations, but by the *actual* refusal of state courts to vindicate federal rights during various periods in American history."[5] To be sure, not all states allowed habeas to issue in the service of liberty. Some Southern states, particularly Mississippi, specifically used habeas to help slave owners to retrieve their property in courts of law. Nevertheless, antebellum federal courts simply did not use their habeas power to free those held unconstitutionally by state governments, as they do today. Not only did antebellum conceptions of federal habeas have little connection to the catalog of substantive rights that we associate with habeas protection today, but they also never imagined habeas to serve as a postconviction remedy for the deprivation of constitutional rights more generally. Constitutional and political support for broad federal habeas corpus for state prisoners to vindicate substantive national constitutional rights was never contemplated by any antebellum political regime.

National political regimes did at times, however, support strategic and limited congressional changes to federal habeas corpus jurisdiction during the antebellum era, and state-level regimes supported strategic changes to habeas to support their particular conceptions of constitutional governance.[6] Particularly after the Compromise of 1850, which among other things provided for more effective national enforcement of Article IV's "fugitive from labor" provisions, some state governments strategically used their habeas powers to pit themselves against the federal government in favor of liberty. As a result, then, state legislatures spurred habeas development as much as, if not more than, their state judicial counterparts. Although unsuccessful, this decidedly political use of habeas by state governments in the antebellum era was crucially important to the development of habeas after the Civil War. National party coalitions also weighed in on habeas, arguing that the use of habeas to frustrate the recovery of fugitive slaves violated federal law and numerous constitutional provisions, and more generally risked the dissolution of the Union. The national judiciary, composed of justices selected and confirmed by these national party coalitions, upheld virtually all slavery-related political compromises and their attendant federal enforcement provisions that ran headlong into state habeas corpus laws.

Like the nation itself during the antebellum period, the trajectory of habeas's development was in no way certain from 1789 to 1860. Before the Founding, state governments provided for habeas in their state constitutions and most were convinced that habeas rights guaranteed in those documents exhausted the writ's liberty-protecting power in restraining unconstitutional governmental actions for both state and federal prisoners. According to William Duker, for example, the fact that the Constitution's habeas clause was originally designed only to allow for the limited suspension of state habeas corpus rights for federal prisoners by the new federal government suggests that a state-centered conception of habeas in the protection of fundamental rights before the Civil War was particularly robust.[7] Because state constitutions already provided for the writ by the time the Constitution was ratified, the assumption was that these state governments were best suited to protect the fundamental rights of their citizens through the time-honored writ. Although federal habeas corpus rights for federal prisoners were quickly established by the first Congress through provisions in the Judiciary Act of 1789, Congress also mandated that federal courts could not review unconstitutional detentions of state prisoners. Up until the early 1870s, state courts routinely entertained habeas petitions for those detained by the federal government, creating at times a double protection for individual rights of federal prisoners. Moreover, congressional modifications of federal court habeas jurisdiction in the antebellum period met with significant criticisms from Northern and Southern states alike. State habeas for federal prisoners also created significant friction within and between antebellum political coalitions and drove the writ's development from the 1840s onward. As a result, there were two different trajectories of habeas development—one state and one federal—that developed side by side in the antebellum era.

Federal, as opposed to state, habeas corpus cases during the antebellum period continued to deal mainly with claims made by those held by the federal government. The only federal habeas review of state detentions before the Civil War occurred as a result of two congressional amendments to the Judiciary Act of 1789. As part of the force bill in the wake of the nullification crisis in South Carolina, the 1833 Habeas Act provided that habeas would issue by federal courts for federal tariff officers if they were detained by state authorities acting in their capacity to enforce federal law. And in response to the McLeod affair in 1842, Congress again amended the Judiciary Act of 1789 to provide for federal habeas corpus for foreign nationals held by states. What is significant about the 1833 act in particular is that it was never subsequently used for its intended purpose. The substantive rights that were at the center of the 1833 act faded away as compromise tariff measures were passed, leaving only the procedural changes to federal and state habeas jurisdiction in place to be applied to new political and legal developments.[8] The 1833 act was never used to rescue tariff officers who were detained by recalcitrant states. Instead, it was used to rescue slave catchers who were arrested and held by state governments, further exacerbating tensions within the Jacksonian political regime.

This use of the writ, combined with state-level habeas changes after 1850 designed to frustrate fugitive slave recovery, came to a head in *Ableman v. Booth* on the eve of the Civil War. There the Supreme Court ruled that state habeas, used in this case, as in others, for antislavery purposes, could not contravene federal habeas writs, here used on behalf of slaveholders and their agents.[9] The two independently developing trajectories of antebellum habeas corpus— one on the state level where key Northern states were using habeas in favor of liberty, and one on the national level where habeas was used to thwart state power and defend slaveholding state interests through the power of the federal government—met head-on in this case with important ramifications. Although national habeas power temporarily contravened state habeas power with respect to the fugitive slave issue in the late 1850s, the structure it created—national enforcement of constitutional rights through habeas for those held by states— became the precedent that congressional Republicans would use to establish broad federal habeas power over state governments during Reconstruction. Broad federal habeas protection for those held unconstitutionally by state governments thus has its roots in a more uncertain and ambivalent developmental history, as the procedural outcome of *Ableman* was soon used to support the substantive content of national habeas rights forged during Reconstruction. Our modern notion of federal habeas thus owes much of its structure and procedure to the ignoble uses of the writ during the antebellum period.

How can we explain these seemingly contradictory developments in antebellum habeas law? In this chapter, I begin to make sense of the sometimes circuitous nature of habeas before the Civil War by placing its development within a political and institutional context. Because our understanding of habeas development is incomplete without a political lens, we need to look to other institutions besides courts in American politics to make sense of the various conceptions and uses of habeas during the antebellum period. Habeas in the antebellum era was used strategically by national and state-level political regimes to enforce their particular conceptions of constitutional governance. Congress, after all, plays an extremely important role in federal court habeas jurisdiction, and presidents at crucial junctures led and supported the congressional charges to expand or contract that jurisdiction. And because of the two-track development of habeas—strong state-level habeas, weak federal habeas—state political regimes also used habeas to enforce their own conceptions of constitutional governance, even approaching nullification of federal law. A wider political lens of habeas history allows us to see how this matrix of multiple institutions affects habeas development because, as we will see, the use of habeas by particular political regimes was often only partly successful in making these changes permanent. The short-term political goals of the regime also often produced long-term habeas developments that cannot square with purely legal understandings of the writ.

THE ESTABLISHMENT OF FEDERAL HABEAS CORPUS

Few arguments concerning the history of habeas in the United States are as contentious as those that try to come to a definitive conclusion about the Framers' purported original understanding of the nature and role of the suspension clause under the new Constitution.[10] There are three important aspects of the nature and scope of the writ that are implicated in debates concerning the original understanding of the suspension clause. The first and most conspicuous aspect is the suspension of the writ during war or rebellion and the concomitant question of presidential versus congressional power to suspend the writ's functioning. The second concern that elicits sharp disagreement is the assertion that congressional or even judicial modification to federal court habeas jurisdiction that result in decreased habeas access for either state or federal prisoners constitutes an unauthorized suspension of the writ. These arguments are applicable both to ordinary peacetime uses of the writ and, as we have seen most recently, to congressional statutes that strip federal courts of habeas jurisdiction for detainees at the Guantánamo Bay naval facility.[11] The third aspect of the writ that spurs inquiries into the original understanding of the suspension clause—and the one that this section deals with explicitly— stems from the fact that the clause seems not to provide directly for federal habeas corpus rights at all. For federal courts to issue the writ, Congress had to provide for the writ through statute, which it did in section 14 of the Judiciary Act of 1789.

Or so it would seem. Contemporary legal scholars are particularly invested in this last debate because at least since the Warren Court's habeas expansions in the 1960s, the modern Republican regime has consistently tried to scale back these changes. Those who criticize habeas rollbacks do so partly on the basis of the argument that these conservative changes, both on and off the bench, constitute not only a suspension of the writ but, more importantly, a misguided reading of habeas's true historical scope and intent. If the suspension clause is read to imply an already existing constitutional basis for broad habeas corpus rights, then congressional and even judicial rollbacks are unconstitutional suspensions. Defenders of the rollbacks argue that broad federal habeas corpus review of state criminal convictions were never part of any original understanding of the scope of habeas, let alone the much more common modern variant of habeas that seeks postconviction review of fundamental constitutional rights in both federal and state courts.[12] Those who currently defend broad federal habeas corpus review for state prisoners fervently contend that the habeas clause was always intended to apply to both federal and state prisoners, both before and after their trials.[13]

These debates are representative of the extent to which political regimes rely on reinterpretations of habeas to justify their legal and political visions of constitutional governance, as both sides are either defenders of Warren Court–era habeas protections or proponents of the Republican Party's habeas rollbacks since the 1970s. In an attempt to uncover some lost or misinterpreted intent on the part of the Founding generation that proves that habeas was forever intended to operate according to one or another regime's contemporary normative constitutional frame, both sides mistakenly read habeas's history backward and ask of the writ's history a set of questions that it cannot answer.[14]

In order to make sense of the admittedly ambiguous Founding-era habeas developments, we have to understand how national and state political institutions—and the regimes that occupied them—initially struggled and ultimately compromised their way to a politically viable construction of federal habeas corpus. Even if there is some evidence in the earliest debates that would support one contemporary side more than another, the fact remains that even the earliest American political regimes—including those that were a part of the Founding generation—never hesitated to choose constructions of habeas that were more acceptable to short-term political considerations than to long-term abstract conceptions of constitutional law.

COLONIAL HABEAS

Habeas corpus in English political and constitutional history had a demonstrable impact on early colonial and state governments. No better example of the American colonial experience with the writ is the fact that habeas was suspended during the American Revolution.[15] In five of the six years of the Revolution (1777–1783), Parliament suspended the writ six times.[16] Debates in England concerning the propriety of suspending the writ pitted none other than

Edmund Burke against the powers of Parliament, a role with which he was more than familiar.[17] Aggrieved by the suspension only in America and not throughout the great realm of the English empire as well, Burke proclaimed, "Liberty, if I understand it at all, is a *general* principle, and the clear right of all the subjects within the realm, or of none. Partial freedom seems to me a most invidious mode of slavery. But, unfortunately, it is the kind of slavery the most easily committed in times of civil discord."[18]

These words were repeated in pamphlets read throughout England and the colonies. There can be no doubt that the colonists were inspired by this defense of habeas rights as guaranteed to all British subjects and citizens. Importantly for our purposes, it would seem that colonists had little doubt that the famous Habeas Act of 1679 applied to them. Otherwise their immediate dissent, as well as Burke's, would have been quite odd.[19]

Interestingly, only three of the original twelve states explicitly provided for the writ in their constitutions by the time of the ratifying convention in 1789, though the other nine certainly entertained habeas writs through common-law proceedings, and most made the writ available after 1790 through either statutory or constitutional provision.[20] What this suggests is that even without enumeration in some state constitutions, the writ was available to citizens from their states before 1790. According to Zechariah Chafee, the most likely reason for the availability of the writ even when a state constitution did not make explicit provision for its availability was that "it had been so long and solidly established in every colony that assertion was probably considered unnecessary."[21]

The significance of the suspension of habeas during the Revolutionary War lies beyond the colonists' immediate feelings of antipathy toward the crown. As Chafee's theory suggests, a formal enumeration of habeas rights was not necessary for courts—and citizens—to believe that the writ was available. But no matter how solidly established habeas access might have been, the fact that the 1789 Constitution did not explicitly provide for habeas leaves room for doubt as to its absolute guarantee during peacetime. This doubt is compounded by the fact that the written Constitution in 1789 in part gained its legitimacy through explicit provisions that guaranteed rights by limiting governmental power.

THE SUSPENSION CLAUSE

The first mention of habeas during the convention came from a series of proposals submitted by Charles Pinckney to the committee of detail on 20 August

1787. James Madison reports that Pinckney's original proposal for a habeas clause in the Constitution stated:

The privileges and benefit of the Writ of Habeas corpus shall be enjoyed in this Government in the most expeditious and ample manner; and shall not be suspended by the Legislature except upon the most urgent and pressing occasions, and for a limited time not exceeding ____ months.[22]

Discussion during the convention concerning habeas would not resume until 28 August, when the following was recorded by Madison:

Mr. Pinckney, urging the propriety of securing the benefit of the Habeas corpus in the most ample manner, moved "that it should not be suspended but on the most urgent occasions, & then only for a limited time, not exceeding twelve months."

Mr. Rutledge was for declaring the habeas Corpus inviolable. He did not conceive that a suspension could ever be necessary at the same time through all the states.

Mr. Govr. Morris moved that "The privilege of the writ of Habeas Corpus shall not be suspended; unless where in cases of Rebellion or invasion the public safety may require it."

Mr. Wilson doubted whether in any case a suspension could be necessary, as the discretion now exists with Judges, in most important cases to keep in Gaol or admit to Bail.

The first part of Mr. Govr. Morris' motion, to the word "unless" was agreed to nem. con.—on the remaining part;

N.H. ay. Mas. ay. Ct. ay. Pa. ay. Del. Ay. Md. ay Va. ay. N.C. no. S.C. no. Geo. No.

The debates are sparse, and the most we can glean from them is that the salient concern was the appropriate duration of suspension, not whether habeas was an independently existing federal right apart from congressional legislation. Moreover, the fact that all of the states already provided for procedural access to the writ, and that each state had its own conceptions of the substantive rights that state habeas served to vindicate, suggests that the clause may have been concerned in the first instance with the suspension of state habeas guarantees by the federal government.[23] Even though he ultimately voted for the clause as ratified, Luther Martin and the rest of the Maryland delegation were initially unconvinced that the federal government should have any right to suspend the writ at all, even during war or rebellion. This sentiment was also echoed in the other two state delegations that voted against the initial construction of the habeas clause. To Martin, as to others, if an invasion occurred that necessitated some kind of suspension, it would occur in one or several of the existing states, which would be more than able to suspend the writ if the situation dictated.

Martin was particularly worried that federal suspension of state habeas would potentially allow the national government to act "whenever the State should oppose its [the federal government's] views, however arbitrary and unconstitutional . . . it would be an engine of oppression in its hands."[24]

To many anti-Federalists in the state ratifying conventions, the absence of a bill of rights in the proposed Constitution was just as problematic as the lack of a positive grant to the right of habeas corpus. The Pennsylvania ratifying convention's minority statement detailed their objections to the Constitution by stating that the omission of a "BILL OF RIGHTS, ascertaining and fundamentally establishing those unalienable and personal rights of man . . . the principal of which are the rights of conscience" that would secure "personal liberty by the clear and unequivocal establishment of the writ of *habeas corpus*."[25] To anti-Federalists, then, the clause did not even implicitly guarantee a right to the writ. As a result, the paucity of debate surrounding the suspension clause leaves us without a definitive conclusion concerning the actual status of habeas. Whether it was an implied but not formally enumerated right, or whether it could only be provided by Congress, would have to be answered by subsequent political necessity and compromise.

HABEAS AND THE JUDICIARY ACT OF 1789

Whether or not the suspension clause explicitly provided for the writ seemed to be answered in the negative when Congress first met in 1789. The politics of the Judiciary Act of 1789 suggest that political compromise motivated and sustained Congress' exercise of its duties under Article III to create a federal court system.[26] Although the Bill of Rights was obviously the most pressing matter of business for the first Congress, the need to establish a federal judiciary—and specify its powers and jurisdiction—was just as important and just as politically sensitive.[27]

In drafting the act, Oliver Ellsworth was forced to find an acceptable middle ground between familiar sides. Federalist conceptions of the judiciary imagined a national court system that was fully commensurate with the Constitution's seemingly broad grant of judicial power, giving to federal courts jurisdiction in "all cases, in law and equity, arising under this Constitution, the laws of the United States, and treaties made, or which shall be made, under their authority." A strong federal government needed a strong federal judiciary in order to compel compliance from recalcitrant states. Anti-Federalists, on the other hand, were intent on limiting as much as possible congressional grants of jurisdiction to whatever lower courts Congress might want to create. In their minds, the fewer federal courts Congress created, the better. They also wanted to retain for state courts original jurisdiction for federal questions, with any appeals moving directly to the Supreme Court.[28]

The structure of the act bears out the political compromises that Ellsworth had to make in order to pass the statute. Aside from setting the number of Supreme Court justices at six and creating district and circuit courts, the act's provisions for federal court jurisdiction were decidedly narrow.[29] All appeals to the Supreme Court on federal questions were granted, but original jurisdiction in most cases remained in state courts and, with the exception of federal criminal cases, federal courts could not exercise common-law jurisdiction. Moreover, for federal court jurisdiction in diversity of citizenship cases, the amount had to exceed $500, and one of the litigants had to be a citizen of the state in which the case was brought. Importantly, section 34 provided a significant concession to anti-Federalists, as it mandated that "the laws of the several states . . . shall be regarded as rules of decisions in trials at common law in the courts of the United States." Section 25 also provided, through writs of error, for Supreme Court review of final decisions of the highest court of any state that ruled against a federal party, invalidated a federal statute or treaty, upheld a state law against charges that it violated federal law, or violated any "title, right, privilege, or exemption" under the Constitution.[30]

The habeas provision in the Judiciary Act similarly tracked these political concessions and compromises. Particularly, section 14 provided

that all the before-mentioned courts of the United States, shall have power to issue writs of *scire facias, habeas corpus,* and all other writs not specially provided for by statute, which may be necessary for the exercise of their respective jurisdictions, and agreeable to the principles and usages of law. And that either of the justices of the supreme court, as well as judges of the district courts, shall have power to grant writs of *habeas corpus* for the purpose of an inquiry into the cause of commitment.—*Provided,* That writs of *habeas corpus* shall in no case extend to prisoners in gaol, unless where they are in custody, under or by colour of the authority of the United States, or are committed for trial before some court of the same, or are necessary to be brought into court to testify.

The congressional grant of power to federal courts to exercise federal habeas corpus is the most conspicuous part of the language of the act. Although the crafting of this provision seems to render moot the question of whether or not Congress needed to provide for the writ, subsequent regime readings of the clause did not hesitate to interpret it to suit their preferred level of federal habeas powers. The second clause remains a persistent source of controversy, especially among those who argue that federal habeas was always meant to review state criminal convictions. Although the clause seemingly prohibits federal review of state detentions through habeas, some argue that the Framers in both Philadelphia and in the first Congress nevertheless meant to provide federal habeas review of state court proceedings. Moreover, Eric Freedman has also argued that because scholars and jurists have accepted Chief Justice Marshall's purportedly erroneous reading of the Judiciary Act of 1789 to prohibit federal habeas for state prisoners in *Ex parte Bollman*, we have since left unexamined the proposition that the act's language thus constituted was either unnecessary or patently unconstitutional.[31]

No explicit provisions were made in the Judiciary Act, moreover, for criminal appeals to the Supreme Court from lower federal courts. According to one of the leading legal scholars of habeas procedure, this omission, combined with the prohibition in section 14 of federal habeas for state prisoners, has led the Court to use habeas as a "substitute for . . . direct review" of many nationally important constitutional issues.[32] Section 25 of the Judiciary Act provided writs of error to the Supreme Court from state courts, but no direct habeas appeal. It also provided no appeal to the Supreme Court for federal prisoners convicted in lower federal courts. To remedy this, James Liebman argues, the Court has consistently used habeas corpus. Of particular importance for Liebman's argument is his contention that the Court has never hesitated to go beyond the purported jurisdictional limitations to habeas, especially those limitations believed by some to have applied during the nineteenth century. The most significant of these limitations to habeas were prohibitions on substantive inquiries into habeas cases after a return to the writ indicated that a prisoner was held by competent jurisdiction, and prohibitions on postconviction habeas review. Many contemporary supporters of habeas rollbacks support them because they see the increased postconviction role of habeas as inconsistent with its original meaning, which they claim was only to test the jurisdiction of the court before conviction and was not designed to review the substance of the petitioner's claims after conviction.[33] With only a few exceptions, most commentators agree that the Judiciary Act of 1789 precluded federal habeas review for state prisoners. But although most would agree that Congress has the authority to adjust federal court habeas jurisdiction, differences continue to persist because neither the suspension clause nor the Judiciary Act explicitly stated that habeas is a right.

ANTEBELLUM FEDERAL HABEAS FOR
FEDERAL PRISONERS

Liebman's argument—that habeas courts did not hesitate to examine the substantive claims of petitioners in the antebellum period—is more right than wrong with respect to the empirical evidence. Before the Civil War, federal courts did not hesitate to go beyond mere questions of lower court jurisdiction in federal habeas cases, but the reasons for this practical effect are found in the larger political conditions that made it possible. Although it is true that federal court habeas power has increased since 1789, the overall increase in scope of federal habeas has never been a continuous or certain development that recognized an ever-increasing set of due process rights. Liebman's analogy of habeas as a limited substitute to direct appeal when no other appellate remedy is provided to either state or federal prisoners thus runs the risk of an overly legal and post hoc generalization of a trajectory of habeas development that has been more circuitous and partial than linear and complete. Moreover, the suggestion that the Court has always used habeas as a substitute for a writ error for nationally important issues is potentially misleading unless we understand the substance of these nationally important issues. As we will see, the use of habeas by federal courts never served to vindicate our modern conceptions of substantive individual rights. Ironically, however, the ignoble use of habeas by these courts before the Civil War became the basis for the national enforcement of a set of individual rights after the war that now seems more familiar.

Federal habeas corpus cases for those detained by the federal government during the antebellum period were more often the products of contingent political considerations than they were of deliberate legal reasoning. As we have seen, the ambiguity of both the suspension clause and the Judiciary Act of 1789 allowed for multiple interpretations of the jurisdictional, procedural, and substantive reach of the writ. For example, all of the nine federal prisoner habeas cases that came before the Supreme Court prior to the Civil War provided both restrictive and expansive interpretations of the Court's habeas powers.[34] The variation is best explained by attending to the politics that created and sustained the Court's earliest habeas cases in the first third of the eighteenth century.

The best examples of this dynamic are two of the most important federal habeas cases decided by Chief Justice John Marshall, *Ex parte Bollman* (1807) and *Ex parte Watkins* (1830).[35] Both the suspension clause and the habeas provisions of the Judiciary Act of 1789 received their first significant readings in *Bollman,* and two important outcomes that have significantly shaped habeas's development ever since emerged from the cases. First, Marshall set the stage for subsequent antebellum habeas development by expansively interpreting federal court habeas power. Nevertheless, the second outcome was that Marshall affirmed the Judiciary Act's prohibition against federal court habeas review for state prisoners, effectively affirming the two-track trajectory of habeas development that created so much friction in the years leading up to the Civil War. Marshall constructed and maintained strong federal court habeas review for federal prisoners partly by ceding federal court habeas power and review for state prisoners. Still, these two outcomes are impossible to reconcile solely through a legal lens. Marshall's legal reasoning in these cases is suspect, but his political and institutional concerns in these cases are clear.[36] Despite a capacious reading of the Judiciary Act's habeas clause in *Bollman,* Marshall reined in his enlarged reading of habeas in *Watkins* when he perceived that larger political support for increased judicial power was nonexistent.

Marshall's *Bollman* and *Watkins* opinions are thus best understood as integral—although immediately inconsequential—parts of the Court's larger political role during the first decades of the nineteenth century. Habeas's role, and the Court's as well, were uncertain during and immediately after the Philadelphia convention, but Marshall was able to engineer the future use of federal court habeas power through a mixture of political calculation and legal maneuvering. The Marshall Court's habeas jurisprudence reflected a concern for establishing judicial power within a political environment that was more generally unsure of the judiciary's role in the new republic.[37] And as we see in *Ex parte Watkins* (1830), which came toward the end of Marshall's tenure, the Court worked hard to maintain its habeas power by continuing to forgo any intimation that it would review state cases through habeas in order to maintain at least some level of judicial independence to issue the writ in the future.

BOLLMAN *AND* WATKINS

Next to John Marshall and Alexander Hamilton, few men played Thomas Jefferson's foil better than Aaron Burr. After fatally shooting Alexander Hamilton in a duel and sizing up the likelihood that Jefferson would jettison him from the presidential ticket in 1804, Burr headed west.[38] Although speculation about his treasonous motives continues even to this day, Burr's Western sojourn was most likely concerned first and foremost with money and power, not perfidy.[39] Nevertheless, Burr's Western exploits quickly drew the attention and suspicion of Jefferson, who suspected that he was secretly working up plans to convince the Western states to secede from the Union and "establish himself as the ruler of a vast empire extending from the Mississippi valley to Mexico City."[40]

Even though he was aware of Burr's exploits for most of the first half of 1806, it was only in November of that year that Jefferson issued a presidential proclamation ordering those who were involved in what he thought were treasonous activities in the West to cease and desist.[41] In January, John Randolph led the passage of a resolution in the House of Representatives demanding that the president come forward with actual evidence of the supposed conspiracy. Jefferson then sent a message to Congress detailing his suspicions and naming Burr as the ringleader. Two other men were named as Burr's coconspirators, Dr. Erich Bollman and Samuel Swartwout. But according to John Adams, Jefferson's message to Congress unfairly and prematurely convicted Burr, permanently jeopardizing any future criminal cases that might be brought against him.

The territorial governor of New Orleans, General James Wilkinson, had already apprehended Bollman and Swartwout by the time Jefferson responded to John Randolph's House proclamation. More importantly, Jefferson failed to tell Congress that Wilkinson had ignored a habeas petition issued by the Supreme Court of the New Orleans territory that had been filed on behalf of Bollman and Swartwout. Aside from the refusal to honor the writ, the pair was denied counsel, and in complying with Jefferson's order to bring them to Washington, D.C., for prosecution, they were also denied their Sixth Amendment rights to be tried in the "state and district wherein [their] crime shall have been committed." As Burr's two suspected coconspirators were transported via Charleston to Baltimore and then to Washington, Wilkinson then disregarded yet another habeas petition, this one issued from the United States district court of South Carolina.

When Bollman and Swartwout arrived in Washington on 23 January 1807, Jefferson directed the United States attorney, Walter Jones, to seek a bench warrant for the two men, charging them with treason. Now aware that Wilkinson had ignored two writs of habeas corpus, and worried that more might follow with similar results, the Senate quickly moved to suspend habeas corpus for three months for those who were charged with "treason . . . or other high crimes or misdemeanors." The measure passed in the Senate with only one dissent. A few days later, and with cooler heads, the House voted down the measure 113–91.[42]

Just a week later, during the first few days of the Supreme Court's opening term, a new habeas petition was filed with the Court on behalf of Bollman and

Swartwout challenging their commitment by the circuit court of the District of Columbia. Aside from the Sixth Amendment question concerning the constitutionality of trying the two men outside of the jurisdiction in which their alleged crimes occurred, the *Bollman* case presented the Court with the first salient question of its power to issue the writ of habeas corpus according to both the Constitution's suspension clause and section 14 of the Judiciary Act of 1789.[43]

For all of the legal maneuvering that characterized Marshall's arguments about the nature of habeas and the ability of federal courts to issue the writ in *Bollman,* one of the most important political facts of the case was that the United States attorney general, Caesar Rodney, declined to argue the case before the Court. Evidently, the Jefferson administration believed that the Court had the authority to issue the writ, and Rodney proclaimed that if the Court should "issue a writ of habeas Corpus he [would] cheerfully submit to it."[44] Although Jefferson was obviously bent on prosecuting Burr, Bollman, Swartwout, and anyone else involved in treasonous activities, the threshold question of whether or not the federal courts—and the Supreme Court in particular—actually had the ability to issue the writ was not disputed. But the Jefferson administration's agreement about the Court's ability to issue the writ did not mean that the case presented Marshall with an easy decision, either politically or legally.

The potentially controversial aspects of the case involved not the ability of the Court to issue the writ, but rather the articulation of the source of that authority. If Marshall located the source of federal court habeas authority in the suspension clause, then that could set the Court up for criticism that it was reading into the language of the clause a power that was not explicitly enumerated. The most likely way that Marshall could give the clause such a reading would be to claim a common-law authority for federal court habeas power, which was an argument advanced in the case by Robert Goodloe Harper, Bollman's counsel. This move would certainly have angered Jefferson to no end, and it could possibly have prompted him to disobey the Court if Bollman and Swartwout were released on an interpretation of habeas derived generally from the common law.[45] Instead, Marshall attributed federal court habeas authority to section 14 of the 1789 Judiciary Act, in which, he argued, Congress specifically gave courts such authority. Disclaiming common-law authority, Marshall instead argued:

Courts which originate in the common law possess a jurisdiction which must be regulated by their common law, until some statute shall change their established principles;

but courts which are created by written law, and whose jurisdiction is defined by written law, cannot transcend that jurisdiction. It is unnecessary to state the reasoning on which this opinion is founded, because it had been repeatedly given by this court . . . that for the meaning of the term habeas corpus, resort may unquestionably be had to the common law; but the power to award the writ by any of the courts of the United States, must be given by written law.[46]

In ceding some federal court habeas power to Congress, then, Marshall was able to avoid a reliance on common-law authority, which was the "old bugaboo of the Republicans."[47] Because federal court habeas authority could only derive from statute (that is, Congress), Marshall even argued that if Congress had not explicitly provided for the writ in the Judiciary Act of 1789, then "the privilege itself would be lost."[48] In other words, the suspension clause did not, by its own force, confer federal habeas rights. This power belonged to Congress alone.

Even though Marshall's interpretation seemingly deferred to Congress, this certainly did not mean that once that power was granted, federal courts were somehow more limited in the exercise of that authority than if the Court's jurisdiction had been derived by common-law readings. Bowing to a habeas authority that had already been conferred actually allowed Marshall the more important long-term ability to interpret this power through common-law notions of habeas practice, a power that was potentially greater. Marshall accomplished this by arguing that while "the power to award the writ . . . must be given by written law [Congress] . . . the meaning of . . . habeas corpus" would be interpreted by the Court according to the "common law."[49] By conceding the power to establish the writ to Congress, then, Marshall was able to leave constructions of its meaning and substance to the Court.

This is exactly how he proceeded to address the second important question concerning the ability of the entire Supreme Court to issue the writ and hear habeas cases. As with the writ of mandamus in *Marbury v. Madison,* the Court was now faced with the question of whether a congressional grant of habeas jurisdiction violated Article III's distinction between the Supreme Court's original and appellate jurisdictions.[50] But unlike *Marbury,* Bollman and Swartwout had not applied for the writ in the first instance from the Supreme Court. The Court's exercise of habeas power in this case was, according to Marshall, a "revision of the decision of an inferior court," which did not run afoul of original and appellate distinctions.[51] Section 14 of the Judiciary Act seemed to indicate that the power to issue the writ to inquire "into the cause of commitment" was limited to individual judges, not entire courts. If this section was construed this way, an individual Supreme Court justice would in effect possess more power than the entire Court itself. For Marshall, this "would be [a] strange" reading.[52] The congressional grant of habeas jurisdiction was thus designed for both individual judges and the federal courts as a whole. Marshall went on to clarify the nature of habeas further, noting that a court's habeas ruling "is always distinct from that which is involved in the cause itself. The question whether the individual shall be imprisoned is always distinct from the question whether he shall be convicted . . . therefore these questions are separated, and may be decided in different courts."[53] On the question of their detention, Marshall found that both Bollman and Swartwout could not be tried in the District of Columbia and that there was not enough evidence to support a charge of treason.[54] Both petitioners were then discharged and released.

With a capacious reading of the Judiciary Act of 1789 that attributed the initial grant of habeas authority to Congress, Marshall simultaneously quelled Republican fears while augmenting the power of federal courts to issue and interpret writs of habeas corpus. In what seems like a further concession, Marshall's reading of federal court habeas power also buttressed the final clause of section 14 of the Judiciary Act, which limited whatever meaning federal courts would subsequently give to the writ only to those petitioners held "under the colour of authority of the United States." Although not in any way related to the case at bar, Marshall bowed to the federalism limitations of the habeas statute—and the states' rights proclivities of his political opponents—by suggesting that federal courts could not use habeas to inquire into state criminal cases.

This more politically sensitive reading suggests that the *Bollman* case is best understood as the first example of the political machinations that always partly drive habeas development and change. The Jeffersonian regime was not hesitant to use habeas for overtly political reasons consistent with its constitutional vision of regime governance. The quick, even rash, push for the suspension of habeas corpus in the House of Representatives, led by stalwart Republican William Giles, shows this to be the case. If only for Federalist representation in the Senate, a three-month suspension of the writ would most likely have occurred. Moreover, on the heels of the impeachment of Justice Samuel Chase, it is likely that Republicans were worried that habeas might be used by Federalist judges to thwart Republican enforcement of Jefferson's prosecution of Burr by claiming for themselves complete judicial independence to interpret the meaning and jurisdiction of federal court habeas power. Only time would tell whether the Federalist judiciary would heed Republican warnings.[55]

Marshall did not completely disappoint Republicans in his reading of habeas in *Bollman* that bowed to noninterference in state detentions. It is likely that Marshall might have miscalculated both congressional and popular support for the subsequent trial of Aaron Burr, which owed its circuitous definition of treason to Marshall's *Bollman* opinion.[56] Threats of impeachment soon surfaced after Burr's acquittal, and William Giles quickly introduced a bill in the House to remove any Supreme Court jurisdiction in criminal cases.[57] Nonetheless, Marshall's opinion helped settle and confirm some Jeffersonian regime principles concerning the nature of the federal judiciary while also establishing the Court's ability to issue habeas writs.[58] Politically, the failed impeachment of Chase provided Marshall with some traction to advance an argument for habeas power that still left significant room for judicial independence. By recognizing congressional authority to grant federal courts habeas authority, Marshall was able to establish the more important power of determining the writ's function and substance.

Marshall would again affirm this settlement of the limits of judicial habeas power twenty-three years later. In *Ex parte Watkins* (1830), he reiterated his *Bollman* argument that while Congress can confer the power of habeas to federal courts, the Court itself can give substantive meaning to the writ.[59] Watkins had been tried and convicted in the circuit court of the District of Columbia and petitioned the Court on habeas, arguing that his indictment presented no charge. Marshall, however, denied the petition and repeated the settlement reached in *Bollman:*

> The court can undoubtedly inquire into the sufficiency of [the cause of commitment]; but if it be the judgment of a court of competent jurisdiction . . . is not that judgment in itself sufficient cause? A judgment, in its nature, concludes the subject on which it is rendered, and pronounces the law of the case. The judgment of a court of record whose jurisdiction is final, is as conclusive on all the world as the judgment of this court would be. . . . It puts an end to the inquiry concerning the fact, by deciding it.[60]

Marshall's self-imposed limitation on Supreme Court jurisdiction in *Watkins* reaffirmed both Congress' power over habeas and the Court's ability to issue the writ. By refusing to release Watkins, Marshall could show that the Court's power could be trusted and limited.

By the time *Watkins* came down in 1830, the political landscape had changed drastically from *Bollman,* and even passive assertions of independent judicial power might have destroyed whatever small advances the Court had achieved. The Jacksonian regime now reigned, and, as Mark Graber has noted, "Marshall Court policymaking ended abruptly in 1829 with the election of Andrew Jackson and the installation of a hostile Democratic party regime in the national government."[61] It is not surprising that Marshall would tread lightly, and it is even less surprising that he would seek to articulate carefully and explicitly the logic of the Court's jurisdictional limitations. Even so, Marshall constructed his argument about jurisdiction only after first arguing that the Court did indeed have the power to issue the writ. "The question is," Marshall added, *"whether this be a case in which it ought to be exercised."*[62]

The Marshall Court did not articulate federal court habeas power for those held by the federal government with countermajoritarian principles in mind, nor did the Court argue for our more contemporary notion of strong federal habeas authority to resolve any constitutional issue raised in either federal or state courts. What the Court did do was carve out a politically and procedurally viable role for federal court habeas authority that was popular enough to survive two large-scale regime transformations between 1800 and 1830. By choosing when to give traction to some important substantive constitutional issues through habeas (such as the Sixth Amendment and the treason clause in *Bollman*), and when not to (*Watkins*), the Court was able to create and preserve an efficient level of judicial independence for federal habeas. It is also likely that the Jeffersonian and Jacksonian regimes were mollified by Marshall's continued support of the Judiciary Act's prohibition against federal habeas for state prisoners.[63] After all, federal habeas power was not the only habeas power available, nor was it understood to be the most important. If states felt that federal prisoners were held in violation of the Constitution, they could—and often did—issue habeas writs to inquire into the cause of their detention.[64]

FEDERAL HABEAS FOR STATE PRISONERS

As the salient Marshall Court habeas cases demonstrate, there were two important Court-imposed limitations on habeas power before the Civil War. The Court's recognition of the power of Congress to provide for the writ might have been politically induced to allow the Court to impose its own conceptions of habeas power in practice, but it nevertheless set the stage for antebellum conceptions of habeas jurisdiction that limited federal habeas changes to congressional statute. The second limitation of habeas power that developed from Marshall's reading of the Judiciary Act of 1789 was an unambiguous reading of the federalism dimensions of federal habeas. Although neither of the two important Marshall-era cases implicated this dimension directly, they both stated in dicta that federal court habeas power was limited only to those held "under colour of authority of the United States," thus precluding any federal habeas review of state court decisions.[65] Marshall's nationalistic jurisprudence aside, he never entertained the possibility that Congress' grant of habeas authority to federal courts allowed them to reach into the domain of state law. The political supports for broad federal court habeas power were difficult enough to develop and then maintain in their own right. Even if Marshall had envisioned federal habeas for state prisoners, he would have been constrained in making the argument by his recognition of Congress' authority to determine the courts' habeas jurisdiction, as well as by the political climate of two regimes—Jeffersonian and Jacksonian—that would certainly have been deeply resistant to any intimation that federal habeas courts could second-guess state legal authority.

Nevertheless, as noted above, there were two important antebellum congressional modifications in habeas jurisdiction for federal courts. In 1833, Congress modified federal court habeas jurisdiction to include habeas petitions from those who might be detained by state authorities when enforcing federal law.[66] In 1842, Congress again expanded federal court habeas authority for foreign nationals detained by state governments.[67] What is most important about the 1833 act is that it was never used for its intended purpose, which was to provide a legal mechanism for the removal of cases involving federal revenue officers who might be arrested by state authorities for enforcing tariff laws. Instead, the 1833 act was used to remove from state to federal courts cases in which federal marshals were arrested by state authorities for enforcing the fugitive slave provisions of the Compromise of 1850. This unintended consequence—which was recognized as such by federal court judges time and again—nevertheless fueled significant backlash from states that were actively using their own newly improved habeas powers to thwart federal fugitive slave legislation and protect their free black populations from kidnapping. The Jacksonian regime's habeas expansion in 1833 might never have been needed after the passage of the force bill, but the provision nevertheless remained law, buttressing both the enforcement of the Democratic Party's vision of constitutional governance with respect to slavery's expansion and a significant state-level Republican backlash during the 1850s.

THE HABEAS ACTS OF 1833 AND 1842

The habeas provision in the force bill of 2 March 1833 provided that

either of the justices of the Supreme Court, or a judge of any district court of the United States, in addition to the authority already conferred by law, shall have power to grant writs of habeas corpus in all cases of a prisoner or prisoners, in jail or confinement, where he or they shall be committed or confined on, or by any authority of law, for any act done, or omitted to be done, in pursuance of a law of the United States, or any order, process, or decree, of any judge or court thereof.

The concern prompting the newly increased reach of federal habeas for those who might be jailed for "acts done . . . in pursuance of a law of the United States" was directly related to the crisis precipitated by South Carolina's threat to nullify federal tariff laws.[68] Although the crisis was averted through a tariff reduction even before the final passage of the force bill and its habeas provision, and no situation ever arose that required federal judges to issue habeas to free those enforcing tariff laws, we still see in the force bill—and the larger crisis—how political regimes transform habeas to enforce their visions of constitutional governance and enforcement.

The fact that the first congressional jurisdictional enlargement of habeas to reach into the legal processes of states came during the nullification crisis is indicative of the use of habeas to enforce regime principles. South Carolina's threat of state nullification of federal law during the 1830s did not arise de novo. Various conceptions of federalism had competed in American politics ever since the Philadelphia convention. Ranging from extreme conceptions of centralized national power to equally extreme conceptions of states' rights, political and constitutional settlements over important national questions almost always involved a compromise that fell somewhere in between these two positions. Threats of state nullification over tariff issues from 1828 onward were no different. In this specific case, the threat of nullification met up with the forging of the Jacksonian political regime. As others have argued, states' rights arguments that pursued radical or extreme positions on other issues during the beginning of Jackson's presidency, such as Georgia's claims in *Worcester v. Georgia,* did not directly confront and challenge the powers of the presidency in the way that South Carolina's threats to use military force did. As such, it was a direct challenge to Jackson's presidential authority.[69]

The centrist position between the two extremes consisted of a conception of federalism that recognized a significant role for both the states and the national government. This position, as Keith Whittington describes it, "leaned toward resolving [disputes] through concession. If the general government had the right to enforce the laws against the states, it should also respect the opinions of those states and voluntarily work to meet their objections."[70] Jackson's more nationalistic position only came to life as a response to the nullifiers, whom he had come to see as the real threat to the Union, and not to states' rights positions more generally. Especially after tariff reductions were negotiated with his support after 1830, the takeover of the South Carolina state legislature by nullifiers who were calling a constitutional convention to continue their plans was seen by Jackson as pure treason. The fact that Jackson demanded the passage of the force bill even after Henry Clay and John Calhoun negotiated new tariffs speaks to its regime-enforcing character. Moreover, even though the substance of the crisis had been resolved, Jackson still believed the force bill's provisions might yet be necessary if nullifiers decided to continue to resist national authority.[71] The theoretical construction of federalism that precipitated from the controversy was thus a regime principle that had to be politically, constitutionally, and legally enforced, and the revision of federal habeas power was an important part of this larger project, even if it was never used.

The second congressional change to federal habeas jurisdiction during the antebellum period came in 1842 as a result of the McLeod affair. Like the 1833 habeas changes, the increased federal habeas jurisdiction provided for in the 1842 act was never used until after the Civil War. Nonetheless, the changes were directly related to the felt need for some mechanism of enforcement for fundamental regime principles. The debates surrounding the passage of the 1842 act, as well as three other Whig-inspired bills increasing federal power at the expense of the states passed during the same congressional term, further demonstrate the political foundations of habeas's change and development.

On 30 December 1837, the American steamboat *Caroline* was destroyed by British troops as it lay moored in Schlosser, New York. Canadian insurgents, who had recently engaged British troops in Ontario, hoped that the *Caroline* would bring much-needed provisions to their resistance efforts. That day, however, British troops sacked the ship, burned it, and sent it over Niagara Falls, killing two people. The Van Buren administration directed Secretary of State John Forsyth to protest the British actions. His protests were met with the response that the United States had failed to quell its citizens' involvement in British and Canadian affairs.[72]

Alexander McLeod, a Canadian, was subsequently arrested by New York authorities for his suspected participation in the assault on the *Caroline*. Angered, the British government demanded that McLeod be released because he was acting on orders directly from the British crown. His actions, according to the British government, were public, not private, and were simply the extension of a sovereign nation. Importantly, in Forsyth's reply, he not only disagreed with the characterization of McLeod's actions as public, which might have precluded his prosecution by the state of New York, but also stated that the federal government did not have the power to reach into the criminal proceedings of states.[73]

When John Tyler assumed the presidency, his secretary of state, Daniel Webster, reversed the United States' previous position on McLeod's actions but still maintained that the federal government did not have the ability to reach into the domain of state criminal law to free McLeod. Convinced that the government was powerless, but sympathetic to Britain's position, Webster even went so far as to enlist the help of Attorney General John Crittenden to aid in McLeod's defense in New York courts. With little subsequent fanfare, McLeod was held over for trial and then subsequently acquitted.[74]

In March 1842, just a few months after McLeod's acquittal, another participant in the raid on the *Caroline* was arrested. In order to avert another international incident, and well aware of similar situations in American history in which foreign nationals were detained by state authorities, President Tyler proposed that Congress remedy this problem through appropriate habeas legislation. As would be expected, the initial wording of the bill from the Senate Judiciary Committee, which provided for the removal of cases from state to federal courts via habeas for "any act done . . . under the law of nations . . . or authority of any foreign State or sovereignty," met with spirited resistance, particularly from Democrats. Not only did these habeas revisions potentially threaten the traditional criminal justice domain of state courts, but in the minds of some Southern members of Congress, they might inspire foreigners to incite slave revolts in states, only to have their cases removed to federal court and dismissed.[75] The final bill, which equally divided Whigs and Democrats, provided that

in all cases of any prisoner or prisoners in jail or confinement, where he, she, or they, being subjects or citizens of a foreign State, and domiciled therein, shall be committed or confined, or in custody, under or by authority of law, or process founded thereon, of the United States or any one of them; for or on account of any act done or omitted under any alleged right, title, authority, privilege, protection, or exemption, set up or claimed under the commission, or order, or sanction, of any foreign State or sovereignty, the validity and effect whereof depend upon the law of nations, or under color thereof.[76]

Three other controversial Whig bills were passed during the same term as the Habeas Act, all of which drew the ire of Democrats, who perceived that the bills would produce, in the words of James Buchanan, "dangerous collision[s] between the Federal and State authorities."[77] The first was the Fiscal Bank Acts, which reinvigorated debates about Congress' power to create a national bank and drummed up old, familiar criticisms of Marshall's decision in *McCulloch v. Maryland*.[78] The second bill was the National Bankruptcy Act, which widened the class of people who could voluntarily file for bankruptcy. And in August

1842, Congress mandated that states choose their congressmen by districts instead of by at-large systems. Of the four controversial bills significantly increasing federal power passed in "rapid succession" by the Whig Congress, Senator Levi Woodbury (D-Mass.), who would soon be appointed to the Supreme Court, further predicted that they would be "fatal towards the States."[79]

What is important to understand about the two antebellum congressional changes to federal habeas court jurisdiction are both the overtly political origins of their changes and their federalism dimensions. Both the 1833 and 1842 acts were engineered by political regimes to meet critical challenges to their ability to govern. For Jackson, habeas changes were necessary to enforce a core regime principle in the form of a centrist federalism that, while deferential to states' rights as a political proposition, was nevertheless unyielding on the basic enforcement powers of the national government. For the Tyler administration, as for others before it, the ability of the federal government to operate with legitimacy and authority on the international stage required habeas changes to remove state cases against foreign nationals to federal courts.[80]

These changes also directly implicated issues of federalism and states' rights, and criticisms of both changes in this regard were swift.[81] Both the 1833 and 1842 acts are often cited by contemporary critics in support of broader arguments about the inevitability of increased federal habeas court supervision of state criminal trials. But there is nothing in the history of these two acts that suggests that they were initiated for reasons other than the enforcement and maintenance of core regime principles of Jacksonian Democrats in the early 1830s and Whigs in the early 1840s. Moreover, the regime principles that were enforced through these changes to habeas were never conceived as having anything remotely to do with the individual rights of the potential habeas petitioners in the ways with which we are familiar today. The removal of state cases to federal habeas courts for federal revenue officers or foreign nationals was a far cry from the use of habeas to vindicate the rights of minority criminal defendants in Southern state courts during the height of Jim Crow. If anything, these changes were solicitous of majorities, not minorities.

ANTEBELLUM STATE HABEAS

State habeas corpus development was much more robust than its federal counterpart before the Civil War.[82] As the early constitutional deliberations surrounding habeas demonstrate, the limited role for federal habeas was most likely premised on the assumption that state habeas was always available for those seeking to challenge their confinement. The reactions to the increased federal jurisdiction in both the 1833 and 1842 acts further show how even minor jurisdictional changes were seen as threatening to state-centered conceptions of states' rights. The question of whether state habeas actually should serve to interfere with federal criminal law, however, was only first answered (and in the negative) in the mid-1850s. States nonetheless continued to exercise their habeas power for those held under federal authority up until 1871.[83] Until then, states never hesitated to inquire into the cause of containment for those held under the color of federal authority. The relative power and autonomy of state habeas before the Civil War allow us to see in sharp relief a pattern of development that foregrounds the writ as a salient tool in the enforcement of various political regimes' conceptions of constitutional governance. More so than with any other issue during the antebellum period, this pattern emerged as the result of free-state resistance to the political and legal controversies involving the enforcement of fugitive slave laws.

To be sure, antebellum state uses of habeas corpus were not limited to the fugitive slave controversy. Either by statute, state constitutional provision, or common-law judicial interpretation, most states precluded the writ for those who were properly held and charged with felonies or treason, and they further prevented the writ from issuing as a postconviction remedy.[84] These bars to habeas access were simply carried forward from the provisions of the English Habeas Corpus Act of 1679, which formed the basis for the understanding of the Great Writ in most states.[85] With respect to state habeas for federal prisoners, McLeod's case is certainly only one example of how state and federal habeas was bound to "bring the federal and State Governments into collision."[86] Other cases demonstrate this as well. For example, Chief Justice Nicholson of the Maryland supreme court released two petitioners on habeas in 1809 who were detained by General Wilkinson in New Orleans during the Burr ordeal.[87] During the War of 1812, Pennsylvania, New York, and Massachusetts courts issued the writ to federal military officers and until 1861 routinely issued habeas to release those serving in the military. A Virginia state judge even released on habeas a petitioner who was a potential witness for the prosecution in the attempted assassination of President Andrew Jackson in 1833.[88]

STATE HABEAS AND SLAVERY

Not surprisingly, no other issue drove habeas development on the state level more dramatically than the politics of slavery. State variation in the use of habeas to adjudicate slave-law-related issues largely tracked the sectional and geographic divisions that characterized slavery's development leading up to the Civil War. Before 1850, Northern states experimented with habeas laws that sought to protect their free black populations from kidnapping, but by and large, they acquiesced to Southern demands to recover fugitive slaves. Northern state governments were as hostile to abolitionist demands as they were loyal to either the Whig or Democratic Party.

However, there were important intrasectional differences in state uses of habeas that speak to the tremendously diverse uses of the writ in the antebellum period. Some Southern states, such as Mississippi, explicitly provided statutory habeas remedies for slaveholders to reclaim their slaves when they were stolen. Mississippi's habeas corpus act provided for the use of the writ to deliver up a slave to inquire into the contested legal ownership and disputed titles of slaves. The act said, in part, that habeas could issue to determine whether "any slave or slaves for life shall be taken or seduced out of the possession of the master, owner, or overseers of such slaves, by force, stratagem or fraud."[89] Habeas in no way was concerned with the freedom of the individual held in this regard or with the legality of her confinement.

In the 1824 case of *Scudder v. Seals,* for example, a habeas corpus petition was issued to bring before the supreme court of Mississippi the bodies of two slaves, Dicey and Daniel, to inquire into the legality of their current owner's title.[90] The court determined that Dicey and Daniel, who had been willed to their former owner's daughter, were effectively stolen from her. The habeas proceeding then returned the slaves to their rightful owner.

The use of habeas to recover stolen property in Mississippi was limited only to the state itself, sometimes confounding owners of slaves in the recovery of their rightful property. In *Nations v. Alvis,* for example, the supreme court of Mississippi refused to release a slave on habeas corpus to her original owner because the theft had occurred in Tennessee and not in Mississippi, where the slave was now held. The court ruled that although the use of habeas to recover stolen slaves was a "prompt and effectual remedy," the notion of state sovereignty "cannot, by any inherent authority, claim respect beyond the jurisdiction of the state which enacts them."[91] The use of habeas to retrieve or recover property was limited to that inquiry only, not only in Mississippi, but also in other Southern states. Legitimate questions concerning the actual freedom of blacks sometimes arose in cases involving their disputed ownership, and most Southern states increasingly determined that jury trials, not habeas proceedings, were the most appropriate legal mechanisms for decisions involving fundamental rights of property.[92] Because most states simply required a return to a habeas writ that could show some legitimate justification for detention, the ubiquitous presumption in slave states that blackness implied servitude significantly limited the utility of the writ for libertarian causes.

In Northern states, habeas laws were enacted in the late seventeenth and early nineteenth centuries as part of Revolutionary era–inspired prohibitions on slavery and in reaction to fugitive slave kidnappings.[93] Here, too, there were important variations. Border states such as Pennsylvania were more likely to be conciliatory toward their slave state neighbors with respect to early fugitive slave issues, while New England states such as Massachusetts explicitly linked habeas to its kidnapping statutes as early as 1785.[94] The differences in the use of habeas in the North reflected the varying degrees of Northern racism as well as legitimate libertarian concerns about the protection of state citizens, whether they were free blacks, suspected fugitives, or white citizens who aided, harbored, or more generally interfered with Southerners' perceived rights of recovering fugitive slaves.[95]

Even as some states were moving toward gradual abolition, states such as New Jersey routinely allowed habeas to issue to resolve disputed claims of title to slaves. In *The State v. Anderson,* for example, the supreme court of New Jersey issued a writ of habeas corpus to inquire into the detention (that is, the enslavement) of a slave child named Silas.[96] Silas's mother, Betsy, was sold pursuant to her owner's will, which stated that she was to remain a slave for only fifteen years after his death. However, during her tenure as a slave for her new owner, she gave birth to a child. The owner then claimed the child as a slave for life, arguing that his property was damaged because it had given birth.[97] The court ultimately ruled that the child was free, and Betsy was also to be free after her fifteen years of service. In the same year, another case came to the supreme court of New Jersey that presented the court with a similar probate question.[98] After the death of his master, a slave, Tom, was sold to a man named Bloomfield, along with the original owner's other slaves. Evidence was presented to the court that argued that Tom's owner had always wished him to be free at his death (at times he was heard to have stated that "they had sucked the same breasts, and that he should never serve another master").[99] The court then issued a writ of habeas corpus. Bloomfield's counsel argued that for a slave to be free, his master must do more than "mention it to a third party." The court, relying again on the owner's complete power over his property, ruled that his verbal intention was enough, and Tom was discharged with his freedom. Just four years later, however, the same court ruled that a verbal intention to free a slave upon an owner's death was not enough for manumission. In the words of the court, the slaves in question "must go with the other property, and legally belong to the defendant."[100] Although the habeas petition failed to free the slaves, the court nevertheless refused to hold those who filed the writ liable for court costs and damages to the defendant. The court justified its position by saying that "they would not in any case compel the prosecutors of these writs to pay costs; it was a laudable and humane thing in any man or set of men to bring up the claims of these unfortunate people before the court for consideration."[101]

Variation in the use of habeas among states to adjudicate contested claims of ownership, however, was not as controversial as the use of habeas by states to frustrate or even prevent the return of fugitive slaves. As Paul Finkelman has argued, few constitutional compromises were as fraught with potential problems as the fugitive slave provision of Article IV.[102] Questions of state versus federal enforcement of Article IV, the potential problems associated with the common-law right of recaption, and the extent to which states could protect their free black citizens from kidnapping through habeas and other legal procedures were simply left unresolved in debate over the clause.[103] Indeed, only a few years after ratification, in response to a dispute between Pennsylvania and Virginia concerning the rendition of slave catchers who were charged with kidnapping, these issues prompted Congress to pass the first fugitive slave act in an attempt to resolve these lingering problems. The resolution of these issues, however, would not be smooth.

The Fugitive Slave Act of 1793 stipulated that state governors were to provide for fugitive extradition by honoring indictments filed in states from which extradition was requested. For fugitive slaves, however, the process was different. Slaves were first seized by owners or their agents. They could then be brought before state or federal judges or local county magistrates. Unlike the extradition process, proof of ownership and the determination of the correct identity of the fugitive in question could be met with a simple affidavit issued from a Southern state judge. The difference between a legitimate indictment and a simple affidavit was significant in that it risked violating the habeas and due process rights of its citizens because of the summary nature of the act's proceedings. It would be expected that an extradited fugitive would return to the state from which he fled to enjoy the rights of a criminal trial, but the prospects for fair trials—if they were provided at all—for fugitive slaves who were returned to slaveholding states were bleak.

These still-unresolved issues of the constitution's fugitive slave provisions would soon develop into full-fledged national controversies that tracked larger antebellum constitutional disputes about states' rights, the nature of the Union, and the extension of slavery. States concerned about the prevention of kidnapping and the general maintenance of law and order soon began to pass laws that significantly increased habeas's reach, reinvigorated the use of the ancient common-law writ *de homine replegiando* (personal replevin), and drew up limitations or even prohibitions on the use of state jails, courts, or personnel for the recovery of fugitive slaves.[104] Usually preceded by controversial fugitive slave renditions and trials, where fugitives were rescued or returned to slavery and slave catchers and abolitionists were arrested, these new state-level provisions—often prominently featuring habeas—allowed states to use legal mechanisms such as habeas to assert and enforce their own interpretations of constitutional governance.

Resistance to the 1793 act in the form of personal liberty laws only gained traction after Northern states failed to convince Congress to pass federal antikidnapping legislation in the years immediately before the Missouri Compromise. Soon after the War of 1812, Congress briefly entertained bills both to amend the 1793 act and to enact national antikidnapping statutes. If Congress had the power to create legislation to enforce Article IV's fugitive clauses, the argument went, they had the power to prevent and punish kidnappings that were perpetrated as a result of their legislation. These bills were ultimately unsuccessful, and combined with prominent fugitive slave cases that were playing out in various state courts (and no doubt spurred on by emerging abolitionist rhetoric), some states began to pass their own laws to protect their free black citizens from kidnapping in the absence of federal legislation.[105]

Pennsylvania's 1826 law, "An Act to give effect to the provisions of the Constitution of the United States relative to fugitives of labor, for the protection of free people of color, and to prevent Kidnapping," was representative of the early state personal liberty laws. The law effectively gutted the 1793 act's provision that allowed slave catchers or owners to present to Pennsylvania courts affidavits from their home states in order to receive a certificate of removal for a captured slave. The Pennsylvania law required that the slave owner or his agent provide witnesses who could verify the owner's claim to the fugitive for state courts to grant a removal certificate. The costs and logistical difficulties made this process prohibitive, and even if the slave owner or agent pursued the other option under the 1793 act by arresting or seizing the suspected fugitive slave and then bringing him before a magistrate, he could still face indictment under the 1826 bill's antikidnapping provisions.[106] These early personal liberty laws effectively challenged much of the extraterritorial application of slave law in Northern states. Although these laws did provide for the return of fugitives, states would only facilitate this process through their own legal systems and state constitutional norms.[107]

Increasing problems with the early personal liberty laws soon made their way to the Supreme Court in a case partly designed by Pennsylvania and Maryland for the Supreme Court to resolve. In *Prigg v. Pennsylvania* (1842), Justice Joseph Story ruled for a unanimous (though deeply divided) Court that personal liberty laws such as the one in Pennsylvania were unconstitutional when they added additional requirements on top of those provided in the 1793 Fugitive Slave Act.[108] As a result, any personal liberty law that even delayed the effective return of fugitives violated slaveholders' property rights. Not only could slave owners or their agents simply present an affidavit claiming ownership of a suspected fugitive, but under the common-law right of recaption—which Story upheld—slave catchers did not even need to comply with these minimal legal requirements. Story went to great lengths to argue that slavery could only exist by positive law, but he nevertheless argued that the Constitution explicitly provided for the rendition of fugitive slaves in Article IV, which, according to Story's slight hyperbole, "constituted a fundamental article, without the adoption of which the Union could not have been formed."[109] Congress thus had a duty to enforce Article IV. Here, in the minds of many, was further evidence of the national government's acquiescence in extending, implementing, and enforcing the extraterritorial application of Southern slave law.[110]

Story nevertheless held that states need not aid in the rendition or recovery process at all, a point on which Chief Justice Roger Taney bitterly disagreed.[111] For Taney, states could pass legislation that aided in the rendition of fugitive slaves as long as those laws did not violate the rights of slave owners. Not only were these types of laws constitutional, argued Taney, but states also had a "duty to protect and support the owner when he is endeavouring to obtain possession of his property found within their respective territories."[112] In effect, *Prigg* did not strike down any state criminal provisions regarding kidnapping more generally, and state courts could still issue habeas writs according to their own state constitutional and legislative processes. What *Prigg* did prohibit was any substantive use of the writ by free states that sought to establish any limitations or prohibitions that were inimical to the laws of slave states, thus establishing the judicial review of the substantive content and reach of state habeas corpus.

Immediate reaction to the *Prigg* decision was mixed. Not surprisingly, abolitionists and antislavery sympathizers, especially in New England, were outraged. John Quincy Adams remarked that the Court had given itself over to the "transcendent omnipotence of slavery in these United States, riveted by a clause in the Constitution." In New York, where the decision effectively struck down its personal liberty law that allowed jury trials in fugitive slave cases, the *New*

York Daily Express concluded that the case was "by no means satisfactory to this part of the country."[113] Southern critics of the opinion immediately picked up on Taney's concerns that states might withdraw all legislation that aided the recovery of slaves. In fact, these concerns were quite prescient: some states, such as Massachusetts and Pennsylvania, began to repeal all laws that assisted in fugitive slave recovery, while other states, such as New York, actually left their now-unconstitutional laws on the books but did not enforce them. Ohio's post-*Prigg* legislative changes hewed as closely as possible to Story's opinion. In 1847, that state's legislature amended its habeas law, which had previously provided that habeas could trigger a full evidentiary hearing on a suspected slave's fugitive status. Now, if a return to a habeas writ was in the form of a certificate of removal from a federal court, the writ was satisfied, but in cases of personal recaption, habeas could still issue and trigger a full hearing.[114]

Significantly, the post-*Prigg* personal liberty laws in the 1840s, especially those that dealt with habeas, did not yet rise to the level of state nullification of federal law. Whether Democrat or Whig, antislavery or doughface, most state legislatures simply took Story's opinion at face value and withheld many state procedures that facilitated the return of fugitive slaves. Moreover, there was general agreement in most states that the Constitution did in fact explicitly provide for the return of fugitive slaves. In support of Union, Northern states held the line in their affirmation of the constitutionality of fugitive slave rendition, although the legal mechanisms to support and enforce that authority would not be routinely facilitated in Northern states, especially when the common-law right of recaption led to violent fugitive slave seizures, as it often did. These state laws that punished the disturbance of the peace in the course of fugitive seizures stayed on the books. To many in the 1840s, the already well-developed notion that the way to end slavery in the United States was through its containment was still the standard view, and state neutrality fit this model nicely. *Prigg*'s nationalistic view of exclusive congressional enforcement of Article IV and the 1793 Fugitive Slave Act was thought by some to have solved the impending collision between state and federal laws, especially competing and contending habeas claims. As the slavery issue worsened, however, this seeming agreement quickly broke down.

HABEAS AND STATE INTERPOSITION

In the last years of the 1840s, larger, more pressing issues involving slavery were beginning to eclipse the specific questions about state response to and compliance with the *Prigg* decision. With the end of the Mexican war in sight, the question of the slave status of the territories acquired from Mexico gripped Congress and state legislatures. The extraterritorial questions concerning the application of slave state laws in relation to non–slave state judicial processes were still a central concern, if only implicitly. Any resolution of the question of the territories would affect this important and unresolved constitutional issue because it could potentially swing sectional control of the House and the Senate. Time and again, Northern states equivocated and accepted at least some extraterritorial application of Southern state slave law to their states. At the very least, they all agreed that at some basic level, fugitive slaves should be returned to their owners. If a resolution of these territorial and fugitive slave problems was not forthcoming, however, state resistance in the form of per-sonal liberty–type laws would be the most likely free-state response.

The Compromise of 1850, which sought to achieve just this type of resolu-tion on all slavery issues that were threatening the Union, was initially viewed with relief by a majority of states, both North and South. Although Southern states were more reserved in their approbation of the fugitive slave provisions of the Compromise, adopting a wait-and-see approach to effective enforce-ment, Northern states were initially willing to agree at least with two proposi-tions: fugitive slaves should be returned, and federal law should be obeyed in a good-faith effort to preserve the Union.[115]

The essential parts of the fugitive slave act in the Compromise of 1850 pro-vided that the act's provisions were to be carried out by commissioners ap-pointed by United States circuit courts who would have authority to issue certificates of removal for fugitive slaves. If United States marshals refused to carry out their duties in reclaiming slaves, they were to be fined $1,000. Mar-shals were also to be held liable for the value of slaves in their custody. Slave owners had two options in reclaiming their property. In the first, the act reaf-firmed slave owners' common-law right of recaption, which would allow them to physically seize their property anywhere, in any state, at any time, and in any way. After the seizure, they could then bring the slave to a United States commissioner, who would issue a certificate of removal. Alternatively, slave owners could first apply for a certificate of removal and then, with the aid of U.S. marshals, who could call forth a *posse commitatus*, physically recover their property. Hearings for certificates before the commissioners could not involve any testimony from slaves themselves.

Most importantly, the act also prohibited any interference in the rendition of fugitive slaves "by any process issued by any court, judge, magistrate, or other person whomsoever." Effectively gutting any meaningfully substantive review of a suspected fugitive's status through habeas corpus, habeas could still theoretically issue, but a certificate of removal was all that was needed to answer the writ. The preclusive nature of this provision was buttressed by a further provision that provided that certificates of removal would automatically issue upon documentation attesting to an owner's title to a fugitive issued from the owner's home state. Here was yet another example of the extraterritorial application of slave state law enforced by the national government. The other two significant provisions were the controversial fee structure paid to commissioners, which remunerated them more for remanding fugitives than for freeing them, and a provision that made aiding and abetting fugitive slaves punishable by fines up to $1,000.[116]

Initial reactions to the Compromise's fugitive slave laws from abolitionists and antislavery men were unsurprisingly negative, but in the main, doubts existed only about its strict constitutionality, not its necessity or utility in preserving the Union. Before signing the bill into law, President Millard Fillmore first requested that his attorney general, John J. Crittenden, advise him on the constitutionality of the bill with respect to its effect on habeas corpus, specifically the very real possibility of the act's de facto suspension of the writ in its prohibitions against legal "molestations." Crittenden's response was that the bill did not jeopardize habeas "in any manner."[117] At issue, of course, was the larger problem of conflicting habeas writs between states and the federal government, as well as the extent to which habeas could be used (on either level) to inquire into the substantive issues associated with detention. The 1850 bill seemed to preclude any use of the writ by states to frustrate the return of fugitive slaves.

In practice, then, the use of the writ to bring the body of a suspected fugitive from the custody of a federal officer to a state court would be prohibited. Since its seeming resolution in *Prigg,* and with subsequent personal liberty laws passed by some Northern states in its aftermath that withheld the use of state jails for fugitive slave rendition, this very political use of habeas was the most likely concern prompting the act's language in this section. But what of those who might be arrested or detained for aiding a suspected fugitive by the federal government? Could state habeas writs issue to inquire into their detentions? Conversely, could federal officers—such as United States marshals—be held by state authorities for violating state personal liberty laws? Could federal courts, via habeas, require state courts to bring up this class of federal defendants charged with violating state laws to federal courts?

Suspecting that collisions between state and federal power were imminent immediately after the Compromise was signed into law, Supreme Court justice Robert Grier and circuit court judge John Kane personally requested that President Fillmore allow them the power to use federal troops in the enforcement of the law. Not wanting to foment Northern uneasiness concerning this issue, Fillmore agreed to provide troops only in emergencies. Nevertheless, he remained committed "to bring[ing] the whole force of the government to sustain the law."[118] As David Potter has argued, the most curious feature of the Compromise of 1850 was that while it was designed to "put a stop to the agitation of the slavery question," it sought to achieve this goal by "adopt[ing] a law to activate the recapture of fugitive slaves." Unlike other forms of compromise that sought to regulate "unpeopled region[s] . . . the Fugitive Slave Act was concerned with men and women in the back streets of New York, Philadelphia, Boston, and many a town and hamlet." Soon these very real cases would eclipse hypothetical ones about slavery's future expansion in the Western hinterlands.[119]

In Massachusetts, two prominent fugitive slave cases quickly brought these issues into sharp relief. A fugitive slave named Shadrach was captured in Boston and brought before Commissioner George Ticknor Curtis in early 1851. Soon thereafter, abolitionists brazenly rescued Shadrach from Curtis's courtroom and took him to Canada. Aghast, President Fillmore provided the assistance of federal troops to authorities in Boston, promising to bring those responsible for the rescue to justice. He then directed United States attorneys in Massachusetts to bring indictments against those involved, although no one was successfully convicted. Aside from the national government's anger, the Shadrach case confirmed Southern suspicion of Northern nonenforcement of the fugitive slave act.[120] To make matters worse from an abolitionist and antislavery perspective, newly appointed but not yet seated Supreme Court justice Benjamin Curtis ruled in a circuit court opinion on the indictment of one of the abolitionists involved in the rescue that his jury was only entitled to return a verdict on the facts, not the substance of the law.[121] John Hale, attorney for Robert Morris, the black defendant charged in the case, had argued to no avail that if a jury thought the pertinent provisions of the fugitive slave act with which the defendant was charged were unconstitutional, then Curtis should direct the jury to acquit on that basis.[122]

As the Shadrach incident was still rumbling, another fugitive slave case again rocked Boston. Thomas Sims had holed himself away in a ship bound to Boston from Georgia.[123] The ship's crew then captured Sims as they entered the Boston harbor and locked him in a cabin until he could be turned over to authorities. After escaping his confines with a pocketknife, he lived for a while on the charity of abolitionists in Boston until his former master, James Potter, received word of Sims's location. Potter then sent a slave catcher to Boston, who petitioned and received from George Ticknor Curtis a warrant for Sims's arrest.

With the doors to the courthouse chained to prevent another escape, and with Sims now confined to the jury room because Massachusetts law would not allow its jails to be used for fugitive slaves, Curtis heard Sims's case. Potter's attorneys produced documents supposedly proving that Sims was a slave, but because the 1850 act prohibited testimony from fugitive slaves, Sims's attorneys were prevented by Curtis from trying to establish Sims's status as a free man.[124] Sims remained in custody for the next week.

The next day, Samuel Sewall petitioned the chief justice of the Massachusetts supreme court, Lemuel Shaw, for a habeas writ on Sims's behalf.[125] Shaw refused, arguing that if he heard the habeas case, he would automatically be bound to remand Sims back to his custodians because according to the Compromise, he had no jurisdiction. Shaw then refused to hear the habeas case on the asserted grounds that the Compromise of 1850 was unconstitutional. In rejecting the petition, Shaw lamented, "When a Court of Justice sits in fetters . . . the ancient and prescriptive safeguards of personal liberty must of course give way."[126] Angered at Shaw's refusal to issue the writ, the Massachusetts state legislature even briefly entertained a bill that would allow habeas to issue for Sims only. Some in the statehouse even suggested that Shaw be impeached, but the bill never materialized.[127]

A few days after Shaw's original refusal to hear Sims's habeas case, advocates again appeared before his court, this time with Richard Henry Dana as Sims's cocounsel. In a unanimous opinion, Shaw again denied the writ and sustained, for the first time, the constitutionality of the Compromise of 1850. Importantly, he argued that the fugitive slave provisions, which many suggested precluded habeas and jury rights, were not violated because the judicial processes set up by the act were only summary in nature and did not constitute a suit at law. Not only was this point doubtful, but Shaw then went on to repeat Justice Story's equally suspect justification in his *Prigg* decision for the Constitution's fugitive slave provisions that they represented a compact among the states that had been vital to the Constitution's ratification.[128] Shaw also suggested that to avoid an "occasion for drawing the authority of the State and United States Judiciary into conflict with each other," the "best adjustment" would be to have all fugitive slave issues decided in federal, not state, courts.[129] In Shaw's mind, this was exactly what the Compromise and its fugitive slave provisions had contemplated and what, he hoped, they would accomplish. In what was by this time a fait accompli, Commissioner Curtis ultimately awarded a certificate of removal to Porter's agents, and Sims was taken back to Georgia, where he bore thirty-nine lashes with the whip upon his arrival.[130] Relieved that the Compromise had been upheld in the case, President Fillmore wrote Daniel Webster to "congratulate [him] and the country upon a triumph of the law in Boston. She has done nobly. She has wiped out the stain of the former rescue [Shadrach] and freed herself from the reproach of nullification."[131]

Although abolitionists were certainly angry with the outcome of the Sims case, most Bostonians, and indeed most Northerners, were, like Fillmore, relieved with the result and remained hopefully optimistic that the Compromise would uphold the Union. This state of affairs in the first two years after the Compromise confirms what Thomas Morris called the "via media," or the "way between submission and revolution" in the face of the extraterritorial application of slave law for free states.[132] Abolitionists who felt morally compelled to stop the rendition process could advocate and uphold personal liberty laws in their states, while those less inclined to this moral extreme could still accept state habeas laws that sought to ensure a legal and constitutional process for the return of fugitive slaves. With the exception of Vermont, which immediately passed a personal liberty law securing suspected slaves a jury trial, no Northern state significantly amended its laws.[133]

This centrism in state legislatures was also reflected in the federal courts' responses to the fugitive slave provisions of the Compromise of 1850, as these justices, regardless of their sectional or partisan identities, consistently sought the middle ground.[134] The sustained equivocation of federal courts only caused more state resistance, however, and ultimately led to the attempted nullification of federal law by states that felt that they had no recourse to the extraterritorial application of Southern slave law. Not more than a few months after the Compromise was passed, Chief Justice Roger Taney ruled for a unanimous Court that the laws of slave states governed questions of freedom in free states. At issue in *Strader v. Graham* was whether slaves who were taken to Ohio from Kentucky were free upon their return to a slave state. Taney unequivocally stated that it was for "Kentucky to determine for itself whether their employment in another State should not make them free on their return."[135] The Court's hands-off position in *Strader,* which represented a bisectional consensus position, would be the opposite approach taken by the same Court in *Dred Scott* just a few years later.

By 1853, the habeas issue was coming to a head. Northern state response to federal judicial decisions began to break away from the compromise position when federal courts began to apply the 1833 Habeas Corpus Act to jurisdictional conflict cases. These cases usually involved United States marshals who were arrested in free states during violent attempts to recover suspected fugitive slaves. Moreover, in May 1853, President Franklin Pierce's ardently pro-Compromise attorney general, Caleb Cushing, developed a policy that anyone arrested "on a warrant of a competent judicial authority of the United States" could not have recourse to a state habeas writ.[136]

The 1833 Habeas Act was first applied to fugitive slave cases in *Ex parte Jenkins* in 1853.[137] Four slave catchers were arrested for trespass in Pennsylvania during a violent seizure of a fugitive slave named Thomas. The marshals then filed a habeas writ in federal circuit court arguing that their detention was unconstitutional. Justice Grier and circuit court justice Kane ruled that the 1833 act allowed the writ to issue from federal to state courts, and the marshals were discharged. The unintended consequence of the 1833 act's use in these types of cases did not escape either judge; in fact, their use of it suggests that they thought that the 1833 act's application to these types of cases was only a natural application of that act's general propositions and intent.[138] It was just this type of state interference with federal law that originally prompted Congress to provide federal habeas relief for tariff officers should they be detained by South Carolina authorities during the nullification crisis. With respect to similar state-level interference with the fugitive slave provisions of the Compromise of 1850, Justice Grier proclaimed, "The extreme advocate of state rights would scarcely contend that in such cases the courts of the United States should be wholly unable to protect themselves or their officers."[139] As the bisectional national political coalition that had countenanced the Mexican war, the Compromise of 1850, and only minor state-level adjustments to personal liberty laws was dissolving, then, federal courts were nevertheless trying to uphold the coalition's bargains, but to little avail. Here again, habeas became a central tool in the larger political processes of sustaining and enforcing core constitutional principles of governance. The use of the 1833 Habeas Act to enforce the supremacy of federal law and authority, however, soon created significant backlash.

The backlash in the states began with Stephen Douglas's Kansas–Nebraska act a year later in 1854. All of the compromises that had facilitated the Jacksonian coalition quickly began to crumble.[140] Many Northern state legislatures immediately passed resolutions condemning the Kansas–Nebraska bill; only Illinois approved of the measure.[141] The political regime that forged political harmony between majorities in both the Democratic and Whig parties since the 1830s soon gave way to an all-out sectional battle over the issue of the extension of slavery that was now more real than ever with the repeal of the Missouri Compromise.[142] Northern state party coalitions, which were now forced to ally with each other on the purely sectional issue of opposition to the extension of slavery, felt that their long-suffering bisectional concessions to Southern states in the name of Union were effectively invalidated.

In terms of the habeas provisions in many Northern state personal liberty laws, the demise of the bisectional coalition was significant. After the Fugitive Slave Act of 1793, the *Prigg* decision in 1842, and the Missouri Compromise in 1850, antislavery forces had tried unsuccessfully to use state habeas laws in ways that challenged the extraterritorial application of slave law in their states. With each attempt, bisectional coalitions of Whigs and Democrats were able to weaken or prevent these habeas provisions (as well as jury trials and writs of personal replevin) from shattering the Jacksonian coalition. However, at no time before 1854 did state habeas laws actually cross the line of nullification. With the possibility of slavery in the new territories foreshadowing continued overrepresentation of Southern interests in national politics, some Northern states now felt compelled—and politically free—to resist, even to the point of nullification.[143]

THE POLITICAL CONTEXT OF ABLEMAN v. BOOTH

These volatile issues started to play out in Wisconsin in 1854 and eventually led to an attempted resolution by the Supreme Court four years later. Habeas's role in *Ableman v. Booth,* a case that Charles Warren proclaimed to be "the most powerful" of all Chief Justice Roger Taney's "notable opinions," served as a proxy for the new sectional politics of the mid-1850s.[144] The specific procedural questions that the Court sought to resolve with respect to the difficult problems of habeas's potential reach from state to federal or federal to state jurisdictions were important enough, but both the state of Wisconsin and the Supreme Court saw much more at stake in the case. Between the initial arrest of Sherman Booth in 1854 and the Court's opinion in January 1859, not only had the Kansas–Nebraska Act been passed, but bloodshed and violence had already stained Kansas. Just as important, *Dred Scott* had been handed down the very same day that the Court accepted Attorney General Caleb Cushing's request for it to hear the *Booth* case on a writ of error.[145] Douglas's bill seemed to suggest that all compromises were now null and void. The Kansas fiasco furthered this belief. *Dred Scott* not only confirmed it, but also led Northern antislavery and abolitionist advocates to the conclusion that the federal government would never side with their position.

As the Jacksonian regime was dissolving, it was increasingly relying on the federal courts, and the Supreme Court in particular, to help insulate, protect, and even advance what it thought were slavery issues that were too delicate to be left in the hands of a Congress that was increasingly showing the symptoms of the larger bisectional dissolution of the party regime. The Kansas–Nebraska Act and the violence of Lecompton had already shown overt signs of this radical and sectional influence.[146] Because the Supreme Court was composed of more moderate Democratic justices, its ability to help maintain a middling coalition was seen by many to be the Union's only hope for survival.[147] Certainly president-elect James Buchanan had believed this to be true, but his secret correspondence with the justices during their consideration of *Dred Scott* before his inauguration, combined with his inauguration day prediction that the Court would finally solve the volatile issue of slavery in the territories, only furthered sectional bitterness toward Southerners and "their" Court.[148]

Federal court application of the 1833 Habeas Act to habeas cases involving state prosecution of federal marshals that began in 1853 was an earlier sign that the Jacksonian-dominated Court was still on board with upholding the national enforcement of slave law in Northern states. But *Dred Scott*'s politically contrived decision forbidding Congress from prohibiting slavery in the territories was immediately cast as a two-front assault on democracy. Taking the issue out of the hands of Congress, no matter how sectionally divided it had become, was seen by many as not only legally wrong, but patently undemocratic. Deferring the issue to a Supreme Court in which "the Democratic Party commanded a majority of the decision makers" and the "South commanded a majority in the party" led some to the conclusion that there was no political or legal recourse to thwart national slave power other than to approach the precipice of state nullification.[149] Although it is true that "Taney did not impose a judicial solution" on the nation because "*Dred Scott* . . . was as majoritarian as any other race or slavery policy made during the 1850's," it was nevertheless this majoritarian vision of constitutional governance, enforced by the extra-territorial application of slave law in Northern states and its related theory of slavery in the territories, that proved too much to bear for some Northern states.[150] It was against this backdrop that a "transvaluation of values" played out in *Ableman* through habeas corpus, as Wisconsin picked up the mantle of the Virginia and Kentucky resolutions and the nullification crisis, and the Southern-dominated Court issued its most nationalistic opinion yet.[151]

ABLEMAN v. BOOTH

In March 1854, abolitionist editor Sherman Booth was arrested by federal marshal Stephan Ableman for violating the fugitive slave law by helping a fugitive slave named Joshua Glover escape from his jail cell and flee to Canada.[152] Booth was brought before a United States commissioner and held over for trial. A few weeks later, Booth petitioned Justice A. D. Smith of the Wisconsin supreme court for a writ of habeas corpus, arguing that the fugitive slave law was unconstitutional. Smith agreed, and Booth was set free. The young and fiery abolitionist Byron Paine, who represented Booth in this first habeas case, tied together the preexisting abolitionist arguments about state personal liberty laws into an ardent defense of states' rights against Southern-dominated national enforcement of slavery in the states:

The North is snapping asunder the bands that have bound it in subjection to the slave power, as Sampson broke the withs of tow! The last link that binds it, is the judicial sanction that power has received! Let that be broken, and the people are free! Can we not have one decision in all this land, that shall vindicate liberty and law?[153]

In the best tradition of Virginia and Kentucky resolutions, upon which, along with James Madison's "Report of 1800," Paine relied, it was a call for state nullification of the federal judiciary's enforcement of slave power.[154]

Stephan Ableman then requested that the habeas decision be reheard by the full Wisconsin supreme court, which on 19 July 1854 upheld Smith's decision. Ableman then immediately sought review of the state supreme court's decision in the United States Supreme Court. The very next day, Ableman again arrested Booth, who had been indicted by a grand jury in United States district court.[155] The district court found him guilty and sentenced him to one month in jail. From this conviction, and while Ableman's writ of error request was pending before the U.S. Supreme Court, Booth once again brought a habeas writ before the Wisconsin supreme court, this time challenging his conviction from the district court. Again, the Wisconsin supreme court freed Booth. In the court's opinion, it warned that "the states never will quietly submit to be disrobed of their sovereignty; submit to the humiliation of having the execution of this compact forced upon them, or rather be taken out of their hands, by national functionaries." The constitutionality of the Compromise of 1850 was squarely denied with the further promise by the court that it would "not become the degradation of Wisconsin, without meeting as stern remonstrance and resistance as . . . may be interpose[d]."[156] In contrast to our modern conceptions of the writ, Justice Smith's argument that "the last hope of free, representative and responsible government rests upon the state sovereignties" to "interpose a resistance . . . to every assumption of power on the part of the general government, which is not expressly granted or necessarily implied in the federal constitution," seems inverted.[157]

In an effort to thwart the Wisconsin court's ruling, Edward Ryan, a Milwaukee attorney whose services were secured at the blessing of Attorney General Caleb Cushing to help the U.S. attorney prosecute Booth's case, wrote Cushing and urged him to help bring the case before the United States Supreme Court.[158] Cushing agreed and filed a motion with the Court to bring the state case up on a writ of error. The Wisconsin court, however, directed its clerk not to file a return to the writ. Unbeknownst to the state court, a copy of the case had already been given to the United States attorney. Cushing then moved to have this copy stand as the answer to the writ of error. The U.S. Supreme Court tried to request the original copy from Wisconsin before allowing the copy to stand in its place. Wisconsin again refused, and the Supreme Court accepted the copy.[159]

Although the *Ableman* case was pending before the Court, and in anticipation of its negative resolution from the perspective of Northern interests, two measures were introduced in Congress that further indicated the increasing tension between states and the federal judiciary. Ultimately unsuccessful, a bill to repeal section 25 of the Judiciary Act of 1789, which provided for writs of error from states to the Supreme Court, was submitted in 1858. Attached to this measure was another provision to repeal the Habeas Corpus Act of 1833, which facilitated the removal of state cases involving federal officers. Ohio abolitionist Philemon Bliss, who attached the 1833 repeal measure to the bill, proclaimed that the 1833 Habeas Act "was a clear usurpation of Federal authority," as people now believed that the federal judiciary was the "right arm of these encroachments."[160] By this point, Taney's *Ableman* decision was all but foreordained.

The administrative recalcitrance on the part of the Wisconsin judges to allow for the writ of error was even more problematic for Taney than the issuance of the two state habeas writs by the state courts. After dispensing with a rather prosaic account of the circuitous path by which the problem of state habeas writs for federal prisoners had reached the Court, Taney said of this move by the Wisconsin courts that they had "not only claimed and exercised this jurisdiction, but have also determined that their decision is final and conclusive upon all the courts of the United States, and ordered their clerk to disregard and refuse obedience to the writ of error . . . pursuant to the [Judiciary Act of 1789]."[161] These "propositions," which were "new in the jurisprudence of the United States," although not explicitly asserted by the Wisconsin judges, could nevertheless be inferred by that court's use "of the writ of *habeas corpus*." As a whole, Taney then asserted, "their commentaries upon the provisions of that law, and upon the privileges and power of the writ of *habeas corpus*, were out of place."[162]

The practical problem with Wisconsin's actions was that it effectively precluded any kind of national enforcement, prosecution, and judicial resolution of national criminal law. If states exercised this supposed authority to use habeas to free those detained, indicted, and prosecuted within their state's territorial jurisdiction, they would quickly undermine any national legislative and judicial power. The result would be that "because State courts would not always agree . . . it would often happen, that an act which was admitted to be an offence, and justly punished, in one State, would be regarded as innocent, and indeed praiseworthy, in another."[163] In terms of the actual procedures of habeas, the Wisconsin courts even violated their state constitution's habeas provisions, because they explicitly prevented habeas from issuing when a prisoner was detained both by "any court or judge of the United States" or when a prisoner was held "by virtue of any final judgment or decree of any competent court of civil or criminal jurisdiction."[164]

Taney's argument then moved to one of the strongest assertions of national power that the Court—let alone a Jacksonian-affiliated Court—had as yet made. Without specific authority to issue habeas for federal prisoners either from their own state constitution or from the national Constitution, it was to be forever understood that "no State can authorize one of its judges or courts to exercise judicial power, by *habeas corpus* or otherwise, within the jurisdiction of another and independent Government." Although both the state and national governments will inevitably exercise their jurisdictional powers within the same territorial limits, Taney then forcefully asserted that these powers are derived from "separate and distinct sovereignties, acting separately and independently of each other, within their respective spheres. And the sphere of action appropriated to the United States is as far beyond the reach of the judicial processes issued by a State judge or a State court, as if the line of division was traced by landmarks and monuments visible to the eye."[165]

Referring next to the supremacy clause, Taney then went on to argue that the "supremacy thus conferred . . . was clothed with judicial power, equally paramount in authority to carry it into execution."[166] The Wisconsin supreme court thus erred when it determined for itself that the Compromise of 1850 was unconstitutional: "[If] it appears that an act of congress is not pursuant to and within the limits of the power assigned to the Federal Government, it is the duty of the courts of the United States to declare it unconstitutional and void."[167]

Importantly, toward the end of the opinion, Taney nevertheless held that states were not prohibited from issuing the Great Writ for those held within their jurisdictions. What they could not do, however, was go beyond an answer to the writ when it was determined that a prisoner was held by authority of the United States. Thus there could not be any substantive inquiry into the constitutionality of the law by which a prisoner was held. This power was reserved to the Supreme Court alone to determine.[168] This assertion of national judicial power to give substantive meaning to the writ built on John Marshall's establishment of this power more generally. With more sympathetic national institutions, the chief justice could assert this power with more assurance. Indeed, Taney's unequivocal defense of "national supremacy" was, in the words of Charles Warren, brought to bear in an "opinion which [John] Marshall himself never excelled in loftiness of tone."[169]

Indignant Wisconsin Republican state legislators immediately passed resolutions condemning the *Ableman* decision as an "arbitrary act of power" that "virtually supersed[ed] the benefit of the writ of habeas corpus and prostr[ated] the rights and liberties of the people at the foot of unlimited power."[170] They also appropriated language almost verbatim from the Kentucky resolutions in their further charge that "the several states which formed that instrument [the Constitution] being sovereign and independent, have the unquestionable right to judge of its infraction, and that a positive defiance by those sovereignties of all unauthorized acts done, or attempted to be done, under color of that instrument is the right remedy."[171] Wisconsin Republicans even went so far as to prevent the renomination to the bench of Chief Justice Dixon, the lone dissenter in Booth's habeas case in Wisconsin district court.[172]

Similar events were playing out in Ohio during the resolution of the *Ableman* case. When slave catchers captured a young boy outside of Oberlin, Ohio, they were quickly met by a hostile group that overcame them and freed the suspected fugitive slave. Prosecuted in U.S. district court, only two of the thirty men originally indicted were convicted. With the ink on the *Ableman* decision not yet dry, the Ohio supreme court entertained a habeas petition again challenging the constitutionality of the Compromise of 1850. This time, however, a majority of the Ohio court upheld the Compromise. This ruling spurred another Republican-led crusade to prevent the renomination of Judge Joseph Swan, one of the court's majority who upheld the act.[173] Ohio Republicans were certainly indignant about the decision, as evidenced by claims that Governor Chase was ready to use troops to enforce the court's decision had it turned out differently.[174] But as in other states, no major legislative changes were made to existing personal liberty laws. Like the national Republican Party itself during the late 1850s, conservative, moderate, and radical members in Northern state legislatures—and especially in border states—could only manage to pass bills and resolutions that sustained a state's ability to protect its citizens through habeas generally, while still recognizing an abstract right of slave owners to recover their fugitives. These measures fell short of outright nullification of federal law.[175]

Even though most Northern state legislatures failed to strengthen their habeas laws further after the *Ableman* case and the Oberlin incident, the damage was done. South Carolina's "Declaration of the Immediate Causes of Secession" summed up nicely their perception of the existing state of affairs:

The General Government, as the common agent, passed laws to carry into effect these stipulations of the States. For many years these laws were executed. But an increasing hostility on the part of the non-slaveholding States to the institution of slavery, has led to a disregard of their obligations, and the laws of the General Government have ceased to effect the objects of the Constitution. In many of these States the fugitive is discharged from service or labor claimed, and in none of them has the State Government complied with the stipulation made in the Constitution. Thus the constituted compact has been deliberately broken and disregarded by the non-slaveholding States, and the consequence follows that South Carolina is released from her obligation.[176]

Despite this failure on the part of some states north of the Mason-Dixon line, habeas nevertheless played an integral role in the development of personal liberty laws as it became a viable political tool to enforce the principles of constitutional governance of Northern states in the face of competing visions of national enforcement of fugitive slave laws. But because habeas was also used as a tool of national political regimes, it also increased the tensions percolating in the dissolution of the Jacksonian regime more generally.[177] Backlash to habeas change is a persistent developmental feature of habeas. The increasing use of habeas to enforce the extraterritorial application of slave law by the Jacksonian regime met an ultimately unsuccessful—but nevertheless persistent and formidable—opponent in the form of Northern personal liberty laws passed by state legislatures that prominently featured the Great Writ. These state-led habeas developments stood as competing alternatives between a dissolving Jacksonian regime and an ascending Republican one.

CONCLUSION

The more political use of habeas on both the state and national levels drove its development during the antebellum period. Federal and state courts played a significant role in this process, but even then, politics, more than law, forged habeas doctrine and jurisprudence. Just as significant, these politically induced antebellum changes to federal habeas corpus would soon be used by Reconstruction political regimes for completely different purposes in the next decade, much as they had when habeas changes during the 1830s were used in ways that those who enacted them never intended. Habeas development in the antebellum period was thus marked by what Karen Orren and Stephen Skowronek refer to as "unintended consequences."[178]

This longer time horizon of habeas development throughout the antebellum era also allows us to see how habeas development was anything but Whiggishly preordained. On the national level, the Jacksonian political regime grafted substantive notions of slaveholders' property rights onto the procedural reach of habeas, most conspicuously after Northern states began to frustrate the national enforcement of the fugitive slave law in the mid-1850s. The use of habeas by federal courts beginning in 1853 to remove state convictions of slave catchers to federal courts created tremendous backlash in many states that felt that their habeas protections for fugitive slaves—and for their free black citizenry—were not only morally but also constitutionally superior.

When the Republican Party that was fighting for habeas protections on the state level during the 1850s was finally able to occupy national political institutions after 1860, they simply grafted their own substantive theories of rights enforcement onto the existing procedural changes to federal habeas corpus. In *Bollman* and *Watkins*, John Marshall deftly asserted federal judicial power to give substantive meaning to habeas, even while conceding that Congress had the power to create federal court habeas jurisdiction. Congress then brought habeas power over state-level detentions within the jurisdiction of federal courts in 1833 and again in 1842. From *Prigg* onward, the federal courts and Congress worked together to enforce and defend federal habeas power against state encroachments. When the Jacksonian regime that forged most of these habeas developments ultimately imploded in 1860 and the ascendant Republican regime gained control of political institutions during the Civil War and Reconstruction, the heavy lifting of creating federal court habeas power to enforce the party's substantive vision of constitutional governance was already primed with ample precedent.

The circuitous developmental path of habeas during the antebellum era also belies characterizations of the Great Writ as a purely court-centered national mechanism for the vindication of individual rights. Although these rights were certainly vindicated at times through habeas before the Civil War, thus providing some precedent for our modern understanding of the writ, the uses of habeas as a liberty-protecting legal mechanism were only successful when particular state-level political regimes fought to make it so. Habeas was always used first as a mechanism to enforce regime power, and whatever effects on rights protection these regime uses of the writ yielded were always only a secondary concern. Even the more libertarian applications of the writ by the Republican Party in various Northern states were never countenanced or supported by the majority of the party.

There is no question that habeas was used in dramatic ways by antislavery forces to enforce their own preferred conceptions of constitutional governance during the fugitive slave controversies of the 1850s. But the constituencies of the Republican Party, which spanned concerns as diverse as the "resentment of southern political power, devotion to the Union, anti-slavery based upon the free labor argument, racial prejudice, [and] a commitment to the Northern social order and its development and expansion," precluded a focused and sustained use of habeas for the vindication of individual rights on the state level.[179] The judicial and political precedents for federal habeas corpus that were produced during the antebellum period were in no way purposively designed by political and legal institutions to operate in the ways that habeas soon would, nor did habeas during this period exhibit the qualities that would lead us to characterize it as a tool of countermajoritarian courts. The only consistent judicial feature of habeas development in the antebellum period was the Supreme Court's determination—forged as much in the political as in the legal realm—to carve out and then guard its ability to issue the writ.

CHAPTER 3

The Reconstruction of Habeas Corpus

Reconstruction precipitated changes to habeas corpus in ways that still reverberate today. Most significant was the Habeas Corpus Act of 1867. Although the 1833 and 1842 habeas acts provided federal court review of state court convictions, they did so in limited ways and under specific circumstances. The 1867 act seemed to transcend these limited and specific categories by providing for federal court habeas review of anyone held by state or federal authorities in violation of the Constitution. Modern advocates of broad federal court habeas review lay claim to the 1867 act's supposed intent in justifying their contemporary claims. The 1867 act, in the words of its House sponsor, was a "bill of the largest liberty" that made "the jurisdiction of the courts and judges . . . coextensive with all the powers that can be conferred upon them."[1] So the argument goes, however, habeas's fate was unfortunately linked to broader goals of Reconstruction that were too quickly abandoned in the 1870s—racial equality; universal suffrage; and equal civil, political, and economic rights for all citizens—only to be subsequently resuscitated by twentieth-century courts. To realize and enforce these goals, the Warren Court and twentieth-century legal scholars relied on habeas corpus as an enforcement mechanism for the constitutional visions of the New Deal and Great Society regimes, in part because they believed that Reconstruction's political coalitions had always envisioned habeas to play this signal role.[2] The Warren Court thus helped secure these lost components of Reconstruction's unfinished revolution. There was no bigger advocate of this reading both on and off the bench than Justice William Brennan, who justified the Court's sweeping habeas changes during the 1960s as simply fulfilling a vision of habeas that was "at first delayed."[3]

The actual development of habeas during and immediately after Reconstruction, however, belies this Whiggish narrative. In fact, habeas's developmental trajectory was anything but certain from the beginning of the Civil War to the informal end of Reconstruction in the late 1870s. And even then, for more than a decade after the election of Rutherford B. Hayes and the beginning of redeemer rule, the exact contours of habeas's new role were still developing. Not until 1886—almost twenty years after the passage of the Habeas Corpus Act of 1867—would Congress and the Supreme Court finally come to an understanding about habeas's role under the 1867 act. When they did, however, the settlement reflected the politics of a different time far removed from the exigencies of war, the imperative of union, the prospective uneasiness of an America without slavery, and most assuredly the moral fervor of Charles Sumner. Even before these momentous political, social, and economic changes doomed Radicals' hopes, Civil War and Reconstruction changes to habeas hardly sprang from rights-protecting and countermajoritarian wellsprings.

Instead, as I show in this chapter, habeas continued to develop from the Civil War through Reconstruction and to the end of the nineteenth century, largely as the result of the same political and institutional dynamics that drove its development during the first half of the century. To be sure, the formal eradication of slavery in 1865 ended habeas's split personality as a tool for enslavement; no longer would the writ serve to enforce the ugliness of the peculiar institution. At times, it would now help to guarantee the very rights that it in part helped to take away. Nevertheless, this particular use of habeas was neither foreordained nor consistently sustained. Federal habeas in the service of individual rights—and particularly freedmen's rights—was the product of a concerted effort by short-lived political coalitions that were only able to achieve their immediate goals when the larger political regime, including the federal courts, countenanced such efforts. Throughout the Civil War and Reconstruction, the Republican regime enacted habeas corpus legislation and enlarged federal court jurisdiction to enforce their preferred vision of constitutional governance. The use of habeas to vindicate fundamental rights in ways that we imagine today was only ever an ephemeral by-product of this larger political reality.

In many ways, then, the only similarity between habeas's use during and after Reconstruction and our more modern conceptions of the writ is that then, as now, it was an effective enforcement tool for political regimes in their attempts to govern. Like the Jacksonian regime before it, Reconstruction Republicans partnered with federal courts through increased grants of habeas jurisdiction against recalcitrant states.[4] Unlike the Jacksonian period, our modern sympathies most likely lie with Reconstruction Republican's national enforcement of regime goals through federal courts. But the fact that the recalcitrant states during the Jacksonian period were Northern states that enacted personal liberty laws in the service of individual liberty should at least give us pause about our sometimes uncritical assumptions that assign a normative role for the national government in the enforcement of rights, especially through habeas.

That our understanding of modern habeas jurisprudence seems to turn almost exclusively on an understanding of the Great Writ during Reconstruction is nevertheless an important feature of habeas development in its own right.[5] The regime use of habeas involves a simultaneous redefinition of the writ's historical function. Like the principles of constitutional governance it enforces, problematic legal precedents and unfavorable historical realities are necessarily pushed aside and even ignored in an attempt to justify a new regime's powers and legitimacy. This dynamic in part explains why uses of the writ during and after the Civil War that call into question the historical veracity of most contemporary accounts are conspicuously absent from the Whiggish narrative that modern supporters of broad federal habeas power advance. As Pamela Brandwein argues, "Reconstruction" itself "has its own history" that is created and advanced to justify contemporary policy and law. As part of this creation, habeas's actual development is often sacrificed for cleaner and more progressive accounts.[6]

I offer a more political account of habeas's development during and after Reconstruction that takes into account the interpretation and use of the writ not only by federal courts, but by other political institutions as well. This allows us to see a how a number of important developmental variables that have always driven habeas's development helped create the foundation for our modern habeas jurisprudence during Reconstruction, not the least of which is the fact that Congress and the executive play extremely important roles in advancing various and often competing roles for the writ apart from the judiciary. This calls into question not only the utility of purely court-centered analyses of habeas, but also any countermajoritarian role for the judiciary. Despite some claims to the contrary, the massive and truly revolutionary changes to American federalism during the Civil War and Reconstruction also suggest that the role of the federal courts in Reconstruction was in important ways developed as a partnership with the elected branches.[7] At the very least, federal courts were able to help enforce national policy against recalcitrant Southern states in ways that were helpful, and in some ways superior to, congressional legislation or executive orders by themselves.[8] Interestingly, the power that federal courts wielded in this partnership was established decades before. The exigencies of war and the unprecedented challenges of Reconstruction might have prompted the Republican regime's partnership with the federal judiciary, but the precedents for this relationship, especially in prior uses of federal court habeas power, were most immediately available from the Jacksonian regime's use of the writ.

Even with this partnership, at important junctures, the Court was able to assert its own particular readings of habeas. When intraparty disputes significantly divided the regime over key issues, as they often did, the Court was able to protect and even entrench further its own independent habeas powers despite its precarious role in the incendiary politics of the Reconstruction era, largely because Congress consistently needed its support.[9] Despite vocal criticism of the Court's opinions—and even isolated threats to its very existence—congressional majorities continued to use federal court habeas power in the second half of the nineteenth century to help enforce their preferred vision of constitutional governance. To be sure, federal courts were not simply the handmaidens of either Congress or the executive. Their ability to protect and craft habeas jurisprudence almost always depended on their cooperation with the regime in power.

This perspective also allows us to begin to understand the writ's role during war or crisis. There is no question that the Civil War and Reconstruction were extraordinary and unprecedented events that pushed American constitutionalism to its limits. It would be a mistake to understand these events as wiping away the preceding, or "ordinary," development of American political and legal institutions.[10] As we will see, the Civil War only made the ordinary developmental variables discussed above play out more quickly and with more intensity than usual. Like accounts of Reconstruction that begin only with Lee's surrender and neglect the possibilities of the war's effects on subsequent Reconstruction politics, we miss much by assuming that events in 1859 had no impact on events in 1861.[11] In important ways, this allows us to see that the triumvirate of wartime jurisprudence cases—*Merryman, Milligan,* and *McCardle*—had less to do with how a seemingly independent judiciary could protect individual rights during war than it did with the extent to which regime-affiliated courts were able to carve out an independent role for themselves despite their dependence on the elected branches.

With these considerations in mind, this chapter does more than explore habeas's role in the salient court cases of the period, including *Merryman, Milligan, McCardle,* and others. It also analyzes the writ's role outside of the Court up to the end of the nineteenth century.[12] What will become clear is that although habeas was indeed "reconstructed" during Reconstruction, these changes not only were modeled on previous regime uses of the writ, but were also short-lived. Contrary to most accounts, these changes and the cases they precipitated were not seen as countermajoritarian, either by the Republican Reconstruction regime in 1867 that expanded the writ's reach or by subsequent regimes that scaled back these changes toward the end of the century. As a tool of regime enforcement, habeas necessarily reflected majoritarian sentiments, which did not always align with the vindication of the rights of numerical or racial minorities as we often assume today.

CONTINUITIES AND DISCONTINUITIES IN EX PARTE MERRYMAN

There is no question that the first shots fired at Fort Sumter marked a turning point in American constitutional and political history. The Constitution of 1787 provided no explicit blueprint for civil war, though many clauses provided direction for war more generally. Even then, the exact role that the president, Congress, the courts, and the states were to play in light of the martial clauses of the Constitution was, and still is, unclear. In his Pulitzer Prize–winning book surveying and accounting for the effects of Lincoln's suspension of habeas corpus, Mark Neely boldly proclaimed that "there is little need to dwell . . . on the uses of the writ [of habeas corpus] before the Civil War" because the "abuses of the writ of habeas corpus in the struggle over slavery were no longer of practical interest."[13] But the institutional conflicts that arose with the sudden onset of civil war—and certainly with the suspension of habeas corpus—are not completely separable from ordinary institutional conflicts that animated the larger constitutional order, nor, as we will see, were the preceding political supports for the judicial uses of the writ wiped cleanly away with the beginning of the war or the advent of Reconstruction.[14] Edward Corwin's characterization of constitutional war powers as "an invitation to struggle" is certainly an empirical reality, but these interbranch struggles and their political contexts are a permanent part of American politics in both war and peace.[15] To understand the structural conflicts in Chief Justice Roger Taney's clash with Abraham Lincoln over the suspension of habeas corpus in *Ex parte Merryman,* then, we need to attend to the continuities with the immediately preceding state of politics, as well as the obvious discontinuities in the polity as the result of the realities of war. This not only allows us to account for differences and similarities, but also pushes us to see how these conflicts continued to shape politics even after the war ended.

At least for the Court, no better example of the impending changes that were to come during war and Reconstruction was the seemingly mundane fact that as the justices began the 1860 term, they now occupied a new and more spacious courtroom in the Capitol building.[16] With the nation divided during their move, and with the need for a new justice to replace Justice Peter Daniel looming large, an editorial in the antislavery *New York Tribune* seemed to augur the future:

The Court consist[s] of five slave-holders and four non-slaveholders with the unscrupulous Taney at its head. This Court, as now arranged, is scandalously sectional, grossly partial, a mockery of the Constitution, a serf of the slave power, and a disgrace to the country. A truly National Administration will not fail to reform it so as to regain for it the confidence of the people, by adapting it to the ends for which it was created.[17]

Republican angst was only worsened when just a few weeks before Fort Sumter, and only a few days after Lincoln's inauguration, the Court ended its term with two opinions that demonstrated important continuities between the existing Court and the one yet to come.

In *Ex parte Kentucky v. Dennison,* the Court ruled that it would not force the governor of Ohio to deliver to Kentucky someone charged with violating Kentucky slave law.[18] And in *Freeman v. Howe,* the Court overturned a decision of the Massachusetts supreme court that allowed private bondholders to recover property seized by a United States marshal in a fugitive slave action.[19] These two opinions continued a developmental trajectory of increasing federal acquiescence to slavery's enforcement and expansion, a power that had reached its apex with the Court's decision in *Ableman v. Booth* just a year before.[20]

The preceding two decades of American constitutional development had witnessed an acute battle over the ability of American national institutions—political as well as judicial—to enforce slave law nationally.[21] As discussed in Chapter 2, habeas played a key role in this battle, as it served as a tool of enforcement for the Jacksonian regime and various Northern state antislavery political coalitions. Federal court habeas power increased during these decades, partly through congressional grants of increased jurisdiction and partly through federal court interpretation of their habeas powers. As a crucial partner in the Jacksonian regime, the Court helped sustain national slave power. With the election of 1860, a new regime was ascending to national control over political institutions. However, the Court was not immediately part of that regime. Indeed, in *Dred Scott,* it effectively held that the salient parts of the platform of the Republican Party were unconstitutional.

Continuity is present between the pre- and postwar constitutional patterns in the aggregate increase in national judicial power, but particularly with respect to federal court habeas jurisdiction. Although certainly critical of this increased judicial power, the ascending Republican regime needed a strong federal court system to buttress its political efforts, particularly one capable of commanding respect and legitimacy throughout the nation, as well as one that could wield its power to create and enforce the emerging visions of constitutional governance of the new regime. Although the Republican Party had not yet formulated their full vision of constitutional governance in 1861—indeed, this process would drive much Civil War and Reconstruction development— it was immediately clear to the party as a whole that federal courts would have to play a role. As Stanley Kutler demonstrated in his powerful revisionist account of the Supreme Court during Reconstruction, the Republican Party's sometimes hostile relationship with the Supreme Court during the 1860s was less a negative reaction to the Court's substantive use of its powers in the past to enforce the nationalization of the slavery question (for example, *Dred Scott*) than a realization of the immediate need to redirect this power for Republican purposes.[22] The Court's new, more spacious courtroom did, in fact, seem to augur an even more capacious role for judicial power.

Abraham Lincoln most likely knew that the already developed power of the federal courts could be an important part of Union victory.[23] Lincoln's reaction to *Dred Scott* was not a wholesale critique of national judicial power per se as much as it was a critique of the substance of the Taney Court's decision and judicial supremacy more generally.[24] Indeed, throughout the war and with the beginning of Reconstruction, Lincoln maintained that his actions would always be subject to some form of judicial review. His goal, then, like the more general goal of the Republican Party, was to direct increased judicial power in support of their new regime. The opportunity for new judicial appointments, combined with the party's desire to recalibrate the federal court system to correct for the overrepresentation of Southern interests, could help change the Court's substantive stance while not sacrificing the increased institutional power gained over the past decade.

From the perspective of habeas corpus, there is yet another continuity that bears on the *Merryman* case. Encomiums to the writ's liberty-protecting foundations in both Taney's opinion and Lincoln's 4 July response were belied by the Court's extant opinions, Lincoln's actions, and the Republican Party's positions on slavery. Despite deep disagreements about slavery's extension during the 1850s, both Democrats and Republicans in 1860 supported the national enforcement of fugitive slave laws, the Corwin amendment, and more general commitments to leave slavery unmolested in the states where it existed.[25] We should remember that increased federal court habeas power in the antebellum period was rarely—if ever—correlated with our more normative ideas of universal rights and freedom.

Aside from the immediate exigencies of war and secession, there were important discontinuities that shaped the context of *Merryman* as well. During John Marshall's tenure, federal court habeas power was partly secured by the

Court's willingness to forego expansive readings of federal habeas for state prisoners in order to maintain national political support for its habeas jurisprudence. During the Taney Court, however, federal habeas power for state prisoners became an increasing reality for federal courts, as it was used to frustrate cases prosecuted by Northern states under their personal liberty laws. Now, however, habeas power would need to be justified horizontally across the federal branches as well as vertically against the states during war and Reconstruction. The difficulty of this task was compounded not only by the realities of an unprecedented civil war, but also by the significant political challenges of accomplishing this move with a Democratically appointed Court that was now pitted against a new Republican Party regime.

EX PARTE MERRYMAN

To speak of the Supreme Court's role in *Merryman* is problematic. Although there are conflicting accounts, Roger Taney's formal role in the events surrounding John Merryman's detention (and even including his opinion in the case) was as a circuit court justice first, and only as chief justice of the Supreme Court by title and by his own willful assertion.[26] Merryman's capture by Union forces in the middle of the night gave Taney—and only by implication the Court he led—an opportunity to hold forth in what would turn out to be the last gasp of national judicial power in the Jacksonian tradition. Carefully bypassing the judiciary when needed, but ever mindful of its necessity to a successful Republican regime in the future, Lincoln deftly brushed Taney—but not the Court—aside.

It is important to highlight the fact that Taney's role was partially manufactured by himself. Of those detained in the earliest days after Lincoln's first suspension of habeas corpus, many were actually allowed to speak with friends and family. Immediately after his arrest, Merryman's family attorney quickly traveled to Washington to petition "The Chief Justice of the United States and presiding Judge of the United States Circuit Court, Baltimore," for the writ. Taney immediately issued the writ to General Cadwalader, the commanding officer of Fort McHenry, where Merryman was detained, but removed his appellation of circuit court justice from the document. He further demanded that Cadwalader produce Merryman's body not in Washington, but in Baltimore, where he immediately traveled after issuing the writ. Taney claimed that he took this course of action because he wanted to spare Cadwalader the burden of traveling to Washington, but other accounts suggest that Taney instead wanted Merryman's habeas petition to rise to the level of a direct confrontation between the chief justice and the new president. Moving the location of the hearing to Baltimore also had the potential added effect of waging this battle in the home city and state of both Merryman and Taney.[27]

The overtly political and confrontational nature of Merryman's habeas case is further evident in the fact that a return to the writ was actually made in the first hearing on 26 May 1861, although it was certainly not complete. General Cadwalader's aide-de-camp, Colonel Lee, wearing full military dress and armed with his sword, appeared before Taney in the general's place. Lee expressed Cadwalader's regret for his absence and presented to Taney Cadwalader's return to the writ, stating therein that Merryman was in his custody and was "charged with various acts of treason, and with being publicly associated with and holding a commission as a lieutenant in a company having possession of arms belonging to the United States, and avowing his purpose of armed hostility against the Government." He further added that the charges could be "clearly established." Lee then went on to inform Taney that he was authorized by the president to suspend habeas corpus—a "high and delicate trust" that "has been enjoined upon him that it should be executed with judgment and discretion." Finally, Cadwalader requested through Morris that Taney postpone any judgment in the case to give him extra time to secure more direction from President Lincoln so he could make a more complete return to the writ. Not surprisingly, Taney refused Cadwalader's request and proceeded to issue an attachment that not only again demanded Merryman's "body," but also declared General Cadwalader guilty of acting "in disobedience to the writ." The chief justice was unflinching in his demands that the writ be honored and that Merryman's body be produced by noon the next day.[28]

The estimated crowd of over two thousand Baltimoreans who gathered in the streets the following day to partake of the spectacle would not see Merryman, however. When the marshal attempted to serve Taney's orders at Fort McHenry, sentries blocked his way, so when Taney, seated alone in the courtroom, asked the marshal, "Have you your return to the writ, sir?," he must have known the answer would be no.

Taney's opinion not only castigated the president for suspending the writ but also asserted that no suspension could ever be authorized by the president alone. Taney began by expressing "surprise" that the writ had been suspended because "no official notice has been given to the courts of justice, or to the public, by proclamation or otherwise." He claimed he listened to Cadwalader's partial return to the writ with surprise because he also assumed it was "one of those points of constitutional law upon which there was no disagreement."²⁹ The point, of course, was the president's assertion of the power to suspend the writ without congressional authorization. Taney justified his position by citing English precedent, which he claimed authorized only parliamentary suspension, and also by citing United States precedent, including Jefferson's explicit deferral to Congress for habeas's suspension during the Burr conspiracy and Justice Joseph Story's assertion of congressional exclusivity.³⁰ Moreover, Taney interpreted the suspension clause's location in Article I, which seemingly constitutes and limits only the legislative branch, as further evidence against executive suspension. The president's duty is to take care that the laws "be faithfully executed," Taney exclaimed.³¹ The suspension, then, was an unconstitutional appropriation of legislative powers.

The most damning criticism, and the one that is most indicative of the extent to which the president's suspension portended further constitutional problems, was Taney's suggestion that there was no reason to suspend habeas in Merryman's case. The courts of Maryland, and of Baltimore in particular, were accessible. If Merryman was suspected of violating United States law, then the information concerning his actions should have been brought to the attention of the local district attorney for prosecution. The very fact that Taney himself was available and able to travel to Baltimore, hear the case, and issue his opinion proved as much. Moreover, the general discretion afforded to military commanders to suspend the writ when they saw fit was also too arbitrary to countenance without concomitant judicial review.

Seeking to limit the president's powers even more, Taney then went on to argue that even if Congress had authorized habeas's suspension, it would only apply to those detained by the military because the Bill of Rights would stand in the way in all other cases.³² Here, Taney was attempting to vindicate the very rights he had torn asunder just four years earlier in *Dred Scott*. Just as Fifth Amendment rights in that case applied only to slaveholders and not to African Americans, they would remain inviolable for the very same people waging war against the United States. These rights could be suspended permanently for some (African Americans), but never for others (Southern slaveholders and their supporters). Taney then ended his opinion knowing well that his decision would likely be ignored: "I have exercised all the power which the constitution and laws confer upon me, but that power has been resisted by a force too strong for me to overcome."³³

Lincoln's retort would come less than two months later in his 4 July 1861 address to Congress, when he posed his famous rhetorical question, "Are all the laws but one to go unexecuted, and the government itself go to pieces, lest that one be violated?" Lincoln did not address Taney or Merryman specifically; he did not even acknowledge that the chief justice had issued a habeas writ or that he even wrote an opinion.[34] Instead, Lincoln bypassed an answer to this oft-quoted phrase, asserting that "it was not believed that this question was presented. It was not believed that any law was violated." Because the habeas clause in Article I was "silent as to which" branch was authorized to suspend during periods of war or rebellion, Lincoln argued that this duty fell to him.[35]

All of this suggests that the *Merryman* case and Lincoln's famous response are best understood not as isolated examples of the more theoretical issues involved in presidential war power and their effects on civil liberties, but rather as the products of political and judicial processes that had been roiling during the past two decades.[36] With Lincoln's election and the advent of Civil War, the Jacksonian regime's ties to the federal judiciary were quickly crumbling, and Taney must have known this. Prospects for executive cooperation with the court, let alone the possibility of deference to its decisions from Lincoln, were unlikely. Considering the state of disarray of the Democratic Party and the complete evisceration of the Whigs over the last half decade, the 1860 election produced a president who famously said that while "the judicial department" and "its decisions on constitutional questions . . . should control . . . the particular cases decided . . . we shall do what we can to overrule [them]."[37] As a reconstructive president, Lincoln's interpretation of his own constitutional powers was thus decidedly departmentalist.[38] Combined with his stance on *Dred Scott* and his departmentalist theory of constitutional interpretation, his assertion of the constitutionality of executive suspension (even with the implicit caveat that he was acting when Congress could not) sought to carve out a coequal role in constitutional interpretation for the executive.[39]

Lincoln's assertion of executive independence in *Merryman* was necessarily a qualified one, and it is directly related to the relationship between the case and the preceding political context.[40] Again, Cadwalader initially asked Taney to give him more time to provide a more complete return to the habeas writ. Presumably, if there was a complete unilateral assertion of executive power, no military representative would have appeared at all. It is also possible that if Taney had agreed to give Cadwalader more time and did not engineer such a spectacle of the proceedings and his role in them, further habeas writs issued by federal judges may have been met with more deference despite the writ's suspension. More importantly, it is quite plausible that even with his assertion that the executive was constitutionally authorized to suspend the writ in situations such as those during the Civil War, Lincoln did not have a completely developed conception of what this proposition actually entailed. Since the initial decision to suspend on 27 April 1861, Lincoln had requested that his Cabinet, and Attorney General Edward Bates in particular, advise him on exactly what was at stake with suspension, and it was only a day after his famous address to Congress that the attorney general submitted in writing the administration's full written position on the constitutionality of suspension. It is more likely that in the trying and unprecedented days immediately after Fort Sumter, Lincoln was simply playing things as they went.[41]

Bates's more detailed justification of suspension begins to make this clear. If the suspension clause is understood to mean "a repeal of all power to issue the writ," he said, "then I freely admit that none but Congress can do it." Instead, he argued that "if we are . . . to understand the phrase to mean, that, in case of a great and dangerous rebellion, like the present, the public safety requires the arrest and confinement of persons implicated in that rebellion . . . the President has lawful power to suspend the privilege of persons arrested under such circumstances."[42] And for the most part, suspensions were limited. In fact, it was not until 24 September 1862, seven days after Congress passed the Militia Act, and over a year after the 4 July address to Congress, that habeas was effectively suspended for the entire country.[43]

Despite the more limited nature of Lincoln's assertion of executive independence in the *Merryman* case, the chief justice and others obviously perceived these actions as bordering on military despotism. Partisan critics in both parties did not hesitate to question and even condemn Lincoln's actions.[44] Taney even wrote in 1863 that he was doubtful of the court's ability to be "restored to the authority and rank which the Constitution intended to confer upon it."[45] And a common refrain among scholars, including many with little sympathy for the chief justice, concludes, as did Charles Warren, "that had the Chief Justice lived" a little longer, "he would have seen the doctrines laid down by him in the *Merryman Case* strongly upheld" in *Ex parte Milligan*.[46]

But we lose a key perspective by casting *Merryman* as purely a case of interbranch struggle during war. To be sure, separation-of-powers issues in *Merryman* would persist through the war and into Reconstruction. Lincoln would spar with congressional Republicans over early conceptions of emancipation and the individual rights of freedmen, and Andrew Johnson would raise this battle to a new level. But as the power and resources of a more sympathetic and regime-affiliated Court became more and more part of the war and Reconstruction effort, the institutional dynamics between the Court and Congress in 1866 (when *Milligan* was decided) would be even less comparable to those in 1861. *Merryman* tells us more about the early period of political and institutional transition between Lincoln's newly ascendant Republican Party and the Jacksonian Court than it does about the future relationship among the branches during Reconstruction.

HABEAS AND CONGRESS, 1862–1864

Although habeas was effectively suspended by the Lincoln administration in matters directly related to the prosecution of the war from 27 April 1861 onward, habeas development continued in other important ways. As a potential tool of regime enforcement, some in Congress believed early in the war that habeas could be used in ways to protect the newly acquired rights of slaves confiscated by Union forces. Although immediately unsuccessful, the role of habeas in the emerging need to protect the legal rights of an increasingly large amount of newly freed slaves, and in the quickening battles between Congress and the president over the substance and procedures of Reconstruction, are important to highlight. These early proposed uses of habeas in the first year of the Civil War would eventually serve as the basis for larger changes to the writ during the height of Reconstruction.

Aside from suspension, the first discussions of habeas corpus revision and extension during the war took shape in the early drafts of the confiscation acts. At the beginning of the war, both Congress and the executive were immediately concerned with depriving the Confederacy of manpower through the confiscation of property, which took the form of the emancipation of slaves for Union military purposes. This was a precarious but necessary tactic—necessary because slaves performed important and meaningful (but nevertheless menial) services for Southern armies (mostly as laborers), and precarious because complete emancipation of slaves was still not a politically popular position.[47] Couched in the language of military necessity, limited emancipation for mostly instrumental reasons was advanced by Lincoln and generally supported by Congress.

The Second Confiscation Act of 1862 sought to pacify those in Congress who wanted limited and controlled emancipation for military purposes and those more radical positions that were already warning of the possible civil and legal deprivations that freed slaves would face without concomitant federal protection. The first version of the act that was reported out of committee would have freed all slaves of anyone who was deemed to be disloyal to the Union, but it failed in the House by a 78–74 vote.[48] Opponents of the bill felt that emancipation of all slaves of disloyal rebels was too drastic a measure to be taken. More radical members of the House voted against the bill because no legal provisions were in place to protect freedmen. In a compromise measure, the House produced a revised version of the bill that limited the scope of emancipation to the slaves of Confederate officers and rebel state officials. It also contained a habeas provision that would allow federal courts to hear habeas petitions for freed slaves who were reenslaved by their former or pretended masters. However, the author of the revised provision, Albert Porter (R-Ind.), advanced it as a much more limited bill that would have two salutary effects. The first would be to reduce the potential influx of freed slaves that could potentially overwhelm the border states of the North—a persistent worry of those states, and one that explains their support of the new provision. The second effect was that by limiting emancipation to those most guilty of rebellion, the domestic state institutions of slavery would remain unchanged. In Porter's words, the purpose of the revised bill was to "deprive the leaders of this rebellion of their property in slaves, but at the same time not destroy the security of the domestic institutions of any of the slaveholding states."[49]

Porter's position helps us clarify his intent with respect to the bill's habeas provisions. If a slave of a Confederate officer or rebel state official was emancipated as a result of the bill and was subsequently claimed as property by another, then they were to be released on habeas corpus by the federal judiciary. Although this habeas provision was certainly monumental in its scope and substance, Porter argued that it was an indispensable enforcement mechanism of this emancipation measure: "In this way a sure remedy is provided to guard against prejudice."[50] Considering his unwillingness to see slavery abolished completely, and considering his general belief that this limited emancipation served military exigencies only, the habeas provision has to be understood as a mechanism to support larger military goals and not as a general provision for ensuring legal equality for freedmen.

We see this argument confirmed as the bill's habeas provisions were then jettisoned in committee. Democrat John Noell of Missouri believed that the grant of habeas to blacks would change their legal status too drastically. Noell drafted the report of the Committee on Emancipation of Slaves and Rebels, which laid out the fundamental objections to the bill's habeas provisions. His fear was that "the substitute [the new habeas provision] treats slaves as *persons* ... not as *property*" and that habeas would not only permanently alter the legal status of slaves but the nature of federalism as well: "Confiscation seizes and condemns *property* as *property,* but does not change the legal status of *persons* in a State, which legal status results from *local* and not *federal* law."[51] Although the act's emancipation of slaves was acceptable, it was so only because they were seized as property and would presumably always be treated as property, "but we cannot ignore their character as *property*, and then alter their status as *persons*."[52] Although Noell's position did not prevent the bill from passing the House, the Senate did not share the House's concerns for legal and civil protections for confiscated property. The final version of the Second Confiscation Act, after revision in the Senate and in joint committee, ultimately provided no habeas protection. Instead, the bill classified confiscated slaves as captives of war and provided the president with the power to use this new labor for whatever purpose he deemed necessary to prosecute the war.

THE HABEAS ACT OF 1863

As the failed congressional attempts to craft meaningful habeas provisions in the first years of the Civil War demonstrate, questions surrounding the legal status of freedmen posed significant challenges to both Lincoln and Congress. Bound up within these challenges were the equally difficult—and increasingly divisive—questions about which branch would lead early Reconstruction efforts. The first successful habeas provisions passed by Congress reflected these emerging problems. Like the failure to include meaningful habeas protection in the Second Confiscation Act, the Habeas Corpus Indemnity Act of 1863 was concerned first and foremost with martial issues, as it indemnified federal officials against Southern state laws and gave congressional imprimatur to habeas's suspension.[53] Habeas's use to thwart recalcitrant state governments—and their state constitutions—was only implicitly designed with freedmen's rights in mind.

Passed on 3 March 1863, just two months after Lincoln's Emancipation Proclamation, the act sought to protect federal officials from prosecutions by Southern state governments and also to put a congressional stamp of approval on habeas's suspension. Not since the Habeas Act of 1833 had Congress used habeas to protect the actions of federal officials. This use of the writ was foremost in the minds of congressional Republicans who, like their Jacksonian predecessors, also used the writ to augment the role of federal courts in aid of their policies.[54]

Incorporating federal courts into the 1863 Habeas Act was a strategic, if risky, move by Congress. The impetus for this strategy was the larger division over early Reconstruction policy between Lincoln and Congress. Presidential war powers loomed large since the beginning of the war, and Congress had already failed to incorporate habeas provisions in the confiscation acts in 1862, largely because the party was divided over emancipation issues as wartime measures.[55] With Lincoln's Emancipation Proclamation, the possibility of a completely executive-led Reconstruction was becoming more and more of a reality. In Louisiana, for example, Lincoln was prepared to recognize a new government under his Ten Percent Plan (issued only five days before the 1863 Habeas Act), which would have left all but top-level Confederates in a position to influence all of that state's political and legal policies.[56] Moreover, the president's early Reconstruction plan was not only led by the military—and not Congress—but would also have allowed the establishment of apprentice-like labor systems for freedmen, a feature that incensed Radical Republicans. With strong Democratic upsurges following the 1862 elections threatening to embolden Southern states, and the simultaneous consideration of Lincoln's conscription bill (which portended even more military centralization), congressional Republicans needed to act. Here, then, was an opportunity for Congress to exert partial control over executive war power through federal courts by setting the terms of habeas's suspension and defining the procedures for indemnifying federal officials.[57]

The strategy had inherent risks, because Chief Justice Taney could hardly be thought of as a natural partner in this endeavor.[58] Despite reservations about Taney, congressional fears and criticisms of the court were far outweighed by an increasing willingness on the part of Congress to turn to the court to help enforce their early Reconstruction agenda. To be sure, Congress was always wary of the Court, especially since at any time it could overturn and frustrate their policies, but this possibility was becoming less likely. Lincoln had already made three appointments to the Court, and during the debate on the 1863 act, the Court was hearing arguments in the *Prize Cases,* and it would issue its favorable opinion in that case just seven days after the passage of the 1863 act.[59]

Section 1 of the 1863 act provided that "during the present rebellion, the President of the United States, whenever, in his judgment, the public safety may require it, is authorized to suspend the privilege of the writ of habeas corpus in any case throughout the United States." Whether this language gave congressional approval to past actions is not clear, but what this section did do was bring Congress in line with Taney's *Merryman* opinion that only that body could authorize habeas's suspension. Significantly, Thaddeus Stevens (R-Pa.), who authored the House version of the act, did not join some of his fellow Republicans who supported Lincoln's and Bates's constitutional justifications for executive suspension of habeas corpus in April 1861. Presumably, then, we can see in the 1863 act a less deferential stance toward executive and military reconstruction, and even an implicit statement that the president's suspension needed congressional approval.[60]

Congressional imprimatur of suspension was seconded by the provisions in the next two sections, which detailed more restrictive procedures for executive suspension. Both the secretary of war and the secretary of state were now required to furnish to federal courts a list of those imprisoned by the executive branch within twenty days of an arrest. If a court did not return an indictment, the prisoner was to be released after swearing a loyalty oath.[61] Even with these provisions—which were enacted to achieve more congressional control over early executive and military reconstruction—many prisoners simply fell out of the processes so established. The definition of "prisoner" in the act was at times disputed, and the military often did not supply the names of those whom it sought to prosecute as criminals under the articles of war, including "bushwhackers, guerillas, saboteurs, and spies."[62] This distinction came to the fore just a month later, when Clement Vallandigham was arrested in Ohio and prosecuted by a military commission. In that case, the Court refused to entertain Vallandigham's writ of certiorari because the Court argued it had no jurisdiction from military commissions so established.[63]

The next sections detailed the procedures for removal of cases against federal officers from state to federal courts. The perceived recalcitrance of Southern state courts, whether or not they were located in areas still in rebellion, was the impetus for these removal provisions. Congress was also aware that state courts might litigate claims against draft officials, because the Enrollment Act (which was a conscription bill) was passed the same day. The defining feature of these sections, and the one that received the most intense criticism, was the fact that it left private citizens in Southern states with virtually no legal recourse, whether civil or criminal, for wrongs or injuries against their person or property.[64] Section 4 provided that any presidential "order" was a "defence ... for any search, seizure, arrest, or imprisonment, made, done, or committed ... under and by virtue of such order, or under color of any law of Congress."[65] The subsequent 1866 revisions of the act, which responded even more forcefully to continued Southern state resistance, would go even further by making state judges liable for continuing civil or criminal complaints against federal officers after removal to federal courts.[66]

The 1863 Act was one of the first of many types of removal legislation passed during the Civil War and Reconstruction. According to James Randall, this means that the act "must be judged in light of the fact that it was originally passed in the very midst of a desperate war" during a "period" when "extreme legislation was characteristic."[67] There is no question that war and rebellion provided the occasion for the 1863 act, but habeas's use by political regimes to protect federal officials had a well-developed history by 1863, both substantively and procedurally. The 1833 act's removal provisions, combined with that act's use in the 1850s to protect federal marshals as they carried out the provisions of the fugitive slave laws, served as an already established procedure to enforce the new Republican regime's substantive goals during the early phases of Reconstruction. That Congress partnered with federal courts to enforce their substantive goals against recalcitrant states further highlights the strategic power of habeas for regimes, even though it is quite likely that part of Congress' strategy in this and other removal legislation was to curb executive power.[68] And as it had during the antebellum period, the increasing regime use of habeas in federal courts would produce federal court habeas opinions wherein justices would seek to confirm their regime's preferred position of habeas while simultaneously protecting their institutional capacity to issue the writ. And this self-regarding dynamic proved to be even more pronounced when the party was divided.[69]

CONTINUITIES AND DISCONTINUITIES IN EX PARTE MILLIGAN

Justice David Davis's majority opinion in *Ex parte Milligan* is often hailed as a paean to individual liberty.[70] Some even go further. Charles Warren, for example, boldly asserted that Taney's *Merryman* opinion was vindicated by Davis in *Milligan:* "Never did a fearless Judge [Taney] receive a more swift or more complete vindication."[71] The image of a completely independent judiciary boldly defending the habeas rights of individuals in the face of tyrannical wartime political institutions, however, is simply wrong. And the assumption that meaningful continuities obtain between Taney's actions in *Merryman* just a few weeks after Fort Sumter, and Davis's majority opinion in 1866 after the end of the of the war, the assassination of Lincoln, and the beginning of the increasingly divisive interbranch battles over Reconstruction, vastly overstates the comparison. The changing political context in which habeas developed between April 1861 and December 1866, when the *Milligan* opinions were made public, suggests that the use of the writ by congressional Republicans to forge their own visions of Reconstruction policy better explains the seemingly countermajoritarian and rights-protecting elements of the opinion. From 1864 to 1867, Congress' Reconstruction agenda moved from checking Lincoln's military programs to checking Johnson's programs with military and judicial legislation.[72] This switch had a significant impact on habeas's development before and after the *Milligan* decision was made public.

The rapidly shifting political context of habeas's development preceding the *Milligan* opinion is first evident in the failed Wade-Davis bill, which sought to shift Reconstruction efforts away from executive and toward congressional control. The Wade-Davis bill was proposed in reaction to what radical Republicans perceived to be an executive prosecution of Reconstruction that, with the exception of the basic abolition of slavery, was tilting toward the status quo ante position of states' rights.[73] Although Lincoln's territorial governments, especially in Louisiana, required the abolition of slavery, critics still felt that without a concurrent plan to enforce and protect legal and civil rights of freedmen, abolition alone would accomplish very little. Abolitionist and radical sentiment toward presidential Reconstruction were summed up by Wendell Phillips, who characterized Lincoln's early Reconstruction effort as one that "frees slaves, but ignores the negro."[74] No provisions were made, except those that would necessarily flow from state courts and legislatures, for their real, meaningful protection. Republicans realized, however, that some kind of civil rights protection was needed, if only because of the unique nature of the status of rebel states as they hung in constitutional limbo since secession. If they did not legislate for the states before they came back into the Union, civil rights would again be under the auspices of state governments. Henry Winter Davis, the architect of the Wade-Davis bill, made this very point in a special speech on the floor of the House on 25 February 1864, in which he sounded a cry for greater legal protection for freedmen through habeas. Without these extra protections, he argued, readmitted states would revert to their old ways:

Slavery is not dead by the proclamation [the Emancipation Proclamation]. What lawyer attributes to it the least *legal* effect in breaking the bonds of slavery? Executed by the bayonet . . . it [presidential emancipation] is undoubtedly valid to the extent of turning them loose from their masters during the rebellion. Reestablish the old governments, allow the dominant aristocracy to repossess the State power in its original plenitude, how long will they be free? What courts will give them rights? What provision is there to protect them? Where is the writ of *habeas corpus*?[75]

The Wade-Davis bill's habeas provisions sought to preempt any state judicial or legislative decision concerning the most basic rights of freedmen, including preventing kidnapping, reenslavement, and all forms of involuntary servitude, most specifically peonage. Considering the potential divisiveness over the institutional control of Reconstruction, it made sense for Congress to partner with federal courts and look to them as another independent enforcement mechanism for their policies through the bill's habeas provisions. However, Lincoln's pocket veto of the bill as the congressional session ended killed the measure. The bill was tabled because fear of losing a Republican in the White House in the November elections outweighed Congress' plans.[76] Once again, meaningful habeas protections were sacrificed.

Interbranch struggles over Reconstruction only continued to worsen. After the assassination of Lincoln and the ascendance of Andrew Johnson to the presidency, it became clear to congressional Republicans that the new president's plans for Reconstruction were problematic. Congressional response to Johnson's amnesty proclamation on 29 May 1865 could only be rhetorical, for Johnson's first major steps toward Reconstruction occurred between May and December 1865, when Congress was in recess. The amnesty proclamation is significant for the policies that it did and did not contain. Johnson provided for "amnesty and pardon, with restoration of all rights of property, except as to slaves," for all except the highest level of Confederate rebels, if supplemented with a loyalty oath.[77] Provisional governors, appointed by Johnson, would then create new state governments. Although each state had to ratify the Thirteenth Amendment, the proclamation provided for no additional legal safeguards for freedmen at a time when black codes had already quickly replaced slave codes in a few states. Presumably, without further protection, every state that followed Johnson's proclamation would do the same.[78] When the Thirty-ninth Congress finally met in December, its skepticism of Johnson's program was revealed in their refusal to seat the congressional delegations from states that met Johnson's requirements.[79] They also created the Joint Committee on Reconstruction, which became the platform for Congress' alternative Reconstruction program.[80]

Two of these legislative initiatives during the first session were the Freedman's Bureau bill and the Civil Rights Act of 1866.[81] Both bills sought to protect freedmen's rights under the Thirteenth Amendment in light of the onerous black codes. The Freedman's Bureau legislation explicitly removed cases of Southern state discrimination to military courts, and when these removal powers were combined with the 1866 Civil Rights Act's more general removal procedures to federal courts, it was evident that Congress sought to enforce their Reconstruction program partly through judicial means. Nevertheless, in the case of the Freedman's Bureau, it became increasingly evident that Congress was beginning to modify its previous stance against military-based Reconstruction measures.[82] Johnson vetoed both laws, and Congress was only able to override the Civil Rights Act's veto.[83] And to make matters worse, four days before the Civil Rights Act veto, Johnson's 2 April 1866 proclamation declared that the "insurrection" was "at an end." He went on to proclaim that "standing armies, military occupation, martial law, military tribunals, and the suspension of the privilege of habeas corpus are, in time of peace dangerous to public liberty, incompatible with the individual rights of the citizen . . . and ought not, therefore, to be sanctioned or allowed except in cases of actual necessity."[84]

It was in the midst of this critical time for congressional–executive relations that the holdings of the *Milligan* decision were announced on 3 April 1866.[85] Interpretations of the opinion that characterize it as a bold vindication of individual rights by the Court against the elected branches most often rely on the admittedly vitriolic but isolated criticisms by radical Republicans that largely occurred only after the justices' opinions were released in December 1866.[86] In April, as William Lasser argued, "There is little wonder that the announcement was largely ignored by the Republicans" because "military rule had just been denounced . . . and the freedmen's security had just been placed solidly in the hands of the civilian courts of the United States rather than those of the military."[87]

EX PARTE MILLIGAN

Negative reaction to Davis's majority opinion in *Milligan* after December 1866 was precipitated by the most recent events that had played out since April and also by speculation about the opinion's portent for congressional Reconstruction in the immediate future.[88] Between April and December, all of Johnson's provisional Southern governments (except his home state of Tennessee) failed to ratify the Fourteenth Amendment. And with Republican victories in the November elections, combined with increasing Southern state recalcitrance, Congress was poised to implement a stronger version of Reconstruction. Nevertheless, a reliance on federal courts, especially through increasing grants of habeas authority, continued to be an important part of their larger policies, even before military reconstruction became a real option for congressional Republicans. Davis's opinion, often hailed as a bulwark of American liberty, cannot be seen as a singular commitment to the blanket protection of individual rights by an independent judiciary. Justice Chase's dissenting opinion, which reads more like a concurrence, further pushes us to see how the Court was working, even if tentatively and partially, with Congress as they both waded through the unprecedented challenges of Reconstruction.

In its rhetorical flourishes, Davis's opinion striking down the jurisdiction of Lambden Milligan's military trial seems to be unwavering. "No graver question," Davis proclaimed, "was ever considered by this court, nor one which more clearly concerns the rights of the whole people."[89] Because of the "late wicked Rebellion . . . the temper of the times did not allow that calmness in deliberation . . . so necessary to a correct conclusion of a purely judicial question." But "now that the public safety is assured, this question . . . can be discussed and decided without passion or admixture of any element not required to form a legal judgment."[90] Although he did not mention the case in his opinion, Davis most likely was referring to *Ex parte Vallandigham,* decided two years earlier, in which the Court, faced with a similar question involving the constitutionality of military tribunals, ruled that it had no jurisdiction in appeals from military trials.[91] Now, with the war over, Davis seemed to suggest that military rule during peacetime, when "courts are open," was unconstitutional.[92]

Yet in important ways, Davis's opinion could be understood to be less definitive about military rule—and hence military reconstruction—than many suggest. For one, his oft-quoted maxim concerning military rule where "courts are open" was immediately followed by the qualification that "their process" had to be "unobstructed."[93] After the opinions were released in December 1866 and criticism of Davis and the Court was reaching a crescendo, Davis even expressed dismay at Republican attacks on the opinion, writing to a friend soon after that his opinion "did not" contain "a word" about "reconstruction, & the power is conceded in insurrectionary States."[94]

However, Davis's private correspondence should not obscure the fact that the Court's opinion was unanimous concerning the unconstitutionality of Milligan's trial and sentence in the military tribunal. Even Chief Justice Chase agreed that Milligan's trial and sentence crossed the line. Nevertheless, the line that was crossed was not the arrest of Milligan or even his future prosecution. Milligan's arrest, like many others, was subject to the provisions of the 1863 Habeas Corpus Indemnity Act, which in part authorized habeas's suspension and also provided for judicial procedures and time limitations for detention. Accordingly, Milligan's case was referred to a federal district court, and no indictment was returned. Pace the provisions of the 1863 act, Milligan should have been released. "If this had been done," Davis said, "the Constitution would have been vindicated, the law of 1863 enforced, and the securities for personal liberty preserved and defended."[95] Formal hostilities were over, and Andrew Johnson was now president. The prospect of military tribunals such as Milligan's now did not sit well, especially since Congress had already brought federal courts into the process. Executive-led martial law, while sometimes necessary because the nation "cannot always remain at peace," was always constitutionally and politically suspect. "Wicked men, ambitious of power," Davis warned, "with hatred of liberty and contempt of law, may fill the place once occupied by Washington and Lincoln . . . the dangers to human liberty are frightful to contemplate."[96]

The most controversial part of Davis's opinion, which in fact prompted Chase to pen his concurrence, was not related specifically to Milligan's case at all. To Chase, this seemed to suggest "that it was not in the power of Congress to authorize" military tribunals in areas where hostilities had ended and courts were opened.[97] Considering Davis's personal correspondence regarding the inapplicability of the opinion's holding to the South and his qualification that courts had to be "unobstructed," Chase's worry might have been moot. Nevertheless, his acceptance of the Court's opinion that Milligan's trial in Indiana was unconstitutional did not prevent him from defending the possibility of the future use of military tribunals established by Congress. In what seemed like an uncanny foreboding of the actual operation of reconstructed Southern courtrooms, Chase argued that these courts "might be open and undisturbed in the execution of their functions, and yet wholly incompetent to avert threatened danger, or to punish, with adequate promptitude and certainty, the guilty conspirators." It must be recognized that Congress had the power to create and provide for military trials because it was still further possible that "judges and marshalls" might "be in active sympathy with rebels, and courts their most efficient allies."[98]

Even with these considerations, which should cause us to discount any characterization of the *Milligan* opinion as completely hostile to executive or congressional war power, both opinions nevertheless refused to abdicate all judicial power in the specific case. The Court was willing to concede some of its habeas power to the proposition that emergency situations might preclude judicial review of detainments, but by the time the case was decided, the emergency situation had passed, at least in Indiana. The fact that Milligan's case centered on the 1863 Habeas Act further suggests that the entire Court was solicitous of the powers conferred by Congress in the supervision of grand juries for those detained by the military. This, after all, was a point on which every justice agreed. Despite Davis's seemingly libertarian rhetoric, then, and even considering Chase's hypothetical deference to congressional power in the future, the Court sought to protect their own habeas powers first. This move by the entire Court, more so than the rather prosaic announcement that certain military trials were unconstitutional after Lee's surrender, was the real exercise of judicial independence by the Court in *Milligan*. With most Republicans generally hostile to executive-led military reconstruction, and with no plans for congressionally led military policies when the case was decided in April 1866, the Court had room to carve out and preserve its habeas powers.

Republican fears about *Milligan*'s possible repercussions for congressional

Reconstruction policies were nevertheless real, even if they ultimately proved to be incorrect. Not long after the decision was released, one of Lincoln's assassins, who had been convicted in a military trial, applied for a writ of habeas corpus before Chief Justice Chase. Although Chase rejected the petition on the grounds that he could not issue the writ outside of his own circuit, the prospects of similar habeas writs in the immediate future did not ease the fears of some in Congress.[99] To make matters worse, Andrew Johnson, who, not unsurprisingly, was sympathetic to an anticongressional reading of *Milligan*, declared an end to all military trials then under way in areas that Republicans still considered belligerent. Even without a congressional consensus about the finer details of future Reconstruction policy hammered out by January 1867, Republicans, now bolstered by electoral victory, were poised to move ahead despite the seeming rebuke by the Court in *Milligan*.[100]

Not more than two months after the opinions in *Milligan* were released, and only a month after most journalistic and Radical Republican attacks on the opinion occupied both editorial pages and floor debates in the House and Senate, Congress passed the Habeas Corpus Act of 1867.[101] The act's origins are to be found earlier the previous year, but it would be odd for Congress to pass a bill such as this if they were as hostile to federal court power as some have assumed.[102] Although the debates surrounding the initial draft of the 1867 act are ultimately unhelpful in determining the exact intent of Congress in enlarging federal court habeas jurisdiction, it is beyond question that habeas's role in congressional Reconstruction was to be one that built on an already increasing relationship between Congress and the federal judiciary.[103] And the Republican regime's reliance on federal courts to enforce and give constitutional legitimacy to its Reconstruction program would continue even though Congress repealed the Supreme Court's jurisdiction under the 1867 act soon after its passage. The key to reconciling this seemingly hostile move, then, is in understanding exactly how Congress imagined federal court regime enforcement through habeas would play out. If Congress was first and foremost concerned with the legal supervision of recalcitrant Southern states with respect to freedmen's issues, and only tangentially concerned with habeas enforcement for federal prisoners, then the seemingly contentious issues in *McCardle* become less problematic.

THE HABEAS CORPUS ACT OF 1867

The Habeas Corpus Act of 1867, the origins of which are admittedly opaque, changed the contour of legal proceedings generally related to the writ and, most importantly, the institutional relationship between state and federal courts. The act not only provided postconviction review of decisions, but also seemingly provided for federal review of state decisions on habeas for anyone held in violation of the Constitution.[104] The 1867 act also had the effect of providing federal court habeas review of state criminal law generally, a function that the 1833 and 1842 acts only implicated by default. Federal court review of state criminal cases was certainly contemplated in the 1833 act's provisions for the removal of state prosecutions of tariff officers to federal courts, but these provisions were not explicitly designed with the view that state criminal law was to fall under its auspices. Even when the 1833 act was used to remove cases involving federal marshals who were arrested for violating state personal liberty laws in the course of their duties in enforcing fugitive slave laws, this was a judicial, not congressional, interpretation of the writ. And although the 1842 act was explicitly designed to remove cases to federal courts involving state criminal prosecutions against foreign nationals acting as agents of a foreign nation, the act never contemplated the more general supervision of state criminal law.

The day after the Thirteenth Amendment went into effect, the House Judiciary Committee was directed to devise legislation to aid Congress in the enforcement of the amendment. Representative Shellabarger moved that the following resolution be passed:

Resolved, That the Committee on the Judiciary be directed to inquire and report to this House, as soon as practicable, by bill or otherwise, what legislation is necessary to enable the courts of the United States to enforce the freedom of the wives and children of soldiers of the United States under the joint resolution of Congress of March 3, 1865, and also to enforce the liberty of all persons under the operation of the constitutional amendment abolishing slavery.[105]

The 3 March 1865 joint resolution referred to in Shellabarger's House resolution was signed by Lincoln on the last day of the Thirty-eighth Congress and declared that the wives and children of those who served during the war were now free. It also conferred freedom upon those in slave states that were not in rebellion, including those slaves who did not fall under the provisions of the Emancipation Proclamation.[106]

The bill that was first proposed to the House Judiciary Committee three weeks after Shellabarger's resolution was, according to Iowa representative James Wilson, designed to "secure the writ of habeas corpus to persons held in slavery."[107] Although the bill died in committee, it suggests that the earliest iteration of what became the 1867 act was decidedly limited in scope. The bill provided that all persons who are held in slavery or involuntary servitude otherwise than for a crime whereof they are convicted shall be discharged on *Habeas Corpus* issued by any returnable before any court or judge of the United States; and if the court or judge refuse the discharge the petitioner may forthwith appeal to the Supreme Court, which court if then sitting or if not at its next term shall hear the case on the first motion day after appeal is docketed and discharge the petitioner if he shall appear to be held in slavery or involuntary servitude contrary to the constitution of the United States.[108]

A different version of what would eventually become the final bill was reported out of committee by Representative James Wilson on 25 July 1866. The relevant parts of the bill are as follows:

The several courts of the United States, and the several justices and judges of such courts, within their respective jurisdictions, in addition to the authority already conferred by law, shall have the power to grant writs of habeas corpus in all cases where any person may be restrained of his or her liberty in violation of the constitution, or of any treaty or law of the United States.

From the final decision of any judge, justice, or court, inferior to the circuit court, an appeal may be taken to the circuit court . . . and from the judgment of said circuit court to the Supreme Court of the United States.[109]

On the same day the bill was reported, it was discussed on the floor of the House. One of the only questions raised was by Representative LeBlond, who was concerned that the bill exempted any person held under military authority.[110] Lawrence's response to the query was that it did not, and then he proceeded to give an explicit restatement of the act's intent:

On the 19th of December last, my colleague introduced a resolution instructing the Judiciary Committee to inquire and report to the House as soon as practicable, by bill or otherwise, what legislation is necessary to enable the courts of the United States to enforce the freedom of the wife and children of soldiers of the United States, and also to enforce the liberty of all persons. Judge Ballard, of the district court of Kentucky, decided that there was no act of Congress giving courts of the United States jurisdiction to enforce the rights and liberties of such persons. In pursuance of that resolution of my colleague this bill has been introduced, the effect of which is to enlarge the privilege of the writ of *habeas corpus,* and make the jurisdiction of the courts and judges of the United States coextensive with all the powers that can be conferred upon them. It is a bill of the largest liberty, and does not interfere with persons in military custody, or restrain the writ of *habeas corpus* at all.[111]

When the bill was reported out of the Senate Judiciary Committee, Senator Lyman Trumbull characterized the act thusly:

The habeas corpus act of 1789 . . . confines the jurisdiction of the United States courts in issuing writs of *habeas corpus* to persons who are held under United States laws. Now, a person might be held under a State law in violation of the Constitution and laws of the United States, and he ought to have in such a case the benefit of the writ, and we agree he ought to have recourse to the United States courts to show that he was illegally imprisoned in violation of the Constitution or laws of the United States.[112]

Despite Trumbull's seemingly clarifying language, determining the exact intent of the bill has proved to be an almost impossible task.[113] One House member, in commenting on the bill, for example, exclaimed, "I would ask whether anybody in this House, when he gives his vote . . . knows what he is voting on? [Laughter]."[114] Aside from intent beyond the text, the 1867 act was a significant development in its own right—this was, after all, an amendment to the Judiciary Act of 1789's habeas provisions. With the exception of the limited and specific classes of defendants specified in the 1833 and 1842 acts, federal court review of state court judgments through habeas was prohibited before the passage of the 1867 act. Now, however, anyone claiming to be held in violation of the Constitution or any federal law or treaty might challenge their detention through a writ of habeas corpus in federal court. Another significant development was that the habeas proceedings would now be permitted to review the facts of cases de novo, when previously de novo review was limited to questions of law.[115]

The act's broad, general language seemed to add yet another important element to federal habeas corpus review for federal prisoners. As discussed at length in Chapter 2, while section 14 of the Judiciary Act of 1789 prohibited federal habeas review of state prisoners, it did provide for habeas review of federal prisoners. Although the language did not explicitly provide for Supreme Court review of federal prisoner habeas appeals, Chief Justice John Marshall rectified that omission in *Ex parte Bollman,* arguing that federal prisoner habeas cases could be reviewed by the Court through the exercise of its appellate powers.[116] The only change with respect to federal prisoners in the 1867 act was the rather prosaic statutory authorization for appeals to the Supreme Court from habeas cases in the lower federal district and circuit courts. Indeed, the 1867 act prefaced the grant of appellate jurisdiction to the Supreme Court with the phrase "in addition to the authority already conferred by law." Providing federal habeas corpus review of state court decisions to federal courts, and further allowing appellate review by the Supreme Court, made sense for state prisoners who had previously been denied federal habeas court access, but its utility—and hence its novelty—for federal prisoner habeas review was questionable at best.

The first case to arise under the 1867 act did little to resolve this problem, although it did seem to confirm the importance of the federalism and racial issues that most likely motivated the act two years before. *In re Turner* seemed to indicate a fairly straightforward understanding of the bill that gave legal support through habeas to both the Civil Rights Act of 1866 and the Thirteenth Amendment.[117] *Turner* involved a habeas appeal from a black minor named Elizabeth Turner who had become a free citizen of Maryland. Before the adoption of the revised Maryland state constitution in 1864, Turner and her mother were the slaves of Philemeon T. Hambleton.[118] But after Maryland's revised constitution was passed and slavery abolished per the Thirteenth Amendment, many freed slaves were immediately bound to their former masters as indentured servants. (Whites were also bound under similar peonage-type arrangements.) Turner's habeas appeal argued that the peonage laws violated the Thirteenth Amendment and the Civil Rights Act of 1866. Under the existing Maryland apprenticeship laws, white apprentices were entitled to an education, and they were not permitted to be arbitrarily transferred to other masters; unlike blacks, they were not legally described as "property and interest." All of these guarantees were not required of black apprentices. Chief Justice Chase, sitting on circuit, found the legal state of apprenticeship as applied to blacks and the legal discrepancies between blacks and whites to be grounds for releasing Elizabeth from her master. Thus habeas, under the 1867 act, was used to uphold the Thirteenth Amendment, its enforcement provisions, and the Civil Rights Act of 1866. Under these circumstances, at least, Chase held that "colored persons equally with white persons are citizens of the United States."[119]

EX PARTE McCARDLE

Like so many other aspects of habeas during Reconstruction, the received understanding of *Ex parte McCardle* overplays the refrain of a seemingly independent Court that advances the bold cause of individual liberty during periods of crisis, only to be quashed by forces out of its control. There is no question that the Court's opinion in the case ultimately deferred to an interpretation of the power of Congress to withdrawal the Court's appellate power as plenary and complete, but this does not mean that the Court completely backed down from Congress, because a close reading of *McCardle* and *Ex parte Yerger,* decided soon after, suggests the opposite.[120] Moreover, Court-curbing legislation was real and palpable, even if most of it never managed to pass. Thus while we should heed the lessons of revisionist historians in seeing these measures, advanced almost exclusively by Radicals, as less indicative of interbranch hostility toward the Court than had previously been thought, there is still reason to account for these measures, if only because they suggest a level of intraparty disagreement within the regime. Such divisions often allow the Court to carve out a more independent role that protects and entrenches their institutional power. *McCardle,* in important ways, shows this to be the case. As a whole, it is likely that Congress did not harbor as much animosity toward the Court in their repealer legislation as some suggest. If we instead interpret habeas's wider Reconstruction role through a federalism lens, with a primary concern for correcting recalcitrant Southern states, then the national-level habeas powers repealed in the 1868 act can be seen as less important to the regime's larger Reconstruction goals.

"Like the rain," Charles Fairman analogized, "the law impartially blesses the just and the unjust."[121] The timing of William McCardle's arrest in 1867 by Union military authorities in Vicksburg, Mississippi, for penning treasonous editorials could not have been more inopportune for congressional Republicans.[122] Now situated in an all-out battle for control of Reconstruction policy with Andrew Johnson, by the time McCardle's habeas appeal came before the circuit court of Mississippi in November 1867, Congress had already passed the Military Reconstruction Act over Johnson's veto, the Tenure of Office Act, and several supplemental bills further specifying the procedures of Reconstruction, all of which would be under control of Congress, and all of which established military rule for states not in compliance. To make matters worse, by the time of the appeal, Congress had also failed in their first attempts to bring impeachment charges against Johnson, further emboldening him to resist Republican policies.[123] With military reconstruction entrenched since March, Democratic forces were already hunting for ways to challenge the constitutionality of congressional Reconstruction with *Milligan*—and the 1867 act—as their benchmark. McCardle's case became a vehicle for this cause.

McCardle's case was dismissed in district court. He then promptly appealed to the circuit court of Mississippi, challenging not only his confinement but, more importantly, the constitutionality of military reconstruction in general as well. Just as significant was that his appeal from the district to the circuit court was justified under the grant of appellate authority for habeas appeals for those detained "in contravention of the Constitution and the laws of the

United States" under the Habeas Corpus Act of 1867. With a denial by the circuit court, the question remained whether the Supreme Court would agree to hear the appeal. In *Ex parte McCardle I,* the Court denied the government's appeal to dismiss, arguing not only that it had the ability to hear habeas appeals aided by its writ of certiorari power under the Judiciary Act of 1789, but that the 1867 act explicitly gave them this authority. Chief Justice Chase said of the 1867 act that it was "of the most comprehensive character. It brings within the *habeas corpus* jurisdiction of every court and of every judge every possible case of privation of liberty contrary to the National Constitution, treaties, or laws. It is impossible to widen this jurisdiction."[124] Chase, however, did not reach the merits of the larger, more important question of the constitutionality of congressional Reconstruction legislation. Chase limited the Court's decision to the purely jurisdictional questions raised.

With the prospect of the Court reaching a decision striking down congressional Reconstruction, and only a few days after oral arguments were concluded in *McCardle,* James Wilson offered an amendment to an otherwise innocuous bill permitting appeals to the Supreme Court in civil cases involving internal revenue officers that would repeal the 1867 Habeas Act's authorization of appeals from circuit courts to the Supreme Court.[125] With no debate in the House, the Senate considered the amendment later that day. Although some in that chamber now felt something was afoot, serious and heated debate on the amendment's true nature only occurred two days later.[126] Despite the pressure of his impeachment trial, President Johnson nevertheless vetoed the bill on 25 March. In his veto message, Johnson defended the Court, stating that even during the "most violent party conflicts," it had always been "deferred to with confidence and respect." The most ironic part of the veto message came when Johnson defended the 1867 act, a bill that he had vetoed, on the grounds that a repeal of the Court's appellate jurisdiction would now be contrary to the act's "wisdom and justice."[127]

In the debate over whether to override the president's veto, Lyman Trumbull, the only senator to comment on the 1867 act when it originally passed, and who was also counsel for the government in *McCardle,* tried to understate the 1867 act's importance, and hence the repealer's significance, only to be met with Democratic responses that chided Radicals for their seemingly wanton power grab.[128] Consistent with the arguments he would advance before the Court, Trumbull contended that McCardle fell within the 1867 act's exceptions for those in military custody, and also that the 1867 act only ever contemplated expansive federal court habeas jurisdiction for state prisoners.[129] Despite Democratic protests, which now put them in the unique, if temporary, position of defending broad federal habeas powers under the 1867 act, the veto was over-ridden on 27 March 1868.[130] With some dissent, the Court moved that the case be postponed and held over until the next term.[131]

When the Court's decision in *McCardle II* was finally announced in April 1869, Chief Justice Chase was clear that the Court had no choice: "Without jurisdiction the court cannot proceed at all in any cause. Jurisdiction is power to declare the law, and when it ceases to exist, the only function remaining to the court is that of announcing the fact and dismissing the cause. And this is not less clear upon authority than upon principle."[132] Although the power of the Court's appellate jurisdiction is derived from the Constitution, that document gives to Congress the power "of making exceptions" to that jurisdiction.[133] This might seem like complete deference by the Court to Congress, as Chase then said of the repealer that the Court was "not at liberty to inquire into the motives of the legislature." However, Chase's last paragraph suggested something quite different:

Counsel seem to have supposed, if effect be given to the repealing act in question, that the whole appellate power of the court, in cases of habeas corpus, is denied. But this is an error. The act of 1868 does not except from that jurisdiction any cases but appeals from Circuit Courts under the act of 1867. It does not affect the jurisdiction which was previously exercised.[134]

The "jurisdiction which was previously exercised" was the habeas doctrine that had developed since Marshall's *Bollman* opinion, at least for federal prisoners. This is not an insignificant distinction, because the 1868 repealer simply withdrew the Court's appellate jurisdiction from circuit courts under the seemingly broad terms of the 1867 act. Combined with that act's new grant of federal court habeas rights for state prisoners, which was not at issue in McCardle's case, this meant that Chase simply affirmed Congress' right to adjust the Supreme Court's appellate jurisdiction for a limited class of petitioners. Federal district and circuit courts could still hear habeas cases for both state and federal prisoners regarding claims that arose under the 1789 Judiciary Act's habeas provisions and the 1867 act.

Significantly for some, the Court could have handed down a decision in the case before Congress overrode the repealer veto. Although there is evidence for claiming that the Court's self-imposed delay in reaching a decision earlier was due as much to political as to legal concerns, the fact remains that the Court interpreted the repealer as a legitimate exercise of Congress' power to determine the appellate jurisdiction of the Court.[135] Even with the Court's acquiescence, there is another explanation for *McCardle*. Although the Congress that passed the 1867 act most likely had in mind freedmen, their families, and federal officers who were unconstitutionally held in Southern states when they expanded federal habeas to include state convictions, it is less likely that they saw an immediate need for increased supervision of federal habeas for federal prisoners. The complete legislative history of the act suggests as much, originating almost a year and a half before the act's final passage as a supplemental piece of enforcement legislation for freedmen only, as does *In re Turner,* the first case heard under the act.[136]

The larger political context of Reconstruction suggests as much as well. It is certainly true that congressional military reconstruction policy implicated important constitutional questions concerning military detentions and trials, but Southern state resistance to congressional Reconstruction, combined with Johnson's resistance at every advance, was a more pressing concern for congressional Republicans. In fact, in the immediate political context of *McCardle,* it is likely that Congress was more concerned with the ratification of the Fourteenth Amendment than it was with a judicial ruling on military reconstruction, whichever way the ruling might go. Even if some Republicans doubted the legality of military detentions, they were willing to live with them in the short term in order to guarantee the long-term federalism changes that were inherent in the Fourteenth Amendment.[137] The fact that Johnson's impeachment trial loomed over the repealer debates might suggest that Congress was engaged in a struggle with the president purely over interbranch control of Reconstruction policies such as the Tenure of Office Act and the constitutionality of further military control of state governments. But these issues were ultimately bound up at every step with larger interbranch disagreements about the ability of the national government to control states more generally.[138]

The more salient concerns with federal judicial supervision of state institutions, rather than federal judicial supervision of national institutions, are also evident in Congress' other Court-related legislation during Reconstruction.[139] Although the 1863 Habeas Act was partly devoted to creating procedures for habeas's suspension, it also sought to remove state cases to federal courts. The Internal Revenue Act of 1866 provided removal for cases involving federal revenue officers from state courts and further allowed federal courts to begin actions de novo. The Separable Controversies Act of 1866, the Local Prejudice Act of 1867, and the 1867 Habeas Act's revision of the federal question doctrine, to name just a few, were completely concerned with state and local resistance.

The congressional partnership with the federal judiciary during the height of congressional Reconstruction is often portrayed in extremes, with *McCardle* serving as the linchpin in both readings. In the first, the Court backed down, and Chase's unequivocal deference, combined with his decision to delay the case, is offered as evidence. In the second, *McCardle* stands as "the quintessence of judicial independence and courage."[140] What is more likely, especially in light of habeas's development during this period, is that while the Court was indeed a true partner with the moderate core of congressional Republicans and each branch was broadly sympathetic with the other, each branch was also deeply concerned with its own institutional independence and was never afraid to stand its ground when it believed that circumstances (real or imagined) would threaten its institutional integrity.[141] Congress needed the Court's habeas power, and the Court depended on Congress for these habeas powers and for other newly instituted removal-related powers as well. When Congress believed that the Court might overturn its military reconstruction program, despite its past and future partnership with the judiciary, it did not hesitate to pass a quick, albeit limited, repealer to the newly granted jurisdiction to ensure its ability to govern. Similarly, the Court felt bound to clarify its ability to hear habeas cases under already well-established congressional and judicial precedents. Even with sympathetic and regime-affiliated Courts, then, we can see that alongside issues that might divide majority parties (such as the extent of congressional military reconstruction), threats to core institutional functions—such as habeas—elicit an institutionally protective response.[142]

POSTREPEALER HABEAS AND THE DEMISE OF RECONSTRUCTION

Large-scale habeas change and development are almost always attributable to the creation and enforcement of new visions of constitutional governance by new political regimes. Although political in their origins, habeas changes are nevertheless adjudicated in a legal world. Combine this reality with the fact that courts, as we have seen, also partly craft habeas jurisprudence in ways that benefit and protect their institutional power, and we can see that the practice of regime enforcement through habeas has the potential to drift away and diverge from the regime's initial visions. This phenomenon only becomes more acute when initial regime changes to habeas begin to come into conflict with new and changing regime priorities.

The Republican retreat from Reconstruction was no different. After 1867, Republican commitment to larger egalitarian goals, including their national enforcement, began to wane. Representative of this pattern was the Ku Klux

Klan Act of 1871, which provided the last congressional authorization for the suspension of habeas corpus during the Reconstruction era.[143] Along with the Enforcement Acts passed the year before, the Ku Klux Klan Act was designed to enforce fundamental national rights in the face of Southern state violence and recalcitrance, particularly the Fourteenth Amendment.[144] Here civil, as opposed to previously provided-for criminal remedies, were now available to prosecute Southern resistance in federal courts. Significantly, section 4 of the act allowed President Ulysses S. Grant to suspend habeas corpus in states where armed violence threatened "to either overthrow or set at defiance the constituted authorities of such State, and of the United States within such State." Subject to the same provisions as Congress' approval of Lincoln's suspension in 1863, where time periods for detentions, names of defendants, and indictment protections were supervised by federal district courts, the act also limited any suspension to one year from the end of the next congressional session. Grant suspended the writ in nine counties, actions partly credited with helping to crush Klan violence in South Carolina.[145]

Despite successful regime use of habeas in 1871, the Republican Party, and the country as a whole, were moving away from a sustained commitment to Reconstruction's purported goals. The Republican Party had barely managed to keep its electoral numbers on par with the height of its power in 1866 and 1867, and Grant's victory in 1868 was most likely the result of black Republican turnout in the South. Democrats had been gaining seats, both in Congress and in state legislatures, since 1868. Even if the Republican Party had never been as radical as some have suggested it was during the party's most powerful years, the fact remained that by 1870, only less radical policies were viable in Congress.[146] The Enforcement Acts of 1870 tracked this pattern, as the financial and military personnel commitments required to fund and oversee the legislation in Southern states shrank considerably from 1868 to the early 1870s.[147] When, in 1870, Congress reenacted the Civil Rights Act of 1866, it did so under its enforcement power derived from the Fourteenth, not Thirteenth, Amendment.[148] The 1872 election further signaled this drift, as Horace Greeley's Liberal Republican Party secured the support of the Democratic Party for his presidential bid. Many former Radical Republicans supported Greeley, and though he lost by a sizable margin, both parties ran on platforms that emphasized economic concerns, states' rights, and the failures of Reconstruction all at the expense of egalitarian rights.[149] The seemingly strong habeas provision in the 1871 Ku Klux Klan Act must therefore be seen in this increasingly decentralizing environment, limited not only in time (one congressional session) but also in scope (solely to the Klan).

Yet even as Reconstruction commitments began to wane in the early 1870s, federal court habeas power continued unabated, with the single exception of the Supreme Court's ability to hear habeas cases on appeal from lower federal courts under the 1867 act. Representative of things to come for federal habeas for state prisoners under these changing political circumstances was *Griffin's Case* in 1869, one of the earliest habeas cases to come before the circuit court under the 1867 act.[150] While sitting on the Virginia circuit court, Chief Justice Chase heard a habeas appeal from a "colored man" named Caesar Griffin who had been convicted of murder in a Virginia state court. The judge in the case, Hugh Sheffey, was one of a series of public officials elected to the Virginia bench before the Civil War who joined the Confederacy at the outbreak of the war, only to return to the bench after Appomattox. Griffin was convicted of murder in Sheffey's court. He then petitioned the federal district court for a writ of habeas corpus under the 1867 act, arguing that the newly ratified Fourteenth Amendment's third section, which made Confederate sympathizers ineligible for public office, rendered Griffin's conviction null and void. The district court agreed, and an appeal was taken to Chase's circuit.

Although Griffin was a "colored man," Chase saw "no allegation that the trial was not fairly conducted, or that any discrimination was made against him."[151] Considering the purported integrity of the trial and the uncontested jurisdiction of the state court, to let a duly convicted man go free, argued Chase, would be an injustice, and was certainly not the intention of the 1867 act. Moreover, the third section of the Fourteenth Amendment should not be construed so as to "annul every official act" of the hundreds of men who would be affected by such a wide reading of its scope. If this was to be the intent of the amendment, "it [would] be impossible to measure the evils which such a construction would add to the calamities which have already fallen upon the people of the states."[152]

Although the retreat from Reconstruction could be characterized partly as a diminishing commitment to the use of national power to guarantee racial equality against recalcitrant states, it was certainly not the case that the Republican Party would let this hard-won national institutional power go to waste.[153] As a concerted push for racial equality decreased, the void was filled with the emerging concerns of the Gilded Age. From the Panic of 1873 onward, it became more difficult to support and defend egalitarian interventionist politics in Southern states, let alone in the rest of the country. Anti-Union hostility and rampant fears of socialism and communism put broad activism on the defensive. Continued concern for the supervision of Southern state governments was already evident in the year or two before the Depression, evidenced in party platforms such as Greeley's Liberal Republican Party that pushed for reconciliation. But increasing calls for state-led economic regulation of the economy to ease unemployment and increase business regulation only made the existing structures of Reconstruction all the more indefensible. As Howard Gillman has demonstrated, the Republican Party then made a concerted effort from the 1870s onward to enforce their new economic nationalism through increased federal court jurisdiction. As federal courts cooperated with Republican Reconstruction policies during the 1860s to thwart Southern state recalcitrance, they would now partner again with the Republican promulgation of Gilded Age economic nationalism that needed a favorably disposed federal bench to resolve problems of state-level intransigence in economic matters.[154]

We can begin to see the role habeas would play in these larger developments not in Mississippi or Georgia, but in California. There, as in other parts of the country, the racial regression resulting from the waning of Reconstruction was only magnified by economic depression. As states began to pass racist legislation in its wake, preexisting legal structures developed during Reconstruction started to create friction within the new post-Reconstruction regime. The ability of lower federal courts to hear habeas state cases under the 1867 Habeas Act quickly became a liability for the regime's new goals. This reality was only compounded in California, where Chinese immigrants were increasingly the victims of racial discrimination that was made worse by the recent economic downturn. The Chinese, however, were in the unique position of benefiting from the rights guarantees of the Burlingame treaty, ratified by Congress in 1868, which became the basis for thousands of habeas cases challenging California's state laws.[155]

Representative of the increasing dissonance created by habeas was *In re Ah Fong,* decided by Justice Field sitting on circuit in 1874. The circuit court struck down a California law that restricted Chinese immigration as violating the Burlingame treaty. The petitioner was denied entry to California because she was declared to be a lewd woman, a status that under the more general police powers of states would normally be found to be within the proper constitutional scope of those powers. Nonetheless, because of the treaty, Field felt bound to overturn the law. Clearly, Field was uncomfortable with his decision, as he lent his sympathies to the state legislature's and people's more "general feeling" against the Chinese, a race that exhibited a "dissimilarity in physical characteristics, in language, in manners, religion and habits" that "will always prevent any possible assimilation of them with our people."[156] Although bound by law, he then recommended that the state's only option would be "recourse . . . to the federal government, where the whole power over this subject lies."[157]

Beyond the Chinese exclusion cases, however, federal habeas cases for state prisoners were increasingly seen as burdensome, both in their sheer volume and, most importantly, in their substantive content. In *Ex parte Bridges,* for example, Justice Bradley, sitting on circuit in Georgia, heard a habeas petition from a former slave who was convicted in a Georgia state court for violating perjury laws in the course of a federal investigation.[158] The question facing the court was whether Georgia could try Bridges for violations of federal law. In Bradley's mind, there was no choice but to grant the habeas petition under the 1867 act because it explicitly allowed for removal to federal courts in cases just like *Bridges.* Bridges was charged by a state court with lying to a federal officer conducting his duties under the Enforcement Acts. Clearly, this was punishable under the laws of the United States, the perjury laws of Georgia notwithstanding. Bridges was charged with lying to United States officials, not Georgia officials. Considering habeas's common-law use to correct decisions by courts without jurisdiction, and the necessary result that his conviction by a Georgia court would then be void, Bradley's decision was not remarkable. Bradley went on to say, "The validity of these acts of Congress [those that treat this type of perjury as a federal offense] is not questioned. It would be a manifest incongruity for one sovereignty to punish a person for an offense committed against the laws of another sovereignty."[159]

Yet Bradley did more than make it explicit that he was troubled by his decision. He also suggested that the 1867 act itself should be changed to show more deference to state court decisions when issues of jurisdiction or overt state court discrimination were not present in the state's decision: "And although it might appear unseemly that a prisoner, after conviction in a state court, should be set at liberty by a single judge on habeas corpus, there seems to be no escape from the law."[160] He made it clear that this present case was not such an instance, but then ended his opinion with the suggestion that Congress repeal the very law that served as the basis for his opinion: "It might, however, be a wise amendment of this law, to provide that in all cases after conviction, the party should be put to his writ of error to the supreme court of the United States."[161]

Soon after, the Supreme Court corrected the problem for itself. In *Virginia v. Rives* (1879), the Court reinterpreted very narrowly the entire class of removal jurisdiction legislation that had been the centerpiece of the Court–Congress partnership throughout Reconstruction. Alleged victims of racial discrimination, such as the defendants in *Rives* who claimed discrimination in the selection of jurors for their trial, would now have to rely on writs of error. Removal legislation was effectively jettisoned and limited to a thin definition of state action.

Before and after it restricted removal case doctrine, the Court also narrowed its enforcement and supervisory role over other racial issues in Southern states. In the *Slaughterhouse* cases, the Court seemed to countenance the reconciliation of North and South that had characterized the 1872 election with a dual citizenship reading of the Fourteenth Amendment's privileges and immunities clause.[162] The Fourteenth Amendment, argued Justice Miller, was not intended to make "this court a perpetual censor upon all legislation of the states, on the civil rights of their own citizens."[163] Two years later, in *United States v. Reese* and *United States v. Cruikshank,* the Waite Court moved even further away from a strong commitment of national enforcement against state-level racial discrimination.[164] In *Reese,* a Fifteenth Amendment challenge to alleged voting discrimination brought under the Enforcement Act effectively gutted that act's legitimacy as an enforcement mechanism of the amendment. The rights allegedly violated by the Kentucky registrar who refused to count the votes of a black citizen, argued the Court, were rights that the state, not the federal government, had a duty to protect.[165] Similarly, in *Cruikshank,* differences between state and national citizenship were coupled with distinctions between official state action and the actions of private individuals to prevent federal indictments of whites who violated both the Fourteenth and Fifteenth Amendment rights of blacks.[166]

Rounding out this oft-cited trilogy of cases that increasingly signaled Reconstruction's demise, in the *Civil Rights Cases,* the Court struck down Charles Sumner's last salvo, the Civil Rights Act of 1875.[167] The Court's ruling seemed almost a fait accompli, as the 1875 act was passed during the lame-duck Forty-third Congress after a Democratic victory in the 1874 elections that gave it almost complete control over the House for the next decade. To make it more palatable, the act was also stripped of its two most controversial features: a ban on discrimination in churches and a ban on segregated education.[168] The act's core features—discrimination at inns, places of public amusement, and theaters—were interpreted as purely private actions among private citizens. Congress' power to regulate discriminatory actions in violation of the Thirteenth, Fourteenth, or Fifteenth Amendment was limited solely to state actions or legislation. Justice Bradley suggested that if the act were to be ruled constitutional and Congress could indeed regulate what he thought to be private, as opposed to public, discrimination, it "would be to establish a code of municipal law regulative of all private rights between man and man in society. It would be to make Congress take the place of the State legislatures and to supersede them. . . . In other words, it steps into the domain of local jurisprudence."[169] The rights guaranteed by the Reconstruction amendments were "guaranteed by the constitution against State aggression," and could not "be impaired by the wrongful acts of individuals. The wrongful act of an individual, unsupported by any such [state] authority, is simply a private wrong."[170] When there was no explicit or demonstrated state action, there was no constitutional justification for national legislation that would seek to regulate it.[171]

To be sure, there was no straight, unbroken line connecting *Slaughterhouse, Cruikshank, Reese,* and the *Civil Rights Cases.* While from 1874 onward the electoral support for Republicans waned and elections became more competitive, support for the party's core principles did not disappear completely. Indeed, many scholars rightly recognize that Reconstruction, albeit in increasingly diminished form, lasted until the 1890s.[172] Others also correctly point out the salient differences among the Chase, Waite, and Fuller Courts in their resolution of the core federalism questions that belie a unified assault on Reconstruction's core values.[173] Two related explanations thus emerge for the doctrinal developments in these cases beyond the now-traditional argument that they completely eviscerated Reconstruction's egalitarian goals. Together, these accounts help to explain habeas's late nineteenth-century changes. The first is that the Court crafted what looked liked thin applications of Reconstruction's goals because those goals were never monolithic in the first place. Intraparty divisions among Republicans during the height of Reconstruction over some of their most fundamental achievements—such as the meaning of the Fourteenth Amendment's privileges and immunities clause—produced multiple accounts of those principles. As a result, the Court had room to craft Fourteenth Amendment jurisprudence with some degree of independence even though it was still largely sympathetic to the Republican regime.[174]

The second, related explanation is that the Court was able to continue to mold Reconstruction ideas well into the 1890s because these core Reconstruction goals were becoming less salient within the party and the country as a whole. Indeed, these goals were often liabilities for Republicans. Increasingly, federal courts could help the Republicans supervise and enforce either Reconstruction's egalitarian goals or the now-pressing goals of the enforcement of national economic development, but not both.[175] This further allowed the Court in the last three decades of the nineteenth century to have significant independence over Reconstruction issues.[176]

THE REPEAL OF THE REPEALER

For the Court to remain an effective partner with the Republican Party on economic issues, however, a critical institutional hurdle had to be overcome. The McCardle repealer prevented Reconstruction issues brought to federal courts under the 1867 Habeas Act from receiving appellate review by the Supreme Court, leaving habeas petitioners access only to lower federal courts. Such cases began to flood federal district and circuit courts, especially the ninth circuit.[177] Aside from the administrative burdens of these cases, the substantive content of most of them, especially those cases involving groups such as the Chinese, were now less pressing because of the increasing racial prejudice of the postwar years, and because of the increasingly dominant preference for national enforcement of economic issues. Without appellate power to revise or correct these cases or, just as importantly, to make new institutional rules for their administration within the federal court system, the Court had to wait for these cases to arrive via writs of error. Otherwise, it would remain a powerless partner with the larger regime on salient habeas issues.

The concerted push by many legal elites for congressional legislation restoring Supreme Court habeas review under the 1867 act was already evident in cases in the 1870s such as *Ex parte Bridges* and *In re Ah Fong*, discussed earlier, where justices riding circuit saw firsthand their potential administrative and political burdens. Beginning in earnest in the early 1880s, states' attorneys general and others pushed for change in what they perceived as a lopsided theory of federalism that now allowed a "single federal judge" to overturn a state conviction on habeas corpus.[178] Legal academics and the American Bar Association also began publishing law review articles that sought to detail this seemingly insulting process.[179]

The most important of these arguments was advanced by Seymour D. Thompson, editor of the *American Law Review*. Thompson argued that the 1867 act's intent had been subverted at the cost of the traditional relationship between the national and state governments. In his report to the committee of the American Bar Association in 1883, reprinted in the *American Law Review* in 1884, Thompson detailed a litany of recent federal habeas corpus cases involving state prisoners. He ultimately concluded, "These cases . . . show that under this act of 1867, the early and long-established idea of keeping the jurisdictions of national and State tribunals distinct and separate . . . is entirely overturned."[180] He then went on to argue that even if the authors of the 1867 act intended a reorientation between national and state tribunals for some cases (that is, newly freed slaves), they never intended the national courts to overturn final state court decisions where proper jurisdiction was arguably present.

Vermont congressman Luke Portland, who was equally troubled by the wide application of federal habeas to state cases, held hearings concerning the application of the 1867 act by the federal circuit courts in 1884.[181] The committee's report began with a lengthy historical recitation of the statutory history of the writ from the Judiciary Act of 1789 to the 1833 and 1842 acts. It then characterized the 1867 act as a product of the "late civil war" that was designed only to ensure that blacks would get a fair and impartial trial:

The overthrow of slavery and the conferring of citizenship upon the colored population were results of the war, and could not be expected to meet favorable conditions by the people of the States mainly affected by these changes. It was felt that these classes could hardly expect to get fair and impartial justice at the hands of local tribunals, and many acts of Congress were passed to extend to them, as far as possible under the Constitution, the protection of the Federal courts. *This act of 1867 was of that class of statutes.* It may be that the danger and necessity of such legislation was [*sic*] overestimated, but that it did exist to some extent was apparent from the condition of things and the ordinary operation of human motives and passions.[182]

The report went on to document how "individual" federal judges (on the district and circuit levels) were able to overturn state decisions single-handedly, effectively giving them final and plenary power over entire state judicial proceedings: "The fact is apparent, that if this jurisdiction is sustained, the final judgments of the highest courts of the States, may be held void and overturned by a single Federal judge of the lowest judicial rank, and from his decision there is no appeal."[183] The recommendation of the committee was to restore the appellate authority of the Supreme Court so it could determine its proper scope and application: "With this right of appeal restored, the true extent of the act of 1867, and the true limits of the jurisdiction of the Federal courts and judges under it, will become defined, and it can then be seen whether further legislation is necessary."[184] As a result of this push, on 3 March 1885, Congress repealed the McCardle repealer, allowing again for Supreme Court appellate review of habeas cases from lower federal courts under the 1867 act.[185]

With appellate power restored, and with an explicit blessing from Congress, the Court was free to set its own standards for habeas in the Gilded Age. The first case to come before the Court on appeal, *Ex parte Royall,* confirmed that the Court would continue to be a partner with the Republican regime.[186] Almost as if the Court were responding directly to the Judiciary Committee's explicit request for advice on how to proceed with habeas statutes, Justice Harlan's decision validated a reading of the 1867 act that was consistent with the withering of Reconstruction. Federal habeas was now limited to a certain class of cases that would not further serve to foster a general and sweeping revision of the relationship between state and federal courts.[187]

Two questions were posed to the Court in *Royall.* The first was whether the circuit court had the necessary jurisdiction to hear a habeas appeal from someone held under state authority for the violation of state laws. The second was whether the federal courts were compelled to grant the writ. Harlan unequivocally found that both the lower federal courts, and through appeal the Supreme Court, did in fact have the requisite jurisdiction to hear the case. The question was whether federal courts were compelled to hear every habeas case from state prisoners who questioned the legality of their confinement. Relying on notions of comity, Harlan dismissed an expansive reading of the 1867 act and instead opted for one that reaffirmed deference to state courts. He said of the unique federal nature of the Union and of the intent of Congress in passing the 1867 act: "We cannot suppose that Congress intended to compel those courts, by such means, to draw to themselves, in the first instance, the control of all criminal prosecutions commenced in State courts exercising authority within the same territorial limits, where the accused claims that he is held in custody in violation of the Constitution of the United States."[188]

Federal courts thus had "discretion" in determining which cases on habeas could be heard. States' rights considerations and notions of "concord," for Harlan, required that those "relations [state and federal] be not disturbed by unnecessary conflict between courts equally bound to guard and protect rights secured by the Constitution." The Court then enumerated two new principles for deciding whether habeas appeals could be brought before a federal tribunal. The first required that appeals in cases from state prisoners first be brought in state courts. No more could habeas appeals be brought on behalf of those held in state custody before the appeal was heard on the state level. The second rule required that habeas petitioners first exhaust all state appellate avenues before even the lowest federal court could entertain the writ. This meant that a case must be fully adjudicated all the way up to a respective state's supreme court and have a disposition. Then—and only then—could the writ be applied for in federal district court. The Court did recognize that the 1867 act made federal habeas review available for anyone who sought to challenge the constitutionality of his detainment and that federal courts had no choice but to adjudicate those claims. However, the Court now had the ability to determine the "time and mode" of those challenges.[189] Apart from exceptional circumstances, where the Court could—and sometimes did—decide to allow a case to come before it on habeas, state prisoners seeking to challenge the constitutionality of their confinement were now left only to writs of error. This allowed the Court to trim the federal courts' habeas docket at the same time that it allowed the Court to choose habeas cases that it felt merited federal court review. Without the Court's acquiescence in responding to Congress' implicit suggestion that habeas was to be scaled back, the Court would not have had the ability to shape its habeas jurisprudence with such latitude.[190]

The Court continued to sustain its creation of procedural habeas rules that would not interfere with or offend the states.[191] In 1891, *In re Wood* held that state courts could adjudicate matters of national and constitutional law co-extensively with federal courts and that habeas appeals (which were already limited by the exhaustion rule) could only be heard if the state courts lacked jurisdiction.[192] This case is poignantly indicative of the late nineteenth-century admixture of race and federalism that informed these new post-Reconstruction rules. Joseph Wood, an African American, was convicted by an all-white jury of murder and sentenced to death. He claimed that criteria for jury selection in the state of New York precluded blacks from serving as jurors. He filed his writ in federal court arguing that his conviction (and, by default, his detention) was unconstitutional. Although the Court had previously ruled that jury discrimination was antithetical to the Constitution and the laws of the United States, it nevertheless held in this case that the constitutionality of New York's jury laws could be adequately determined by the state supreme court.[193] The determination of racial discrimination and civil rights violations was, in Harlan's words, a question "which the [state] trial court was entirely competent to decide, and its determination could not be reviewed by the Circuit Court." Justice Field's concurring opinion is even more indicative of the racial components that went into these habeas rollbacks. Reiterating his dissent in *Neal*, he said:

> there is nothing in the late amendments to the Constitution, the Thirteenth, Fourteenth and Fifteenth, which requires that colored citizens shall be summoned on juries . . . in order to secure to persons of their race justice and equality in the administration of the law; and, further, that the manner in which jurors to serve in the state courts shall be selected, and the qualifications they shall possess, are matters entirely of state regulation.[194]

By the 1890s, then, habeas's role as a potent tool of regime enforcement for recalcitrant Southern states receded into the background as Congress and the federal judiciary deliberately chose to redirect federal judicial power—and habeas power in particular—away from Reconstruction's initial goals and toward new challenges at the turn of the century.

CONCLUSION

Habeas's development during and after the Civil War belies contemporary accounts of the writ. When habeas was used to vindicate fundamental rights during and after Reconstruction, it was only when both the Court and Congress were in agreement that the writ served that function. The use of the writ in similar cases was therefore not as countermajoritarian as many today imagine. In *Turner,* for example, the use of the writ to free a former slave who was bound to her former master in an apprentice-like arrangement that bordered on slavery was a regime principle that a majority of Republicans—and the country as a whole—could easily tolerate and support. The 1867 Habeas Act was an enforcement tool of the Republican regime that sought to discipline outlier states, not large national majorities. This almost majoritarian use of the writ was soon confirmed in the repealer passed in the wake of the impending *McCardle* decision. The repealer, we must remember, was designed almost exclusively to eliminate Supreme Court jurisdiction specifically for federal prisoners such as McCardle. Federal court habeas access under both the 1789 Judiciary Act and the 1867 act were still available for both state and federal prisoners more generally. This reality hardly lends credence to a portrait of a hostile Congress bent on stripping the Court of its newly granted habeas powers.

The wartime development of the writ should also push us to look for continuities in habeas's development in the immediately preceding periods of normal political development. In *Merryman* especially, Lincoln's seemingly extraordinary actions were as much the products of the Republican Party's extant conceptions of departmentalism as they were of the exigencies of civil war. Lincoln and the Republicans were also aware of the necessity of federal court power in the prosecution of the war and Reconstruction. The precedents for federal court habeas power in particular had in any case already been developed during the Jacksonian period. To be sure, the war necessitated new and unprecedented actions on the part of American political institutions, but at least in the case of habeas, the policies eventually developed—such as indemnity and removal—had their origins in earlier developments before the outbreak of civil war.

CHAPTER 4

From the Extraordinary to the Ordinary: 1915–1969

Habeas corpus, which was effectively marginalized as a key regime tool as a result of the nation's abandonment of Reconstruction by the beginning of the twentieth century, was again transformed into a powerful tool of regime enforcement by the mid-1960s. After the 1880s, habeas ceased to be an important regime enforcement tool for the supervision and correction of recalcitrant states in matters of racial justice. This meant that the Court was left to craft habeas jurisprudence largely independent of either Congress or the president. Until the 1960s, however, the Court's habeas jurisprudence hewed almost exclusively to a conception of the writ's purpose as protecting only the most egregious due process violations.

Importantly, neither the Court nor the New Deal regime up to the beginning of the 1960s believed that the writ should serve as an enforcement mechanism of specifically defined due process criminal rights. The rights habeas enforced before then were only the most fundamental due process trial rights. The Court's use of habeas from 1960 onward, then, was never foreordained, and it contained within itself increased tensions, as the use of the Great Writ to enforce and protect only the most basic rights in the face of extraordinary violations morphed into an ordinary enforcement mechanism for what quickly became extraordinarily unpopular criminal procedure rights.

During the first five decades of the twentieth century, the Court managed to expand and formalize a role for habeas in monitoring increasingly egregious criminal procedure due process violations in three cases now recognized to be seminal: *Frank v. Mangum* (1915), *Moore v. Dempsey* (1923), and *Brown v. Allen* (1953). In these cases, habeas was only ever understood to function as an extraordinary legal remedy that could "come in from the outside" and "cut through all the forms and go to the very tissue" of patently unconstitutional detentions.[1] Although the Court expanded the causes and review procedures for federal habeas review of state due process violations in these cases, we should not see them as part of a linear or increasingly progressive development that somehow ineluctably led to the Warren Court's revolutionary habeas changes.[2] Rather, in the first half of the twentieth century, the Court attempted to establish only the broadest outlines of minimal fundamental criminal due process rights. These three cases are really of a piece with habeas's role as it was developing since the 1880s. No political regime or Court before 1960 had a fully developed notion of the specific criminal procedure due process rights that the Warren Court would eventually develop, so even when the Court suggested that habeas could overturn mob-dominated trials in the South starting in 1915, we should not see the writ's potential scope here as temporarily limited by backward or yet-to-be-defined progressive conceptions of due process rights, as Whiggish advocates of habeas on the Warren Court asserted in the 1960s.[3] Habeas's scope was only ever as wide as the Court's notion of the most basic requirements of constitutional fairness, and the Court's notion was limited to only the most basic fair trial rights.

Nevertheless, the Court was increasingly confronted with significant due process questions beginning in the 1920s. The Court's response was to craft habeas jurisprudence in ways that allowed it to define and protect these fair trial rights independent of pressures from the larger political regime. No matter how much racial prejudice permeated the Jim Crow and Progressive orders, and no matter how sympathetic justices might have been personally and ideologically to those prejudices, some due process violations were simply unacceptable. This meant that the Court would protect and even expand its ability to define the procedural contours of habeas access even though it was reluctant to expand the substantive rights that the writ could protect and enforce.

These cases and others also had the further—and unintentional—effect of heightening the country's awareness of its worsening problem with racial inequality, which would only serve to undermine the country's legitimacy at home and abroad during a period when the realities of fascism and national socialism were garnering national attention. The Court's policing of exceptionally egregious cases helped magnify the similarities between racist American institutions and their supposed antithesis in totalitarian states, pushing the Court and the country to define with more specificity the rights that habeas would soon come to enforce.

Although early signs of an increasing concern for the protection and further elaboration of substantive due process rights were evident immediately after the revolution of 1937 and the advent of the New Deal constitutional order, particularly in *Carolene Product*'s (1938) famous footnote 4, they were really only prospective, for the lingering problems of race would continue to haunt habeas during World War II.[4] Even the fundamental outlines that marked the most basic commitments to rights and liberties that were developed over the preceding two decades were largely ignored by the Court during the war. Some World War II habeas cases, such as *Ex parte Endo* and *Duncan v. Kahanamoku,* served to vindicate the fundamental rights of the petitioners involved, but as we will see, they did so in only most procedurally limited ways, allowing the Court to sidestep larger, more important constitutional questions such as the basis for internment and martial law.[5] In other cases, the Court upheld executive and military actions as it did in *Hirabayashi* and, most famously, in *Korematsu.* As during periods of war and crisis before, habeas's use (or nonuse) during World War II reflected both the governing regime's preferences and preexisting conceptions of the scope of individual rights. The World War II habeas cases suggest that even a decade after the Court's first prospective steps into the realm of individual substantive due process rights in 1938, there was hardly an immediate trajectory toward an ever-increasing catalog of rights established by the Court or the country.

After World War II, domestic and international pressure to provide more effective enforcement of fundamental rights, especially for minorities, pushed the Court to move from simply tracing the outlines of these rights to defining them with more precision. But this push yielded no significant advances, as Court majorities refused to replace the amorphous standards of "ordered liberty" or "shocks the conscience" doctrines with the more specific criminal process provisions of the Bill of Rights as workable definitions of due process.[6] Habeas also reflected these limits: the Court in *Brown v. Allen* (1953) continued to affirm habeas's role in correcting state-level due process violations during trials, but it went no further in specifying exactly what those rights were beyond trials "consonant with standards accepted by this Nation as adequate to justify their convictions."[7] With no larger regime vision of what these rights were, and with no Court majority willing to go any further than affirming only the fundamental due process rights, the Court assumed a holding pattern.

Starting in earnest in 1960, however, the Warren Court incorporated more criminal process provisions of the Bill of Rights against the states via the due process clause of the Fourteenth Amendment. Now a solidly liberal Court by 1962, the justices of the "real" Warren Court recast federal habeas corpus in 1963 to allow the federal judiciary to use habeas to enforce not only their incorporation agenda, but also the prophylactic rules that the Court would develop to further clarify the contours of these rights.[8] Although national majorities outside of the South might have countenanced and even welcomed the Court's earlier attempts to define and enforce basic fair trial rights, an increasingly divided nation was almost immediately resistant to the Warren Court's seeming overreach. To most Americans, it now seemed that the lone black teenager who was beaten into a forced confession in a backwoods Southern jail was worthy of habeas corpus and due process protections that would remove his case to a neutral federal court, but the new face of the violent inner-city black criminal who used newly created habeas rules to frustrate, delay, and eventually free himself was now seen in a far different light.[9]

Almost as quickly as it began this project, the Great Society regime that the Court sought to support began to lose momentum. From 1960 onward, the Warren Court's criminal procedure and equal protection revolution led many Americans to believe that the Court—and the New Deal/Great Society regime that underwrote it—had moved far beyond simply enforcing basic and largely popular due process rights in the area of criminal justice, so much so that Richard Nixon could argue in 1968 that to be free from Court-created and -sanctioned "domestic violence" was the "first civil right of every American."[10] Most importantly, Republicans increasingly zeroed in on habeas corpus as the procedure in American liberalism that needed the most reform. Partly as a result of the Court's actions, a retooled Republican Party, poised to counter the regime's every move, seized on the Warren Court's incorporation and habeas jurisprudence to rally momentum against the perceived excesses of Great Society liberalism, as well as the supposed threat to finality and federalism that the Court's new habeas jurisprudence posed.[11]

The rules and procedures for federal habeas review of state due process violations developed by the Court up until the 1960s were largely uncontroversial. The substantive content of due process until then simply meant the right to a fair trial free from mob domination or the right not to have the contents of your stomach forcibly removed by police officers in their search for evidence.[12] The extension of these habeas rules to newer substantive rights, such as *Miranda* rights and the exclusionary rule, certainly helped the Democratic Party announce and enforce its new vision of constitutional governance in the 1960s, but it also created a backlash to habeas corpus rights in the United States in ways that still reverberate today.[13]

HABEAS AT THE TURN OF THE CENTURY

After the Court's creation of the exhaustion rule in *Ex parte Royall* (1885), the Court was left to craft habeas's rules and procedures independently of either Congress or the executive.[14] Although the Great Writ would no longer be used as the preferred enforcement mechanism for a sustained national enforcement of racially egalitarian policies against recalcitrant Southern states, as it had during the height of Reconstruction, the Court did not altogether abandon habeas in the late nineteenth century. In *Yick Wo v. Hopkins* (1886), for example, the Court struck down a California law that effectively prohibited only Chinese residents from obtaining building permits as violating the equal protection clause of the Fourteenth Amendment.[15] "The conclusion cannot be resisted," asserted Justice Matthews, "that no reason for [the legislation] exists except hostility to the race and nationality to which the petitioners belong."[16] But *Yick Wo* was the exception that proved the rule, for although many constitutional claims were indeed litigated in the Court through habeas after *Royall,* none of any significance was resolved in favor of the petitioner.[17] Unwilling and unable to ignore the Habeas Act of 1867's commands and, quite simply, the most basic duties and responsibilities of judging, the Court did not abandon federal habeas review but linked it only to the most fundamental constitutional violations.[18]

That the Court did continue to hear—even if only to reject—fundamental constitutional challenges through habeas is an indication that it was motivated less and less by overt regime influences after 1885. Certainly the Court rejected most of these habeas challenges on grounds that were consistent with the larger mood of late nineteenth- and early twentieth-century politics, most specifically a renewed deference to states' rights that was indicative of the larger political regime's retreat from Reconstruction and the emergent doctrine of economic substantive due process that overwhelmingly occupied the Court's agenda. In *Felts v. Murphy* (1906), for example, the Court rejected a Fourteenth Amendment challenge through habeas by a deaf state defendant who could not hear any of the testimony presented against him, partly because "that Amendment . . . did not radically change the whole theory of the relations of the state and Federal Governments to each other and of both governments to the people."[19] Nevertheless, there are certain fundamental aspects of the judiciary, as there are with any political institution, that its members believe can never be compromised. Partly because of the unique nature of the judiciary itself, partly because of the larger regime's hands-off approach to issues of criminal justice and racial egalitarianism, and partly because any institution has idiosyncratic commitments independent of its relationship with other institutions, the Court found it hard to look past increasingly egregious due process violations and patently unconstitutional state statutes during the late nineteenth and early twentieth centuries, such as the ones in *Yick Wo,* that allowed the exercise of "purely personal and arbitrary power."[20] Even before *Royall,* for example, the Court had established minimum criteria for constitutional fairness in the prohibition against racial discrimination in juries.[21]

Considering the realities of racial oppression in the first few decades of the twentieth century, the Court's protection of these fundamental due process rights through habeas was important in another way, for it suggests that explanations for the Court's behavior in these and other race cases during this period cannot easily be explained solely by the policy preferences of the justices, or even by the Court's general sympathies with the larger political order.[22] When the rule of law and the legitimacy of legal institutions themselves are threatened by legislation that patently discriminates against a particular group, or by sham trials dominated by hostile mobs, or by the hijacking of minimal judicial procedures by vigilantism, courts have little choice but to face these threats head-on. Judicial decisions in these cases stemmed from what Rogers M. Smith calls the "institutional perspectives" that represent "purposes and principles" that are based on "conceptions of duty or inherently meaningful action" rather than the pull of other political institutions, or from the preferences or predilections of individual justices.[23] The habeas jurisprudence that the Court increasingly developed in the late nineteenth century, then formalized in *Frank* and *Moore* in the first two decades of the twentieth century, was a reaction to egregious threats to the most basic guarantees of constitutional fairness, or what Michael Klarman calls "minimalist constitutional interpretations—the very least that a straight-faced commitment to constitutionalism entailed."[24] Any Court, with almost any assemblage of justices, at any time, would have done the same.[25]

This internal institutional perspective developed as much from the Court's reaction to egregious due process violations on the state level as it did from larger legal and political developments during this period. Consider just one example of this process—the effects of the Court's *Lochner*-era jurisprudence on its race and habeas decisions—which could plausibly be attributable to the nature of that era's judicial activism.[26] Benno Schmidt makes the important observation that the Court's increasing judicial activism in support of economic substantive due process produced in the Court an increased "institutional conviction and confidence" that it was the "custodian of constitutional values." This new view of its "institutional capacity" led the Court to have added confidence that "its commands must be respected" and that its decisions "should not be circumvented by legislative verbalisms and pretexts" and "that forms must not overtake constitutional substance."[27] Schmidt's point about the larger degree of judicial independence, confidence, and more general self-conception of its institutional mission that was derivative from the Court's increased judicial activism complements and reinforces the argument that the Court's habeas jurisprudence during this period was largely derived from internal solutions to egregious and explicit threats to the integrity of the rule of law, and not directly the result of a desire by the Court to bring itself in line with the concerns of the larger political regime. Unlike the Court's actions during the 1960s, which were linked to the larger regime's visions of constitutional governance, these early twentieth-century habeas cases were largely institution regarding.

FRANK v. MANGUM *IN CONTEXT*

Like other habeas cases during the late nineteenth century, but much more so during the first fifteen years of the twentieth century, *Frank v. Mangum* stands as an important marker of the outermost limits of criminal procedure due process violations during the Progressive era.[28] Although the Court ultimately found no constitutional violations by the state of Georgia in Leo Frank's habeas petition, the Court, including the dissenters, nevertheless agreed that mob-dominated trials violated the due process clause of the Fourteenth Amendment. But just what the opinion means now, or even what it meant then for habeas's development, still puzzles many legal academics and historians.[29] The answer lies in the larger political and legal contexts of the Progressive period, although it would be a mistake to see the ugly realities of the period as eliciting in the justices changed or changing ideological sympathies for those who were victims of larger racist structures and attitudes. What the Court reacted to instead were only the worst abuses of a regime with which they were otherwise sympathetic that threatened the institutional legitimacy of judicial institutions and the rule of law. In other words, the factors that influenced the Court in *Frank* were the institutional threats and challenges to judicial integrity and legitimacy that the era's politics produced, not the direct substance of those politics.

Even the broadest sketch of the rise and establishment of Jim Crow from the turn of the twentieth century to Leo Frank's case in 1915 confirms Michael Klarman's assessment that during the Progressive era, "racial attitudes and practices seemed to have reached a post–Civil War nadir."[30] C. Vann Woodward partly accounts for this as a "decline in the effectiveness of restraint" in the South. Abhorrent racism was always present in the South, Van Woodward argued, but at the dawn of the twentieth century, the forces that had always kept the worst aspects of this ugly propensity in check pulled back.[31] These extremes soon forced the Court to establish some basic boundaries. Despite racial prejudices, which surely affected individual justices as much as anyone else during this time, the Court felt bound to enforce minimum notions of constitutional fairness, if only to maintain the legitimacy of its institutionally specific mission.

The most salient threats to the integrity and administration of justice in the United States during the Jim Crow and Progressive eras were the disturbing rise in lynchings and the pervasive—and often nostalgic—notions of vigilante justice more generally. Lynching, which was not confined solely to the South, as the formation of the White Caps in New England and the ubiquitous cultural influence of the Western frontiersman demonstrate, was an extralegal system of justice that was increasingly difficult to square with the modern bureaucratic state. During the years leading up to the *Frank* case, lynching and vigilantism were so pervasive that their mystique spread into popular culture in ways that reverberated well into the twentieth century. Owen Wister's 1902 novel, *The Virginian,* for example, which depicts the uniquely American drama of the literal execution of justice in the midst of a corrupt justice system, was adapted into a movie four times (once with Gary Cooper in 1929) and was a popular television show from 1968 to 1971.[32] Southern politicians, many of them Progressives, proclaimed the benefits of the ugly practice, but even national politicians were effectively indifferent. For example, although President Theodore Roosevelt publicly denounced lynching, he nevertheless remained convinced that blacks were ultimately to blame, thus reinforcing and perpetuating the common myth that lynchings, while gruesome, would stop if only black crime—and rape in particular—would decrease. Summing up the feelings of the era, Roosevelt said in a letter to Owen Wister that he felt blacks "as a race and a man are altogether inferior to whites."[33]

Roosevelt's feelings were more than idiosyncratic, as the Progressive era witnessed the resurgence of scientific theories of racial development that seemed to confirm the failed ethos of Reconstruction at the same time that they helped foster a new reconciliation between North and South, especially as both sections together took up the white man's burden in Cuba and the Philippines.[34] The Dunning school of Reconstruction historiography soon followed, with historians and political scientists providing an academic imprimatur to the supposed failures of Reconstruction. They were seconded by colleagues in sociology and anthropology, including Robert W. Shufeldt, whose *The Negro: A Menace to Civilization* was published in 1907.[35] The next year, William Howard Taft became the first Republican presidential candidate to bring his campaign directly to Southern whites, and, making good on those promises as president, he soothed the South's fears about the reach of the Fifteenth Amendment, dragged his feet over grandfather clauses in Oklahoma, and said of blacks in general that they were "a race of farmers, first, last and for all time."[36]

The concrete political effects of the pervasive racism of Jim Crow in the United States were devastating. Disfranchisement, which had begun in earnest in the 1890s, reached its apex in the first few years of the twentieth century, as Oklahoma, North Carolina, South Carolina, Alabama, Louisiana, Virginia, and Georgia followed the lead of Mississippi in establishing property and literacy requirements—both buttressed by threats of violence—to block all effective black political participation in the South. The establishment of the white primary system, one of the many racially induced Progressive-era "reforms," soon helped bring black registration to zero in states such as Louisiana and Texas.[37] State disfranchisement schemes that otherwise fell short of the most blatant types of discrimination were often sustained by the Court, but those involving the permanent enumeration of grandfather clauses, such as those in Oklahoma, proved too much for the Court to countenance. In *Guinn v. United States* (1915), decided the same year as *Frank,* a unanimous Court, led by former Klansman and Louisiana-bred chief justice Edward Douglas White, struck down Oklahoma's grandfather clause.[38] As others have noted, cases such as *Guinn* were not as groundbreaking as they might initially seem. Most states had already repealed their grandfather clauses, and most legal and political elites were in agreement that they were unconstitutional, so the effect of the case for the prospects of more effective black voting rights was minimal at best.[39] But what is significant is that even an otherwise racially indifferent Court was forced to establish and then enforce minimum protections against statutes and practices that blatantly disregarded basic constitutional rights. And aside from blatant violations of the Fifteenth Amendment, the Court in the Progressive and Jim Crow eras also struck down Thirteenth Amendment violations involving labor contract laws and criminal surety schemes to return blacks to an effective state of slavery.[40]

These cases were blatant threats to the integrity of law and adherence to constitutional language. But even the fact that at least some racially discriminatory actions were neutralized was revolutionary in that much of the immediate political context was infected with some of the worst racism in American history. By 1915—the same year as *Frank* and *Guinn*—President Woodrow Wilson, a proud son of the South, had already filled his Cabinet with the very Southern Progressive politicians who had delivered him the presidency, and he further fed the ugly flames of Jim Crow with a concerted and blatant effort to bring Jim Crow to the United States government's civil service positions.[41] That same year also saw the publication of Maurice S. Evans's *Black and White in the Southern States: A Study of the Race Problem in the United States from a South African Perspective,* in which he compared the American South to his native South Africa. One of Evans's many suggestions for improvements in the South, where its court systems produced "violence and injustice," was the direct appointment of more professional judges and attorneys.[42]

The year 1915 also marked the debut of D. W. Griffith's *The Birth of a Nation,* which redefined and set the standard for the motion picture for decades to come and still serves as a useful window into the political, legal, and social world of the first fifteen years of twentieth-century America.[43] Adapted to the screen from Thomas Dixon's two novels, *The Clansman* and *The Leopard's Spots,* and replete with politics, race, and sex, the film chronicles the reconciliation between two families, one Northern and one Southern, amid the upheavals of post–Civil War America. The fictional arc of *The Birth of a Nation* is the triumph of an ultimately united white nation over the disastrous effects of an unnecessary civil war and the evils of Reconstruction. The advent of the Civil War rips apart young lovers in Pennsylvania and South Carolina, reunites them, and then challenges their unity through the trials of a disastrous Reconstruction. Blacks are depicted as depraved and sexualized predators who use their illegitimate political power (one scene depicts Negro legislators as unruly monkeys) for their own aggrandizement, forcing even Republicans (who are depicted as punishing the South by propping up black governments) to join the newly formed Ku Klux Klan. The infamous final scene, where a risen Christ fades in to consecrate the trinity of a triumphant Klan, a defeated horde of blacks, and a unified nation, acts as a coda not only for the film but for the now-dominant state of race relations in the United States.

With little subtlety, then, the overt racism of Jim Crow was replete at the turn of the century. From the acerbic racist rhetoric of national political leaders to quotidian popular culture, vigilantism and institutionalized racial hierarchy were now the dominant motif of politics and culture. Despite this ugly reality, however, legal institutions were still expected to operate with objectivity and fairness.

FRANK v. MANGUM

It was during this low point of race relations that *Frank v. Mangum* made its way to the Supreme Court. The case encapsulates the Progressive- and Jim Crow–era political and legal development in the United States. Thematically, the case touched on lynching and vigilantism, Southern working-class economic angst, fear of Northern industrialism (Leo Frank was a transplanted Northerner), and most importantly for our purposes, the increasing challenge that Southern mob-dominated justice posed to judicial legitimacy at the turn of the twentieth century.

Leo M. Frank was a Northern Jew who moved to Atlanta to manage his parents' pencil factory. He settled in a Jewish section of the city and was a leader in his local synagogue. Mary Phagan was a thirteen-year-old girl who worked at the factory with Frank. Although she had been laid off from her position at the factory, on 13 April 1913, she came to the factory to collect $1.20 in lost wages and was murdered. Frank was charged with the murder largely on testimony from the factory's janitor, Jim Conley, who claimed to have found her battered body, although many believe he was the real killer. Frank's trial was clearly dominated by a mob—so much so that for his own safety, and with his consent, the trial judge suggested that Frank not be present in the courtroom when the verdict was delivered. The unsurprising verdict was guilty, and Frank was sentenced to death.[44]

The mob-dominated atmosphere of the trial and the absence of Frank during the jury's reading of the verdict became the bases for Frank's appeals through the Georgia appellate process. All of his claims were adjudicated by subsequent state appellate courts, and his guilty verdict was upheld at every step of the appeal process. Frank then applied for a writ of habeas corpus in federal district court, arguing that the mob-dominated trial, combined with his absence from the courtroom at the reading of the verdict, violated due process. Not only did the original trial judge allow spectators brandishing weapons to fill the courtroom, but the jury and the judge could hear crowds yell threats through the court's open windows, with cries of "hang the Jew, or we'll hang you" bellowed during the trial. The local chapter of the B'nai B'rith took up Frank's cause and mounted a public defense, but they were outmatched by populist journalist and Southern firebrand Tom Watson, who went to great lengths to portray the virginal qualities of young Mary Phagan in the pages of his widely read *Watson's Monthly*.[45] The district court denied Frank's habeas claim, and he appealed to the Supreme Court.

Justice Pitney's majority opinion largely confirmed the traditional procedural and jurisdictional limitations of the writ, stating that habeas could not issue to challenge mere legal errors, nor could it serve to take the place of a writ of error. At the same time, however, he also seemed to advance a more capacious conception of both jurisdiction and due process. Pitney as much as admitted that Frank's first trial was dominated by a mob, thus producing an atmosphere that effectively violated the most basic due process procedural requirements. But because habeas could only be issued to challenge the jurisdiction of a court that never had jurisdiction to begin with or that had lost it during the proceedings through constitutional violations, Frank had to show that at no point in the appellate process were the facts of the case or the particulars of the trial itself reviewed free from mob domination. Pitney went on to say that because the case was appealed, and the facts and testimony were reviewed by the appellate courts of Georgia, the initial trial was "corrected." With this in mind, he remarked that "it would be clearly erroneous to confine inquiry to the proceedings and judgment of the trial court. . . . The laws of the state of Georgia . . . provide for an appeal in criminal cases to the Supreme Court of that state upon divers grounds, including [the assertion] that the trial court was lacking jurisdiction."[46]

Importantly for Pitney and the Court, mob domination of a trial was the most basic example of Fourteenth Amendment due process violations, and federal habeas courts could "look beyond forms and inquire into the very substance of the matter" to determine for themselves whether a constitutional violation had occurred.[47] The fact that the Georgia courts did review Frank's claims free from mob domination was the only reason that its judgment was upheld. However, drawing on notions of comity and federalism, the Court still left state courts ample room to determine and correct these questions of constitutional law themselves. The jurisdictional nature of habeas claims thus still remained, although slightly qualified. Although federal courts could determine due process violations in state courts, the entire state procedural mechanism must nevertheless be given the opportunity to address and correct violations. Even though Frank's petition contained a "narrative of disorder, hostile manifestations, and uproar" concerning the actions of the original trial court, "the entire [habeas] petition," including the review by the Georgia appellate courts, which was unarguably free from this disorder, must be taken into consideration and ultimately deemed corrective of the original constitutional violations. Nevertheless, the majority opinion considered Fourteenth Amendment violations in their substantive and procedural forms. Mixed questions of law and fact could not serve as a barrier to federal court habeas review of sham trials or gross constitutional violations, but if they were somehow corrected, the Court would defer. Jurisdiction, the key component of habeas, was only lost permanently by state courts if they failed to undo or correct violations at any time during the appellate process. Thus even though the petition was denied, Pitney nevertheless reminded the state of Georgia that their own courts' determination of whether or not constitutional violations occurred was not *res adjudicata,* and federal courts could make factual as well as legal determinations de novo. The 1867 act, Pitney pointed out, widened the scope of the writ and replaced "the bare legal review that seems to have been the limit of judicial authority under the common-law practice [of habeas]" with "a more searching investigation" that could, but did not necessarily have to, accept the factual and legal determinations of other courts.[48] Any other position concerning the scope of federal court habeas power would result in the "impropriety of limiting . . . the authority of the courts of the United States in investigating an alleged violation by a State of the due process of law guaranteed by the Fourteenth Amendment."[49]

For Justices Holmes and Hughes in dissent, "The loss of jurisdiction is not general but particular, and proceeds from the control of hostile influence."[50] Much more forcefully than Pitney, Holmes cited federal civil cases that precluded state corrective processes as res judicata with respect to federal questions. Therefore, in criminal matters, especially those involving capital punishment (such as this one), criminal law should follow the same logic.[51] Holmes justified the loss of jurisdiction at any point in the state process despite future corrective processes as uniquely vindicated by habeas corpus: "Habeas corpus cuts through all forms and goes to the very tissue of the structure. It comes in from the outside, not in subordination to the proceedings, and although every form may have been preserved opens the inquiry whether they have been more than an empty shell."[52]

For Holmes, no corrective appellate process could serve to vindicate the due process violations in *Frank*. Rejecting the majority's conclusion that jurisdiction was lost by the original trial court only to be regained by the appellate courts, Holmes held to a more capacious understanding of due process, arguing that mob-dominated trials were unarguably a complete violation of due process. Though many disagree as to what due process violations actually entailed, there could, in his mind, be no disagreement that a "mob intent on death" qualified.[53] Just as important, deference to state courts on questions of fact were problematic, especially during mob-dominated trials. Determinations of the voluntariness of confessions, for example, allowed state courts in some instances to create law themselves. "When the decision of the question of fact is so interwoven with the decision of the question of constitutional right that the one necessarily involves the other," Holmes said, "the Federal court must examine the facts."[54] Without federal court habeas review, including the ability to review legal as well as factual claims, the due process right would be "barren."[55]

Nonetheless, with his habeas claim denied and his death sentence upheld, Leo Frank was left with no other option than to petition Georgia's governor,

John M. Slaton, for clemency. Inundated with sympathetic petitions from other states and newspaper editorials demanding a pardon, Slaton, a skilled lawyer, researched Frank's case personally. His investigation revealed numerous discrepancies in the case that ultimately led him to conclude that Frank was innocent. Slaton then commuted Frank's sentence to life in prison. The mob influence during Frank's trial was seconded only by the reaction to Slaton's commutation, as hordes of protestors stormed the governor's mansion soon after Frank's commutation. In an effort to protect himself and his family, Slaton was forced to declare martial law, making him the first governor in American history to do so only to protect himself.[56] Soon after the violence at the Georgia governor's mansion, a band of vigilantes calling themselves the Knights of Mary Phagan kidnapped Leo Frank from the jail in Milledgeville, Georgia, and lynched him. He bled profusely while hanging from a tree, although he most likely died from wounds he received in a fight a few days before.

The coda to *Frank* brings full circle the depths of racism during the Jim Crow and Progressive eras and the emergence of extralegal threats to the judicial function in the United States. Just after the Atlanta premiere of *The Birth of a Nation,* itinerant preacher William J. Simmons, with the help of the Knights of Mary Phagan, reestablished the Ku Klux Klan in Georgia in the fall of 1915, just a few months after Leo Frank's horrible death. Evidently inspired by Dixon's fictional account of Klan cross burnings depicted throughout the film, the upstart Georgia Klan highlighted their debut by burning a cross atop Stone Mountain for all of Atlanta to see.[57]

MOORE v. DEMPSEY

Holmes's dissent in *Frank* would eventually become the majority opinion in *Moore v. Dempsey* eight years later.[58] *Moore* arose from race riots in Phillips County, Arkansas, in 1919. Black sharecroppers attempted to form an agricultural union to protect themselves against what they perceived as unfair labor and peonage practices imposed by the white minority in the county. Black leaders who were assembled in a local church were met with gunfire by a white mob and returned fire, killing one white man. Whites from surrounding counties then went on a vigilante rampage, where some estimates suggest that as many as 250 blacks were killed. Seventy-nine blacks were prosecuted and twelve were convicted of murder. Five of those death sentence appeals were brought in the consolidated case of *Moore* to the Supreme Court.[59] The defendants in *Moore* argued that their due process rights had been violated through mob domination and systematic exclusion of blacks from the grand and petit juries.[60]

As in *Frank,* the Court confronted the question of whether Southern state courts were able to provide due process of law when trials were dominated by mobs. After a lengthy recitation of the history of the case, Holmes began his majority opinion not with a substantive analysis of the claims or with an announcement of a new doctrine concerning habeas, but rather with the holding of *Frank.* He argued quite simply that if there was evidence of mob domination in the trial, due process is violated.[61] Moreover, he quoted from Pitney's opinion the holding that if the state fails to provide for any "corrective process," then due process is again violated. In the very next sentence, Holmes affirmed this model:

We assume in accordance with that case [*Frank*] that the corrective process supplied by the State may be so adequate that interference by habeas corpus ought not to be allowed. . . . But if the case is that the whole proceeding is a mask . . . neither perfection in the machinery for correction nor the possibility that the trial court and counsel saw no other way of avoiding an immediate outbreak of the mob can prevent this court from securing the petitioners their constitutional rights.[62]

The fact that mob intimidation was present throughout the appellate process showed that the state's appellate courts were unable to conduct their inquiries with regard to the due process requirements encompassed in the laws of Arkansas and in the due process requirements of the Fourteenth Amendment. Thus although habeas could be used to challenge mere "mistakes of law" during trials, it was nevertheless necessary for the writ to issue when "the whole proceeding is a mask—that counsel, jury and judge [are] swept to the fatal end by an irresistible wave of public passion."[63]

Justice McReynolds's dissenting opinion in the case (with Sutherland concurring) suggested that Holmes was overturning the corrective process model of *Frank.* McReynolds believed that the lower federal district court, such as the one in *Frank,* did not err when it denied habeas to Moore and the other defendants because the state courts of Arkansas had fully reviewed the facts of the case wholly apart from the valid accusations of mob domination in the original trial. Moreover, he also pointed to the fact that other defendants besides the ones in this case had their cases overturned for lack of evidence, thus supporting his argument that the appellate process had not been tainted.[64] He also worried that Holmes's position would open the floodgates for state prisoners who would similarly claim that their trials were dominated by mobs. This possibility, he said, would delay "prompt punishment," and the Court's ruling "probably will produce very unfortunate consequences."[65]

But together, the habeas changes announced in *Frank* and *Moore* were not as radical a departure from the traditional understanding of the jurisdictional requirements of habeas jurisprudence as some suggest, although the cases did, in the limited circumstances of asserted mob domination of trial courts, slightly broaden habeas access.[66] We only need to understand that Holmes, as quoted above, twice put forth the corrective process model in both cases to see the similarities between them. Corrective process assumed that if state appellate processes took into account the assertions of mob domination and sought to examine the facts apart from it, traditional habeas jurisdiction was still controlling. The fact that Holmes believed that these processes did not adequately take this into account represents more an affirmation, rather than an overturning, of the rules set down in *Frank*.

Frank and *Moore* still continue to divide habeas scholars. But reading them through a lens that focuses on the larger threats to judicial legitimacy that vigilantism and mob-dominated trials posed to courts in the first third of the twentieth century unifies the cases in an institutional sense. The fact that Holmes's dissenting opinion in *Frank* became the majority opinion in *Moore* was thus arguably the understandable—and indeed institutionally necessary— by-product of the increase in Southern mob-dominated courtrooms, the failure of antilynching legislation in Congress during the interwar period, and the Court's more purely legal shift to the acceptance of mixed factual and legal considerations.[67] No explanation recognizes these institutional concerns of the Court in establishing minimum criteria for due process trial rights. To be sure, the Court's adoption in *Moore* of Holmes's dissent in *Frank* was greatly influenced by extralegal contextual factors. But those factors are best understood as pushing the Court to protect and defend the integrity of their own institution in the face of structural threats to the most basic due process requirements in criminal trials rather than a more general move on their part in the direction of ensuring legal equality for minorities.[68]

HABEAS CORPUS AND WORLD WAR II

That habeas development was not transformed in the first third of the twentieth century so much by a new commitment to racial egalitarianism on the part of individual justices or the Court as a whole as it was by more institutional concerns is further evident during World War II. The Court's personnel changes after 1937 linked it more closely to the New Deal coalition in ways that few Courts had ever been linked to dominant national coalitions in American history. Aside from cooperation in the economic realm, Congress and the Court overwhelmingly supported Roosevelt's vision of constitutional governance, especially in the area of increased executive power during World War II.[69] Nevertheless, Roosevelt's Court still exhibited a concern for its institutional independence even as it sought to affirm the New Deal regime's principles of constitutional governance.[70] This dynamic is evident in the habeas cases that challenged Japanese internment and martial law in Hawaii, as well as postwar cases examining the extraterritorial jurisdictional reach of the constitution. Even when the Court seemingly vindicated individual liberty through habeas in cases such as *Endo* and *Duncan*, it did so without reaching a decision on the constitutionality of internment or martial law in general, two core regime commitments during the war. Moreover, despite rhetoric to the contrary in *Korematsu*, which announced the now-familiar doctrine of strict scrutiny for racial classification, racial distinctions were countenanced. But even with Court deference to the New Deal regime, the Court's own institutional ability to issue the writ and make independent determinations of unconstitutional detention through habeas was never sacrificed completely. These cases show us how the Court balanced its own institutional commitments and concerns with its allegiance to the governing regime through habeas. They also serve as further evidence that habeas was not developing in an increasingly progressive direction before the Warren Court's civil rights and civil liberties revolution.

JAPANESE INTERNMENT

On 19 February 1942, almost two and a half months after the bombing of Pearl Harbor, President Roosevelt signed Executive Order 9066, authorizing the secretary of war and certain military commanders to define certain military areas from which certain "persons" could be excluded.[71] Then, on 2 March 1942, General DeWitt, commander of the Western Defense Command, established Military Areas 1 and 2, comprising the entire Pacific coast of the United States. And on 21 March 1942, legislation was enacted that gave a congressional imprimatur to the exclusion order. After congressional authorization, two military orders were issued that excluded Japanese Americans (with citizenship) and Japanese resident aliens from the areas while simultaneously preventing them from leaving these designated areas. These contradictory orders were resolved by requiring all Japanese first to report to civil relocation stations and then to relocation camps, where they were resettled outside the military zones.

HIRABAYASHI v. UNITED STATES

Gordon Hirabayashi was an American citizen of Japanese ancestry. Although his parents were born in Japan, he was born and raised in the United States; in fact, he had never been to Japan. While a senior at the University of Washington, Hirabayashi knowingly refused to report to the relocation center in Seattle, Washington, on 11 and 12 May, choosing instead to remain at home. He was subsequently arrested, charged, and convicted of violating the military order that demanded that he report to the center. Another charge, that of violating a curfew order requiring Japanese Americans and residents to remain in their homes between 8:00 P.M. and 6:00 A.M., was also added.

His conviction was appealed to the Supreme Court, where he argued that the curfew orders were an unconstitutional delegation of legislative authority by the president to the military, and also that the general exclusion orders violated the due process clause of the Fifth Amendment. However, because Hirabayashi's sentence of three months for each count was to run concurrently, the court sidestepped the larger question of the constitutionality of the exclusion order, instead limiting its decision to the legality of the curfew order.[72]

On the curfew question alone, Chief Justice Stone found that it was a constitutional delegation of legislative power to military commanders in the field because congressional legislation affirmed Executive Order 9066. The question the Court was asked to determine was whether the president and Congress together had the authority to implement curfews in this particular case. He again found that they did. The justification was based on military necessity and race.

Although for Stone "distinctions between citizens solely because of their ancestry are by their very nature odious to a free people," during war, the realities of espionage and sabotage "call upon military authorities to scrutinize every relevant fact bearing on the loyalty of populations in these dangerous areas."[73] Though these "facts" might problematically suggest that one nationality is more dangerous than another, they should not prevent the executive from defending the nation. In an awkward justification, Stone cited John Marshall's famous assertion that "we must never forget that it is *a constitution* we are expounding . . . a constitution intended to endure for ages to come, and, consequently, to be adapted to the various *crises* of human affairs."[74] In the days after Pearl Harbor, argued Stone, the possibility of Japanese invasion was particularly acute on the West Coast. Our knowledge of Germany's advance through Europe gave us the further knowledge that fifth column activities were routinely used in this process.[75] Moreover, the president's commission that had investigated the Pearl Harbor bombings indicated that some "in sympathy" with the Japanese in Hawaii had acted in concert with the Japanese empire to facilitate the attack during the preceding days.[76] Therefore, the belief that similar circumstances could exist on the West Coast, where 112,000 of the 126,000 Japanese (citizens and noncitizens) resided, was to the Court not inconsequential.

The idea that Japanese in the United States were capable of fifth column activities was further based on the view that their peculiar economic and social history in the United States had prevented their assimilation. Stone observed that "a large number of children of Japanese parentage are sent to Japanese language schools," which were sources of "Japanese nationalistic propaganda, cultivating allegiance to Japan."[77] Moreover, many Japanese who were American citizens had dual citizenship with the Japanese empire, and those who were merely residents but not citizens were "of mature years and occupy positions of influence in Japanese communities."[78] For the Court, this provided a rational basis for the military's imposition of a curfew. As a result, the Court did "not need [to] attempt to define the ultimate boundaries of the war power."[79] Even the most critical concurrence, by Justice Murphy, condoned the immediate action of military officers in the field when a real crisis was imminent. Murphy, however, went to great lengths to argue that the racial classifications, and the rights that they necessarily curtail, while temporarily constitutional during the conflict, must be fully restored when the "danger is past."[80]

KOREMATSU v. UNITED STATES

Although the Court sidestepped the question of the constitutionality of the relocation program in *Hirabayashi*, it did engage the question of the exclusion program of Executive Order 9066 in *Korematsu v. United States* (1944). Fred Korematsu, an American citizen who lived in California all of his life, was charged with disobeying the general exclusion order that excluded all Japanese from designated military areas after 9 May 1942. Like Gordon Hirabayashi, Korematsu remained at home rather than reporting to a relocation center. Thus, in the words of Justice Jackson's dissenting opinion, Korematsu was convicted of "being present in a state whereof he is a citizen, near the place he was born, and where all his life he has lived."[81]

Justice Black's majority opinion extended the logic of *Hirabayashi*, predicating the opinion on the exigencies of military decision making during times of crisis. He also distinguished the decision on the charges of violating the exclusion order from questions concerning the legality of relocation and detention. Although Black argued that legal restrictions that apply to particular racial groups are "immediately suspect" and require the utmost "strict scrutiny," he nevertheless determined that the exclusion order, which was specifically directed toward all Japanese, was not racially discriminatory.[82] The military's response to the possibility of imminent attack necessitated a judgment that Japanese persons should be removed from designated areas because the United States was at war with Japan, not because there was "hostility to him or his race."[83] Concerning the question of Korematsu's American citizenship, Black noted that "citizenship has its responsibilities as well as its privileges, and in time of war the burden is always heavier." To Black, Korematsu's exclusion was a responsibility of citizenship.[84]

The dissents, especially those of Murphy and Jackson, attacked the patently racist conclusions of the decision, not only with respect to the exclusion order, but also concerning detention and relocation. Murphy in particular argued that the majority's opinion "falls into the ugly abyss of racism" and charged that the commander's actions in determining exclusion, relocation, and detention were not the result of "bona fide military necessity" but rather of the "erroneous assumption of racial guilt."[85] Murphy pointed out that General DeWitt's comments before a naval subcommittee, as well as his written orders, proved the racial animus behind the government's actions. In the original exclusion order, DeWitt had referred to all Japanese as "subversive" and as belonging to an "enemy race whose racial strains are undiluted."[86] In his testimony before the House Naval Subcommittee, he said, "I don't want any of them here. They are a dangerous element. It makes no difference whether he is an American citizen, he is still Japanese. American citizenship does not always determine loyalty."[87]

EX PARTE ENDO

With these two cases in mind, we can now better understand the grant of habeas corpus in *Ex parte Endo,* which was decided the same day as *Korematsu.*[88] Mitsuey Endo's habeas petition presented a different, but no less important, set of circumstances considering the entire program of Japanese internment. Endo had been excluded and then relocated, first to the Tule Lake war relocation facility in Modoc County, California, and then to another facility in Topaz, Utah. Those Japanese who were detained could ostensibly leave the facility, though their leave required a series of petitions and procedures that were subject to a final approval by the war relocation authority in conjunction with military intelligence and the Federal Bureau of Investigation. The application for leave clearance was a lengthy process, and even when completed, it did not necessarily allow the petitioner to leave the detention facilities. Instead, another petition had to be filed for indefinite leave. Each applicant was investigated to determine whether his or her leave would "affect the war program."[89] Nine factors were used to determine whether a detainee would qualify for leave clearance, some of which included taking oaths of allegiance and foreswearing the same to the Japanese empire, identification of records of attempts to expatriate, records of military training in Japan, and having had no more than three trips to Japan since the age of six. Even if these criteria were met, leave still might be denied if the detainee was set to relocate in an area where he or she was still excluded, or, more importantly for the government's contention in this case, leave might not be granted if the petitioner desired to settle in an area where sentiment against Japanese was determined to be too hostile. This point in particular was the crux of the government's argument for detention. The relocation of Japanese away from the coasts to the interior mountain states, including Colorado, Nevada, and Utah, they argued, had created "unease" among the white civilian population, including state governments, who faced the prospect of being inundated with relocated Japanese. Some governors had even suggested that they "would not be responsible for maintenance of law and order" unless those granted release remained under military or civilian surveillance.[90]

Endo applied for leave clearance, and the war authority granted it to her. However, this did not allow her true leave. Before she applied for indefinite clearance, she petitioned the federal district court for a writ of habeas corpus, arguing that she was a loyal citizen who had committed no civil, criminal, or military crime and was being held unconstitutionally. Her petitions were denied, partly based on the fact that her indefinite leave petition was still pending, but also because the district court believed that it could not grant her habeas because of the executive and congressional approval of exclusion and relocation.

Writing for the majority, Justice Douglas ruled that habeas corpus should issue, and Endo should have her freedom. The Court effectively ruled that the civilian rules and regulations that resulted in detention of concededly loyal American citizens were unconstitutional. However, the decision was distinguished from other constitutional questions (racial distinctions, equal protection, and due process) as well as the reach of habeas on these questions. Most importantly, the Court refused to rule as unconstitutional the presidential and congressional sanctioning of exclusion, evacuation, and relocation. Because the war relocation authority was a civilian agency, the Court was able to distinguish the grant of habeas in this case from the denial of habeas for those detained by military tribunals, which would presumably still be a constitutionally permissible action. Therefore, the executive order and the accompanying congressional legislation were constitutional. It was only the actions of the civilian agency that were not, leaving intact detention, exclusion, and relocation.

Endo's conceded and proved loyalty were the crucial factors in the decision, even more than her United States citizenship. The executive order authorizing exclusion and evacuation, combined with the legislation accompanying it, had allowed the delegation of these powers to military commanders on the basis of the necessity of preventing "espionage and sabotage," even with respect to American citizens. Two distinctions emerge in this part of the decision. The first is that the military determination of who commits or might commit espionage or sabotage is not to be questioned and is presumably valid. And second, citizens can fall into this category. However, the distinction is not citizenship per se, but rather loyalty: "A citizen who is concededly loyal presents no problem of espionage or sabotage. Loyalty is a matter of the heart and mind, not race, creed, or color. He who is loyal is by definition not a spy or a saboteur. When the power to detain is derived from the power to protect the war effort against espionage or sabotage, detention which has no relationship to that objective is unauthorized."[91]

Douglas went on to qualify this distinction even further, leaving open the possibility for the detainment, without habeas corpus, of citizens by the military: "The authority to detain a citizen or to grant him a conditional release as protection against espionage or sabotage is exhausted *at least when his loyalty is conceded.* Detention which furthered the campaign against espionage or sabotage is one thing. But detention which has no relationship to that campaign is of a distinct character."[92]

The concurrences in the case read more as dissents. For Murphy, the entire presidential and congressional program of exclusion, evacuation, and detention was an example of an "unconstitutional resort to racism."[93] Even with her freedom granted through habeas, Endo was still excluded from her home according to the exclusion orders that remained in effect, thus denying her the right to "pass freely from state to state."[94] Not mincing words, Murphy's final salvo to the World War II internment of Japanese Americans did not let the Court, Congress, or the president off the hook for what he perceived to be patently racist policies that still prevented Endo from enjoying all of her rights: "For the government to suggest under these circumstances that the presence of Japanese blood in a loyal American citizen might be enough to warrant her exclusion from a place where she would otherwise have a right to go is a position I cannot sanction."[95]

DUNCAN v. KAHANAMOKU

No other case during World War II better demonstrates the Court's institution-regarding posture in habeas cases than *Duncan v. Kahanamoku*. The petitioners in *Duncan v. Kahanamoku* were civilians who were convicted of crimes and tried in military courts in Hawaii when martial law was partially suspended.[96] Under the initial suspension order by the governor after the attacks on Pearl Harbor, all civil courts were closed and were replaced by military courts. Over the next few months, civil courts were authorized to open for some civil trials that required juries. However, through a series of military and executive orders (from the governor), military courts were still prosecuting certain crimes. Duncan was charged with assaulting a naval sentry, and a co-defendant, a stockbroker, was charged with embezzlement. They were tried in military courts without juries, convicted, and imprisoned. In their habeas corpus appeal to the Supreme Court, they challenged their convictions, arguing that the military courts set up as a result of the original declaration of martial law and simultaneous suspension of habeas corpus were unconstitutional.

Justice Hugo Black's decision to grant habeas to both Duncan and White was limited to the question of the provisions of the Hawaii Organic Act concerning the suspension of habeas and the imposition of martial law. Black carefully distinguished the grant of habeas here from what he otherwise considered to be legitimate wartime detention and trial, including the detention and trial through military tribunals of citizens interfering with "military functions" or those tried under temporary military governments. The question that Black addressed was simply whether the Organic Act's provisions for suspension of habeas allowed for the supplanting of civil by military courts when trying civilians not connected in any way with the military or its functions.[97] Black ruled that when Congress provided for declarations of martial law and suspension of habeas in the Organic Act, it granted them only to the extent that they would be used to restore civil government and repel invasion. For the Court, Duncan

and White, charged and convicted after most martial law provisions were removed, were therefore deserving of trials in civil courts, and deserving of the
habeas petition that removed them from the military's detainment.[98]

If not for Justice Murphy's concurring opinion, the case would not have
addressed some of the core arguments advanced by the Hawaiian attorney
general, who advocated the continued use of military courts to try civilians,
even though the civil courts were open and functioning. The attorney general suggested that, among other problems, the presence of "tens of thousands
of citizens of Japanese ancestry" prevented the civil courts from constituting
adequate juries. Their "doubtful loyalty" posed not only serious military concerns, but because they could not be constitutionally excluded from juries,
Hawaii had no alternative but to forego jury trials altogether in civil cases.
Murphy called this process a "deplorable . . . use of the iniquitous doctrine of
racism." Any justification advanced that was based on racist assumptions only
serves to "strike down individual rights . . . and aggr[avate] rather than solv[e]
the problems toward which it is directed."[99]

Again, in the majority opinion, many constitutional questions were jettisoned even though habeas served to vindicate the individual petitioners.
Foremost among these questions was the majority's sanction, admittedly under limited circumstances, of detainment and trial of American citizens by the
military. Equally important, however, was the majority's consistent refusal to
acknowledge the racial bases that often accompanied these arguments.

The World War II habeas cases confirm the pattern of wartime habeas cases
more generally. War and crisis certainly produce unique political and legal
challenges to governance, but the political and legal concerns of the immediately preceding period of normal political development often influence wartime politics. Japanese internment was no different. The preceding peacetime
conceptions of Japanese racial inferiority and suspicion infected the wartime
regime's adjudication of individual rights through habeas.

To see these habeas cases as simply deferential to the New Deal regime prevents us from also marking the limits of the cooperation between the Court
and the larger political regime, especially during war or crisis. Even though
the Court seemed to bend over backward to accommodate Japanese internment, they never surrendered their power to review wartime actions through
the writ. Like the *Frank* and *Moore* Courts before it, the World War II Court
partly crafted its wartime habeas jurisprudence with its own institutional concerns and duties in mind. Even if only implicitly, the Court was willing to
countenance racist influences in upholding Fred Korematsu's conviction, but
it was not willing to condone habeas's suspension in *Duncan,* where it justi-

fied granting the defendant's habeas petition because Hawaii's argument for continuing the writ's suspension was "so obviously contrary to our political traditions and our institution of jury trials."[100] Sympathetic Courts, even during war or crisis, will still only go so far in supporting regimes with which they are allied. When the legitimacy of the judicial institution is threatened at its core—when its most basic powers of review are in doubt—the Court will draw a line of judicial independence in the political sand.[101]

POSTWAR HABEAS AND THE RISE OF CIVIL RIGHTS AND CIVIL LIBERTIES

As a result of *Frank* and *Moore*, by the end of World War II, habeas underwent two minor changes in terms of its traditional jurisdictional qualities. First, due process claims concerning alleged mob domination of trials were held to be violations of the Fourteenth Amendment and therefore cognizable on habeas corpus. As a result, a state's failure to supply an adequate "corrective process" in its appellate processes could cause it to lose jurisdiction. Second, the Court was more willing to review questions of law and fact in the service of vindicating these basic due process rights, though it did not identify any other specific rights beyond settings in which mob domination overtook an otherwise legitimate trial that would trigger this type of habeas review.[102] These changes suggest that habeas's development before the 1960s was not the result of a progressive development of ever-increasing concerns for the rights of individuals generally. Instead, they are best explained as institutionally protective judicial responses to egregious due process violations. The salient jurisdictional component of habeas—courts of competent jurisdiction would only lose that appellation when they violated fundamental rights—thus remained, but now what counted as an exceptional circumstance that would cause a court to forfeit its jurisdiction became increasingly important.

But according to some, the Court's decision in *Brown v. Allen* (1953), one of the most significant habeas cases of the pre–Warren Court era, set the Court off on a course that far exceeded the rules developed in *Frank* and *Moore*.[103] The competing interpretations of *Brown*'s role in habeas's development center on the impact that the case has had in the years since the decision was rendered. After habeas was transformed by the Warren Court from 1963 onward, and in an attempt to account for and criticize this move by those opposed politically and legally to increased federal habeas corpus rights for state prisoners, *Brown* has been singled out as a case that made it easier for state defendants to challenge alleged due process violations by state trial courts. What these critics overlook is that although it might have seemed that the Court announced new broad federal habeas corpus rules for state prisoners, these rules were merely formalizations of earlier rules developed in cases such as *Frank* and *Moore* after the turn of the century.[104] Just as important, the Court formalized these rules before broader—and certainly more controversial—criminal procedure due process rights (which would eventually rely on habeas for their enforcement) were announced. As such, the Court's most important arguments in *Brown*, advanced by Justice Felix Frankfurter (certainly no advocate of judicial activism), put forward positions that were by then widely acknowledged, which were that federal constitutional questions could trigger federal habeas review, and that if a petitioner was denied certiorari on direct review, it did not preclude habeas review.[105] The significance of *Brown v. Allen* stems from the fact that what counted as due process violations changed dramatically in the decades after the decision.

BROWN v. ALLEN: *DEVELOPMENT OR AFFIRMATION?*

Brown had been charged, convicted, and sentenced to death for murder in North Carolina. He asserted in his state and federal appeals that his confession had been coerced and that the grand and petit juries in his trial were tainted by discriminatory practices that violated his due process and equal protection rights under the Fourteenth Amendment. Specifically, he charged that North Carolina's use of a tax list to select prospective jurors was discriminatory because it contained almost no blacks. His appeals were denied by the state and lower federal courts, which also denied his habeas petitions.[106]

The majority opinion was written by Justice Reed with Justice Frankfurter concurring. Brown's Fourteenth Amendment claims were fully litigated by the state courts, which found no violations. Up until *Brown,* the court had only agreed to hear habeas cases for constitutional violations for mob-dominated trials within a racially charged atmosphere. However, this decision potentially broke new ground because it provided that all federal questions, when brought on habeas to district courts, were fully reviewable, even though the state courts on every level had fully litigated and determined the federal constitutional claims.

On one level, *Brown* seemed to indicate a seismic change in the nature of habeas corpus. Up until then, when state courts adjudicated questions that implicated federal constitutional rights on habeas, lower federal courts would not revisit the state's judgment of the facts of the case. There were exceptions, but as we have seen, they were limited to egregious due process violations such as the mob-dominated trials in *Frank* and *Moore*. Now any federal question raised on an application for habeas corpus in the district courts of the United States could trigger "*de novo* review of legal and mixed legal–factual claims."[107] "The state court cannot have the last say," Frankfurter argued, "when it, though on fair consideration and what procedurally may be deemed fairness, may have misconceived a federal constitutional right."[108]

Frankfurter's justification for allowing federal questions to be heard again by federal district judges was not a revolutionary call for expanded habeas jurisprudence, but rather a particular reading of how habeas corpus cases should be adjudicated by lower federal courts, given the obvious implications that this already developed position posed to federalism issues. Throughout his opinion, he recognized that criminal adjudication was fundamentally a state power, and after admonishing the lower federal court for denying habeas because the Supreme Court had denied certiorari in the case, he seemed to lessen the potential blow of the ruling's implications for rehearing federal claims that had been fully adjudicated in state courts. "Most [habeas claims] are without merit," he argued, and are "adequately dealt with in State courts." He then went on to cite court statistics that indicated that in recent years only 67 of 3,702 habeas applications were granted, and in only a small portion of those was the state prisoner ultimately released. Considering the paucity of legitimate claims, federal habeas for state prisoners posed a potential problem for normal state adjudication of criminal matters and those extraordinary times in which federal constitutional rights are called into question and federal courts need to intervene. Therefore, particular care needed to be paid to the holding in this case: "The complexities of our federalism and the workings of a scheme of government involving the interplay of two governments, one of which is subject to limitations enforceable by the other, are not to be escaped by simple, rigid rules which, by avoiding some abuses, generate others."[109]

Nevertheless, Congress had provided the district courts of the United States the power to hear habeas claims from state prisoners, and the Court had to provide procedures to guarantee the right. Frankfurter then recounted the expanded habeas jurisdiction granted to the federal courts as a result of the Habeas Corpus Act of 1867. Although Congress could have left all residual power over criminal matters to the states that they had always possessed (as they are equally as responsible as federal courts to enforce the Constitution), Frankfurter stated that "it is not for us to determine whether this power should have been vested in the federal courts."[110] He then cited Justice Bradley's opinion in

Ex parte Bridges that "although it may appear unseemly that a prisoner . . . after conviction in a state court should be set at liberty by a single judge on habeas corpus, there seems to be no escape from the law."[111] With this in mind, he approvingly acknowledged how the Court had deferred to state courts in the form of the exhaustion rule, but then went on to admit that federal habeas for state prisoners was still precarious. The job of the Court in Frankfurter's mind was to craft a rule or set of acknowledged procedures for habeas that gave due consideration to the historical workings of federalism, particularly adjudications and judgments of state courts in criminal procedure cases, while recognizing the changes Congress had made to the writ: "If we are to give effect to the statute and at the same time avoid improper intrusion into State criminal process by federal judges—and there is no basis for thinking there is intrusion unless 'men think dramatically, not quantitatively,' [quoting Holmes]—we must direct them to probe the federal question while drawing on available records of prior proceedings to guide them in doing so."[112]

The procedures that Frankfurter enumerated were consistent with an approach that sought a balance between the jurisdictional limitations to habeas and the ability of federal judges to rehear state determinations of constitutional questions. The first guideline for federal judges was an obvious one: the habeas claim must state a federal question. Second, the habeas claim must have exhausted the respective state's procedures for habeas appeals, consistent with *Ex parte Royall.*[113] Third, the federal judge had the option, when using his "legal judgment under the habeas statute," to decide whether to rehear parts of the state's case. Frankfurter asserted that although the judge could call up the whole record of the case and even rehold hearings, it was still within his discretion not to do so. Some cases, he suggested, were so frivolous that "it seems unduly rigid to require the District Judge to call for the record in every case," but some claims are legitimate enough that they would need to be reheard.[114] Fourth, keeping with the spirit of the third rule, the district judge was to have the independent power to decide whether to have de novo factual hearings even if they had already been heard and adjudicated by the state. This decision would turn on the question of whether there was a "vital flaw . . . found in the process of ascertaining such facts in the State court," but with the caveat that state courts could not have the final say on federal law under the habeas statute. Fifth, when the facts in question in a state habeas claim called for "interpretation of the legal significance of such facts," then the district judge "must exercise his own judgment."[115] Frankfurter cited *Powell v. Alabama* (1932), in which the Court ruled that the Fourteenth Amendment's due process clause required states to furnish defendants in capital criminal cases with counsel consistent with the Sixth Amendment, to illustrate this point.[116] Although nominally represented by counsel, the state only provided this help the day before the trial was to begin. The Court held that *Powell* had been denied his Sixth Amendment and state rights to counsel, which the Alabama constitution required. Frankfurter used this case because if the federal judge was presented with state facts that indicated counsel was denied, he should be able to accept the state court's determination. If, however, the case did not deal with a capital crime, then the judge should still have the ability to determine whether there were other circumstances that might have contributed to error in a case where a state defendant was not represented by counsel, such as the age of the defendant, his mental condition, and his familiarity with legal proceedings, all in an effort to ensure that fundamental procedural fairness had occurred in the course of the trial.[117] Finally, federal judges could take into account prior denials of habeas corpus by other federal courts, although they might still entertain them if they chose. In sum, the rules were "addressed as they are to the practical situation facing the District Judge" so he can "give weight to whatever may be relevant in the State proceedings, and yet preserve the full implication of the requirement of Congress that the District Judge decide constitutional questions presented by a State prisoner even after his claims have been fully considered by the State courts."[118]

At the end of his opinion in *Brown*, Frankfurter made two points that suggested the limits of the Court's position.[119] The first was a reiteration of the argument that these new standards were necessary because Congress had mandated that federal courts, via habeas, could hear state claims of constitutional violations. The second point was more telling. As a result of the discretion now afforded district judges under habeas, some might fear that the "prison doors would open" and that the guilty would go free, thus subverting and frustrating the administration of criminal justice on the state level. This argument was a "bogeyman" for Frankfurter because, as he noted, only five state prisoners were released from 1948 to 1952 through habeas.[120]

In an encomium to habeas corpus at the end of the opinion, we see further just how little the traditional conception of habeas corpus had changed in Frankfurter's mind. We also get a glimpse of the extralegal context that influenced the opinion:

The uniqueness of habeas corpus in the procedural armory of our law cannot be too often emphasized. It differs from all other remedies in that it is available to bring into question the legality of a person's restraint and to require justification for such detention. Of course this does not mean that prison doors may readily be opened. . . . Its history and function in our legal system and the unavailability of the writ in totalitarian societies are naturally enough regarded as one of the decisively differentiating factors between our democracy and totalitarian governments.[121]

Frankfurter's concern with ensuring the procedural mechanics of due process through habeas corpus was partly a product of the larger political realities of post–World War II America, as well as his more general process-oriented jurisprudence. The contrast between democracy and totalitarianism at the end of *Brown v. Allen* is indicative of World War II's more general effects on the Court.[122] Just a year later, in *Brown v. Board of Education,* these effects, magnified by the perceived exigencies of the cold war, would manifest themselves both in the Court's unanimous opinion and in the briefs of the Eisenhower Justice Department.[123] Frankfurter's legal process leanings are also evident in the opinion, as is his belief that the Fourteenth Amendment's due process clause should not be straightjacketed by the fixed standards of a wholesale incorporation of the Bill of Rights.[124] But in an important way, the Court's more self-regarding institutional concerns about its ability to maintain and police the integrity of due process trial rights—which no justice denied—cannot also be excluded as a meaningful influence.

As we examine the extralegal context of these habeas decisions in the next section, we will see that this particular concern, which often hewed to federalist concerns about the relationship between state and federal courts, combined with the political realities of race in American politics by the middle of the twentieth century, yielded backlash and dissent even before the Warren Court's revolutionary habeas changes in the early 1960s.

RESISTANCE BEGINS

Changes to the procedural reach of federal habeas for state prisoners from the Progressive period to the beginning of Earl Warren's ascent to chief justice did not represent a significant departure from the traditional jurisprudence of habeas. The *Frank, Moore,* and *Brown* decisions only sought to reinforce and buttress habeas with respect to exceptional violations of only the most fundamental criminal trial due process rights, such as the appointment of inadequate counsel and mob-dominated trials. Habeas was thus only meant to help correct outlier cases, mainly in the South, that blatantly violated the rights of mostly indigent black defendants.[125]

But this does not mean that criticisms of even these exceptional habeas remedies were not forthcoming before the momentous changes by the Court during the 1960s. Even before Paul Bator's seminal critique of habeas appeared in 1962 (which became the foundation for later Republican critiques of habeas), resistance to federal habeas review of state court convictions was evident in Justice Robert Jackson's *Brown v. Allen* concurrence, which was partly influenced by his law clerk during the 1952 to 1953 term, William H. Rehnquist.[126] Jackson's opinion in *Brown,* while concurring in the decision not to award the writ, nevertheless questioned the legitimacy of the Court's developing habeas jurisprudence. Jackson worried that "the fact that the substantive law of due process is and probably [remains] . . . vague and unsettled" would create the impression among many observers that the "Court no longer respects impersonal rules of law" and was instead "guided in these matters by personal impressions which from time to time may be shared by a majority of Justices."[127] Aside from this attack on the Court's role in the increasingly uncomfortable world of due process after 1937, Jackson's second concern was with the low probability of actual innocence among those state prisoners who now seemingly had easier access to federal district courts. Jackson feared that the Court's decision transformed habeas's role from adjudicating only "probable constitutional grievance[s]" to those that were a "mere gamble [on] persuading some indulgent judge to let him out of jail." The result for Jackson was that habeas's extraordinary role was cheapened: "It must prejudice the occasional meritorious application to be buried in a flood of worthless ones. He who must search a haystack for a needle is likely to end up with the attitude that the needle is not worth the search."[128]

Importantly, Jackson's opinion was decidedly influenced by Rehnquist. In a memo to Jackson concerning another habeas case that term that was dismissed on procedural grounds soon before *Brown v. Allen,* entitled "HABEAS CORPUS, THEN AND NOW, Or, 'If I can just Find the Right Judge, Over these Prison Walls I shall Fly,'" Rehnquist detailed for Jackson his views on recent habeas developments.[129] Lamenting the difficulties that any federal district judge—let alone any state judge—would encounter in discerning the exact nature of increasingly vague standards of substantive due process that habeas could then be used to enforce, Rehnquist suggested that federal habeas for state prisoners should only issue in exceptional circumstances, such as those when the "denial of the right to counsel made meaningless the opportunity to litigate questions." Otherwise, state court judgments should be considered final. In another memo soon thereafter, Rehnquist went even further in justifying this position and putting it into a larger perspective concerning the role of the Court since 1937:

For many years this ct exercised a strict supervision over state economic legislation, rate-making, etc. That day is now gone. . . . But the very factions which most loudly damned the old court for its position on property rights are the most vocal in urging that this ct and other federal cts strictly supervise the state cts on matters of "civil liberties" and procedural due process. This inconsistency is apparently justified on some preferred position theory. What these forces fail to recognize is that the vice of the old court was not that it imposed the wrong views on the states, but that it imposed any views at all. In the fields of liberty as well as property, the states must be left to work out their own destinies within broad limits. If innocent people are regularly sent to jail, this ct or other federal cts may intervene; but subject to that limitation, there is no more reason for making this ct or other federal cts into a "super legal-aid society" than there was for elevating the doctrine of freedom of contract into a constitutional principle. For this ct to relax the federal grip on state criminal justice would be a step in the same direction as was taken by the case which overruled *Lochner v. New York*.[130]

Moreover, aside from this kind of internal dissent after *Brown v. Allen*, both the Judiciary Committees of the House and the Senate heard almost yearly testimony concerning attempts for bills that would further seek to limit the minimalist changes to habeas jurisdiction that had developed since *Moore*.[131] One such bill, H.R. 5649, considered in the House in 1955, sought to limit habeas appeals from those held under state custody unless certain conditions had been met by the defendant. The most significant part of this legislation would have limited federal habeas for state prisoners to "substantial constitutional" questions. Whatever these substantial questions were, the bill further limited them to the following three conditions: first, the claims in question on an application for federal habeas had to have been raised during trials on the state level; second, if the claims had not been raised, the habeas petitioner must show that he was somehow prevented from raising them; and, third, if it was found that the petitioner simply failed to raise them and was not prevented from raising them, these new claims on habeas could not be heard.

The House Judiciary Committee held hearings on the merits of the bill in June 1955. Testifying in favor of the bill were groups that had always been concerned with the effects that a widening scope of habeas would have on federalism and states' rights, especially the National Association of State Attorneys General. Testifying against the proposed bill was Thurgood Marshall, then special counsel of the NAACP. Howard Fatzer, who was representing the state attorneys general, argued that the proposed limitations to habeas appeals were necessary because the increased volume of habeas appeals from state prisoners was not only creating an unmanageable case load for both state and federal courts, but also because he and others sought to return habeas to its proper role in a federal system.[132] To Fatzer, the enlargement of habeas over the last decade had precipitated "an attendant loss of prestige and respect by all citizens for the judiciary—State and Federal—and its ability to administer criminal justice."[133] He recounted the conditions in Kansas jails, where he claimed prisoners were becoming "experts in the law of habeas corpus" and were enlarging "the avenues of possible escape from the penitentiary."[134] Other groups, including the Conference of State Chief Justices, echoed Fatzer's claim that the bill's limits to habeas appeals would ensure that the writ would not continue to offend "basic constitutional rights [that can be protected] without paralysis of the administration of the States' criminal codes."[135]

Thurgood Marshall also testified at the hearing as special counsel for the NAACP. Without publicly accusing the authors and supporters of the bill of overt racial discrimination, he nevertheless felt that its passage would "all but completely eliminate" the power of state criminal defendants to remove their cases via habeas to the federal courts. Marshall was deferential to issues of comity and states' rights but still felt that the integrity of the criminal justice process—especially when issues of federal constitutional rights of the accused are raised—benefited from and required the continued protection of habeas corpus. To those who argued that habeas appeals were too burdensome for both state and national courts, Marshall proclaimed that "the attorney generals of the States have a lot of work to do and the State's attorneys have a lot of work to do," but "frankly it does not impress me at all."[136] Instead, "the courts should bend over backward to be certain that they do not take a life without due process. I think a man's life is more important than dollars or cents or labor."[137]

The relatively minor changes in habeas that precipitated from *Brown v. Allen* quickly produced a backlash founded on dual federalism concerns with respect to state criminal procedure and focused squarely on the role of the Supreme Court in American politics. Since 1937, the Court increasingly faced the dilemma of justifying the same level of scrutiny and oversight of civil rights and civil liberties issues that it had only recently promised to abandon in the realm of economic substantive due process. The prospect of an about-face on this promise was partly fought out in terms of habeas corpus.

HABEAS, HISTORY, AND THE WARREN COURT

Even with these concerns looming large, the Warren Court chose to enlarge habeas doctrine even further at the same time that it sought to enlarge the scope of the rights that would now be applied to the states through the due process clause of the Fourteenth Amendment. In 1963, just a year after the beginning of "history's Warren Court," the Court in *Fay v. Noia* and its companion case, *Townsend v. Sain,* announced new habeas rules that were designed to enforce the rights revolution of the larger New Frontier/Great Society political regime with which it was now firmly allied.[138] The fears of some—and certainly of those who advocated more state-level control of criminal justice— were more than realized as a result of these two habeas cases. Indeed, partial and limited changes to the rules laid down in these cases have been central to the criminal procedure jurisprudence of both the Burger and Rehnquist Courts that followed.

Although habeas was chosen to aid in the enforcement of the Warren Court's larger criminal procedure revolution, there had been one criminal procedure case two years earlier, before these momentous habeas changes were announced, that in many ways portended the widespread dissatisfaction and backlash that the Court would face in the ensuing years. *Mapp v. Ohio,* handed down in 1961, made the Fourth Amendment's exclusionary rule applicable to the states, overturning *Wolf v. Colorado,* which had allowed illegally seized evidence in criminal prosecutions.[139] Abe Fortas said of the opinion in 1961 that it was "the most radical decision in recent times."[140] *Mapp's* controversy partly stemmed from internal criticisms from other justices who rightly noted that none of the briefs filed on Mapp's behalf raised the issue of excludable evidence, except for one line in an amicus brief filed on her behalf by the American Civil Liberties Union. The case was also perceived as an assault on federalism and state criminal adjudication and procedure. Half of the states had already precluded the admissibility of illegally obtained evidence, but half also allowed it. The fallout from *Mapp* produced the inevitable response: guilty criminals would go free on mere technicalities, severely hampering the states' traditional duties and responsibilities in the criminal justice arena. The gradual, but not complete, incorporation of most of the criminal procedure provisions of the Bill of Rights that followed increasingly became a problematic jurisprudential and political position for the Court to justify. This problem was only compounded when unenumerated provisions, such as the exclusionary rule or Miranda warnings, were applied as well. And by linking habeas to their enforcement, the Court set both incorporation and habeas on a collision course with an increasingly vocal legal class, both conservative and liberal, that was already uneasy with the Court's justification of judicial review since 1937.[141]

THE HABEAS TRILOGY

The Supreme Court's 1963 term produced three significant habeas cases: *Fay v. Noia, Townsend v. Sain,* and *Sanders v. United States. Fay* and *Townsend* were issued the same day as one of the most famous civil liberties cases during the Warren Court, *Gideon v. Wainwright.*[142] In the Warren Court's other major constitutional victory earlier in the previous decade—*Brown v. Board of Education*—a concomitant enforcement mechanism was also devised to ensure compliance. Accompanying *Brown* and other civil rights cases, such as *Reynolds v. Sims,* was a simultaneous implementation of federal equity power.[143] This meant that the federal courts provided more than just a legal remedy for litigants in a particular case, as the power and threat of injunctive penalties would accompany the Court's mandate that separate but equal was unconstitutional.[144] When a county, governor, or school board refused to implement or hampered a district court's desegregation plan, equity courts would serve to correct, implement (enjoin), and, if necessary, punish.[145] Thus the Court's monumental desegregation decisions had the added benefit of remedial force to back them up. The injunctive power of equity courts and lower district courts did not, however, accompany the court's criminal procedure and incorporation decisions. Instead, habeas corpus was chosen as the court's remedial vehicle to ensure that its decisions would be carried out and obeyed.

Unlike the outlier Southern cases of *Frank* and *Moore,* the Court in *Gideon* was now poised to move beyond the more corrective role of bringing these states into line with due process standards throughout the rest of the country and into the arena of overt criminal procedure supervision of states by the federal government. Clarence Gideon's moving story inspired best-selling books and popular movies, but two other factors are important to consider.[146] First, unlike the earlier Southern outlier cases, Clarence Gideon was white. Second, most states already had provisions in their state constitutions by 1963 that provided indigent defendants with the right to counsel. Not only were there only three states that did not provide counsel, but many states that did actually filed amicus briefs in Gideon's behalf. But the incorporation of right to counsel was certainly far less controversial than other criminal procedure rights that the Court would soon announce, and then seek to enforce, through habeas. Moreover, the incorporation decisions that soon followed applied to every state, not just outlier ones in the South. The trilogy of habeas cases decided in 1963 was not limited to right-to-counsel cases but further supervised both frontline criminal procedure by the police and the legal processes of state-level adjudication throughout the entire country. In a larger sense, the trilogy represented the Great Society regime's attempt to announce and then enforce new regime principles of constitutional governance, as the cases sought to give legal legitimacy to the now more specific catalog of rights and liberties that were to be protected by the Court.

Fay in particular represented a dramatic expansion of habeas. It not only confirmed but also moved past the developments in *Brown v. Allen.* In *Brown,* prisoners were still barred from raising issues in their federal habeas appeals if those issues had not been fully litigated in state court. As a result of *Fay,* the Court, led by Justice Brennan, ruled that the habeas petitioner had only to exhaust the remedies still available to him. If the state appellate process had changed procedures since the original sentence, as was the case in New York, the defendant was not barred from proceeding with successive habeas petitions based on the new procedures. *Fay* also significantly altered the "independent and adequate state grounds" rule.[147] Now state prisoners who never raised federal constitutional questions through their entire state appellate process had the ability to raise them de novo in federal habeas petitions. Brennan admitted that federal courts, and particularly the Supreme Court, would usually defer to state procedures independent of federal law as long as they are not "evasive of or discriminatory of federal rights."[148] In his view, this was done for mainly practical reasons, including "the unfamiliarity of members of this Court with the minutiae of 50 States' proceedings; the inappropriateness of crowding our docket with questions turning wholly on particular state procedures; the web of rules and statutes that circumscribe our appellate jurisdiction; and the inherent and historical limitations of such a jurisdiction."[149] But this rule would now have no relevance in federal habeas hearings.

The second case issued that day was *Townsend v. Sain.*[150] As ambitious as *Fay,* this case, decided by Chief Justice Warren, considered whether and under what conditions a federal habeas court could hear new cases based on evidence and facts already determined in state courts. The Court held that federal habeas courts could hear them de novo if the case fell under one of six new rules enumerated in the case. First, a new hearing could be had if the facts of the case were never fully resolved in the state hearings; second, the state's determination was not supported by the entire record of the proceedings; third, the procedures used in the state process were not supportive of a full or fair hearing; fourth, there were substantial allegations of new evidence; fifth, the facts were not developed adequately enough during the state hearings; and sixth, there was no reason to suspect that the court did not give the defendant a fair hearing of the facts.[151] These determinations were to be made by the district judge who first heard the habeas petition. The final case in the habeas trilogy of 1963 was *Sanders v. United States.*[152] In *Sanders,* Brennan in essence ruled that an unlimited amount of successive federal habeas petitions could be made to district courts, even if previous ones had been denied, as long as the new petition raised a different question from the previous ones, and as long as one of the six criteria in *Townsend* were met.

These three cases significantly enlarged both state and federal prisoners' access to the Great Writ. But as we have seen, significant change in habeas is almost always in the service of larger extrajudicial regime principles. Historical accuracy never stood in the way of John Marshall or Abraham Lincoln in their readings of habeas, and the same continued to be true of the Warren Court. By ignoring statutes and selecting only those cases that fit a particular doctrinal vision of habeas as an ever-increasing bastion for the protection of individual liberty on the federal level, the Court created an account of habeas's development to justify its decisions.[153]

The most sustained exposition of the Court's revisionist historiography was Brennan's opinion in *Fay.* After a recitation of the facts of the case at hand, Brennan devoted a large chunk of the opinion to his reading of the historic function of habeas corpus. He quoted the most venerable jurisprudential authorities in asserting the writ's historic importance. According to Blackstone, habeas was the "most celebrated writ in the English law."[154] For John Marshall, "there was no higher duty than to maintain it unimpaired."[155] To Brennan, "these are not extravagant expressions" because "behind them may be discerned the unceasing contest between personal liberty and government oppression."[156] Although he next conceded that the writ was first used simply as a "mode of procedure," he then asserted that it "became inextricably intertwined with the growth of fundamental rights and personal liberty."[157] Moving ahead a few hundred years, he then proclaimed that "vindication of due process is precisely its historic office."[158] Admitting that "of course standards of due process have evolved over the centuries," this did not change the fact that "the nature and purpose of habeas corpus have remained remarkably constant."[159] After dispensing with the obvious fact that habeas had been historically limited to questions of jurisdiction for most of its history in the United States by relying on an equally questionable reading of English common-law history, he said that "at all events it would appear that the Constitution invites, if it does not compel, a generous construction of the power of federal courts to dispense the writ."[160] He justified this position by arguing that because Congress had originally granted federal courts power to issue the writ (although they did so only for federal prisoners), they never explicitly defined the writ, leaving us to search the common law for its use. To Brennan, its historic common-law use was amazingly broad.

As problematic as his reading of the writ's common-law use was his reading of the writ's overall development in American constitutional law. Although the case law before the Habeas Corpus Act of 1867 made clear the separation of state from federal habeas, Brennan glossed over this fact, characterizing seventy-eight years of law thusly: "The development of the law in this area was delayed." After the 1867 act, he rightly claimed that the power of federal courts to hear habeas petitions from state prisoners was removed, but during the McCardle repealer era (1868–1885), he nevertheless suggested that lower federal courts "did not hesitate to discharge state prisoners whose convictions rested on unconstitutional statutes or had otherwise been obtained in derogation of constitutional rights." In support of this bold claim, he cited seven lower federal court opinions.[161] Although these cases did in fact involve state prisoners who had applied for federal habeas and who had been granted release as a result, they are hardly indicative of the sweeping and unbroken development of habeas that he asserts. In fact, with some scrutiny, they suggest just the opposite.

One of the cases, *Ex parte Bridges,* has already been discussed in Chapter 3.[162] In this case, Justice Bradley, sitting on circuit, did in fact release the defendant on habeas corpus, but he also lamented the fact that he actually could release him, because he felt that it was an affront to federalism and states' rights. He even went on to argue that the very law (the 1867 act) that allowed him to issue the opinion should be modified, making this a questionable endorsement of federal habeas for state prisoners. Also in support of his assumption of the ever-increasing liberalization of the writ are four cases from the district and circuit courts of California in 1880, all involving challenges to California state laws that discriminated against Chinese nationals.[163] The defendants in these cases, charged with crimes ranging from the exhumation of dead bodies to violations of employing Chinese immigrants against state law, all claimed Fourteenth Amendment violations. However, the assumption that these cases all turned completely on Fourteenth Amendment rationales is questionable. All of the Chinese national cases also asserted that federal habeas should be issued because of the statutory requirements of the Burlingame treaty, which gave China and its immigrants most favored nation status. *In re Wong Yung Quy* made this point clear: "Whether he [the petitioner] is in custody in violation of the constitution or treaty [Burlingame] is the very question to be investigated."[164] The possible limitations posed to any analysis by the Court of habeas's development vis-à-vis the Fourteenth Amendment were never acknowledged, because recognizing that the defendants were in a special class relative to other habeas petitioners might seriously detract from Brennan's account.

Although these seven cases hardly square with Brennan's argument, there were nevertheless cases on the district and circuit court level during the repealer period in which the 1867 act was given a fairly wide interpretation.[165] However, as we saw in the previous chapter, these cases were increasingly criticized by groups such as the American Bar Association, eventually leading to Congress' repeal of the repealer in 1884. Returning habeas jurisdiction under the 1867 act to the Supreme Court in 1885 was seen by many—including Congress and the court—as a way to limit habeas appeals and restore what was thought to be the proper balance between the adjudication of state and federal criminal law.

One of the other limitations that Brennan claimed prevented habeas from developing as neatly as it was meant to was that the Fourteenth Amendment was only recently "deemed to apply some of the safeguards of criminal procedure contained in the Bill of Rights to the States."[166] As these rights were applied further in the twentieth century, the Court, Brennan argued, had been "led to find correspondingly more numerous occasions upon which federal habeas corpus would lie."[167]

Aside from the Court's, and particularly Brennan's, controversial and still-unsettled incorporation jurisprudence, these cases implicated larger federalism questions for the ascending Great Society regime.[168] Just two years before his decision in *Fay*, Brennan addressed the fundamental issues of incorporation, federalism, and habeas corpus jurisprudence in a lecture at the University of Utah law school.[169] His argument attempted to justify an enlargement of habeas review by federal courts as an inevitable result of the fact that "under one formulation or another, the Supreme Court has extended to state prisoners many of the procedural safeguards of the federal Bill of Rights." As "the Supreme Court brings state criminal proceedings more and more within the protections and limitations of the Federal Bill of Rights, federal habeas corpus jurisdiction will correspondingly expand."[170] Incorporation was thus here to stay, and traditional notions of federalism would have to change. To Brennan, this was a natural development. He argued that the federal system exists to protect individual liberty by protecting the individual from the excesses of any one power, including state governments. The discord between state and federal governments in areas of criminal procedure, and particularly habeas corpus, had a simple solution: states and their judiciaries must change their procedural rules governing criminal procedure to bring them more in line with the development and application of new fundamental individual rights. Once states acknowledged the inevitability of incorporation, they would then realize that they "have it within their power substantially to reduce occasion for resort by state prisoners to federal habeas corpus."[171] This could be achieved by providing more procedural safeguards for those charged with crimes, including more postconviction remedies that sought to "vindicate . . . violations of fundamental constitutional rights," thus reconciling federalism, habeas, and individual rights.

The difficulties involved in federal habeas corpus appeals were further clouded by a jurisprudential dilemma faced by the federal circuit and district court judges who heard the bulk of habeas appeals from state prisoners. As lower federal courts mostly apply settled constitutional law with well-developed precedent, habeas presents a choice for the judge to decide between deferring to state sovereignty and vindicating perceived fundamental national rights. This art of judging consisted not only in choosing, but in choosing well. This might explain Brennan's final thoughts on habeas development in *Fay*, where he admitted that habeas precedent has not "always followed an unwavering line in its conclusions as to the availability of the Great Writ."[172] Although precedent had not always been completely clear, there was nevertheless a correct model of judging: the fundamental constitutional rights of the individual had to remain the basis of habeas corpus. If fundamental individual rights are the writ's antecedent, then as they increase (through incorporation and the Fourteenth Amendment), so should the availability of the writ. For Brennan, these rights were settled and inevitable, but for others, as we will see, these fundamental constitutional rights were not only vague, but were never meant to apply to the states.

FROM ENFORCEMENT TO DISSOLUTION

Fay, Townsend, and *Sanders* not only enlarged the writ's scope but also aided in the enforcement of the Court's Fourteenth Amendment incorporation agenda. The seemingly innocuous result at the time in *Brown v. Allen* (1953), which held generally that any constitutional violation could be vindicated through habeas, meant that habeas had now reached the apex of its procedural reach and substantive breadth. As more of the rights accorded federal prisoners were applied to state prisoners, and as more substantive rights were recognized by the Court, habeas would serve these rights and ensure that they were given a judicial forum for their enforcement. Importantly, the Court's expectation of an inevitably positive relationship between habeas and the rights it was now poised to protect and enforce hung both on the legitimacy of this tidal change in constitutional interpretation with respect to habeas appeals and unenumerated rights and on the larger and more difficult acceptance of the propriety of applying these changes directly to the states. Thus the efficacy of enlarged habeas was directly tied to the continuing acceptance of the Court's and the Great Society regime's vision of constitutional governance.

We can see just how tenuous this relationship was in two nonhabeas cases decided soon after the Warren Court's habeas trilogy. *Escobedo v. Illinois* (1964) and *Miranda v. Arizona* (1966) expanded the definition of the substantive rights that the procedural changes in the habeas trilogy cases would now cover. They seemed further to push the Court's incorporation and criminal procedure jurisprudence to their political limits and hasten an already burgeoning backlash to the Warren Court.[173] *Gideon v. Wainwright* (1963) had incorporated the Sixth Amendment right to counsel generally, but the specifics of when and where the right accrued, aside from representation of counsel at trial, had not been articulated by the Court. At issue in *Escobedo* was the point at which the right to counsel begins. Was it before, during, or after questioning by police? Did it obtain before a charge was brought?

The decision, written by Justice Arthur Goldberg, stated that when police interaction with citizens ceased to be investigative and became accusatory (that is, when the police begin to elicit confessions), the right to counsel kicked in.[174] Goldberg's opinion struck directly at the interview and interrogation process, the most fundamental tool that law enforcement had in the execution of its duties. With time as a critical factor in criminal investigations, and considering the real difficulties in obtaining immediate physical proof in the form of criminal instrumentalities (evidence), the one-on-one interaction between police and suspects was seen by many in law enforcement as the only real chance they had to confront suspects, elicit confessions, and develop investigative leads. The confession was thus the cornerstone to efficient (although not always accurate) law enforcement. If everyone had the right to counsel during investigations and before charges were even brought, then this tool would be limited. Goldberg railed against a system (ingrained in every state) that relied almost exclusively on the confession. He admitted that when confronted with the possibility of incrimination, almost everyone would request the service of counsel. He felt that the need to protect the fundamental right of counsel outweighed the burden of law enforcement to solve crimes. In his words, "a system of criminal law enforcement which comes to depend on the confession will, in the long run, be less reliable and more subject to abuses than a system which depends on extrinsic evidence independently secured through skillful investigation."[175]

The ensuing backlash to *Escobedo,* which mirrored subsequent attacks on the Warren Court's habeas changes, was presaged in Justice Potter Stewart's dissenting opinion, where he warned that the decision would prevent society from enjoying the benefits of meaningful and honest police investigation of crime. For the most part, police confront and question citizens before they have established attorney–client relationships. Asserting the right to counsel at the moment investigation reaches the stage of accusation might be devastating to investigative tactics in many of those situations. This is why Justice Stewart's dissent was so caustic. To him, even purely voluntary confessions (whether elicited or not) would now be inadmissible. The traditional test of confessions, according to Stewart, had been a voluntary–involuntary standard. In the Court's quest to constitutionalize its ideas of the Fourteenth Amendment's due process clause, it was crafting a "rule wholly unworkable and impossible to administer unless police cars are equipped with public defenders."[176] Worse yet, habeas could now be summoned to protect this new and controversial right.

Reaction was swift.[177] William Parker, chief of police of Los Angeles, stated that the decision had the effect of "handcuffing police." Michael Murphy, chief of police of New York, quipped that *Escobedo* was "akin to [requiring] one boxer to fight by the Marquis of Queensbury rules while permitting the other to butt, gouge and bite."[178] Soon after the decision, public opinion of the Warren Court began to decline rapidly. Decisions such as *Mapp* and especially *Escobedo* spurred "Impeach Earl Warren" bumper stickers and billboards, and ascendant politicians, such as presidential candidate Barry Goldwater, saw the Court's incorporation and due process decisions as contributing to increasing crime in cities while preventing police and states from prosecuting obviously guilty parties.[179]

Soon after *Miranda* and *Escobedo,* Senator Sam Ervin introduced a constitutional amendment that would allow the admission of any voluntary confession in criminal cases. In introducing the amendment, Ervin lamented, "When one reads some recent decisions of the nation's highest court and realizes that under them perpetrators of the foulest crimes are turned loose in society to repeat their crimes, he is tempted to exclaim: 'Enough has been done for those who murder and rape and rob! It is time to do something for those who do not wish to be murdered or raped or robbed.'"[180] With state and local governments crying foul as a result of *Escobedo,* familiar groups, including the American Law Institute and the American Bar Association, began to develop plans that would seek to challenge the Warren Court's authority in dictating the prearraignment procedures of the investigative process. Headed by Harvard law school professors James Vorenberg and Paul Bator, the ALI proposed, with the ABA's support, an alternative plan that would allow state legislatures to enact a "comprehensive code [that could] evaluate and adjust the various interrelated portions" of criminal processes more faithfully and accurately than the Court could.[181] The conservative bent of the ALI was obvious in that its proposal would defer to state legislatures in crafting criminal procedure codes for determining the exact rules for counsel in prearraignment circumstances.

Habeas's link in this chain was evident in the fact that Bator had written forcefully in the *Harvard Law Review* criticizing *Brown v. Allen* in 1962.[182] There he argued that federal habeas should only be available when the state loses jurisdiction because it failed to provide adequate procedural processes for deciding federal questions. It should not be available simply because a federal court thinks a state's decision was incorrect. Instead, Bator emphasized the necessity of "finality" in the criminal process, so that matters that had been fully and fairly litigated on one level (the state level) were not forced into redundancy at the cost of justice by another court (a federal one).[183] Other members of the ALI, including federal court of appeals judge Henry Friendly, also wrote prestigious and influential articles criticizing the Warren Court's habeas and incorporation jurisprudence. Friendly argued that for all the concern over due process in criminal procedure on the state level, the ultimate decision for granting or denying federal habeas corpus for state prisoners should be the innocence of the defendant. If mere technicalities violated perceived constitutional rights, then they could be addressed by means short of freeing the guilty.[184]

Before the ALI and the ABA could vote on their plan that would advocate for legislative, as opposed to judicial, determination of proper constitutional prearraignment procedures, the Warren Court beat them to the punch with arguably the most controversial criminal process case of the Court's tenure, *Miranda v. Arizona,* which would serve as a lightning rod for the Court's reform of state-level criminal justice.[185] To get a sense of just how far the Court had moved in terms of its criminal procedure jurisprudence that habeas would now enforce, Scot Powe points out that *Gideon* required that only five states change their criminal procedure rules (as twenty-seven amicus briefs from states encouraging the court to apply the Sixth Amendment to the states); *Mapp v. Ohio* required half of the states to change their exclusionary rule procedures; but *Miranda* required every state to change its most basic frontline criminal process procedures.[186] Of all the decisions issued by the Warren Court, *Miranda* produced the most visceral reactions. From police chiefs to state judges to presidential candidates such as Barry Goldwater and later Richard Nixon, many now believed that the Court had abandoned its constitutional duty of deciding cases between litigants on the basis of precedent and traditional notions of federalism in favor of crafting legislation out of thin air.

Miranda required that before any questioning by police, suspects be informed of their right to remain silent and other rights accruing to them as a result of their encounter with law enforcement, including the fact that any admissions to questions can be used by law enforcement if prosecution results. Chief Justice Warren portrayed the decision as almost inevitable considering the Court's correction of courtroom abuses earlier in the twentieth century. In those largely Southern cases, he said, "the police resorted to physical brutality—beating, hanging, whipping—and to sustained and protracted questioning incommunicado in order to extort confessions."[187] What was different about *Miranda* was not only that it now applied throughout the country, but that it also involved the creation of an entirely new right, now incorporated against the states and potentially enforced through habeas, that was nowhere to be found in the text of the Constitution. Applying enumerated Bill of Rights provisions to the states was controversial enough, but the further application of unenumerated rights—now understood as preventive or prophylactic devices—appeared to be judicial lawmaking, pure and simple. In his dissent, Justice Harlan seemed to foresee the backlash, as he warned that the decision could "return a killer, a rapist or other criminal to the streets . . . to repeat his crime whenever it pleases him."[188]

Miranda—and the Court's habeas agenda developed during the 1960s—came at a bad time for the Court.[189] As crime became a central issue in the 1968 presidential campaign, public opinion polls showed that most Americans felt the Court was "soft on crime."[190] In 1968, Congress passed the Omnibus Crime Control and Safe Streets Act, which, among other goals, sought to overturn *Miranda*.[191] It mandated that voluntary confessions without *Miranda* warnings were to be evaluated by federal courts on appeal under a "totality of circumstances" test, a procedure that had governed pre-*Miranda* appellate processes. Viewing the constitutionality of the legislation as questionable, Attorney General Ramsey Clark directed the Justice Department not to comply with the legislation, but the bill became a poster child for Nixon's and even George Wallace's anticrime stance in 1968.[192]

The racial significance of freeing criminals was also a real, though covert, part of the unpopularity of the Court's habeas and incorporation agendas. Race riots were featured prominently on nightly newscasts, and the reality that those guilty of such crimes might go free through habeas corpus technicalities was perceived as a perversion of the criminal justice system. George Wallace's statement in 1968 seemed to sum things up: "If you walk out of this hotel tonight and someone knocks you on the head, he'll be out of jail before you're out of the hospital, and on Monday morning, they'll try the policeman instead of the criminal."[193] By 1968, he could have added that the legal tool that could now routinely free the guilty was the writ of habeas corpus, transformed from an extraordinary tool of law into an ordinary one.

CONCLUSION

From the turn of the twentieth century to the end of the 1960s, habeas moved from an extraordinary to a routine tool of regime enforcement. The waning commitment to increased enforcement of egalitarian principles through habeas that reflected the nation's larger retreat from Reconstruction in the last third of the nineteenth century allowed the Great Writ to serve as an enforcement mechanism for only the most egregious violations of due process. In this role, habeas was used to correct outlier behavior in state criminal justice adjudication, mainly in the South, that stood out as vastly out of touch with the rest of the nation in its disregard for the most basic due process trial rights. In both *Frank v. Mangum* and *Moore v. Dempsey,* the Court reacted to these due process violations from an institutionally protective position in which concern for the rights of individuals coincided with a broader, growing concern for the integrity of legal adjudication. The Court's mild liberalization of habeas in the years between *Frank,* when federal habeas for a state prisoner was denied, and *Moore,* when it was granted under similar circumstances, was only a positive development to the extent that the Court was more aware than ever of the destabilizing threats that sham trials, vigilantism, and racist state-level criminal justice systems posed to the integrity of legal adjudication in the United States. To account for these habeas changes as simply reflective of the Court's—and the country's—increasing realization of the evils of racism in the Jim Crow South misses the mark. Extralegal factors certainly influenced the Court's habeas jurisprudence, especially the rise of mob-dominated trials that all too often ended in lynchings and vigilante justice. But the Court's habeas changes were made less out of concerns for any strong version of egalitarianism and equal protection than out of establishing minimal requirements for any trial to be perceived as fair.

That the Court was no egalitarian or countermajoritarian hero is further confirmed in the habeas cases during World War II.[194] As it had during war and crisis before, habeas during World War II was used by the dominant national political regime to advance and protect its view of constitutional governance during war. It also reflected the preceding development of normal politics. Discrimination against Asians had a long history in the United States, dating back at least to the use of Chinese labor in the construction of the transcontinental railroad in the 1840s. This ugly reality continued to fester throughout the nineteenth century as the United States witnessed an influx of immigrants after the Civil War. It should come as no surprise that habeas reflected this more general state of affairs in cases such as *Duncan, Hirabayashi, Endo,* and even *Korematsu.* Even though habeas was used as an enforcement tool of the regime during World War II, we still saw the Court refusing to relinquish its own institutional power to issue the writ.

The Court's concern with its own institutional legitimacy continued to influence habeas development after World War II. Beginning with *Brown v. Allen,* the Court continued the logic of *Moore v. Dempsey* by allowing federal district courts to hear habeas cases from state prisoners when they determined that due process trial rights were violated in state proceedings. Rather than a novel development, *Brown v. Allen* simply confirmed the Court's concern that it should always have the option to remove state cases to federal courts if necessary.

It was a relatively uncontroversial move for the Court to ensure that it had the power to supervise state trials through habeas when it perceived egregious due process violations, but when the content of due process itself began to change rapidly during the 1960s, the rules laid down in *Brown v. Allen* became problematic. As the Court and the larger Great Society regime began to announce new and more controversial criminal process rights, habeas became enmeshed with emerging Republican criticisms of the 1960s more generally. The Court's protection of the most basic due process trial and criminal process rights through habeas in the first half of the twentieth century quickly gave way to the use of habeas to protect new and controversial due process rights at a time when many perceived that rising crime rates, particularly in the inner cities, were the result of a misguided and naive program of constitutional governance enforced through habeas corpus. Summing up the seemingly failed use of habeas by the Great Society regime, and poised to assert a new role for habeas in the Republican Party's vision of constitutional governance, presidential candidate Richard Nixon wrote in a 1967 article in *Reader's Digest* that "far from being a great society, ours is becoming a lawless society."[195]

CHAPTER 5

Innocence and Guilt: Habeas from Burger to Rehnquist

Because sentence against an evil deed is not executed speedily, the heart of the sons of men is fully set to do evil.

—Ecclesiastes 8:11, quoted by Senator Sam Ervin, Subcommittee on Constitutional Rights of the Committee on the Judiciary, considering S. 895, the Speedy Trial Act of 1971

During the 1968 presidential campaign, candidate Richard Nixon promised to change what he and a majority of the country perceived as a Supreme Court that favored criminals over victims and law enforcement. His answer was to replace activist judges with those who would interpret the Constitution according to strict construction.[1] In his acceptance speech for the Republican nomination for president in 1968, Nixon expounded on "the problem of order in the United States":

Let us always respect, as I do, courts and those who serve on them. But let us also recognize that some of our courts in their decisions have gone too far in weakening the peace forces as against the criminal forces in this country and we must act to restore that balance. Let those who have the responsibility to enforce our laws and our judges who have the responsibility to interpret them be dedicated to the great principle of civil rights. But let them also recognize that the first civil right of every American is to be free from domestic violence, and that right must be guaranteed in this country.[2]

To many, the Warren Court's incorporation of most of the criminal procedure guarantees of the Bill of Rights, especially in controversial decisions such as *Miranda* and *Mapp*, stacked the deck against law and order in favor of criminals.[3] But these were not wholly new arguments. Academic lawyers such as Henry Friendly and Paul Bator, as well as an increasingly vocal cadre of interest groups, had been making this sort of critique for two decades.[4] By 1968, however, these critiques now had the support of the Oval Office.

The Speedy Trial Act of 1971 encapsulated the incipient Republican regime's backlash against the Warren Court's criminal justice revolution. Among its provisions, the Speedy Trial Act of 1971 sought to guarantee the Sixth Amendment's right to a speedy trial by mandating changes in federal district court procedures. Its most important change would have been the requirement of a sixty-day maximum time period between charge and trial. Various witnesses were called to comment on the bill before the Senate, but one witness, and his suggestions for making the bill stronger, stood out. On 14 July 1971, the Senate called the assistant attorney general of the United States in the Office of Legal Counsel, William H. Rehnquist, to offer testimony on behalf of the Department of Justice.[5] Rehnquist supported the bill in theory but thought it did not go far enough. What was needed, he argued, was an additional measure that would also mandate reforms to the existing rules governing federal habeas corpus for state prisoners. According to Rehnquist, the Sixth Amendment's guarantee of a speedy trial was most hampered by increased access to habeas corpus for state prisoners in federal courts.[6] His concern about habeas jurisprudence as it had developed since the Warren Court was that it prevented "finality" in criminal procedure adjudication and ignored the low probability of the actual innocence of the defendant, a critique that had been gaining currency since the controversial decisions of *Mapp* and *Miranda*.[7] Habeas petitions had so clogged federal courts, he went on to argue, that in 1971, district courts received almost 11,000 habeas petitions.[8] He proposed that Congress change the existing habeas law according to the arguments of Henry Friendly and Paul Bator (whose law review articles he cited in his testimony), who suggested that the actual guilt or innocence of the defendant, as well as a desire for finality in criminal adjudication, should govern access to habeas.[9] Habeas claims that relied on newly applied (or discovered) rights, such as the Fourth Amendment's exclusionary rule, or misapplied *Miranda* rights, which only relate to technical procedures and did not establish or suggest innocence, should be barred.

Rehnquist's reading of the development of the writ suggested that the Warren Court had taken minor habeas expansions in outlier due process cases at the beginning of the century that granted habeas during mob-dominated trials (*Frank v. Mangum* and *Moore v. Dempsey*) and made them the rule for all constitutional challenges.[10] In other words, the use of habeas to examine extraordinary trials with no due process whatsoever had been transformed into a mechanism by which any state-level trial, no matter how perfect or seemingly free from error, could be questioned on any federal ground, ultimately delaying conviction and preventing justice. He said of these types of early cases, "Hard cases make bad law."[11]

In his testimony, Rehnquist argued that although federal habeas corpus for state prisoners should always be available, it should be reserved only for the most egregious due process violations, not for new Court-created rights such as those of *Mapp* and *Miranda:* "The principal types of claims which would be barred under such legislation [limiting habeas corpus] would be those stemming from the case of *Miranda v. Arizona,* and those stemming from claims of unlawful search and seizure. It is generally agreed . . . that the exclusionary rule based on *Miranda* and on *Weeks v. United States* and *Mapp v. Ohio* is not designed to insure the fairness of the trial, but rather designed to discipline police officers."[12]

At the end of Rehnquist's testimony to the committee, Senator Sam Ervin engaged him in a conversation about the Warren Court's most controversial rulings: *Mapp* and *Miranda.* After complaining that the Warren Court overstepped its duties in these two cases, Ervin agreed with Rehnquist that it had also wrongly expanded federal habeas for state prisoners. Ervin said he had always admired Justice Jackson's opinion in *Brown v. Allen,* where, in describing the flood of frivolous habeas petitions to federal district courts, Jackson said, "It must prejudice the occasional meritorious [habeas] application to be buried in a flood of worthless ones. He who must search a haystack for a needle is likely to end up with the attitude that the needle is not worth the search."[13] Rehnquist said he remembered that portion of the argument very well because he was Jackson's clerk at the time he wrote the opinion.[14]

Rehnquist would not see formal congressional changes to habeas until 1996, when Congress passed the Antiterrorism and Effective Death Penalty Act. With no congressional majority able to make the changes (although there were bills presented almost every year for habeas reform), the Burger and Rehnquist Courts were left to fashion their own changes to habeas jurisprudence.[15] In many ways, Rehnquist was the perfect man for the job. If the Burger Court (and later Rehnquist's own Court) were to overturn and refashion a habeas jurisprudence that had been overstretched and manipulated by the Warren Court, they would have to guide the Court to a return to the pre-1963 understanding of habeas, specifically the dissenting opinions to the 1963 trilogy cases of *Fay, Townsend,* and *Sanders,* thereby offering a competing vision for the role of habeas corpus. And in many ways, this is the path that the Burger and Rehnquist Courts followed until the 1996 Antiterrorism and Effective Death Penalty Act (AEDPA) codifications. These new visions, and the steps the Court, Congress, and the executive would take to realize it, are the subject of this chapter. The Court's rollbacks of the Warren Court's habeas jurisprudence took on the same institutional concerns that previous courts had adopted. Although habeas was weakened, at no time did any Court majority suggest that habeas or its own control over its processes should be completely eliminated. Conservative or liberal, the Court fought to keep itself in the game.

The jurisprudential justifications for habeas rollbacks took their cue from the concerns expressed in Jackson's opinion in *Brown v. Allen* and in subsequent academic commentary on the Warren Court's habeas jurisprudence: finality, federalism, and actual innocence. If the Warren Court rewrote out of whole cloth the historical development of the Great Writ of Liberty as always increasing toward more unfettered liberty, then arguments against the Warren Court's habeas jurisprudence would have to reformulate an alternative version of habeas's intended use.

PRECURSORS TO ROLLBACK: RECOVERING FINALITY AND ACTUAL INNOCENCE

Paul Bator's influential 1962 article in the *Harvard Law Review* continues to this day to be an important source of legal and theoretical arguments concerning the proper application of habeas corpus for those who support rollbacks of the Warren Court's habeas jurisprudence.[16] More than with any other academic commentator, proponents of habeas rollbacks on the Court continue to rely on Bator's conceptions of the proper scope of habeas corpus review. Bator's arguments, as well as those developed by federal circuit court judge Henry Friendly, constitute the intellectual origins for the Burger and Rehnquist Courts' attempt to restore habeas to its purported roots as a tool for the federal adjudication of only the most egregious state-level due process violations.[17]

Writing at the height of the cold war, Bator recognized that his arguments for finality in the criminal procedure process had to tread slowly. Considering this reality, he said, "The notion that a criminal litigation has irrevocably ended may have been an acceptable one in an age with a robust confidence in (or, if you prefer, complacency about) the rationality and justice of the basic process itself." He went on to argue that in our age of "dictators," we as a nation were less likely to believe that final legal judgments are always correct and just. However, he maintained that it was nevertheless possible to identify and justify some theoretical precepts concerning the point at which a judgment becomes final. This becomes easier, he asserted, when we understand two things. First, we had to realize that our hesitation concerning the finality of legal judgments was of "recent origin," identifiable mostly as a response to experiences in postwar Europe and our realization at home of the challenges to fundamental justice faced by African Americans, particularly in Southern state courts. Second, his arguments concerning finality were forward-looking, and imagined a time when distrust of courts (for example, Southern ones) might not always be necessary.[18]

Related to this second point was his more general institutional and process-oriented argument that our federal system divides jurisdiction and review of that jurisdiction between state and national courts, and is designed to have limits on that review. Ultimately Bator's arguments concerning finality rested on an epistemological assumption: no court, whether state or federal, will ever be able to determine in all certainty the factual truths of any case. Regardless of the ability of federal courts to rehear and test the assertion of errors made in determining federal law by state courts, they too will always be unable to determine with complete accuracy whether errors or violations of law occurred. What are the prerequisites for the determination of when, and whether, a lower court's decision should be deemed final, with the caveat that finality is not certainty?

His answers were framed negatively, but they nevertheless provide us with a suggested baseline for accepting finality as an important conceptual tool as we search for limits in criminal procedure adjudication. The first is what he called "failure of process." The test was "whether the conditions and tools of inquiry were such as to assure a reasoned probability that the facts were correctly found and the law correctly applied."[19] Examples of failed processes were those cases in which judges are bribed or guilty pleas are coerced by torture. The second proposition was that jurisdiction matters. In terms of the historical functioning of habeas, jurisdiction had always been a core feature, but Bator's concern here was simply that identifying legal errors before first considering the appropriateness of the relevant court's jurisdiction ignored the federal system's design. By extension, absent a cause to question jurisdiction, errors in a court's decision should not be construed to delay its final decision. As a whole, his argument suggested nothing about the actual innocence of the habeas petitioner. Instead, he was more interested in constructing a process-oriented model of habeas adjudication that sought to determine when, and under what conditions, habeas decisions should be considered final.

Henry Friendly's arguments concerning habeas, which have been equally influential, go beyond the formalism of Paul Bator's process-oriented model.[20] Although Friendly agreed with Bator's larger concerns regarding finality, he went even further, suggesting that the most important criterion for habeas review should be the potential innocence of the petitioner: "collateral attack [habeas in this case] must show a fair probability that, in light of all the evidence, including that alleged to have been illegally admitted (but with due regard to any unreliability of it) and evidence tenably claimed to have been wrongly excluded or to have become available only after trial, the trier of facts would have entertained a reasonable doubt of his guilt."[21] Aside from the more general proposition that innocence, not mere error, should govern habeas, this was a clear broadside against the exclusionary rule laid down in *Mapp v. Ohio* in 1961. Friendly, who at the time had been a federal circuit judge for eleven years, immediately sought to buttress this criterion for a colorable showing of innocence by asserting that in these years as a circuit court judge, he had only seen "a half dozen" cases on habeas in which he actually doubted the guilt of the petitioner. To bring his argument home, he further argued that *Miranda* claims on habeas did not conform to the innocence model.

Friendly found the most compelling support for his argument in two Supreme Court cases. The first was Justice Jackson's opinion in *Brown v. Allen* in 1953. In that opinion, Jackson worried that the already high caseload of frivolous habeas petitions from state to federal courts was preventing these courts from vindicating the few meritorious claims that managed to make their way into federal courts. At the time, Jackson quoted figures that showed 541 habeas petitions from state to federal courts. If 541 was considered "inundating" in 1953, Friendly asserted, what should we make of the approximately 7,500 petitions filed in 1969? He also garnered more recent support for his argument in Justice Black's dissent in *Kaufmann v. United States* in 1969, one of the last habeas cases decided by the Warren Court.[22] In that case, the Court ruled that, consistent with its earlier habeas decisions, Fourth Amendment exclusionary arguments could still trigger habeas review. Black, however, argued that Fourth Amendment claims were "crucially different from many other constitutional rights" because even illegally obtained evidence "often . . . establishes beyond virtually any shadow of a doubt that the defendant is guilty."[23] Black further wondered why it seemed that it was becoming "more difficult to gain acceptance for the proposition that punishment of the guilty is desirable."[24]

Although Bator's and Friendly's arguments were used by subsequent courts to justify exceptions and curtailments to the Warren Court's liberalization of habeas, their arguments are not interchangeable. Bator's process-oriented arguments about finality are most conducive to arguments concerning federalism, specifically the writ's impact on the integrity of state judgments. Even though Bator's epistemological skepticism concerning the elusive quest for error-free trials was not wholly a federalist argument, his point was nevertheless construed by both the Burger and Rehnquist Courts to bolster claims that state court judgments should be accorded more respect, especially as larger theories of federalism were reinvigorated in subsequent years.[25] Friendly's "colorable innocence" argument further served to limit habeas development; it would soon become the ideological basis on which limitations and exceptions were made to the Warren Court's incorporation decisions—specifically *Mapp* and *Miranda*—without formally overruling these cases. The low probability of "actual innocence" would also be applied to death penalty habeas cases such as *Furman v. Georgia, Gregg v. Georgia,* and *McCleskey v. Kemp.*[26]

Aside from Bator, Friendly, and the resurgence of arguments relying on and citing Jackson's *Brown* concurrence, there is yet another source relied on by the Burger and Rehnquist Courts in their habeas rollbacks. After the trilogy of 1963 cases that dramatically enlarged federal habeas review of state cases (*Fay, Townsend,* and *Sanders*), Congress modified the existing habeas corpus statute in 1966. The *Townsend* case in particular provided that "a district judge may, in the ordinary case in which there has been no articulation, properly assume that state courts decided facts and constitutional questions correctly."[27] The congressional codification of the habeas statute slightly modified this language by providing that state findings of fact "shall be presumed correct" by federal courts unless a district judge finds them not to be correct.[28] The key point here, and the one that will be an important source of development in subsequent cases, is the amount of actual discretion that federal district judges have in deciding whether the state trials were free of errors. This modified codification of *Townsend* by Congress in 1966 thus allowed the Burger and Rehnquist Courts to justify their habeas rollbacks as simply applying the 1966 amendments, as district judges, who look to the Supreme Court for guidance, saw increasingly rigid guidelines instituted by the Burger and Rehnquist Courts in determining the types of habeas cases that could be heard.

HABEAS AND THE BURGER COURT

The Burger Court produced piecemeal changes to the Warren Court enlargement of the Great Writ, but three areas in particular—custody, exhaustion, and grounds—were quickly reinterpreted by the Burger Court in an effort to chip away at the writ's availability.

The notion of custody has always been a central component of habeas corpus jurisprudence. The grand rhetoric that accompanies the writ has most often focused our attention squarely on the individual who is being held unconstitutionally. Without the actual physical custody of the individual, however, there is no one to whom a court can direct the presentment of the individual's body (*corpus*) in order to determine the legality of its confinement. The major precedent that governed this concept with respect to habeas up until the Warren Court was *Wales v. Whitney*.[29] Wales was a naval doctor who, at the time of his habeas petition, was stationed in the District of Columbia. He was subsequently charged with a court-martial, and because he was not relieved of his medical duties, he was ordered to stay within the confines of the district. Whitney argued that he was being held unconstitutionally, but the Court, in an opinion by Justice Miller, denied the writ, arguing that Whitney was in no way being held under physical custody pending his court-martial because he was free "to walk the streets of Washington with no one to hinder his movements."[30]

In the 1960s, the Warren Court significantly enlarged the notion of custody as actual physical restraint. In *Jones v. Cunningham*, the Warren Court expanded the notion of custody well beyond the traditional notion.[31] Jones was a recent parolee who had initiated a habeas petition while he was serving a ten-year prison sentence. The original writ was directed to the warden of the penitentiary, the traditional custodian for habeas petitions. However, during the petition proceedings, Jones was paroled. Jones then asked to have his original petition revised to include the parole board, which he now claimed had custody of his body. In a unanimous opinion, the Court reasoned that the common law had "always" envisioned an expansive definition of custody that included children in the custody of their parents and indentured servants who, although not in actual physical custody, were nevertheless held against their will in one form or another: "History, usage, and precedent can leave no doubt that, besides physical imprisonment, there are other restraints on a man's liberty, restraints not shared by the public generally, which have been thought sufficient in the English-speaking world."[32] Although paroled, Jones could not drive a car or leave his county, was forced to report to his parole officer, and was subject to visits from the parole board at his place of employment. The Court considered this custody because his parole "imposes conditions which significantly confine and restrain his freedom."[33]

The Burger Court revisited the custodial aspects of habeas again in the 1973 case of *Hensley v. Municipal Court*.[34] Although it upheld the earlier rulings of the Warren Court with respect to custody, we see in this case a partial revolt by Rehnquist against the Warren Court's custody changes. Hensley was charged with granting doctoral degrees in divinity without a license, in violation of California law. He contended that the law violated his First and Fourteenth Amendment rights. However, his application was made after he was released on his own recognizance by the state court. The question was whether he was still in physical custody. In a 6–3 decision, the Court upheld the expanded notion of custody in *Jones* and allowed the habeas petition to issue. Arguing that habeas had undergone such drastic and expansive change over the last decade, the Court felt that the enlarged notion of custody for criminal matters must keep pace: "We have consistently rejected interpretations of the habeas corpus statute that would suffocate the writ in stifling formalisms or hobble its effectiveness with the manacles of arcane and scholastic procedural requirements."[35] The dissenters in the opinion, Rehnquist, Powell, and Burger, showed early signs of their resistance to the habeas expansions that had occurred over the past ten years. Rehnquist summarily rejected the majority's argument. After arguing that "this is simply not 'custody' in any known sense of the word," Rehnquist said, "The Court apparently feels, such as Faust, that it has in its previous decisions already made its bargain with the devil, and it does not shy from this final step in the rewriting of the statute."[36] Although they are not explicit in the dissent, we can nevertheless see the seeds of change in Rehnquist's dual critique that the Court was rewriting history at the same time that it was overextending the traditional limits of habeas corpus.

If the Court in 1973 remained favorably postured toward toeing the Warren Court's line in terms of the custodial aspects of habeas, the rising opposition nevertheless had enough momentum to start chipping away at another procedural avenue, particularly the amount of discretion that federal habeas courts had with respect to portions of state trials that had already been adjudicated. These cases determine the grounds on which habeas petitions can reach federal courts. Their most recent precedent was *Townsend v. Sain* and the 1966 congressional codification of that decision discussed earlier. Again, while *Townsend* suggested that federal district judges had the ability to review the facts of cases brought on habeas if the judge felt that it would further the "ends of justice," the Court still left this discretion with the particular judge. The congressional codification of that decision in 1966 seemed to accord even more deference to state courts, as it mandated that state court records be given a presumption of correctness unless it could be shown that the factual dispute was not fully resolved in the state courts. This question of just how much deference the federal judge could give to state determinations of fact (for example, the constitutionality of confessions, jury makeup, and adequate counsel) was answered in *LaValle v. Delle Rose.*[37] Here, the district judge was confronted with a habeas petition in which Delle Rose argued that his original confessions to police were coerced and his detention was unconstitutional. The charge that the confessions were coerced was denied by subsequent state courts.

The question the Court faced was the extent to which, under the 1966 codifications, state courts' fact-finding processes should be presumed correct by federal habeas judges. When the original state court had reviewed the allegations of coerced confessions, it rejected them, but it gave no sustained reason for its decision. For the majority of the Court, this was enough to sustain the presumption of correctness as they read the 1966 statute. In support of the conclusion, the Court took into consideration the fact that the state judge's rejection of the claim occurred before *Miranda v. Arizona* and *Escobedo v. Illinois* and thus relied on the "totality of circumstances" test to determine that no Sixth Amendment rights were violated. The dissent, which consisted of all of the justices who were on the Court during the Warren Court's criminal justice revolution, saw the majority's opinion as a clear repudiation not only of the 1966 statute, but also of the goals of *Townsend* and the other habeas cases from the 1963 term.

In a footnote, Justice Marshall took on the majority concerning what he perceived to be an overly narrow and ultimately rights-contracting reading of habeas: "*Townsend* indicates that 'the district judge *may,* in the ordinary case in which there has been no articulation, *properly assume*' that the state court reached a constitutionally permissible conclusion. Today, however, the Court effectively indicates that the district court *must assume* in such cases that the proper standard was applied. . . . These matters are properly left largely to the discretion of the district judge."[38] Marshall argued that because the state court judge who determined that the confessions were adequate made no argument or justification as to why he thought they were acceptable, the federal judge should rehear all of the arguments on the question of Delle Rose's confession. The difference in the relative degree of deference toward state courts and their appellate processes had obviously changed as a result of this case. The majority reasoned that because the state judge who reheard the evidence to determine if the confession was coerced did not find any violation, then it should be determined as correct. Many of the same states' rights arguments that had been made for years about the integrity of state courts and their ability to determine whether constitutional rights had been violated had now found a rather sympathetic Court, willing to read the 1966 statute that codified some of the most drastic habeas expansions in a very narrow way. A simple rejection by a state judge rehearing a constitutional claim was now all that was needed to satisfy *Townsend* and the 1966 congressional statutes in the eyes of the Burger Court.

Another technical area of habeas that was slowly refined by the early Burger Court was exhaustion, which required that federal habeas petitions first show that available state procedures for appeal (as well as state habeas processes) had been fully exhausted before the federal appeal could be entertained. The exhaustion requirement, which has its roots in the 1886 case of *Ex parte Royall,* was in many ways a doctrine developed in the wake of mobilization by federalist concerns against what was perceived as an imbalance in traditional state–federal relations.[39]

Even Justice Brennan, in a relatively uncharacteristic 1971 decision, held true to these basic requirements. In *Picard v. Connor,* the defendant had originally been indicted by a Massachusetts grand jury under the name of John Doe.[40] At a later date, the state amended the indictment to reflect the defendant's real name. He then petitioned for a writ of habeas corpus in state court, then in federal court, arguing that the process of amendment to the indictment violated both Massachusetts law and the Fifth Amendment. The federal district court denied his habeas petition, but the federal appeals court granted it on equal protection grounds, a claim that Connor and his attorney had never made. Speaking for the majority, Brennan overturned the appeals court's decision granting habeas, arguing that at a bare minimum, the state must have a full and fair opportunity to hear constitutional challenges. Moreover, the appeals court should never have asserted a constitutional violation (the equal protection claim) when the defendant had never raised it. Brennan spoke of the exhaustion rule's role in "our federal system." Quoting *Darr v. Burford,* he said it would be "unseemly in our dual system of government to upset a state court conviction without an opportunity to the state courts to correct a constitutional violation."[41] In dissent, Justice Douglas pithily stated that "in this case we carry the rule of exhaustion of state remedies too far."[42] For Douglas, due process and equal protection in habeas appeals from state prisoners were "not mutually exclusive" because "they stem from our American ideal of fairness."[43] The fact that only the due process claim was raised by the defendant, not the equal protection claim introduced by the appeals court, was not sufficient to prevent habeas from issuing.

Though Brennan disagreed in that case, his reading of exhaustion would not continue to be so literal. In *Murch v. Mottram,* exhaustion, as well as the related concern of "deliberate bypass" of state remedies, was considered by the Court.[44] The defendant in the case originally filed a federal habeas petition to challenge his conviction and confinement, but then amended it to challenge the conditions of his parole. In a 6–3 decision, the Court ruled that the defendant deliberately bypassed established state procedures, a choice that precluded federal habeas review of his charges. The state of Maine, where his convictions and parole were adjudicated, required that constitutional challenges be argued all at once. Because the defendant chose to file successive and factually different challenges, the Supreme Court argued that he was trying to dispute parts of his conviction "piecemeal." Justifying its denial of habeas, the Court said, "In this sensitive and ofttimes strained area of federal-state relations, a state prisoner may not deliberately 'elect' not to comply with the interpretation of the state procedural statute."[45] The Court explicitly read the Warren Court's decision in *Fay v. Noia* in a restrictive way that, again, seemed to limit the discretion that federal district judges had in redetermining factual matters of constitutional challenges. In *Fay*, Brennan suggested that it was up to federal district judges to determine whether or not the defendant deliberately bypassed state procedures on habeas when federal claims were raised, and the presumption was that the federal judge would hold a de novo trial to determine the facts for himself when considering a claim that the issue had already been fully resolved by a state court judge. For the Burger Court, this same standard continued to apply, except that the Court would now be more willing to accept determinations that were more deferential to state courts' decisions on federal constitutional matters, at least when these technical issues of exhaustion and bypass were at issue.

Another somewhat technical but no less important area of habeas review is the question of whether a defendant has grounds to bring a federal habeas petition even if he pleaded guilty, and even if his constitutional challenge on federal habeas was never raised during his state appellate trials. These questions, as well as the Burger Court's willingness to hear challenges on habeas considering race, were considered in *Tollett v. Henderson* in 1973.[46] The defendant, a black man, was convicted in Tennessee in 1948, and with advice from his counsel, he pled guilty and accepted a ninety-nine-year prison sentence— a sentence presumably less drastic than the alternative, death. Twenty years later, he filed a habeas petition attacking his conviction on the grounds that the grand jury that indicted him excluded and discriminated against blacks in its selection of grand jury members. The majority opinion, authored by Rehnquist, held that Henderson's petition must be denied for two reasons.

First, although Rehnquist admitted that discrimination in the composition of grand and petit juries had been held to be unconstitutional since *Strauder v. West Virginia* in 1880, none of the challenges brought under these cases came from defendants who actually pled guilty.[47] For Rehnquist, there was a distinction between those who are convicted or charged with a crime by unconstitutional grand and petit juries but nevertheless claim innocence, and the defendant in this case, where innocence was not formally questioned in the habeas appeal. Rehnquist ruled that a guilty plea should distinguish this case unless the defendant could show that his attorney's advice was "outside the range of competence demanded of attorneys in criminal cases."[48]

Second, the fact that there were only allegations of discrimination in the selection of the grand jury that indicted Henderson, and not the jury that convicted him, prevented habeas from issuing. In effect, asserted constitutional violations that antedate guilty pleas were off the table. As Rehnquist summed up the entire case, "When a criminal defendant has solemnly admitted in open court that he is in fact guilty of the offense with which he is charged, he may not thereafter raise independent claims relating to the deprivation of constitutional rights that occurred prior to the entry of the guilty plea."[49]

Marshall's dissent painted a quite different picture concerning the role of race. As mentioned above, one of Rehnquist's arguments was that Henderson's attorney did not raise claims of grand jury discrimination during the original trial and appellate process in 1948. Rehnquist ruled that the attorney's actions were within the range of competence for attorney conduct. Marshall pointed out that one of Rehnquist's justifications for this belief was a statement from a Tennessee judge in the state habeas proceedings who excused Henderson's attorney from error in not originally claiming jury discrimination. The appellate judge remarked, "No lawyer in this State would have ever thought of objecting to the fact that Negroes did not serve on the Grand Jury in Tennessee in 1948."[50] Marshall contended instead that Henderson's attorney either was unfamiliar with the case law in the state at the time, which included many similar challenges from similarly situated blacks, or simply was negligent. Moreover, the fact that a guilty plea was made by a defendant within the larger discriminatory practices of the Tennessee criminal justice system in the 1940s rendered the plea illegitimate. Marshall claimed that "plea bargaining rests on an exchange," and if the state had such a monolithic discriminatory practice, then "no bargain [the plea] is possible."[51]

Moving past the more technical aspects of exhaustion, grounds, and standing, in 1973 the Court in *Schneckloth v. Bustamonte* began to tackle the habeas jurisprudence of the Warren Court that specifically dealt with the incorporation of the Bill of Rights. Aside from *Miranda* and *Escobedo*, *Mapp v. Ohio*'s exclusionary rule, and its larger role in the criminal justice system, had been brewing as a source of controversy since *Kaufman v. United States* in 1969.[52] In dissent in *Kaufman*, Black argued that the Fourth Amendment, and the exclusionary rule gleaned from it, should not prevent the prosecution of the patently guilty criminal.[53] *Schneckloth* addressed this issue with the finality and innocence arguments of Bator and Friendly, which increasingly became the intellectual foundation of the Court's new habeas jurisprudence.

Bustamonte, along with five other Hispanic men, was a passenger in a car when it was stopped for traffic violations. The driver of the car could not produce a valid driver's license, and the officer asked all of the occupants to step out of the vehicle. The officer then asked another man (not Bustamonte) if he could search the car. By all accounts, even those of the other passengers, the driver casually consented to the search, and even helped the officer open the car's glove compartment and trunk. During the search of the trunk, stolen checks from a car wash were discovered. Ultimately, Bustamonte was charged with a crime. Bustamonte appealed his conviction in the California state courts, where it was upheld, and then filed a habeas petition in federal court, claiming that the search violated his Fourth Amendment, Fourteenth Amendment, and *Miranda* rights. Although consent was given, it was given without knowledge of these rights. Only the last habeas petition to the ninth circuit court of appeals was successful. The Supreme Court reversed the decision.[54]

The majority opinion, authored by Justice Potter Stewart, only addressed the relationship of consent to the exclusionary rule in regard to these types of noncustodial searches. Stewart distinguished *Miranda* by arguing that none of the defendants was in custody. He further argued that *Miranda* specifically excepted these types of searches from requiring the now-familiar enumerations of rights. The consent given to law enforcement still needed to be reviewed, but the "totality of circumstances" of the consent and the search must be taken into consideration by the judge determining constitutionality: "While knowledge of the right to refuse consent is one factor to be taken into account, the government need not establish such knowledge as the *sine qua non* of an effective consent." For Stewart, the question was one of balancing the needs of police in effectuating searches and guaranteeing that these searches were free from coercion. Most important for Stewart was his belief that no "talismanic test" could be devised to determine consent. Therefore, the strict application of the exclusionary rule was detrimental.

The concurring opinion of Burger, Powell, and Rehnquist was an attack on the exclusionary rule and on the Warren Court habeas decisions more generally. Just as important was their assertion of actual innocence, finality, and federalism as the new criteria for habeas. Throughout the opinion, Bator and Friendly were heavily referenced. Powell began the opinion with what he felt was a much-needed revision of the revisionist history of habeas that was the cornerstone of the Warren Court's enlargement of the writ in the 1963 trilogy of habeas cases. Drawing on Dallin Oaks's work on habeas in the early American colonies, Powell argued that the historic common-law notion of the Great Writ had always favored deference in jurisdiction to the original court where the case was adjudicated (in this case, state courts generally). The circuit court's grant of habeas to Bustamonte "goes well beyond the traditional purpose of the writ of habeas corpus" because the proper historic role of the writ is "tempered by a due regard for the finality of the committing court."[55] He then went on to criticize Brennan's *Fay* opinion, which he characterized as rereading the history of habeas as an ever-increasing mechanism by which the unconstitutionality of restraint was vindicated by federal courts. "If this were correct," he said, "the wide scope accorded the writ would have arguable support. . . . However, recent scholarship has cast grave doubt on *Fay*'s version."[56] He relied on arguments that suggested that deference had traditionally been given to lower courts (state or federal) and their decisions, and to support this position further, he relied on John Marshall's opinion in *Ex parte Watkins,* where Marshall proclaimed that "the judgment of a court of record whose jurisdiction is final, is as conclusive on all the world as the judgment of this court would be."[57] Introducing the language of "finality" into the analysis, Powell conceded that the issues of "federal–state" relations did not confront the nineteenth-century Court as they do now. He then quickly explained away the seemingly expansive language of the Habeas Corpus Act of 1867 by quoting Paul Bator, who argued that the Reconstruction Congress did not intend to "tear habeas corpus entirely out of the context of its historical meaning and scope and convert it into an ordinary writ of error with respect to all federal questions in all criminal cases."[58] This was further confirmed, he argued, by Congress' and the court's habeas restrictions in 1884 and 1885. Although he detailed the changes to habeas by the Court from *Frank* to *Brown,* suggesting the Court obviously should not feel "imprisoned by every particular of habeas corpus as it existed in the late 18th and 19th centuries," Powell nevertheless held to the idea that finality in habeas should be a core feature of its adjudication.[59]

The arguments of unconstitutionality in this case, specifically the exclusionary rule and the *Miranda*-type warnings that should accompany noncustodial searches, did not fall within the historical functions of the writ. Claiming that "recent decisions . . . have tended to depreciate the importance of finality . . . in criminal cases," Powell argued that these cases provide inappropriate guides for distinguishing between those cases where an "evolution" in habeas might be appropriate and those cases where it was not.[60] Fourth Amendment claims fell into this latter category.

On top of the Bator-style finality argument, Powell then added the Friendly-style innocence argument to the process of distinguishing search-and-seizure cases. Powell nevertheless conceded that "history reveals no exact tie of the writ of habeas corpus to a constitutional claim relating to innocence or guilt."[61] This was a crucial admission, and one that suggests that like the Warren Court, the Burger Court was not afraid to tread new ground in constructing historically questionable accounts of constitutional developments. Although innocence was not historically identifiable as a criterion in habeas's history, Powell nevertheless felt that the Court was now "faced . . . with the task of accommodating the historic respect for the finality of the judgment of the committing court with recent Court expansions of the role of the writ. This accommodation can best be achieved . . . by recourse to the central reason for habeas corpus: the affording of means, through an extraordinary writ, or redressing an *unjust* incarceration."[62] Invoking what he called a "perceptive analysis," he quoted directly from Henry Friendly in search of a rule for distinguishing between proper and improper uses of habeas: "With a few important exceptions, convictions should be subject to collateral attack [habeas] only when the prisoner supplements his constitutional plea with a colorable claim of innocence." The exclusionary rule as applied in this case detracted from this important aspect of habeas. Bustamonte was guilty of stealing checks, regardless of the constitutionality of the search. The continued application of habeas in exclusionary precustody cases thus offended the system itself: "Habeas corpus review of search and seizure claims thus brings a deficiency of our system of criminal justice into sharp focus: a convicted defendant asserting no constitutional claim bearing on innocence and relying solely on an alleged unlawful search, is now entitled to federal habeas review of state conviction and the likelihood of release if the reviewing court concludes that a search was unlawful."[63]

Finally, Powell's arguments also used a federalism component. The Warren Court's habeas decisions "tend[ed] to undermine the values inherent in our federal system of government . . . and render[s] the actions of state courts a serious disrespect in derogation of the constitutional balance between the two systems." Much like the American Bar Association, the National Association of Attorneys General, and the American Law Institute over the preceding decades, Powell relied on statements by the National Center for State Courts' president, Justice Paul Reardon, for evidence of the insulting impact of habeas on state courts and judges who claimed "humiliation of review from the full bench of the highest state court [of Massachusetts]."[64]

With this new link between the purported recovery of habeas's common-law roots in finality and claims of a guilt/innocence dichotomy now read into the writ as a remedy for the Warren Court's revisionism, the Court seemed to be set to deal a final blow to the exclusionary rule and its main vehicle of adjudication in the form of the Great Writ. All that was needed was a true majority on the bench to achieve the desired change.

STONE v. POWELL *AND JUDICIAL INDEPENDENCE*

When the majority-formed change came, it was in arguably the most important habeas case of the Burger Court: *Stone v. Powell*, along with its companion case, *Wolff v. Rice*.[65] All of the Nixon appointees, as well as Justice Potter Stewart, joined in the majority's opinion. Chief Justice Burger wrote a concurring opinion that, although in complete agreement with the majority, argued that the exclusionary rule as a whole needed complete revision.[66] *Powell* shows how the Court partly responded to larger regime changes. Even though a sympathetic Court majority was willing to implement many of the dominant regime's anti–Warren Court changes to habeas, sympathetic courts will never entirely sacrifice their fundamental power to review cases through habeas. In many ways, *Stone* formally reversed the Warren Court's due process cases that struck at the core of state criminal procedure processes, but not without some significant exceptions.[67]

To many, the substance of both cases brought in *Powell* was a quintessential example of the Fourth Amendment exclusionary rule and habeas run amok. The defendants had their state habeas cases denied, and then both applied for federal habeas review in the federal district courts, where they were again denied. However, the circuit court granted their habeas appeals and argued that the evidence used to convict them of murder was illegally obtained. *Powell's* case in particular signaled the extent to which the Burger Court was willing to permit wide latitude in police searches.

Powell was convicted of murdering the wife of a liquor store owner during a robbery in California. Police officers in Henderson, Nevada, arrested Powell many hours later. The officers, with no knowledge of Powell's involvement in the California robbery, stopped and arrested Powell for violating Nevada vagrancy and loitering ordinances. As a result of the arrest, a gun was found in Powell's possession; it was ultimately linked to the murder.[68] Powell's attorneys argued that the Nevada ordinance was unconstitutional, and that as a result, the evidence seized was inadmissible.[69]

Justice Powell began the opinion in much the same way that he began the opinion in *Schneckloth:* by reciting his understanding of historical case law development of habeas. Again, his reading of the expansion of the writ was wholly negative, at least in the sense that the earlier due process cases, such as *Frank* and *Moore*, only corrected obvious due process violations, while later cases from the Warren Court, especially *Fay* and *Kaufman*, overextended the proper historical reach of the writ. The Warren Court's enlargements were only complicated by the fact that the Court's incorporation decisions from

Mapp to *Miranda* now added more rights that could be challenged on habeas. Particularly with respect to *Mapp*'s exclusionary rule, the Court had not had "occasion fully to consider the validity" of the view that federal habeas should issue for state prisoners who, though convicted, challenge their convictions on Fourth Amendment search-and-seizure grounds. Powell summarily rejected the view that this was the proper role of habeas in Fourth Amendment jurisprudence: "We hold, therefore, that where the State has provided an opportunity for full and fair litigation of a Fourth Amendment claim, the Constitution does not require that a state prisoner be granted federal habeas corpus relief on the ground that evidence obtained in an unconstitutional search or seizure was introduced at the trial."[70] This explicitly overturned the *Kaufman* rule, which held that the "federal habeas remedy extends to state prisoners alleging that unconstitutionally obtained evidence was admitted against them at trial."[71]

The deference to state courts was evident in Powell's reversal, but importantly, the Court did not completely block habeas petitions from state prisoners. If the state did not provide a full and fair opportunity for review of these constitutional claims, federal habeas could still issue. The limits were instead ones crafted with deference to state courts' ability to review decisions with the objectives of finality in mind, as well as their ability to adjudicate fundamental issues of due process. Without completely jettisoning incorporationist doctrine, the Court nevertheless deferred significantly to state adjudication of these rights.

After Powell's new rules for habeas were announced, he addressed the use of the exclusionary rule. The question of the relationship between habeas and *Mapp*-style arguments was answered by "weighing the utility of the exclusionary rule against the costs of extending it to collateral review of the Fourth Amendment."[72] For Powell, these costs were too great in criminal trials because the "attention of the participants therein, are diverted from the ultimate question of guilt or innocence that should be the central concern in a criminal proceeding."[73] Also, the supposed utility of the exclusionary rule as a deterrent to unconstitutional police conduct was further perverted by appeals and delays through habeas, specifically because the conduct that was to be corrected had sometimes occurred years before the constitutional question was decided by courts. Again, the Court was not arguing that the exclusionary rule was no longer a valid constitutional rule, but only that collateral challenges through habeas are now curtailed because these concerns had already been adjudicated.[74] In doing so, the Court relied directly on Bator's finality argument and Friendly's and Justice Black's guilt/innocence assertions.

Larger federalism arguments were also advanced as justification for undoing federal habeas review. In answering the defendant's claims that the exclusionary rule provided an "educative" role in deterring and supervising police, Powell responded with a classical explanation of the role of state courts in the federal system:

The argument is that state courts cannot be trusted to effectuate Fourth Amendment values through fair application of the rule. . . . Despite differences in institutional environment and the unsympathetic attitude to federal constitutional claims of some state judges in years past, we are unwilling to assume that there now exists a general lack of appropriate sensitivity to constitutional rights in the trial and appellate courts of the several States. State courts, like federal courts, have a constitutional obligation to safeguard personal liberties and to uphold federal law. In sum, there is "no intrinsic reason why the fact that a man is a federal judge should make him more competent, or conscientious, or learned with respect to the [consideration of Fourth Amendment claims] than his neighbor in the state courthouse."[75]

The dissenting opinions in this case, all authored by Warren Court justices, recognized the attack. Brennan in particular portrayed the majority's opinion as effectively ushering in a brand of federalism that he had worked so hard to correct:

Enforcement of *federal* constitutional rights that redress constitutional violations directed against the "guilty" is a particular function of *federal* habeas review, lest judges trying the "morally unworthy" be tempted not to execute the supreme law of the land. State judges popularly elected may have difficulty resisting popular pressures not experienced by federal judges given lifetime tenure designed to immunize them from such influences, and the federal habeas statutes reflect the congressional judgment that such detached federal review is a salutary safeguard.[76]

Such "salutary safeguards" were properly located in the federal courts through habeas review, regardless of the guilt or innocence of the defendant. For Brennan, the greater evil would not be freeing the guilty on habeas, but rather offending the Constitution by the Court's complicity in preventing the vindication of fundamental rights such as the Fourth Amendment's exclusionary rule.

The next substantial revision to the Warren Court's habeas jurisprudence, and one that again turned on reinvigorated notions of federalism, occurred in *Wainwright v. Sykes* in 1977.[77] The defendant in *Sykes* failed to raise a constitutional claim in his state trials and instead raised it in the federal habeas phase. The state of Florida, however, had specific procedural rules that mandated that defendants object to perceived constitutional violations (coerced statements and confessions) during trial, or their claims could not be raised on appeal.[78] Rehnquist's opinion affirmed the procedural requirements of Florida, holding that they amounted to adequate and independent state grounds, thus denying the habeas writ that was brought to examine the constitutionality of the defendant's statements.

Importantly, the *Sykes* court did not preclude the availability of federal habeas generally, though it did continue to carve out exceptions and limitations. The Court still made room for federal habeas review, but it also developed a "cause and prejudice" test to limit state habeas appeals. Defendants seeking habeas who did not conform to independent state procedures in raising constitutional claims in their state trials must now show adequate cause as to why they bypassed state rules, as well as demonstrate that the violation caused "actual prejudice" to their trial.[79] Rehnquist distinguished parts of *Fay v. Noia* as narrowed, but not overturned, by the decision: "It is the sweeping language of *Fay v. Noia*, going far beyond the facts of the case eliciting it, which we today reject."[80] Florida's contemporaneous-objection rule, if decided with the broad rule of *Fay*, would not respect the "coordinate jurisdiction within the federal system" and would not allow its benefits to accrue because it prevented successive appeals on habeas and contributed to "finality."[81]

The increased respect the Burger Court accorded to state criminal processes was also buttressed by a concurrent deference to states' civil processes and institutions just two years later. In *Moore v. Sims*, a complicated child-abuse custody case, Rehnquist again relied on notions of federalism and comity to hold that federal district courts should not entertain habeas petitions from state civil proceedings when those proceedings were still being adjudicated.[82] In this case, the parents of the children who were taken into custody by state officials on suspicion of child abuse filed a habeas petition in federal court while they were already involved in civil litigation challenging the legality of the state procedures that took custody of their abused children. Linking civil to criminal habeas enlargement over the last two decades, Rehnquist stated, "The basic concern—that threat to our federal system posed by displacement of state courts by those of the National Government—is also fully applicable to civil proceedings."[83] State criminal courts, state governments and their political subdivisions, and state civil institutions, such as the Texas Department of Human Services, were now accorded the respect that the Court thought they deserved from the overreaching enlargement of habeas corpus.

The same year, race and habeas were again linked with federalism concerns, although this time egalitarian racial concerns were just barely vindicated. We see again in the dissenting opinions that notions of finality and guilt/inno-

cence played a large role. In *Rose v. Mitchell,* the defendants claimed Fourteenth Amendment equal protection violations against the state of Tennessee
in its selection of foremen for grand juries.[84] The charge was that Tennessee
discriminated against blacks, as testimony of grand jurors revealed that no
blacks had been selected in recent memory. The Court ruled that equal protection violations could be brought on habeas to federal district courts for review,
but that the defendants in this case had failed to show that Tennessee's selection procedures were discriminatory. However, the dissents and the partial
concurrences in the case centered on the use of habeas in cases of factual guilt.
Rehnquist in particular agreed that habeas was the proper vehicle to determine
whether jury selection practices violated the equal protection clause, but he
argued that alleged discriminatory practices in grand juries, which only serve
to establish prima facie evidence that charges and trial are necessary, should be
excepted. This argument goes to the core of the continued assertion by some
on the Court that guilt and innocence, not general rights protection, should
determine habeas adjudication. The defendants in *Rose* did not charge that the
jury that convicted them was selected in a discriminatory method, but only the
grand jury that indicted them. Justice Stewart's opinion, in which Rehnquist
concurred, argued that a grand jury "is not a proceeding in which the guilt or
innocence of a defendant is determined. . . . Any possible prejudice to the defendant . . . disappears when a constitutionally valid jury trial later finds him
guilty beyond a reasonable doubt."[85]

Three more habeas cases over the next six years, leading up to the end of
Warren Burger's tenure as chief justice, specified even further the extent to
which the Court had chipped away habeas from within the very Warren Court
opinions that enlarged it. In *Rose v. Lundy* in 1982, the exhaustion rule was
again confirmed as the controlling procedural limitation on habeas from state
to federal courts.[86] However, the Warren Court holdovers (Marshall, Brennan,
and White) wrote separate dissents for the majority's new interpretations of
the exhaustion rule, which consisted of arguments that neither party in the
case had raised.

Newly appointed associate justice Sandra Day O'Connor's majority opinion
laid out a new, more stringent rule concerning the exhaustion of state remedies
in federal habeas cases. In an effort to prevent what she called "piecemeal habeas litigation," she ruled that a federal district court judge, who was presented
with a habeas petition from a state prisoner after some of the challenges had
been exhausted, should dismiss the writ and remand the challenges back to
the respective state court for adjudication of the unexhausted challenges. This
part of the opinion was acceptable even to Brennan and Marshall. However,

O'Connor also asserted that the prisoner now ran the risk of "abusing" habeas when he subsequently filed another petition in federal court. This was, once again, a tightening of Warren Court habeas jurisprudence. In *Sanders,* one of the habeas trilogy cases in 1963, the Court said it would not countenance the deliberate withholding of certain claims in successive petitions to federal courts in order to "vex, harass, or delay."[87] O'Connor's new rule effectively required not only that state remedies be completely exhausted before federal courts would hear claims, but also that a defendant make all of his or her constitutional arguments in a single habeas petition. If he or she did not, then the courts could, if so inclined, rule that the claims in the writ were forfeited. Again, her argument was based on the assumption that these new rules will "promote comity."[88]

That same term, O'Connor again wrote for the Court in limiting habeas access, this time applying the "cause and prejudice" test developed in *Wainwright v. Sykes.* In *Engle v. Isaac,* the Court was presented with the question of retroactive application of state criminal procedure rules. Isaac was charged, tried, and convicted of homicide in Ohio. After his trial, conviction, and appeals, Ohio changed its rules for explaining to juries how the concept of burden of proof was to be interpreted. Obviously, at the time of trials and appeals, Isaac's lawyers never raised objections to the jury instructions because the new rule was not in effect. In Isaac's federal habeas petition, he argued that Ohio's new rule should be applied retroactively and that he should either be given a new trial or be freed. The majority summarily denied the habeas petition, arguing that there was no "cause or prejudice" shown during the trial, and that retroactive application of state-level procedural rules was not appropriate through habeas.[89]

O'Connor began her opinion with rhetorical deference to the Great Writ, suggesting that it "indisputably holds an honored position in our jurisprudence." However, she immediately qualified this: "We have always recognized, however, that the Great Writ entails significant costs . . . [and] extends the ordeal of trial for both society and the accused."[90] The adverb *always* is, of course, an arguable assertion, but one that the Court was now determined to advance and prove. Her footnote relied on none other than Henry Friendly, whom she quoted further in support of her argument: "The proverbial man from Mars would surely think we must consider our system of criminal justice terribly bad if we are willing to tolerate such efforts at undoing judgments of conviction."[91] The costs to society were too great to continue to allow habeas petitions to challenge convictions. Just as importantly, these costs come at the expense of federalism: "The Great Writ imposes special costs on our federal system. The States possess primary authority for defining and enforcing criminal law. In criminal trials they also hold the initial responsibility for vindicating constitutional rights. Federal intrusions into state criminal trials frustrate both the States' sovereign power to punish offenders and their good-faith attempts to honor constitutional rights."[92]

In one of the last habeas opinions of the Burger Court, it once more affirmed its strict interpretation of the exhaustion rule and its deference to state procedural rules. Again writing for the court in *Murray v. Carrier,* O'Connor ruled that an attorney's failure to raise a claim in the state court trial and appeal process precluded him from raising it in a federal habeas petition. Relying on the cause and prejudice test developed by Rehnquist, she argued that the attorney's failure to raise the claim was not prevented by the state courts.[93]

The failure of attorneys to raise constitutional claims, and the Court's unwillingness to view this as grounds for habeas access to federal courts, continued to provoke controversy in habeas throughout the next decade. Especially with respect to death penalty cases, in which minorities and indigent defendants are at the mercy of low-paid and overworked public defenders who are not always familiar with labyrinthine state procedural rules, these three cases made it more difficult to have federal district courts review the constitutional claims of state prisoners. *Murray* in particular seemed to relegate concerns that state-level trial errors that might reveal a defendant's innocence to the now well-developed concerns for finality, federalism, and process.

THE REAGAN ADMINISTRATION'S HABEAS OFFENSIVE

Congressional, executive, and interest group proposals to limit habeas corpus during the Burger and Rehnquist Courts serve as further evidence of the attempts by the Republican regime to transform habeas corpus.[94] Although these proposals were initially unsuccessful, they nevertheless represented an attempt to redefine the underlying principles that conservatives argued should govern access to the Great Writ. These proposals confirmed the more general notions of finality, actual innocence, and renewed respect for states' rights that had been slowly mounting since the late 1960s. They also show that Court-centered conceptions of habeas access and purpose are determined as much by extrajudicial political pressures as they are by strictly legal and Court-centered considerations. Even with these pointed attacks by the Republican regime, however, the Court never fully capitulated to the most drastic restrictions of habeas by regime leaders.

One case in particular reflected the drive during the beginning of the Reagan administration to reform habeas through a call for extrajudicial action.

United States ex rel. Jones v. Franzen, authored by circuit court judge Richard Posner, was a habeas case that had risen through the ranks of the Illinois court system and the federal district court.[95] Jones and others, who were already jailed prisoners, were convicted of stabbing to death three prison guards during a riot. They alleged numerous constitutional errors in their state trial as well as in their appeals. All were denied. They then filed habeas writs in federal district court, where, without even looking at the claims of alleged constitutional errors, the district court denied habeas. The three-judge court of appeals reversed the lower court's denial of habeas and ordered that the evidence in question be reviewed.

Posner asserted that the only reason he voted to grant the writ (thereby overturning the denial on the district level) was that as a circuit court judge, he was bound by the Supreme Court's opinion in *Townsend,* as well as by Congress' codification of that opinion's rule that federal courts were not bound by state courts' conclusions as to facts that implicate constitutional violations. In the first paragraph, Posner explained that he thought "it unfortunate as a matter of fundamental principle that we have to reverse the dismissal of the petition for habeas corpus in this case." "I want to explain why I think it unfortunate," he continued, "in the hope that Congress will consider reforms in the habeas corpus statute."[96] Posner argued that *Townsend* was a "product of its time," created to monitor and check Southern state recalcitrance to the Warren Court's larger race and incorporation agenda, but the requirements of *Townsend* were now "outmoded" because it is "doubtful that the standard laid down in Townsend" would be decided the same way by the current Court:

Townsend was a product of its time. The southern states' resistance to court-ordered desegregation had induced a widespread skepticism concerning the willingness of government in those states, including the courts, to protect the federal constitutional rights of their black citizens; and blacks were then as they are now disproportionately represented in the population of criminal defendants. Moreover, the process whereby the Supreme Court has progressively constitutionalized state criminal procedure, by reading the criminal-procedure provisions of the Bill of Rights expansively and applying the expansive readings to the states through the Fourteenth Amendment, was then just beginning, and the number and variety of constitutional claims that state prisoners would be able to raise in habeas corpus proceedings was [*sic*] not foreseen. Times have changed.[97]

For Posner, the defendant in the case had a fair opportunity to raise his claims— and in fact, he did raise them in a full appeal. His frustration was with the continued appeals and rehearings that habeas had now produced. His opinion ended, as it began, with a plea: "If this is what Congress wants, it is not for us to complain; but I cannot believe it is what Congress has ever wanted."[98]

Congress and the executive heard Posner's plea. As Larry Yackle has detailed, at least seven different bills from 1981 to 1982 were introduced in Congress that in some way sought to reform habeas corpus. Not surprisingly, considering the recent resurgence of federalism arguments on the bench concerning the writ, most of the legislation originated in the Senate under the guidance of Strom Thurmond of South Carolina.[99] One bill, S. 2216, the Habeas Corpus Reform Act of 1982, was indicative of the Reagan administration's larger approach to habeas reform. Attorney General William French Smith submitted a letter to the Senate detailing the administration's goals with the bill. While asserting that the administration was "firmly committed to the enforcement and protection of federal rights including the federal rights of criminal defendants in state proceedings," he went on to say that "there is no justification in the present day for the availability of federal habeas corpus as a routine means of review of state criminal convictions."[100] Smith's justifications for reforming habeas were threefold. His first argument was that many states had since reformed their appeal processes to reflect changed notions of due process, most likely as a result of the incorporation decisions of the Warren Court. Second, federal habeas offends the "integrity of state procedures." And third, because state courts are "trustworthy expositors of federal law," they are fully capable of vindicating and overseeing the protection of fundamental national rights.[101]

Although this bill and others during the Reagan years never became law, the administration was not deterred and continued to argue for new limits to habeas. From 1986 to 1988, the Department of Justice's Office of Legal Policy produced a series of reports to Attorney General Edwin Meese detailing its vision for constitutional governance more broadly and habeas reform specifically.[102] Reading the historical function of the Great Writ much differently than the Warren Court had, the report argued that legislation should be enacted that returned habeas to its proper role in the federal system.

As other regimes had before, the ascendant conservative Republican regime sought to reinterpret habeas's historical development, a necessary prerequisite to achieving a conception of the writ that conformed to the regime's conceptions of constitutional governance.[103] The report's general proposition was that there were now two habeas corpus writs. The original writ, which was now only a shadow of its former self, was only ever meant to issue before trials, and then only in cases involving extraordinary detentions by executives. This is the writ, the report argued, that the Framers had in mind when they enumerated the habeas provisions in Article I, section 9, of the Constitution.[104] The writ that had developed since the Warren Court, however, was something quite different. Because of the Warren Court's "innovative decisions which held, contrary to earlier precedent, that most of the specific provisions of the Bill of Rights applied in state proceedings," the traditional limitations of jurisdiction had been jettisoned, and now any and all seeming constitutional violations were repeatedly reviewed at both the state and federal levels.[105]

Just as important was the report's reliance on the new legal academic readings of habeas that had been developing since the early 1960s. Paul Bator's argument concerning finality, with its concomitant deference to state courts' findings of fact and adjudication of federal constitutional questions, was prominently featured. So too were Henry Friendly's arguments about innocence. Noting that "the objectives of accuracy and substantive justice" were "disserved" by the current form of habeas, the report was firm in its conviction that the Court should now direct its habeas jurisprudence to the task of ensuring "that guilt shall not escape or innocence suffer."[106]

The report ultimately suggested the elimination of habeas altogether, a position that former attorney general William French Smith had staked out during Reagan's first term. However, the report did suggest limitations in lieu of complete abolishment, including limiting appeals to one year from state court conviction, more deference to state courts' determinations of facts relating to alleged constitutional violations, and limits on habeas for Fifth and Sixth Amendment claims, among others.[107] Tellingly, the report suggested that limited forms of Supreme Court review of state court decisions, which were certainly necessary at times, not take the name "habeas corpus"; instead, Congress and the Court should refer to this type of review as a "writ of federal review."[108]

The same year as the Department of Justice report, former Supreme Court justice Lewis Powell was appointed by Justice Rehnquist to lead the Ad Hoc Committee on Federal Habeas Corpus in Capital Cases.[109] The report of this committee, as well as Powell's published remarks to the American Bar Association the following year, made clear the frustration that was felt by many with the time delays in death penalty cases by habeas corpus appeals from state prisoners.[110] Powell argued that the deterrent effects of the death penalty since *Gregg*, which allowed states to resume capital punishment, were stymied by habeas petitions in federal courts.[111] He argued that "the evidence . . . is compelling that a large majority of our people consider that capital punishment is appropriate for certain crimes," and that the delay in fulfilling this felt need stems from "our unique system of dual collateral review of criminal convictions."[112] Congress established this review in the 1867 Habeas Act, according to Powell, and the judiciary "federalized" the supervision of the death penalty as a result of its decision in *Furman v. Georgia* by allowing federal constitutional challenges in almost all death penalty cases.[113] He did acknowledge the problems attendant in obtaining qualified counsel in death penalty challenges, especially among indigent and incarcerated defendants. One of his proposed solutions—congressional legislation that would impose a statute of limitations on habeas appeals—also provided for an exception for defendants who could not obtain qualified counsel. Nevertheless, he continued to argue that habeas reforms were needed to speed up the time from prosecution to execution because of the "alarming murder rate that prevails in this country."[114]

The American Bar Association's habeas reform proposals during this period further reflected some of Powell's suggestions, although not without important differences, as the federalism and finality arguments were decidedly absent from many of its proposals. However, its concern about time delays through habeas petitions was evident, as it too advocated legislation that would impose a statute of limitations on habeas appeals. The similarity to Powell's suggestions came in the American Bar Association's concerns about inadequate representation of counsel for death penalty defendants. Its proposals advocated that states mandate specialized training for death penalty attorneys, as well as more adequate compensation, presumably for public defenders, to whom most of the burden of representation continued to fall.

HABEAS AND THE REHNQUIST COURT: 1986–1996

The jurisprudential changes to habeas during the Burger and Rehnquist Courts were incremental, but formal congressional codification of these rollbacks would not be realized until the passage of AEDPA in 1996. The eventual habeas changes that Congress made in 1996 were directly informed by the executive and congressional proposals to limit habeas throughout the 1980s. Timing matters here. The changes to habeas in the Courts starting in the early 1970s finally overlapped with both sympathetic and energetic Reagan and Bush administrations, as well as a receptive conservative majority in Congress after the 1994 Republican victories in Congress. Though AEDPA was passed during the Clinton administration, the act reflected the legislative, executive, and judicial changes in habeas jurisprudence that had been brewing since the Warren Court.[115]

On 25 September 1991, Warren McCleskey, a black man, was executed by the state of Georgia for the murder of a white Atlanta police officer during a robbery. Just five months earlier, the Supreme Court had denied his second habeas corpus petition in *McCleskey v. Zant,* sealing his fate and also reaffirming more restrictive limitations on habeas petitions.[116] Before we turn to the facts and significance of McCleskey's final, fatal habeas case, we need to consider the landmark decision in his first attempt on habeas to have his conviction overturned.

McCleskey v. Kemp marked the formal ascendance of notions of finality and innocence that had been methodically linked to attempts to transform habeas adjudication.[117] McCleskey's first habeas petition to the Supreme Court involved a Fourteenth and Eighth Amendment challenge to his death sentence based on the results of the Baldus study, a complex study of death penalty cases in the state of Georgia during the 1970s. Baldus's study suggested, among other findings, that there was a correlation between "race of the victim" cases and the imposition of the death penalty. The study indicated that black defendants charged with crimes against white victims were 4.3 times more likely to receive a sentence of death from juries than were white defendants, regardless of the race of their victims. On the basis of the study, McCleskey filed a habeas petition in federal district and circuit courts, where it was denied. The Supreme Court then considered the case on habeas.

Justice Powell began the opinion by stating, "Our analysis begins with the basic principle that a defendant who alleges an equal protection violation has the burden of proving 'the existence of purposeful discrimination.'" He went on to buttress this "basic principle" by arguing that McCleskey must somehow show that "decisionmakers in *his* case acted with discriminatory purpose."[118] The proof offered, in the form of inferences that could be drawn from the Baldus study, did not prove that any state actor had such intent. Although the study might indicate generalized trends, it did not directly relate to the facts of McCleskey's particular circumstance. Powell's basic principle of proving specific discriminatory state action for equal protection violations thus rendered McCleskey's entire argument moot.

With considerations of race deferred temporarily as irrelevant, Powell then addressed the Eighth Amendment claim.[119] On the basis of his reading of both *Furman* and *Gregg,* the imposition of the death penalty for murder was fully consistent with both federalism and society's long-held traditions, which suggested approval of capital punishment. The bifurcated trial–sentencing schemes developed in *Gregg* were designed to alleviate the racially based concerns advocated in this case. Quoting *Gregg,* Powell defended the current process of death penalty adjudication in Georgia: "Considerations of federalism, as well as respect for the ability of a [state] legislature to evaluate . . . the moral consensus concerning the death penalty and its social utility as a sanction, require us to conclude, in the absence of more convincing evidence, that the infliction of death as a punishment for murder is not without justification and thus is not unconstitutionally severe."[120] Building on these federalism arguments, the bifurcated Georgia procedures actually provided for adequate opportunity for race and prejudice to be rooted out, if they existed at all. Moreover, these types of arguments, which implicated state-level functions and duties, were "best presented to legislative bodies," not the courts, who must apply their decision-making duties on a "case-by-case" basis.[121]

Another important consideration in the denial of the writ, and the finding of no constitutional violations, was that the study, if accurate, would "question the principles that underlie our entire criminal justice system." Thus it would prevent the Court from creating a "limiting principle" for other types of discriminatory claims that could result from the Court's decision. Worse yet, statistical studies might possibly show gender discrepancies, other minority sentencing anomalies, and, by extension, discrepancies based on "facial characteristics."[122] These discrepancies, he argued, might exist, but these challenges would force states to meet the unrealistic expectation that their respective adjudicative systems be perfect.

Two years after *McCleskey v. Kemp*, the Court further solidified its new habeas jurisprudence, this time concerning the retroactive application of new rules developed by the Court and their ability to be raised in habeas petitions. *Teague v. Lane* (1989) involved a challenge to the selection of jury members based on their race during a trial for attempted murder.[123] Teague argued that the prosecutor used his peremptory challenges to purposefully exclude blacks from the jury. After Teague was convicted, the Court decided *Batson v. Kentucky,* which set rules for the kind of threshold evidence that was required to prove equal protection violations in jury selection. Teague's federal habeas petitions had been denied by the district and circuit courts on the basis of their reading of the decision that *Batson* overruled. The new rules provided that the defendant only had to show that he was a "member of a cognizable racial group" and that the prosecutor removed similar members from that group during voir dire.[124]

Writing for the Court, Justice O'Connor denied the writ. She ruled that habeas petitions could be granted only if the charges were clearly contrary to existing case law at the time of the defendant's conviction.[125] This meant that petitions would be denied if they claimed violations on the basis of subsequent changes to constitutional rules. The only exception to the new retroactivity decision was that the habeas petitioner could apply a new rule if that rule "breaks new ground" or if that rule was not "dictated by precedent" at the time of conviction.[126] Thus only a few habeas cases could potentially fit into this category.[127] Finally, she argued that this new retroactivity decision was produced to make sure that state prosecutions would square with federal law. Otherwise, continued relitigation of new rules would undermine finality and federalism.[128]

That same term, the Court further carved out exceptions to the Warren Court's criminal procedure revolution in another habeas context, as it again qualified the extent to which *Miranda* rights had to be conveyed by police to suspects, in *Duckworth v. Eagan*.[129] Eagan had confessed to police that he stabbed a woman nine times after she refused to have sex with him. While in custody, he was Mirandized, but the police did not use the classic wording. Instead, they told the defendant he could have a lawyer "if and when" he went to court. His habeas petition argued that this violated his right to counsel. Rehnquist held that *Miranda* never held that police must repeat certain wording exactly, only that they "touch all of the bases required by *Miranda*."[130] The statement that a lawyer will be provided "if and when" one goes to court conformed to the respective state's actual criminal procedure processes. The state of Indiana provided counsel at the defendant's first court appearance, and therefore Eagan's questioning as to when his attorney would be present was "anticipated" by police in their answer. Consequently for the Court, *Miranda* rights were only prophylactic, not "talismanic."[131]

The limiting effects of the new retroactive limitations on habeas announced in *Teague* would be seconded the next year in *Sawyer v. Smith*.[132] The death row inmate in this case challenged comments made by the prosecutor during his trial, who told the jury that the sentencing decision in this case would be made by another jury, and that their charge was only to establish guilt or innocence. The defendant argued that this had the effect of diminishing the jury's own sense of gravity in their decision-making process. The argument was based on *Caldwell v. Mississippi* (1985), a case that the Court had heard after the defendant's conviction and sentence.[133] The question was whether this new decision could be retroactively applied under *Teague*. Writing for the majority, Justice Kennedy denied the writ, arguing that the decision relied on did not produce a "watershed" rule that was "fundamental to the integrity of the criminal proceeding."[134] Although a recent decision allowed challenges based on a prosecutor's supposed unconstitutional statements, this case did not fall within *Teague*'s exceptions. Relying on Henry Friendly, Kennedy ruled that the "application of constitutional rules not in existence at the time a conviction became final seriously undermines the principle of finality which is essential to the operation of our criminal justice system."[135]

The following year, Warren McCleskey filed the last habeas petition of his life. The basis of this habeas challenge was his contention that one of the witnesses in his original case—his cellmate—had elicited testimony from him (a supposed admission of guilt), in violation of his Sixth Amendment right to counsel. The Court not only reaffirmed its "cause and prejudice" test as developed in *Sykes* to deny the habeas petition, but also took the opportunity to reaffirm and strengthen its abuse of the writ doctrine announced in *Sanders* in 1963.

In his first federal habeas petition, McCleskey only raised the federal question of Eighth and Fourteenth Amendment equal protection violations, not a specific Sixth Amendment challenge concerning his supposed jailhouse confession. Justice Kennedy considered this new petition an abuse because McCleskey should have combined both challenges in the original federal habeas petition. Moreover, even this new challenge did not establish that the prosecution acted with "cause and prejudice." The abuse of the writ had become overwhelming, according to Kennedy, because, as Brennan had suggested in his 1963 *Fay* opinion, the federal court had not "always followed an unwavering line in its conclusions as to the availability of the Great Writ."[136] The Court would now "define the doctrine of abuse of the writ with more precision."[137] The new standards held that the habeas petitioner must somehow show that he was either prevented from raising the claim or that, consistent with notions of innocence, new evidence had come to light after his prior petitions. Neither of these criteria was met, according to the majority. Again, the justification relied on the developing notions of finality and the costs that habeas exacts from society and its limited resources.[138]

The extent to which the Court's developing notions of actual innocence would apply on habeas when it was actually asserted had yet to be seen. Presumably, on the basis of the case law developed since the beginning of the Burger Court, we should expect that, absent an egregious affront to finality (for example, abuse of the writ through successive petitions), claims of actual innocence on habeas would be welcomed by the Court.

This question was confronted by the Court in *Herrera v. Collins* in 1993.[139] Herrera was convicted of murder in 1982 and sentenced to death in Texas. Ten years later, he filed a habeas petition asserting that new evidence (the deathbed confession of his brother) proved his innocence. However, absent a showing in the petition that a constitutional violation had occurred, the Court ruled that habeas could not issue. Rehnquist argued that habeas was not intended to cor-

rect errors of fact; it only served to vindicate those held or imprisoned in violation of the Constitution. Without a concurrent showing that his state trial and
appeals were tainted, Herrera could not be released by the Court on habeas.
Rehnquist further argued that the denial of the writ served to show deference
to states, as they were the proper and traditional repositories of criminal adjudication.[140] For the Court to override the states' traditional domain of criminal
procedure, there must be a violation that "offends some principle of justice so
rooted in the traditions and conscience of our people as to be ranked as fundamental."[141] Herrara's only option, absent a rehearing of the entire case by the
state of Texas, was to seek clemency from the governor. Leonel Herrera went
to the electric chair still claiming his innocence.

AEDPA: AN IMPRIMATUR OF THE REPUBLICAN
REGIME'S HABEAS OFFENSIVE

The ascendant Republican regime largely realized its habeas reform agenda in
AEDPA, which became law on 24 April 1996 in the wake of the bombing of
the Alfred. P. Murrah Federal Building in Oklahoma City.[142] Although it was
passed to help combat terrorism both at home and abroad, it instead represented a wish list of many habeas opponents since the mid-1960s.[143] More specifically, it represented the codification of a more conservative, states' rights–
oriented political philosophy that had been developing since the 1960s. The act
was thus a product of the Republican regime's overall vision of constitutional
governance through habeas, with its most specific roots in the suggestions for
reform detailed by the Office of Legal Counsel (OLC) during the tenure of
Edwin Meese.

In many ways, AEDPA's provisions finalized the Republican-led habeas
counterrevolution. It established a one-year time limit for filing petitions from
state to federal courts and eliminated the "successive petitions" rule established in *Sanders* by allowing only one chance for federal review of constitutional challenges. AEDPA further provided that "a determination of a factual
issue made by a State court shall be presumed correct. The applicant shall have
the burden of rebutting the presumption of correctness by clear and convincing evidence."[144] Striking at one of the writ's core features since the late nineteenth century, it modified the existing rules concerning exhaustion by allowing federal courts to deny a habeas petition from a state defendant even if he
or she had not exhausted his or her state's appellate processes. But the most
controversial provision was the one governing the types of cases that federal

courts could now entertain through the writ. Now there were only two types of circumstances under which habeas could issue. These were habeas petitions that either "resulted in a decision that was contrary to, or involved an unreasonable application of, clearly established Federal law, as determined by the Supreme Court," or "resulted in a decision that was based on an unreasonable determination of the facts in light of the evidence presented in the State court proceeding."[145]

AEDPA's habeas provisions surely reflected the regime's attempt to re-create habeas's function along the lines of the regime's vision of constitutional governance, but the circumstances surrounding the bill's passage also show how habeas's extraordinary use during times of crisis—in this case, the country's reaction to the Oklahoma City bombing and the 1993 attacks on the World Trade Center—is informed more by the preceding period of normal politics than by the crisis at hand. When we again consider AEDPA's most salient provisions, we can see in them a fairly direct link to the Reagan Justice Department's proposals for habeas rollbacks. Aside from the OLC's recommendation for the complete abolition of federal habeas corpus for state prisoners (which was never seriously considered), the report suggested many legislative options that were included. The report recommended a one-year time limit "running from the exhaustion of state remedies," a proposal that was included in AEDPA. AEDPA's provision concerning a state's determination of fact was also a proposal of the OLC. Both the report and the act also included provisions allowing federal district courts to deny habeas claims before state processes were exhausted, as well as provisions allowing only courts of appeals to issue certificates of probable cause in habeas appeals.[146]

But the most direct link between AEDPA and the preceding normal development of habeas is the fact that the act's salient provisions were overwhelmingly designed to curtail the use of federal habeas for state prisoners. The legislative history of what eventually became AEDPA is important here. Introduced as the Effective Death Penalty Act as part of the congressional Republicans' Contract with America, this first iteration of the bill received little movement in committee until the 19 April 1995 bombing. Soon after the attacks, Republicans amended the bill and attached it to a Clinton administration bill detailing antiterrorism measures. In this form, the bill was renamed the Antiterrorism and Effective Death Penalty Act.[147] As James Liebman characterizes the act's inauspicious development, it "was the product of the bizarre alignment of three ill-starred events: Timothy McVeigh's twisted patriotism and disdain for 'collateral damage,' the Gingrich Revolution in its heyday, and the Clinton Presidency at the furthest point of its most rightward triangulation."[148] It is no surprise that the act's original impetus stemmed from Gingrich's Contract with America, which was in many ways a paean to the reinvigoration of states' rights that the Republican Party had been featuring in its party platforms since the 1960s. Prominently featured in the OLC report was the argument that most of its habeas reform proposals were based on "deference to adequate state processes."[149] The awkward justification of the bill's supporters for its necessity in combating terrorism and establishing more efficient and fair rules for its prosecution becomes even more obtuse when we consider the fact that both Timothy McVeigh and Ramzi Youseff were federal, not state, prisoners whose jurisdictional status had never been questioned.[150]

CONCLUSION

As it had been before, habeas was used as a tool of regime creation, enforcement, and dissolution from the beginning of the Warren Court to the codification of many of the ascendant Republican regime's habeas proposals in AEDPA. Both regimes during this period countered the other with new readings of the writ's historical development. Both regimes then reinterpreted habeas's procedures to enforce their respective visions of constitutional governance. Each responded to the other's successful enforcement with counternarratives that attacked the core governing principles of the dominant regime.

The Court's role in each regime's use of the writ was not simply one of deference. To be sure, the Warren Court after 1962, and the Rehnquist Court from the mid-1980s onward, fashioned habeas jurisprudence that was largely in tune with the dominant national regime of its time. The Warren Court reinterpreted the writ's historiography broadly to reflect New Deal and Great Society concerns for individual rights, both enumerated and unenumerated. The Burger and Rehnquist Courts also reread the writ's historical trajectory, but they did so narrowly and with equal disregard for historical accuracy, recasting the writ to square with the ascending Republican Party's concern for law and order, states' rights, and equally important project of resisting and partly dismantling the post-1937 mantra of special judicial protection for minorities.

But each Court also established important limits to its habeas jurisprudence that suggests an important degree of Court-centered independence from the dominant regime. This is most evident in the Burger and Rehnquist Court's habeas rollbacks. Certainly poised to undo much of the Warren Courts' expansive habeas rulings, the Burger Court in *Stone v. Powell* nevertheless refused to eliminate federal habeas review for state prisoners more generally.[151]

The Court would continue to adopt the Republican regime's larger theories of habeas review from both the legal academy and the Reagan administration's Justice Department, but it never adopted—or ever seriously considered—the administration's preferred choice of the complete elimination of federal habeas review. Indeed, in important cases after *Stone* where we might expect the Court to continue to erode habeas corpus review in areas beyond the exclusionary rule, it refused to apply that case further in important areas. In these cases, moreover, the Court hewed to a conception of the writ that sought to protect only the most egregious due process violations and thus the most basic trial rights and procedures, including allowing habeas to issue in challenges involving ineffective counsel or jury discrimination.[152] These areas in which the Court's habeas jurisprudence was left intact sought to protect the very core of the judiciary's functions: the fair trial.[153] No matter how sympathetic a Court might be to the forces dominating American politics, it has always stopped short of supporting the regime when its own institutional legitimacy was at stake.[154]

Conclusion: The Not-So-Great Writ of Liberty

The account of habeas corpus in American political development offered in this book is predicated on the assumption that while habeas is often understood to be a purely legal mechanism, there have been as many if not more political determinants that have shaped the Great Writ of Liberty. Thus while the writ is adjudicated by courts, the story cannot begin or end with them. Courts in the United States are partly political and partly legal. If only because Supreme Court justices and federal judges are appointed and confirmed by the executive and the Senate, we should expect at least some symmetry between federal courts and the larger political regimes that have governed for any meaningful period of time in the United States.[1] Looking past purely legal accounts of habeas, we see that the writ not only has played an important role in the larger political struggles of American political development more generally, but has also been shaped by these struggles.

Several important features of habeas corpus in the United States thus stand out as important factors that almost always drive the writ's development over time. The first and most important is that our understanding of the admittedly arcane operation of the writ in courts of law, replete with a legal vernacular that sometimes seems daunting and prohibitive to the layperson, cannot continue to be purely court centered. The empirical history of the writ's development overwhelmingly proves that other institutions, including Congress, the executive, state governments, interest groups, and academics, also may shape the writ's meaning. The salient cases that legal academics identify as important markers in the development of the writ's jurisprudence are almost always only the final steps in a larger ongoing political process.

A broader political lens also allows us to see that habeas corpus—the purported Great Writ of Liberty—has not been so great. Habeas is simply not the countermajoritarian check against executives or political majorities that we assume. Because the writ is primarily a tool of political regimes, it serves the priorities of majoritarian politics first. We can better understand the writ's operation and development if we also see habeas as a procedural, not a substantive, right. The real power of the writ is its ability to serve as a procedural instrument for changing conceptions of substantive rights. This means that although the writ has the potential to enforce conceptions of rights that are consistent with the best ideals of American politics, it means that it also has the potential to enforce our country's worst aspects. As an umbrella right, habeas largely serves as a repository for changing conceptions of different sets of substantive rights. Thus when we try to understand changes to habeas procedure, we also always need to account for the sets of rights that are implicated as a result of these changes.

No better example of this aspect of habeas development in American history is the use of the writ to enforce the institution of chattel slavery. The use of habeas by Southern slave states to enforce slave law and protect the property rights of slave owners shows that the writ's real history belies Whiggish narratives of its liberty-protecting past. It also shows us how increased federal habeas protection has not always been in the service of those substantive rights that we naturally find so appealing today. Although not directly related to the slavery controversy, the two major habeas developments before the Civil War were used by federal courts to bring before them state habeas cases involving the rescue of fugitive slaves, only to be resolved not in favor of liberty, but in favor of slavery. Our modern conception of habeas corpus as best protecting substantive individual rights through the removal of state cases to federal habeas courts is thus not always the best structure for habeas adjudication.[2]

That habeas has not always been used to vindicate minority rights, and that it has played a significant role in enforcing the ugly side of American politics, also suggest that the writ's history—so often portrayed as always widening toward more protection of the most important and most fundamental rights that Americans hold so dear—is less linear and progressive than we have imagined. Although the Whiggish histories of the writ that almost always foreground case law are empirically false, they nevertheless demonstrate the writ's capacity to serve political interests, both good and bad. The unintended consequences of the 1833 Habeas Act's use first to protect slave catchers in the 1850s and then to enforce the rights of freedmen by the Republican Reconstruction regime after 1867 certainly bear this out.

But it would be a mistake to think that the writ's use by political regimes as a tool in the process of creating and then enforcing new visions of constitutional governance through the idiom of case law means that courts simply translate those visions in the ways that dominant political forces wish. As the writ's political history demonstrates, courts will only go so far in their support of the regime through habeas jurisprudence. This is a particularly important component of habeas's development not only because it provides us with a fairly predictable baseline for the future reductions or enlargements of federal habeas corpus, but also because this feature of habeas development allows us to begin to understand the limits of the Supreme Court's relationship to the larger political environment. Time and again, the Supreme Court has refused to bow to political forces—even ones with which they are otherwise largely sympathetic—that push for the elimination of their habeas jurisdiction. In an important way, this more institutional reality may be the only permanent check against otherwise politically influenced and politically saturated uses of the writ in the future.

HABEAS, THE WAR ON TERROR, AND THE FUTURE OF HABEAS CORPUS

To make sense of these points in the most relevant and timely way, and to show further how these institutional features continue to shape the development of habeas, we need only look briefly at the writ's role since the terrorist attacks on the World Trade Center on 11 September 2001. However, we first need to look backward.

As I have argued throughout this book, one of the most common mistakes in attempting to understand the history and development of habeas is the persistent framing of a false dichotomy between so-called extraordinary periods of war or crisis and ordinary periods of relative peace.[3] This overstated distinction prevents us from seeing the continuities between the writ's ordinary development during peacetime and its actual operation during extraordinary periods of war or crisis. As we have seen during both the Civil War and World War II, conceptions of habeas from the immediately preceding period of relative peace had tremendous influence on the regimes that shaped habeas during war. Memories of the use of the writ by federal courts to frustrate Northern state liberty laws in the 1850s, for example, were never completely erased from the minds of Lincoln and the Republican Party in 1861, and the ugly history of Asian American discrimination in the United States certainly informed the politics of Japanese internment during World War II. In both instances, we cannot begin to understand wartime uses of the writ apart from the ways in which courts and other political institutions had already been grappling with arguments concerning the proper use of the writ. The use (or nonuse) of the writ since 9/11 has been no different. We cannot fully understand the important habeas cases in the last few years without seeing them as extensions of an already well-developed conservative critique of habeas expansions since the Warren Court.

The current prosecution of the war on terror has so far been marked by many important and challenging constitutional questions, including warrantless wiretaps, domestic spying, and the rendition of terrorist suspects to foreign countries that use torture. However, the most contentious—and the most litigated—question has been the ability of the executive branch to hold terrorist suspects indefinitely. When litigated, this question of detainment has most often been challenged through writs of habeas corpus, as we have seen most recently in *Hamdi v. Rumsfeld, Rasul v. Bush, Hamdan v. Rumsfeld,* and *Boumediene v. United States.*[4] Moreover, both the executive and Congress have also weighed in on their respective conceptions over habeas access in the Detainee Treatment Act, the Military Commissions Act, and President George W. Bush's executive orders concerning enemy combatants tried by military commissions. Like it has before, habeas continues to transcend purely Court-centered analyses.

Although there is much disagreement over habeas access for terrorist suspects, the substance of the debate surrounding the writ's reach—even for terrorist suspects—is not new. As I have detailed, arguments about meaningful access to the writ had been swelling for the past fifty years of ordinary constitutional and political development in the United States. Beginning with the Warren Court's criminal procedure revolution, the contemporary habeas debate as we know it was born. Almost from the Warren Court's first habeas decisions with respect to criminal process cases, scholars, legal practitioners, and politicians on the state and national levels began to criticize the Court for providing too many procedural rights to seemingly guilty criminals.

Increasingly, broad habeas access was challenged throughout the next three decades. Beginning with President Richard Nixon's war on crime, conservative political coalitions chose habeas as a principal tool to remake the criminal justice system in their image. The appointment of more conservative justices to the Supreme Court, particularly Warren Burger, William Rehnquist, Sandra Day O'Connor, Antonin Scalia, Anthony Kennedy, and Clarence Thomas, further spurred this change. Beginning with *Stone v. Powell,* the Court signaled that the preceding enlargement of habeas was coming to an end, as the Court ruled that Fourth Amendment claims could not be relitigated through federal habeas courts if the state court in which the claim originated had already ruled on the admissibility of evidence.[5]

The intellectual origins of the regime's changes are found in the works of Paul Bator and Henry Friendly. Paul Bator emphasized the necessity of finality in the criminal procedure process so that matters that have been fully and fairly litigated and determined on one level (the state level) are not forced into redundancy at the cost of justice by another court (a federal one).[6] Henry Friendly also wrote a prestigious and still influential article criticizing the War-ren Court's habeas developments.[7] Friendly argued that for all the concern over due process in criminal procedure on the state level, the ultimate decision for granting or denying federal habeas corpus from state prisoners should be the innocence of the defendant. If mere technicalities violate perceived con-stitutional rights, they could be addressed by means other than freeing the guilty through habeas corpus. And with the election of Ronald Reagan to the presidency in 1980, a solidified conservative regime further advanced these and other arguments to curtail habeas access, as the justice departments of William French Smith and Edwin Meese sought to implement legislation to carve away further meaningful access to habeas.[8] Although most of the executive and con-gressional proposals during the 1980s failed, they were nevertheless informed by the earlier arguments that suggested that Warren Court habeas expansions skewed the criminal justice system toward criminal defendants who were most likely guilty. As a result, the criminal justice system would be burdened by a flood of habeas petitions that, according to its critics, would not be meritori-ous, thus resulting in an abuse of the Great Writ.

With Republican congressional victories in the House and Senate in 1994, these habeas proposals were poised to make traction. Just two years later, Con-gress passed the Antiterrorism and Effective Death Penalty Act (AEDPA).[9] AEDPA represented the legal codification of many of the restrictive habeas cases that the Burger and Warren Courts had decided to narrow—but not overrule—from the Warren Court's attempt to utilize habeas as its oversight mechanism for enforcing its incorporation and criminal procedure jurispru-dence. These preceding developments cannot be separated from any analysis of habeas as we try to make sense of the serious challenges to the constitution-ality of the Bush administration's detainment of terrorist suspects in the war on terror. These arguments about habeas access advanced during ordinary periods of peace were simply carried forward by the Republican regime into our current extraordinary period of the war on terrorism.

HAMDI v. RUMSFELD

In the first challenge to Bush administration policies, *Hamdi v. Rumsfeld,* ha-beas was used to challenge the detainment of Yasser Hamdi, a United States citizen raised abroad, as an enemy combatant.[10] Captured on the battlefield in Afghanistan in November 2001 by the Northern Alliance, Hamdi was initially transported to the United States Naval Base at Guantánamo Bay, Cuba. Upon learning of his U.S. citizenship, the military transferred Hamdi to a naval brig in Charleston, South Carolina. Designated as an enemy combatant by executive order, Hamdi then challenged the president's authority to hold him absent explicit congressional authorization. At issue was whether the executive, using his Article II war powers combined with Congress' 2001 Authorization for the Use of Military Force (AUMF), had the ability to detain and classify U.S. citizens as enemy combatants. The majority in *Hamdi* did not side with the extreme unilateral executive position advanced by the Bush administration, instead holding that those classified and detained as enemy combatants could challenge this classification through habeas. The treatment of habeas by the Court and by the executive reflected well-trodden ground. Though the Bush administration did not argue that Hamdi was precluded from challenging his enemy combatant classification through habeas, they did argue that the president's and the military's evidence presented against Hamdi was enough to meet the requirements of a habeas petition. The Court majority ruled that Hamdi had the right to challenge the evidence presented against him as to why he should continue to be held as an enemy combatant. The Court also ruled, however, that the traditional procedural rules of the courtroom would not have to be met. Hearsay evidence, for example, could be used, and the traditional notions of burden of proof could be shifted to the defendant to prove that he or she should not be classified as an enemy combatant and held indefinitely. Consistent with the preceding normal political development of habeas jurisprudence, defendants were to have access to the writ but could not use it to frustrate, delay, or hide from justice.

This understanding of habeas as only a minimal constitutional necessity is also visible in the congressional and executive reactions that followed. The first congressional response was the passage of the Detainee Treatment Act (DTA), which attempted to strip federal courts of habeas jurisdiction for noncitizen enemy combatants.[11] Military commissions, or combatant status review tribunals (CSRTs), would consider detainees' cases, and although the DTA allowed one appeal from the decisions of tribunals or commissions, it gave exclusive jurisdiction to hear these appeals in the circuit court of the District of Columbia. In *Hamdan v. Rumsfeld,* the Court held that the DTA did not apply to cases that were already pending before the act. Congress then passed the Military Commissions Act (MCA), which again authorized the use of commissions and tribunals; more importantly, it explicitly prohibited habeas petitions from aliens held outside the United States seeking to challenge their detainment, including those whose cases were pending before the passage of

the DTA.[12] Extremely telling is the concern that the DTA's congressional spon-
sors raised concerning the potential flood of habeas petitions to federal courts
from noncitizens that might result if detainees were afforded habeas access,
a concern that stretched as far back as Justice Jackson's concerns in *Brown v.
Allen* (1953):

Congress enacted the DTA to bring order to the chaos that resulted from the ava-
lanche of anticipatory lawsuits under general statutes that were not suitably tailored to
the circumstances. Allowing the current detainees—all of whom had pending actions
when the DTA was enacted—to continue to pursue those actions would utterly defeat
the DTA's purpose. It would, moreover, defeat Congress's purpose of channeling cases
through the military administrative process as a condition precedent to judicial review,
as it would perpetuate the resolution of important legal issues without the benefit of
concrete determinations by the military and Executive Branch on a properly developed
record.[13]

Considering the arguments about habeas access that had characterized the
preceding decades, this argument about the role of habeas during war was
not that different. Habeas access in general had already been limited in both
statute and court precedent. Limiting habeas further for United States citizens
classified as enemy combatants, and possibly denying it altogether for aliens
held outside of the United States, was a move that required little extension
beyond the normal preceding habeas jurisprudence.

BOUMEDIENE v. BUSH

In *Boumediene v. Bush,* the most recent habeas case to come before the Court,
the central component of both the DTA and the MCA was challenged.[14] The
Court ruled that Congress' habeas jurisdiction-stripping provisions in both
acts violated the suspension clause. Most recent commentary on *Boumediene*
has emphasized the Court's justification of its decision as premised on separation-of-powers concerns.[15] This is more right than wrong, but the specific
concerns of the Court also led it to find the relevant portions of the MCA unconstitutional because they threatened the most basic judicial functions altogether, up to and including de facto suspension of the writ. *Boumediene* thus
serves as a perfect example of the dynamics of habeas advanced in this book. A
regime-affiliated Court tried its best to hew to the Bush administration's and
Congress' preferred policies in the war on terror. Still, the Court only followed
the regime's wishes until its preferred policies prevented federal court partici-

pation through habeas corpus altogether. The point at which judicial sympathy with the political regime stopped and judicial institutional independence began occurred when the Court perceived that its institutional power to issue habeas writs was jeopardized and when bare minimum judicial functions were jettisoned by the regime.

We see the Bush administration's position clearly in their *Boumediene* brief, authored by United States solicitor general Paul Clement, who laid out three points of defense against the argument that the MCA violated the Constitution's suspension clause. The first objection was cast in familiar rhetoric: he argued that habeas had been so transformed over the last three decades that it now had the potential to tip the scales of justice in the favor of patently guilty defendants who, with the help of meddlesome courts, were now asking for even more rights: "The detainees now enjoy greater procedural protections and procedural and statutory rights to challenge their wartime detentions than any other captured enemy combatants in the history of war. Yet they claim an entitlement to more."[16] The second argument was a further attempt to legitimize congressional intent in stripping—or modifying—the Supreme Court's habeas jurisdiction as a matter of right and replacing appeals from CSRTs with review in the District of Columbia circuit court. In justifying this position, the administration argued that, consistent with the World War II habeas case of *Johnson v. Eisentrager*, enemy alien combatants held abroad had never been afforded habeas rights and should not now have access to them.[17] This position also served as the foundation for the administration's linchpin argument that Guantánamo Bay is not under the jurisdiction of the United States. The final objection in the administration's *Boumediene* brief was one that had been levied most often by those who sought to curtail habeas access over the preceding decades. The concept of exhaustion in habeas jurisprudence requires that the substance of habeas petitions—the actual claims of unconstitutional action against the detaining authority—first be made and adjudicated in lower courts according to established processes. Although exhaustion is most commonly understood through the lens of federalism, as it requires those seeking federal review of constitutional claims to have these claims adjudicated completely on the state level before they can be heard by federal courts, the Bush administration's extension of exhaustion to the Guantánamo petitioners reflected their desire to prevent habeas claims by federal courts of any stripe, instead relegating them to adjudication by military courts or tribunals that are created solely by the executive branch. These three objections buttressed the Bush administration's arguments against granting habeas to enemy combatants in the war on terror.

Led by Justice Anthony Kennedy, the Court rejected these arguments and held that the DTA and the MCA involved unconstitutional suspensions of habeas corpus and that the CSRTs provided were inadequate substitutes for the writ, making it the first case ever in which the Court held that Congress had unconstitutionally suspended the writ.[18] Kennedy began his opinion by considering the administration's arguments that federal habeas could not reach Guantánamo Bay, Cuba. It was one thing to give deference to Congress and the president in matters touching on "formal sovereignty and territorial government," he said, but "to hold the political branches have the power to switch the Constitution on and off at will is quite another."[19] The writ of habeas corpus plays a central role not only in matters of individual rights, the Court argued, but also in monitoring the separation of powers, especially when the questioned governmental action implicates judicial processes.

Next, the Court distinguished the World War II case of *Johnson v. Eisentrager* from the facts here, partly to develop its position that the CSRTs were inadequate substitutes for habeas, and partly to justify habeas for Guantánamo detainees. As he did throughout the opinion, Kennedy trod carefully, conceding that Guantánamo's location outside of sovereign United States territory "weigh[ed] against" the detainees' suspension arguments. Nevertheless, there were important differences between the two cases, including the fact that the *Eisentrager* detainees did not contest their status as enemy aliens. Here, the detainees were questioning their imputed status as enemy combatants. Also, the defendants in *Eisentrager* had already been convicted in military commission proceedings, where there had been a "rigorous adversarial process to test the legality of their detention," and wherein they were provided with a detailed list of charges, the benefit of counsel, and the ability to introduce evidence and cross-examine witnesses.[20] None of these basic trial features was provided through CSRTs. Instead, detainees were assigned personal representatives, not traditional counsel. Moreover, the government's evidence in CSRTs was considered presumptively valid, and while defendants could present "reasonably available" evidence in their defense, the ability to rebut the government's charges was questionable because of the lack of traditional counsel. Just as important, while defendants could seek review of the CSRT's decisions, this review need not "cure all defects in the proceeding."[21] Combined with the fact that detention in Guantánamo seemed indefinite, the limits of suspension were still in "full effect."[22]

So what were the standards for determining whether or not the writ was suspended, absent an explicit congressional provision? The answer, the Court said, was hard to know because "most legislative enactments pertaining to habeas corpus have acted not to contract the writ's protection but to expand or hasten resolution of prisoners' claims."[23] There were recent exceptions, including AEDPA, and the Court had upheld their constitutionality in terms of the suspension clause.[24] But these limitations to federal habeas were different from the instant cases "where no trial has been held" at all.[25] Without even the most basic involvement of federal courts, Congress' actions here simply "circumscribed" the writ.

Furthermore, unlike AEDPA limitations, the appeals process for detainees from the CSRT decisions did not allow the reviewing court (here, the District of Columbia circuit court) to "inquire into the legality of detention" on its own. It was instead limited to assessing whether CSRTs "complied with standards and procedures specified by the Secretary of Defense." Moreover, the MCA's provisions granting exclusive jurisdiction to the District of Columbia circuit court were also problematic because normally any federal justice or any federal circuit could issue the writ as well as remand a case to a district court for more fact finding. Here, these traditional functions of habeas corpus were severely limited.[26] At a minimum, a federal habeas court (or any process designed to approximate one) should have the power to release a defendant, though the Court pointed out that this would not mean that this would be the end of any further process against the defendant. To Kennedy, this power was so basic that it was "an easily identifiable attribute of habeas" jurisprudence.[27] Habeas's common-law use, moreover, suggested that great deference was to be given to prior court determinations, but in this instance, no federal court had heard any cases at all. The effective result was that the CSRTs were simply executive, not judicial, processes. Even if wide latitude was given to these sorts of processes, CSRTs still fell short: "Habeas corpus proceedings need not resemble a criminal trial, even when detention is by executive order. But the writ must be effective. The habeas court must have sufficient authority to conduct a meaningful review of both the cause for detention and the Executive's power to detain."[28]

Even though the Court determined that the jurisdiction-stripping provisions of the MCA, along with the CSRT processes so established, violated the suspension clause, the Court did not completely shut the door on the Bush administration. At times, the Court went out of its way to suggest that habeas, at least in terms of its common-law use, was flexible enough to justify processes that were unique to exigent circumstances, even suggesting that "innovation" in habeas was possible.[29] What was required was not only that federal courts have some independent power in any process, but also that those processes conform to the most fundamental notions of procedural fairness. Unchecked executive power to detain individuals for an unlimited period of time may sometimes be necessary, but "few exercises of judicial power are as legitimate or as necessary as the responsibility to hear challenges to the authority of the Executive to imprison a person" by courts.[30]

THE NOT-SO-GREAT WRIT

These most recent habeas cases, along with the larger account of habeas's development offered in this book, might seem to suggest that habeas, like the courts that adjudicate it, simply follows the election returns. There is a great deal of truth to this proposition, not the least of which is the extent to which political regimes in the United States continue to reinterpret the writ's history, function, and reach to help enforce their own visions of constitutional governance. Justice Kennedy's questionable assertion in *Boumediene* that habeas changes have almost always tended to expand access to this important judicial remedy is only the most recent example of this pattern. When we actually trace the writ's development, we might conclude that the many Whiggish readings of habeas's history are simply masking a more nefarious role that the writ has, and will continue to play, in American political development. In this sense, the writ's most famous moniker, the Great Writ of Liberty, might more accurately be modified to the Not-So-Great Writ.

However, this understanding of the writ's role is fundamentally wrong. Although the writ's history does present a more circuitous trajectory that has been marked by as many ugly uses of the writ as it has by more noble ones, and although the writ has more often been used to mirror majoritarian interests rather than minority ones, the fact remains that there were, and still are, important institutional limits to the complete appropriation of the writ by purely political interests. Of course federal courts—and particularly the Supreme Court—have interpreted the writ according to the preferences of identifiable political regimes in American history when they might have instead worked to develop a jurisprudence of habeas that hewed more to our more modern conceptions of individual rights. But time and again, the judicial conception of the normative institutional role of courts has prevented them from following the political winds to the point of obliterating the habeas privilege completely. This more institutional reality of the judicial role in American constitutionalism, which envisions at least some minimally acceptable procedures of fairness along with some inviolable rights of individuals that courts must always seek to protect, might be the basic guarantee we have that habeas will continue to be at least a good writ, if not a great one.

Notes

PREFACE

1. 542 U.S. 507 (2004).
2. 542 U.S. 466 (2004).
3. 553 U.S. (2008).

CHAPTER 1. HABEAS CORPUS AND HISTORY

1. *Boumediene v. Bush*, 128 S. Ct. 2229, 2294 (2008).

2. Larry Yackle, *Federal Courts: Habeas Corpus* (New York: Foundation Press, 2003), 283. Barry Friedman has lamented that "habeas doctrine has lost its way." Barry Friedman, "A Tale of Two Habeas," *Minn. L. Rev.* 73 (1988): 252. In *Brecht v. Abrahamson*, 113 S. Ct. 1710 (1993), Justice Byron White similarly claimed that habeas jurisprudence had taken on the appearance "of a confused patchwork." See also Evan Tsen Lee, "The Theories of Federal Habeas Corpus," *Wash. U. L. Q.* 72 (1994).

3. See, for example, Richard Fallon and Daniel Meltzer, "Habeas Corpus Jurisdiction, Substantive Rights, and the War on Terror," *Harv. L. Rev.* 120 (2006).

4. The most recent account of habeas's early British and American use is Paul D. Halliday, *Habeas Corpus: From England to Empire* (Cambridge: Harvard University Press, 2010). See also Paul Halliday and G. Edward White, "The Suspension Clause: English Text, Imperial Contexts, and American Implications," *Va. L. Rev.* 94 (2008).

5. The standard-bearers of habeas's legal history include William F. Duker, *A Constitutional History of Habeas Corpus* (Westport, Conn.: Greenwood Press, 1980); Francis Paschal, "The Constitution and Habeas Corpus," *Duke L. J.* 1970 (1970); Neil Douglas McFeeley, "The Historical Development of Habeas Corpus," *Sw. L. J.* 30 (1976); Dallin H. Oaks, "The Original Writ of Habeas Corpus in the Supreme Court," *Sup. Ct. Rev.* 1962 (1962); Steven Semeraro, "Two Theories of Habeas Corpus," *Brook. L. Rev.* 71 (2005); Larry Yackle, "Federal Habeas Corpus in a Nutshell," *Hum. Rts.* 28 (2001); Larry W. Yackle, "Explaining Habeas Corpus," *N.Y.U. L. Rev.* 60 (1985); James S. Liebman, *Federal Habeas Corpus Practice and Procedure* (Charlottesville, Va.: Michie, 1994); James S. Liebman, "Apocalypse Next Time? The Anachronistic Attack on Habeas Corpus/Direct Review Parity," *Columbia Law Review* 92, no. 8 (1992).

6. Notable exceptions include Larry W. Yackle, "The Reagan Administration's Habeas Corpus Proposals," *Iowa L. Rev.* 68 (1982); Larry W. Yackle, "A Primer on the New Habeas Corpus Statute," *Buff. L. Rev.* 44 (1996); Cary Federman, *The Body and the State: Habeas Corpus and American Jurisprudence* (Albany: State University of New York Press, 2006).

7. Consider, for example, Paul Halliday's evaluation of the writ: "Habeas corpus did not evolve. Judges made it, transforming a common device for moving people about in aid of judicial process into an instrument by which they supervised imprison-

ment orders made anywhere, by anyone, for any reason." Halliday, *Habeas Corpus,* 9. For a recent review and critique of the legal academy's separation of law from politics, see Barry Friedman, "The Politics of Judicial Review," *Tex L. Rev.* 84 (2005). But see Brian Z. Tamanaha, *Beyond the Formalist–Realist Divide: The Role of Politics in Judging* (Princeton: Princeton University Press, 2010).

8. Article I, sec. 9, provides that "the privilege of the writ of habeas corpus shall not be suspended, unless when in cases of rebellion or invasion the public safety may require it."

9. For a defense of the Court's inherent right to issue the writ, see Paschal, "The Constitution and Habeas Corpus." The classic example is *Ex parte McCardle*, discussed at length in Chapter 3. See also Henry M. Hart Jr., "The Power of Congress to Limit the Jurisdiction of Federal Courts: An Exercise in Dialectic," *Harv. L. Rev.* 66 (1952).

10. Consider, for example, the observation of Felix Frankfurter and James Landis: "For law and courts are instruments of adjustment, and compromises by which the general problems of federalism are successively met determine the contemporaneous structure of the federal courts and the range of their authority." Felix Frankfurter and James M. Landis, *The Business of the Supreme Court: A Study in the Federal Judicial System* (New Brunswick, N.J.: Transaction Publishers, 2007), 59–60.

11. The Court-centered search for rights is neither new nor limited to the American case. See, for example, Ran Hirschl, *Towards Juristocracy: The Origins and Consequences of the New Constitutionalism* (Cambridge: Harvard University Press, 2004).

12. See Robert G. McCloskey, *The American Supreme Court* (Chicago: University of Chicago Press, 2005). Some argue that there is a fourth era in which conceptions of rights are advanced after the New Deal. See, for example, Richard A. Primus, *The American Language of Rights* (New York: Cambridge University Press, 1999). And some argue that Ronald Reagan's conservative coalition might be the extant constitutional regime. See Mark V. Tushnet, *The New Constitutional Order* (Princeton: Princeton University Press, 2003). For a slightly broader chronology, see Morton Keller, *America's Three Regimes: A New Political History* (New York: Oxford University Press, 2007). See also John Herbert Aldrich, *Why Parties? The Origin and Transformation of Political Parties in America* (Chicago: University of Chicago Press, 1995), 241–283.

13. For accounts that employ similar characterizations for each regime, see Bruce A. Ackerman, *We the People* (Cambridge, Mass.: Belknap Press of Harvard University Press, 1991); Akhil Reed Amar, *The Bill of Rights: Creation and Reconstruction* (New Haven, Conn.: Yale University Press, 1998); Stephen C. Lamb and Charles M. Halpern, "The Supreme Court and New Constitutional Eras," *Brook. L. Rev.* 64 (1998); Primus, *American Language of Rights*; Tushnet, *New Constitutional Order;* William M. Wiecek, *Liberty under Law: The Supreme Court in American Life* (Baltimore: Johns Hopkins University Press, 1988).

14. Karen Orren and Stephen Skowronek, *The Search for American Political Development* (New York: Cambridge University Press, 2004), 123.

15. Walter Dean Burnham, *Critical Elections and the Mainsprings of American Politics* (New York: Norton, 1970); Richard Funston, "The Supreme Court and Critical Elections," *American Political Science Review* 69, no. 3 (1975); John B. Gates, "Supreme Court Voting and Realigning Issues: A Microlevel Analysis of Supreme Court Pol-

icy Making and Electoral Realignment," *Social Science History* 13, no. 3 (1989); V. O. Key Jr., "A Theory of Critical Elections," *Journal of Politics* 17, no. 1 (1955); Robert G. Scigliano, *The Supreme Court and the Presidency* (New York: Free Press, 1971); James L. Sundquist, *Dynamics of the Party System: Alignment and Realignment of Political Parties in the United States* (Washington: The Brookings Institution, 1973). For a general critique of the realignment literature, see David R. Mayhew, *Electoral Realignments: A Critique of an American Genre* (New Haven, Conn.: Yale University Press, 2002). For a defense of the critical realignment literature, see Peter F. Nardulli, "The Concept of a Critical Realignment, Electoral Behavior, and Political Change," *American Political Science Review* 89, no. 1 (1995).

16. See also Jack M. Balkin and Sanford Levinson, "Understanding the Constitutional Revolution," *Virginia Law Review* 87, no. 6 (2001). The five party systems are Federalist-Jeffersonian (1789–1828); Jacksonian (1828–1860); First Republican (1860–1896); Second Republican (1896–1932); and New Deal (1932–1968). See Sundquist, *Dynamics of the Party System*. For a critique of the standard periodization of party systems in the early nineteenth century, see Joel H. Silbey, *The American Political Nation, 1838–1893* (Stanford, Calif.: Stanford University Press, 1991).

17. See Stephen Skowronek, *The Politics Presidents Make: Leadership from John Adams to Bill Clinton* (Cambridge, Mass.: The Belknap Press of Harvard University Press, 1997); Keith E. Whittington, *Political Foundations of Judicial Supremacy: The Presidency, the Supreme Court, and Constitutional Leadership in U.S. History* (Princeton: Princeton University Press, 2007); Keith E. Whittington, "Presidential Challenges to Judicial Supremacy and the Politics of Constitutional Meaning," *Polity* 33, no. 3 (2001); Geoffrey P. Miller, "The President's Power of Interpretation: Implications of a Unified Theory of Constitutional Law," *Law and Contemporary Problems* 56, no. 4 (1993).

18. Keith Whittington, *Political Foundations of Judicial Supremacy*, 50.

19. Orren and Skowronek, *Search for American Political Development*, 127.

20. Ibid., 125.

21. For an excellent account of the positive and negative roles the judiciary has played in state building generally and in regime building specifically, see Paul Frymer, "Law and American Political Development," *Law and Social Inquiry* 33, no. 3 (2008).

22. With respect to the difficult project of wielding and legitimating the prerequisite authority needed for true political development, Orren and Skowronek add that "governing authority in any given period presents itself as a complex web of relations, a composite of controls gotten up at different times for different purposes . . . and for this reason likely to engage conflicting institutional mandates and methods of execution." Orren and Skowronek, *Search for American Political Development*, 125.

23. Orren and Skowronek, *The Search for American Political Development*, 108. See also Frymer, "Law and American Political Development," 785.

24. See, for example, Ackerman, *We the People*. For an argument that relates the emergence of new constitutional eras to exogenous shocks to the polity, see Lamb and Halpern, "The Supreme Court and New Constitutional Eras."

25. Karen Orren and Stephen Skowronek, "Regimes and Regime Building in American Government: A Review of Literature on the 1940s," *Political Science Quarterly* 113, no. 4 (1998). The maintenance of the New Deal coalition was beset by economic, racial,

and regional problems. See, for example, Kevin J. McMahon, *Reconsidering Roosevelt on Race: How the Presidency Paved the Road to Brown* (Chicago: University of Chicago Press, 2004).

26. See, for example, Stanley I. Kutler, *Judicial Power and Reconstruction Politics* (Chicago: University of Chicago Press, 1968). Michael Les Benedict, *A Compromise of Principle: Congressional Republicans and Reconstruction, 1863–1869* (New York: Norton, 1974). Eric Foner, *Reconstruction: America's Unfinished Revolution, 1863–1877* (New York: Harper & Row, 1989). Rogers M. Smith, *Civic Ideals: Conflicting Visions of Citizenship in U.S. History* (New Haven, Conn.: Yale University Press, 1997), chap. 10.

27. For a discussion of party decline in the years leading up to the 1860 election, see Sundquist, *Dynamics of the Party System.*

28. Eric L. McKitrick, *Andrew Johnson and Reconstruction* (Chicago: University of Chicago Press, 1964). See also Klinkner with Smith, *The Unsteady March: The Rise and Decline of Racial Equality in America*, who refer to this as the obstructed phase of Reconstruction.

29. Act of 5 February 1867, 14 Stat. 385. There were, of course, other statutory changes made to habeas during Reconstruction, specifically the Habeas Corpus Act of 1863 and the so-called McCardle Repealer in 1868, which stripped the Supreme Court (but not lower federal courts) of habeas power under the 1867 act. Also, President Lincoln suspended habeas in 1861, and Congress retroactively authorized these and future executive suspensions in 1863. See Chapter 3 for a detailed discussion of these changes.

30. For an excellent overview of the habeas debates in Congress during Reconstruction, see William M. Wiecek, "The Great Writ and Reconstruction: The Habeas Corpus Act of 1867," *Journal of Southern History* 36, no. 4 (1970); and William M. Wiecek, "The Reconstruction of Federal Judicial Power, 1863–1875," *Am. J. Legal Hist.* 13 (1969). Some argue that even radical Republicans were never as committed to broad Reconstruction principles as some believe they were. See, for example, Benedict, *A Compromise of Principle.* Michael Les Benedict, *Preserving the Constitution: Essays on Politics and the Constitution in the Reconstruction Era* (New York: Fordham University Press, 2006).

31. 117 U.S. 241 (1886). For a detailed discussion of *Royall,* see Chapter 3.

32. This is the effect of what Orren and Skowronek refer to as the "limits, contingencies, varieties, and incongruities of order." Orren and Skowronek, *Search for American Political Development,* 15.

33. In a similar vein, Gerard N. Magliocca refers to this process as a "feedback effect" in the sense that "each generation [regime] carries the seeds of its own destruction, as its very success eventually triggers a backlash." Gerard N. Magliocca, *Andrew Jackson and the Constitution: The Rise and Fall of Generational Regimes* (Lawrence: University Press of Kansas, 2007), 7.

34. See, for example, the contending approaches and views on habeas set forth by Edwin M. Meese III, former attorney general in the Reagan administration, and Justice William Brennan. Edwin Meese III and Rhett DeHart, "Reining in the Federal Judiciary," *Judicature* 80 (1996). William J. Brennan, "Federal Habeas Corpus and State Prisoners: An Exercise in Federalism," *Utah L. Rev.* 7 (1960). William J. Brennan Jr., "The Bill of Rights and the States: The Revival of State Constitutions as Guardians of Individual Rights," *N.Y.U. L. Rev.* 61 (1986).

35. See, for example, Henry J. Friendly, "Is Innocence Irrelevant? Collateral Attack on Criminal Judgments," *University of Chicago Law Review* 38, no. 1 (1970). Paul M. Bator, "Finality in Criminal Law and Federal Habeas Corpus for State Prisoners," *Harv. L. Rev.* 76 (1962). Lewis Mayers, "The Habeas Corpus Act of 1867: The Supreme Court as Legal Historian," *U. Chi. L. Rev.* 33 (1965). Oaks, "Original Writ of Habeas Corpus"; Dallin H. Oaks, "Habeas Corpus in the States—1776–1865," *U. Chi. L. Rev.* 32 (1964); Dallin H. Oaks, "Legal History in the High Court—Habeas Corpus," *Mich. L. Rev.* 64 (1965).

36. Robert M. Cover and Alexander Aleinikoff, "Dialectical Federalism: Habeas Corpus and the Court," *Yale Law Journal* 86, no. 6 (1977).

37. Erwin Chemerinsky, "Thinking about Habeas Corpus," *Case W. Res. L. Rev.* 37 (1986); Alan Clarke, "Habeas Corpus: The Historical Debate," *N.Y. L. Sch. J. Hum. Rts.* 14 (1997); Cover and Aleinikoff, "Dialectical Federalism"; Friedman, "A Tale of Two Habeas"; Barry Friedman, "Pas de Deux: The Supreme Court and the Habeas Courts. The Future of Habeas Corpus: Reflections on *Teague v. Lane* and Beyond," *S. Cal. L. Rev.* 66 (1992); Joseph L. Hoffmann and William J. Stuntz, "Habeas after the Revolution," *Sup. Ct. Rev.* 1993 (1993); Lee, "The Theories of Federal Habeas Corpus"; Liebman, "Apocalypse Next Time?"; Daniel J. Meltzer, "Habeas Corpus Jurisdiction: The Limits of Models. The Future of Habeas Corpus: Reflections on *Teague v. Lane* and Beyond," *S. Cal. L. Rev.* 66 (1992); Paschal, "The Constitution and Habeas Corpus"; Herbert Wechsler, "The Political Safeguards of Federalism: The Role of the States in the Composition and Selection of the National Government," *Colum. L. Rev.* 54 (1954); Yackle, "Explaining Habeas Corpus"; Larry W. Yackle, "The Habeas Hagioscope," *S. Cal. L. Rev.* 66 (1992).

38. Brennan, "Federal Habeas Corpus and State Prisoners"; Brennan, "The Bill of Rights and the States"; Gary Peller, "In Defense of Federal Habeas Corpus Relitigation," *Harv. CR-CL L. Rev.* 16 (1982). Eric M. Freedman, *Habeas Corpus: Rethinking the Great Writ of Liberty* (New York: New York University Press, 2001). Liebman, *Federal Habeas Corpus Practice and Procedure.*

39. See generally Yackle, "The Reagan Administration's Habeas Corpus Proposals."

40. See, for example, Halliday, *Habeas Corpus;* Halliday and White, "Suspension Clause"; David Cole and James X. Dempsey, *Terrorism and the Constitution: Sacrificing Civil Liberties in the Name of National Security,* 3rd ed. (New York: New Press, 2006); Fallon and Meltzer, "Habeas Corpus Jurisdiction, Substantive Rights, and the War on Terror"; Freedman, *Habeas Corpus;* Clinton Rossiter, *Constitutional Dictatorship: Crisis Government in the Modern Democracies* (Princeton: Princeton University Press, 1948); John Yoo, *The Powers of War and Peace: The Constitution and Foreign Affairs after 9/11* (Chicago: University of Chicago Press, 2005); John Yoo, *War by Other Means: An Insider's Account of the War on Terror* (New York: Atlantic Monthly Press, 2006).

41. See, for example, Brennan, "The Bill of Rights and the States"; Brennan, "Federal Habeas Corpus and State Prisoners." Warren E. Burger, "Post Conviction Remedies: Eliminating Federal–State Friction Criminal Law," *J. Crim. L. Criminology and Police Sci.* 61 (1970); Warren E. Burger, "Report on the Federal Judicial Branch—1973 Report," *A.B.A. J.* 59 (1973); Warren E. Burger, "The Need for Change in Prisons and the Correctional System," *Ark. L. Rev.* 38 (1984).

42. This debate is framed around contending accounts of habeas's history more generally, but specifically its history since the Habeas Corpus Act of 1867, in which Congress provided for the first time ever broad postconviction habeas power for federal courts. The classic defense of broad postconviction habeas review is Peller, "In Defense of Federal Habeas Corpus Relitigation." See also Brennan, "Federal Habeas Corpus and State Prisoners." Arguments for limited postconviction habeas power from a historical perspective include Mayers, "Habeas Corpus Act of 1867." See also Bator, "Finality in Criminal Law and Federal Habeas Corpus for State Prisoners." Friendly, "Is Innocence Irrelevant?"

43. The classic account of Whiggish history is Herbert Butterfield, *The Whig Interpretation of History* (London: G. Bell and Sons, 1931). See also Kenneth Kersch, *Constructing Civil Liberties: Discontinuities in the Development of American Constitutional Law* (New York: Cambridge University Press, 2004). In this sense, most accounts of habeas also have the tendency to replicate the various "mythologies" that Quentin Skinner argues beset attempts to synthesize political thought more generally. Quentin Skinner, "Meaning and Understanding in the History of Ideas," *History and Theory* 8, no. 1 (1969).

44. Alfred H. Kelly, "Clio and the Court: An Illicit Love Affair," *Sup. Ct. Rev.* 1965 (1965). See also Charles A. Miller, *The Supreme Court and the Uses of History* (Cambridge, Mass.: Belknap Press of Harvard University Press, 1969); William M. Wiecek, "Clio as Hostage: The United States Supreme Court and the Uses of History Bicentennial Constitutional and Legal History Symposium," *Cal. W. L. Rev.* 24 (1987).

45. Similar charges have been leveled against legal history for decades. See, for example, Robert W. Gordon, "Historicism in Legal Scholarship Symposium on Legal Scholarship: Its Nature and Purposes," *Yale L. J.* 90 (1980); Laura Kalman, "Border Patrol: Reflections on the Turn to History in Legal Scholarship," *Fordham L. Rev.* 66 (1997); Larry D. Kramer, "When Lawyers Do History, Marbury and Its Legacy: A Symposium to Mark the 200th Anniversary of *Marbury v. Madison*: The Constitutional Origins of Judicial Review," *Geo. Wash. L. Rev.* 72 (2003); Paul L. Murphy, "Time to Reclaim: The Current Challenge of American Constitutional History," *American Historical Review* 69, no. 1 (1963); G. Edward White, "The Arrival of History in Constitutional Scholarship," *Va. L. Rev.* 88 (2002). For a defense of law office history, see Cass R. Sunstein, "The Idea of a Useable Past," *Colum. L. Rev.* 95 (1995). My goal is not to levy more criticism but simply to characterize law office accounts of habeas as part of the regime-building process more generally.

46. The definitive account of the mistaken link between habeas and the Magna Carta is Daniel J. Meador, *Habeas Corpus and Magna Carta: Dualism of Power and Liberty* (Charlottesville: University Press of Virginia, 1966). See also Justin J. Wert, "With a Little Help from a Friend: Habeas Corpus and the Magna Carta after Runnymede," *PS: Political Science and Politics* 43, no. 3 (2010); Halliday, *Habeas Corpus*, 15–17; Duker, *Constitutional History of Habeas Corpus*, chap. 1.

47. For accounts detailing similarly Whiggish readings of the origins and development of Magna Carta, see Edward Jenks, "The Myth of Magna Carta," *Independent Review* 4 (1904); C. H. McIlwain, "Due Process of Law in Magna Carta," *Colum. L. Rev.* 14 (1914); Max Radin, "The Myth of Magna Carta," *Harv. L. Rev.* 60 (1946); Meador, *Habeas Corpus and Magna Carta.*

48. Meador, *Habeas Corpus and Magna Carta*. See also Oaks, "Habeas Corpus in the States—1776–1865."

49. A more sympathetic view would characterize this not as Whiggish history but as forensic history. See John Phillip Reid, *The Ancient Constitution and the Origins of Anglo-American Liberty* (DeKalb: Northern Illinois University Press, 2005).

50. Barry Friedman, "The History of the Countermajoritarian Difficulty, Part One: The Road to Judicial Supremacy," *N.Y.U. L. Rev.* 73 (1998).

51. Alexander M. Bickel, *The Least Dangerous Branch: The Supreme Court at the Bar of Politics* (Indianapolis: Bobbs-Merrill, 1962), 16.

52. *United States v. Carolene Products*, 304 U.S. 144 (1938). The definitive account is John Hart, *Democracy and Distrust: A Theory of Judicial Review* (Cambridge: Harvard University Press, 1980).

53. Ronald Dworkin, *A Matter of Principle* (Cambridge, Mass.: Harvard University Press, 1985).

54. Robert H. Bork, *The Tempting of America: The Political Seduction of the Law* (New York: Free Press, 1990).

55. Freedman, *Habeas Corpus*, 1.

56. Zechariah Chafee, "The Most Important Human Right in the Constitution," *B.U. L. Rev.* 32 (1952).

57. St. George Tucker, *Blackstone's Commentaries: With Notes of Reference, to the Constitution and Laws, of the Federal Government of the United States; and of the Commonwealth of Virginia* (1803), 4:131.

58. Alexander Hamilton, James Madison, and John Jay, *The Federalist Papers* (New York: Bantam, 2003), No. 84.

59. *Ex parte Bollman*, 8 U.S. 75, 95 (1807); *Bowen v. Johnston*, 306 U.S. 19, 26 (1939).

60. 75 U.S. 85, 95 (1868)

61. *Fay v. Noia*, 372 U.S. 391, 400–401 (1963).

62. *Frank v. Mangum*, 237 U.S. 309, 346 (1915).

63. See, for example, *Gideon v. Wainwright*, 372 U.S. 335 (1963); *Boumediene v. Bush*, 128 S. Ct. 2229 (2008).

64. The most famous example is *Ex parte Merryman*, 17 F. Cas. 144 (1861).

65. *Fay v. Noia*, 372 U.S. 391, 402 (1963).

66. The characterization of habeas as a double-edged sword is from Mark E. Neely, *The Fate of Liberty: Abraham Lincoln and Civil Liberties* (New York: Oxford University Press, 1991).

67. Robert A. Dahl, "Decision-Making in a Democracy: The Supreme Court as a National Policy-Maker," *J. Pub. L.* 6 (1957). Howard Gillman, "Courts and the Politics of Partisan Coalitions," in *The Oxford Handbook of Law and Politics*, edited by Keith E. Whittington, R. Daniel Kelemen, and Gregory A. Caldeira (Oxford: Oxford University Press, 2008), 644. See also Cornell Clayton and David A. May, "A Political Regimes Approach to the Analysis of Legal Decisions," *Polity* 32, no. 2 (1999); Cornell W. Clayton and J. Mitchell Pickerill, "Guess What Happened on the Way to Revolution? Precursors to the Supreme Court's Federalism Revolution," *Publius* 34, no. 3 (2004); J. Mitchell Pickerill and Cornell W. Clayton, "The Rehnquist Court and the Political Dynamics of Federalism," *Perspectives on Politics* 2, no. 2 (2004); Thomas M. Keck, "Party Politics

or Judicial Independence? The Regime Politics Literature Hits the Law Schools," *Law and Social Inquiry* 32, no. 2 (2007).

68. Dahl sidestepped the Court's judicial review of state legislation, saying, "I propose to pass over the ticklish question of federalism and deal only with 'national' majorities and minorities." Robert A. Dahl, "Decision-Making in a Democracy."

69. Dahl, "Decision-Making in a Democracy," 279.

70. See, for example, McCloskey, *American Supreme Court*, chap. 1. Martin Shapiro, "Judicial Modesty: Down with the Old—Up with the New," *UCLA L. Rev.* 10 (1962); Howard Gillman, "Martin Shapiro and the Movement from 'Old' to 'New' Institutionalist Studies in Public Law Scholarship," *Annual Review of Political Science* 7 (2004).

71. Mark A. Graber, "The Nonmajoritarian Difficulty: Legislative Deference to the Judiciary," *Studies in American Political Development* 7, no. 1 (1993). On legislative deferrals more generally, see George I. Lovell, *Legislative Deferrals: Statutory Ambiguity, Judicial Power, and American Democracy* (New York: Cambridge University Press, 2003). Howard Gillman and Keith Whittington have further mapped the contours of this process. Gillman, "How Political Parties Can Use the Courts to Advance Their Agendas"; Keith E. Whittington, "'Interpose Your Friendly Hand': Political Supports for the Exercise of Judicial Review by the United States Supreme Court," *American Political Science Review* 99, no. 4 (2005).

72. Gillman, "Martin Shapiro and the Movement from 'Old' to 'New' Institutionalist Studies," 377. See also Whittington, "Interpose Your Friendly Hand."

73. On criminal procedure, see Lucas A. Powe, *The Warren Court and American Politics* (Cambridge, Mass.: Harvard University Press, 2000); Michael J. Klarman, "Rethinking the Civil Rights and Civil Liberties Revolutions," *Va. L. Rev.* 82, no. 1 (1996); Michael J. Klarman, "The Racial Origins of Modern Criminal Procedure," *Mich. L. Rev.* 99, no. 1 (2000). On *Brown v. Board of Education,* see McMahon, *Reconsidering Roosevelt on Race.* On federalism, see Pickerill and Clayton, "The Rehnquist Court and the Political Dynamics of Federalism"; Clayton and Pickerill, "Guess What Happened on the Way to Revolution?" On voting rights, see Whittington, "Interpose Your Friendly Hand." On executive power, see Justin J. Wert, "Nothing New under the Sun: Habeas Corpus and Executive Power during the Bush Administration," *American Review of Politics* 29 (2009). On abortion, see Graber, "The Nonmajoritarian Difficulty." See generally Mark A. Graber, "Constructing Judicial Review," *Annual Review of Political Science* 8, no. 1 (2005); David G. Barnum, "The Supreme Court and Public Opinion: Judicial Decision Making in the Post–New Deal Period," *Journal of Politics* 47, no. 2 (1985); William Mishler and Reginald S. Sheehan, "The Supreme Court as a Countermajoritarian Institution? The Impact of Public Opinion on Supreme Court Decisions," *American Political Science Review* 87, no. 1 (1993).

74. In a variant of this argument, Balkin and Levinson explain the existence of regime-affiliated Courts from the fact that "judges—and particularly Supreme Court Justices—tend to reflect the vector sum of political forces at the time of their confirmation." Balkin and Levinson, "Understanding the Constitutional Revolution," 1069.

75. Clayton and May, "Political Regimes Approach," 246.

76. See, for example, Jeffrey Allan Segal and Harold J. Spaeth, *The Supreme Court and the Attitudinal Model Revisited* (New York: Cambridge University Press, 2002).

77. Cornell W. Clayton and J. Mitchell Pickerill, "The Politics of Criminal Justice: How the New Right Regime Shaped the Rehnquist Court's Criminal Justice Jurisprudence," *Geo. L. J.* 94 (2005): 1391.

78. See Keck, "Party Politics or Judicial Independence?"; Thomas M. Keck, "Party, Policy, or Duty: Why Does the Supreme Court Invalidate Federal Statutes?," *American Political Science Review* 101, no. 2 (2007). Keck's criticism is directed mainly at three recent applications of the regimes approach: Klarman, *From Jim Crow to Civil Rights;* Tushnet, *New Constitutional Order;* Jeffrey Rosen, *The Most Democratic Branch: How the Courts Serve America* (New York: Oxford University Press, 2006). See also Barry Friedman, *The Will of the People: How Public Opinion Has Influenced the Supreme Court and Shaped the Meaning of the Constitution* (New York: Farrar, Straus and Giroux, 2009). Others who find fault with this literature include Stephen M. Feldman, "The Rule of Law or the Rule of Politics? Harmonizing the Internal and External Views of Supreme Court Decision Making," *Law and Social Inquiry* 30, no. 1 (2005); and George Thomas, *The Madisonian Constitution* (Baltimore: Johns Hopkins University Press, 2008), 12–13.

79. Keck, "Party Politics or Judicial Independence?"; Gary King, Robert O. Keohane, and Sidney Verba, *Designing Social Inquiry: Scientific Inference in Qualitative Research* (Princeton: Princeton University Press, 1994), chap. 3.

80. Keck, "Party Politics or Judicial Independence?," 535.

81. Ibid., 540. Keck, "Party, Policy, or Duty," 323, 335. Robert McCloskey argued that in constitutional history, the "Court can be observed struggling to formulate a judicial role that will reinforce those interests and values within the subtle limits of judicial capability." McCloskey, *American Supreme Court,* 15.

82. Critiquing purely political understandings of courts, Robert McCloskey made a similar point: "Judges have usually known what students have sometimes not known — that their tribunal must be a court, as well as seem one, if it is to retain power. The idea of fundamental law as a force in its own right, distinguishable from today's popular will, can only be maintained by a pattern of Court behavior that emphasizes the separation." McCloskey, *American Supreme Court,* 13.

83. Vincent Blasi, *The Burger Court: The Counter-Revolution That Wasn't* (New Haven, Conn.: Yale University Press, 1983).

84. *Mapp v. Ohio,* 367 U.S. 643 (1961); *Stone v. Powell,* 428 U.S. 465 (1976).

85. 428 U.S. 465, 495.

86. Rogers M. Smith, "Political Jurisprudence, the 'New Institutionalism,' and the Future of Public Law," *American Political Science Review* 82, no. 1 (1988): 95. See also Howard Gillman, "The Court as an Idea, Not a Building (or a Game): Interpretive Institutionalism and the Analysis of Supreme Court Decision-Making," in *Supreme Court Decision-Making: New Institutionalist Approaches,* ed. Cornell W. Clayton and Howard Gillman (Chicago: University of Chicago Press, 1999).

87. See Clayton and Pickerill, "Politics of Criminal Justice," 1424; Keck, "Party, Policy, or Duty," 335; Wert, "Nothing New under the Sun."

88. This institutionally protective posture is evident in *Hamdi v. Rumsfeld,* 542 U.S. 507 (2004); *Rasul v. Bush,* 542 U.S. 466 (2004); *Hamdan v. Rumsfeld,* 548 U.S. 557 (2006); and *Boumediene v. Bush,* 128 S. Ct. 2229 (2008).

89. Paul Frymer argues that "because institutions do not refract interests directly but instead represent an amalgam of historically produced and institutionally entrenched archeology, the actors within them do not mirror society. Government institutions and actors come to play roles that are meaningfully autonomous from society. . . . These government institutions create an analytically distinct set of interests and politics that cannot be explained without attention to the rules and incentives inherent within the institutions that motivate individual behavior and outcomes." Frymer, "Law and American Political Development," 785.

90. *Fay v. Noia*, 372 U.S. 391, 409 (1963).

91. 237 U.S. 309 (1915); 261 U.S. 86 (1923).

CHAPTER 2. ANTEBELLUM HABEAS

1. My account of the Matson slave case is drawn from John J. Duff, *A. Lincoln: Prairie Lawyer* (New York: Rinehart, 1960), chap. 9.

2. *Bailey v. Cromwell*, 4 Ill. 70 (1841). See Stephen B. Oates, *With Malice toward None: The Life of Abraham Lincoln* (New York: Harper & Row, 1977), 101–102.

3. Quoted in Duff, *A. Lincoln*, 139.

4. Oates, *With Malice toward None*, 101.

5. Gary Peller, "In Defense of Federal Habeas Corpus Relitigation," *Harv. CR-CL L. Rev.* 16 (1982): 582.

6. It should be noted that jurisdiction in habeas cases is not equivalent to the concept of jurisdiction more generally that courts may or may not possess. In habeas cases, the concept of jurisdiction has a few different meanings. It can refer simply to an attack on the competency of a court or an individual to detain someone. It can also refer to situations when courts lose jurisdiction because some action or actions (most often constitutional violations) cause them to forfeit their otherwise competent and legitimate jurisdiction. This concept of jurisdiction, in particular, is the most controversial aspect of habeas jurisprudence because courts can lose their legitimate jurisdiction when new substantive rights are violated.

7. William F. Duker, *A Constitutional History of Habeas Corpus* (Westport, Conn.: Greenwood Press, 1980), 8.

8. On the tariff issue generally, see Joel H. Silbey, *The American Political Nation, 1838–1893* (Stanford, Calif.: Stanford University Press, 1991); Keith E. Whittington, *Constitutional Construction: Divided Powers and Constitutional Meaning* (Cambridge, Mass.: Harvard University Press, 1999), chap. 3.

9. 62 U.S. 506 (1859).

10. Article I, sec. 9, provides that "the privilege of the writ of habeas corpus shall not be suspended, unless when in cases of rebellion or invasion the public safety may require it." See generally Dallin H. Oaks, "The Original Writ of Habeas Corpus in the Supreme Court," *Sup. Ct. Rev.* 1962 (1962).

11. Detainee Treatment Act (DTA), 119 Stat. 2739, and the Military Commissions Act (MCA), 120 Stat. 2600.

12. Oaks, "Original Writ of Habeas Corpus"; Paul M. Bator, "Finality in Criminal Law and Federal Habeas Corpus for State Prisoners," *Harv. L. Rev.* 76 (1962); Henry J.

Friendly, "Is Innocence Irrelevant? Collateral Attack on Criminal Judgments," *U. Chi. L. Rev.* 38, no. 1 (1970).

13. Francis Paschal, "The Constitution and Habeas Corpus," *Duke L. J.* 1970 (1970); Peller, "In Defense of Federal Habeas Corpus Relitigation"; William J. Brennan, "Federal Habeas Corpus and State Prisoners: An Exercise in Federalism," *Utah L. Rev.* 7 (1960); Eric M. Freedman, *Habeas Corpus: Rethinking the Great Writ of Liberty* (New York: New York University Press, 2001).

14. In the most recent defense of the position that the suspension clause supports modern conceptions of broad federal postconviction habeas review, Eric Freedman argues that our interrogation of Founding-era habeas records "has not been accompanied by any greater insights into specifics of original intention on matters *of particular interest today—as those matters did not happen to be the ones particularly in controversy among the debaters of the time*" (italics added). Freedman, *Habeas Corpus,* 13–14.

15. See Paul D. Halliday, *Habeas Corpus: From England to Empire* (Cambridge: Harvard University Press, 2010), 250–253; Paul Halliday and G. Edward White, "The Suspension Clause: English Text, Imperial Contexts, and American Implications," *Va. L. Rev.* 94 (2008): 644–651; John H. Hatcher, "Martial Law and Habeas Corpus," *W. Va. L. Q.* 46 (1939).

16. Halliday and White, "Suspension Clause," 644.

17. See, for example, Edmund Burke's "Speech on Conciliation" (1775), in *Edmund Burke: Selected Writings and Speeches,* ed. Peter J. Stanlis (Washington, D.C.: Regnery, 1997).

18. Quoted in Halliday and White, "Suspension Clause," 650.

19. Halliday and White make this observation against claims to the contrary that the 1679 act did not apply in the colonies. Halliday and White, "Suspension Clause," 645n206

20. The constitutions of North Carolina, Georgia, and Massachusetts had enumerated provisions guaranteeing the writ. The standard account of state habeas is Dallin H. Oaks, "Habeas Corpus in the States—1776–1865," *U. Chi. L. Rev.* 32 (1964).

21. Zechariah Chafee, "The Most Important Human Right in the Constitution," *B.U. L. Rev.* 32 (1952): 146.

22. James Madison, *Notes of Debates in the Federal Convention of 1787* (New York: Norton, 1987), 486.

23. This position, which is most fervently articulated and defended by William Duker, is of course heavily criticized by those who argue for broad federal habeas corpus rights for state prisoners. Duker, *Constitutional History of Habeas Corpus.* For the opposite position, see Paschal, "The Constitution and Habeas Corpus," and Freedman, *Habeas Corpus.*

24. Max Farrand, *The Records of the Federal Convention of 1787* (New Haven, Conn.: Yale University Press, 1911), 3:213.

25. "The Address and Reasons of Dissent of the Minority of the Convention of Pennsylvania to Their Constituents" (18 December 1787), in Ralph Ketcham, *The Anti-Federalist Papers and the Constitutional Convention Debates* (New York: New American Library, 1986).

26. For excellent accounts of the Judiciary Act of 1789, see Charles Warren, "New

Light on the History of the Federal Judiciary Act of 1789," *Harv. L. Rev.* 37 (1923); Wythe Holt, "To Establish Justice: Politics, the Judiciary Act of 1789, and the Invention of the Federal Courts," *Duke L. J.* 1989 (1989); Erwin Chemerinsky, *Federal Jurisdiction*, 4th ed. (New York: Aspen, 2003), 9–11; Robert N. Clinton, "A Mandatory View of Federal Court Jurisdiction: Early Implementation of and Departures from the Constitutional Plan," *Colum. L. Rev.* 86 (1986).

27. The Judiciary Act of 1789 is still considered by many to be almost as authoritative as the Constitution itself by virtue of the fact that many in the first Congress were also drafters of the Constitution. See, for example, *Wisconsin v. Pelican Ins. Co.*, 127 U.S. 265, 297 (1888), in which the Court explained that the Judiciary Act of 1789 "was passed by the first Congress assembled under the Constitution, many of whose members had taken part in framing that instrument, and is contemporaneous and weighty evidence of its true meaning." And in *Ames v. Kansas*, 111 U.S. 449, 463, Chief Justice Waite asserted that the first Congress consisted of "many who had been leading and influential members of the convention, and who were familiar with the discussions that preceded the adoption of the Constitution by the States and with the objections urged against it."

28. Stanley M. Elkins and Eric L. McKitrick, *The Age of Federalism* (New York: Oxford University Press, 1995), 62–64.

29. Ibid., 63.

30. 1 Stat. 73, 25 (1789).

31. Freedman further suggests that scholars' historical investigations of the Founding generation's understandings of habeas have "not been accompanied by any greater insight into the specifics of original intention *on matters of particular interest today*" (italics added). Freedman, *Habeas Corpus*, 13.

32. James S. Liebman, *Federal Habeas Corpus Practice and Procedure* (Charlottesville, Va.: Michie, 1994), 39.

33. The claim that habeas was originally understood only to apply before conviction, or after conviction only if the original court lacked jurisdiction, is most forcefully made by Bator, "Finality in Criminal Law and Federal Habeas Corpus for State Prisoners." See also Lewis Mayers, "The Habeas Corpus Act of 1867: The Supreme Court as Legal Historian," *U. Chi. L. Rev.* 33 (1965); and Oaks, "Original Writ of Habeas Corpus."

34. The nine federal habeas cases that came before the Supreme Court during this period were *United States v. Hamilton*, 3 U.S. 17 (1795); *Ex parte Burford*, 7 U.S. 448 (1806); *Ex parte Bollman*, 8 U.S. 75 (1807); *Ex parte Kearney*, 20 U.S. 38 (1822); *Ex parte Watkins*, 28 U.S. 193 (1830); *Ex parte Watkins II*, 32 U.S. 568 (1833); *Ex parte Milburn*, 34 U.S. 704 (1835); *In re Kaine*, 55 U.S. 103 (1852); and *Ex parte Wells*, 59 U.S. 307 (1855).

35. 8 U.S. 75 (1807); 28 U.S. 193 (1830).

36. For accounts detailing Marshall's strained legal logic more generally, see Christopher L. Eisgruber, "John Marshall's Judicial Rhetoric," *Sup. Ct. Rev.* (1996); Susan Bloch and Maeva Marcus, "John Marshall's Selective Use of History in *Marbury v. Madison*," *Wis. L. Rev.* 1986 (1986); David P. Currie, *The Constitution in the Supreme Court: The First Hundred Years, 1789–1888* (Chicago: University of Chicago Press, 1985); William E. Nelson, "The Eighteenth-Century Background of John Marshall's Constitutional Jurisprudence," *Mich. L. Rev.* 76 (1977); G. Edward White and Gerald Gunther, *The Marshall Court and Cultural Change, 1815–35* (New York: Macmillan, 1988).

37. See generally Gordon S. Wood, *Empire of Liberty: A History of the Early Republic, 1789–1815* (New York: Oxford University Press, 2009), 437–441; Mark A. Graber, "Establishing Judicial Review? Schooner Peggy and the Early Marshall Court," *Political Research Quarterly* 51, no. 1 (1998); Mark Graber, "Federalist or Friends of Adams: The Marshall Court and Party Politics," *Studies in American Political Development* 12, no. 2 (1998).

38. See generally Joseph J. Ellis, *Founding Brothers: The Revolutionary Generation* (New York: Alfred A. Knopf, 2000), chap. 1.

39. Cf. ibid., 38–39; Jean Edward Smith, *John Marshall: Definer of a Nation* (New York: Holt, 1996), 352–354.

40. Smith, *John Marshall*, 352. See also Robert G. Scigliano, *The Supreme Court and the Presidency* (New York: Free Press, 1971), 29–31.

41. Although Jefferson never mentioned Burr by name in the proclamation, he did so privately in correspondence, referring to Burr as "Our Catiline," who will "place himself on the throne of Montezuma." Smith, *John Marshall*, 353.

42. Smith, *John Marshall*, 354–355.

43. *Ex parte Bollman* and *Ex parte Swartwout*, 8 U.S. 75 (1807). But see also *Ex parte Burford*, 7 U.S. 448, 449 (1806).

44. Freedman, *Habeas Corpus*, 21.

45. For an excellent overview of Harper's argument, see Freedman, *Habeas Corpus*, 21–23. See also Smith, *John Marshall*, 355.

46. 8 U.S. 75, 93 (1807).

47. Smith, *John Marshall*, 355.

48. 8 U.S. 75, 95 (1807).

49. 8 U.S. 75, 93 (1807).

50. 5 U.S. 137 (1803).

51. Ibid., 101.

52. Ibid., 96.

53. Ibid.

54. Marshall's distinction was between a conspiracy to commit treason and the actual act itself. Wood, *Empire of Liberty*, 439–440.

55. On the Chase impeachment, see Whittington, *Constitutional Construction*, chap. 2. See also Lucas A. Powe, "The Politics of American Judicial Review: Reflections on the Marshall, Warren, and Rehnquist Courts," *Wake Forest L. Rev.* 38 (2003).

56. See Robert K. Faulkner, "John Marshall and the Burr Trial," *Journal of American History* 53, no. 2 (1966); Smith, *John Marshall*, 357–374; Graber, "Federalist or Friends of Adams," 251–252.

57. Smith, *John Marshall*, 357; Donald Grier Stephenson, *Campaigns and the Court: The U.S. Supreme Court in Presidential Elections* (New York: Columbia University Press, 1999), 46–52.

58. Whittington, *Constitutional Construction*, 65; Robert G. McCloskey, *The American Supreme Court* (Chicago: University of Chicago Press, 2005), 30.

59. 28 U.S. 193 (1830).

60. Ibid. at 202–203. See also Duker, *Constitutional History of Habeas Corpus*, 229; Liebman, *Federal Habeas Corpus Practice and Procedure*, 39n101.

61. Graber, "Federalist or Friends of Adams," 259.

62. 28 U.S. 193 (1830) at 201.

63. Mark Graber argued that both the *Bollman* case and Burr's trial were exceptions to the Marshall Court's otherwise regime-sympathetic doctrine. Graber, "Federalist or Friends of Adams." Graber also argues that Marshall might have misjudged public and congressional opposition to Burr.

64. Rollin C. Hurd, *A Treatise on the Right of Personal Liberty: And on the Writ of Habeas Corpus and the Practice Connected with It: With a View of the Law of Extradition of Fugitives* (Albany: W. C. Little, 1858); Duker, *Constitutional History of Habeas Corpus;* Oaks, "Habeas Corpus in the States—1776–1865"; Charles Warren, "Federal and State Court Interference," *Harv. L. Rev.* 43 (1929).

65. It should be noted again that this limitation on federal court habeas power did not preclude writs of error from state courts on federal questions. See Liebman, *Federal Habeas Corpus Practice and Procedure,* 34–35. Freedman, *Habeas Corpus,* 27.

66. 4 Stat. 632 (1833).

67. 5 Stat. 539 (1842).

68. See, for example, the excellent accounts of the controversy in William W. Freehling, *The Road to Disunion* (New York: Oxford University Press, 1990); Whittington, *Constitutional Construction;* David F. Ericson, "The Nullification Crisis, American Republicanism, and the Force Bill Debate," *Journal of Southern History* 61, no. 2 (1995); and Richard B. Latner, "The Nullification Crisis and Republican Subversion," *Journal of Southern History* 43, no. 1 (1977).

69. *Worcester v. Georgia,* 31 U.S. 515 (1832). Whittington, *Constitutional Construction,* 87. Whittington contends that "Jackson could remain passive in the face of Georgia's recalcitrance to court orders, since Georgia's actions did not directly challenge presidential authority," whereas South Carolina's actions "threatened to disrupt" and directly challenge presidential authority.

70. Whittington, *Constitutional Construction,* 86.

71. Latner, "Nullification Crisis," 33.

72. For an excellent account of the incident and its influence in international law, see David J. Bederman, "The Cautionary Tale of Alexander McLeod: Superior Orders and the American Writ of Habeas Corpus," *Emory L. J.* 41 (1992). See also Duker, *Constitutional History of Habeas Corpus,* 188–189.

73. Bederman, "Cautionary Tale," 518.

74. Ibid., 526.

75. Ibid., 528nn68, 69.

76. Act of 29 August 1842, 5 Stat. 539.

77. Quoted in Charles Warren, *The Supreme Court in United States History* (Washington, D.C.: Beard Books, 1999), 2:374.

78. 17 U.S. 316 (1819).

79. Warren, *Supreme Court in United States History,* 2:375.

80. For historical examples before the McLeod affair where state criminal cases against foreign nationals were disruptive of international affairs, see Bederman, "Cautionary Tale," 526–527.

81. See, for example, Justice Brennan's opinion in *Fay v. Noia,* 372 U.S. 391 at 401, n9 (1963).

82. See generally Oaks, "Habeas Corpus in the States—1776–1865."

83. *Tarble's Case*, 80 U.S. 397 (1871). See also Seymour D. Thompson, "Abuses of the Writ of Habeas Corpus," *Am. L. Rev.* 18 (1884).

84. Oaks, "Habeas Corpus in the States—1776–1865," 254.

85. See Halliday, *Habeas Corpus;* Dallin H. Oaks, "Legal History in the High Court—Habeas Corpus," *Mich. L. Rev.* 64 (1965); Daniel John Meador, *Habeas Corpus and Magna Carta: Dualism of Power and Liberty* (Charlottesville: University Press of Virginia, 1966).

86. Warren, "Federal and State Court Interference," 355.

87. 2 Hall's Am. L. J. 195–196 (1809).

88. *Ex parte Pleasants*, 19 F. Cas. 864 (1833). Thompson, "Abuses of the Writ of Habeas Corpus," 354–355.

89. Miss. Comp. Stats., sec. 11. See Oaks, "Habeas Corpus in the States—1776–1865," 278.

90. 1 Miss. 154 (1824). See also *Hardy v. Smith,* 11 Miss. 316 (1844), in which a similar course of events played out.

91. 13 Miss. 345 (1845).

92. See, for example, *Thornton v. Demoss,* 13 Miss. 609 (1846); *Weddington v. Sam Sloan (of color),* 54 Ky. 147 (1854); *Ruddle's Ex'or v. Ben,* 37 Va. 467 (1839).

93. On manumissions during and immediately after the Revolutionary War, see generally Philip A. Klinkner with Rogers M. Smith, *The Unsteady March: The Rise and Decline of Racial Equality in America* (Chicago: University of Chicago Press, 1999), chap. 1.

94. Thomas D. Morris, *Free Men All: The Personal Liberty Laws of the North, 1780–1861* (Baltimore: Johns Hopkins University Press, 1974), 11.

95. See Leon F. Litwack, *North of Slavery: The Negro in the Free States, 1790–1860* (Chicago: University of Chicago Press, 1961).

96. 1 N.J. L. 41 (1790).

97. The new owner's argument also rested on the argument that children of black female slaves were automatically slaves for life.

98. *The State v. The Administrators of Prall,* 1 N.J.L. 4 (1790).

99. Ibid., 6.

100. *State v. Frees,* 1 N.J.L. 299.

101. Ibid., 300.

102. Article IV in part provides that "no Person held to Service or Labour in one State, under the Laws thereof, escaping into another, shall, in Consequence of any Law or Regulation therein, be discharged from such Service or Labour, but shall be delivered up on Claim of the Party to whom such Service or Labour may be due."

103. Paul Finkelman, "The Kidnapping of John Davis and the Adoption of the Fugitive Slave Law of 1793," *Journal of Southern History* 56, no. 3 (1990).

104. For a detailed discussion of the writ *de homine replegiando* and personal replevin, see William F. Duker, "The Right to Bail: A Historical Inquiry," *Albany L. Rev.* 42 (1977): 43–44; Morris, *Free Men All,* 11–12; Oaks, "Habeas Corpus in the States—1776–1865," 281.

105. See generally Morris, *Free Men All;* William R. Leslie, "The Pennsylvania Fu-

gitive Slave Act of 1826," *Journal of Southern History* 18, no. 4 (1952); Paul Finkelman, "Story Telling on the Supreme Court: *Prigg v. Pennsylvania* and Justice Joseph Story's Judicial Nationalism," *Sup. Ct. Rev.* 1994 (1994).

106. Leslie, "Pennsylvania Fugitive Slave Act," 443.

107. To some, the extraterritorial application of slave law, enforced by the national government, was the central legal and constitutional issue that led to the Civil War. See Arthur Bestor, "State Sovereignty and Slavery: A Reinterpretation of Proslavery Constitutional Doctrine," *Journal of the Illinois State Historical Society* (1961).

108. 41 U.S. 539 (1842). See also Earl M. Maltz, *Slavery and the Supreme Court, 1825–1861* (Lawrence: University Press of Kansas, 2009), 93–113; Finkelman, "Story Telling on the Supreme Court."

109. 41 U.S. 611 (1842). See Finkelman, "Story Telling on the Supreme Court," 256.

110. Earl Maltz characterizes the *Prigg* decision as "an effort to defuse sectional tensions" over the issue of fugitive slaves. Maltz, *Slavery and the Supreme Court,* 112.

111. For a defense of Story's opinion as antislavery, see Christopher L. Eisgruber, "Justice Story, Slavery, and the Natural Law Foundations of American Constitutionalism," *U. Chi. L. Rev.* 55 (1988). For the argument that Story's opinion was proslavery, see Finkelman, "Story Telling on the Supreme Court."

112. 41 U.S. 539, 627 (1842).

113. Quoted in Warren, *Supreme Court in United States History,* 359–360.

114. Morris, *Free Men All,* 124–125.

115. For an overview of public opinion toward the Compromise of 1850 and its fugitive slave provisions, see Stanley W. Campbell, *The Slave Catchers: Enforcement of the Fugitive Slave Law, 1850–1860* (Chapel Hill: University of North Carolina Press, 1970), chaps. 3 and 4.

116. Campbell, *Slave Catchers,* 23–25.

117. Ibid., 96–97.

118. Quoted in ibid., 98.

119. David M. Potter, *The Impending Crisis, 1848–1861* (New York: Harper & Row, 1976), 130.

120. Campbell, *Slave Catchers,* 99.

121. *United States v. Morris,* 26 F. Cas. 1323 (1851).

122. Warren, *Supreme Court in United States History,* 500–503.

123. The most thorough account of the Sims case, from which most of my account derives, is Leonard W. Levy, "Sims' Case: The Fugitive Slave Law in Boston in 1851," *Journal of Negro History* 35, no. 1 (1950).

124. The Compromise provided that "in no trial or hearing under this Act shall the testimony of such alleged Fugitive be admitted as evidence."

125. For a more in-depth analysis of Justice Shaw's role in fugitive slave cases more generally, see Robert M. Cover, *Justice Accused: Antislavery and the Judicial Process* (New Haven, Conn.: Yale University Press, 1975).

126. Quoted in Levy, "Sims' Case," 50–51.

127. Ibid., 53.

128. 6 Mass. 285, 310. On the questionable basis of Story's argument, see Finkelman, "Story Telling on the Supreme Court."

129. Quoted in Levy, "Sims' Case," 59–60.

130. Morris, *Free Men All,* 153.

131. Quoted in Campbell, *Slave Catchers,* 99–100.

132. Morris, *Free Men All,* 159.

133. Vermont's law, as Morris argues, was the exception that proved the rule. Massachusetts and Pennsylvania legislatures, intent on upholding the Compromise, were only able to repeal some of the personal liberty laws passed after *Prigg.* Even with partial repeals, bills did not pass unless some concessions were made to antislavery interests. See Morris, *Free Men All,* 158–164.

134. See also Maltz, *Slavery and the Supreme Court,* 142, 148; Mark A. Graber, *Dred Scott and the Problem of Constitutional Evil* (Cambridge: Cambridge University Press, 2006), 36–37.

135. 51 U.S. 82, 94 (1851). See also Warren, *Supreme Court in United States History,* 498–499; McCloskey, *American Supreme Court,* 61.

136. Campbell, *Slave Catchers,* 105.

137. 13 F. Cas. 445 (1853).

138. Judge Kane argued that "the phraseology of the [1833] statute is unequivocal in its import, and entirely consonant with its apparent object. It applies in broad and general terms to all officers of the United States, by whatever law or authority confined." 13 F. Cas. 445, 451.

139. 13 F. Cas. 445, 448 (1853). See also *Ex parte Robinson,* 30 F. Cas. 965 (1856), and *Ex parte Sifford,* 22 F. Cas. 105 (1857), in which the Habeas Act of 1833 was also used to discharge federal officers involved in fugitive slave renditions.

140. Graber, *Dred Scott,* 154; Potter, *Impending Crisis,* 246–247.

141. Morris, *Free Men All,* 167.

142. Michael F. Holt, *The Rise and Fall of the American Whig Party: Jacksonian Politics and the Onset of the Civil War* (New York: Oxford University Press, 1999), 804–835; Graber, *Dred Scott,* 158, 163–166; James L. Sundquist, *Dynamics of the Party System: Alignment and Realignment of Political Parties in the United States* (Washington: The Brookings Institution, 1973).

143. My description of the demise of the bisectional Jacksonian coalition as precipitated in part by the political calculations of changing demographics is informed by Graber, *Dred Scott.*

144. 62 U.S. 506 (1859). Warren, *Supreme Court in United States History,* 3:58.

145. U.S. 393 (1857). Morris, *Free Men All,* 178. Warren, *Supreme Court in United States History,* 55.

146. Freehling, *Road to Disunion,* chap. 10.

147. Freehling, *Road to Disunion.* Graber, *Dred Scott,* 33–35. Mark A. Graber, "The Nonmajoritarian Difficulty: Legislative Deference to the Judiciary," *Studies in American Political Development* 7, no. 1 (1993): 46–49.

148. Freehling, *Road to Disunion,* 115–116. McCloskey, *American Supreme Court,* 63.

149. Freehling, *Road to Disunion,* 121–122.

150. Bestor, "State Sovereignty and Slavery."

151. McCloskey, *American Supreme Court,* 63. See also Eric Foner, *Free Soil, Free Labor, Free Men: The Ideology of the Republican Party before the Civil War* (New York: Oxford University Press, 1970), 134–135.

152. My account of the *Ableman* case is largely drawn from H. Robert Baker, *The Rescue of Joshua Glover: A Fugitive Slave, the Constitution, and the Coming of the Civil War* (Athens: Ohio University Press, 2006). Maltz, *Slavery and the Supreme Court;* Warren, *Supreme Court in United States History,* 532–536. Morris, *Free Men All,* 173–179. Campbell, *Slave Catchers,* 159–160.

153. *Arguments of Byron Paine,* quoted in Morris, *Free Men All,* 174.

154. See Baker, *Rescue of Joshua Glover,* 118–121. See also Foner, *Free Soil,* 134. Warren, *Supreme Court in United States History,* 533.

155. After his arrest on the federal indictment, Booth unsuccessfully petitioned the Wisconsin supreme court for a habeas writ on the charge. It was denied. See Campbell, *Slave Catchers,* 159n37.

156. *In re Booth,* 3 Wis. 1 (1854).

157. Ibid., 31.

158. Baker, *Rescue of Joshua Glover,* 137.

159. Warren, *Supreme Court in United States History,* 54–55. Campbell, *Slave Catchers,* 160.

160. Warren, *Supreme Court in United States History,* 57–58.

161. 62 U.S. 506, 514 (1859).

162. Ibid., 514.

163. Ibid., 515.

164. Ibid.

165. Ibid.

166. Ibid., 517.

167. Ibid., 520.

168. Ibid., 522.

169. Warren, *Supreme Court in United States History,* 60.

170. Ibid., 63. See also Morris, *Free Men All,* 180.

171. *Wisconsin House Journal,* 1859, 864, quoted in Morris, *Free Men All,* 180. The legislature substituted the term "positive defiance" for "nullification." See also Warren, *Supreme Court in United States History,* 63.

172. Foner, *Free Soil,* 135.

173. See Foner, *Free Soil,* 137. Morris, *Free Men All,* 187.

174. Warren, *Supreme Court in United States History,* 67.

175. Foner, *Free Soil.*

176. "Declaration of the Immediate Causes Which Induce and Justify the Secession of South Carolina from the Federal Union, December 24, 1860." See Bestor, "State Sovereignty and Slavery," 2n2.

177. Maltz, for example, argues that the "Southern dominated *Ableman* Court was ultimately successful in resisting the challenge to its authority only because it had the firm support of the executive branch." Maltz, *Slavery and the Supreme Court,* 285–286.

178. Karen Orren and Stephen Skowronek, *The Search for American Political Development* (New York: Cambridge University Press, 2004), 29.

179. Foner, *Free Soil,* 310.

CHAPTER 3. THE RECONSTRUCTION OF HABEAS CORPUS

1. *Congressional Globe*, 39th Cong., 1st sess. (8 January 1866), 135 (Rep. Lawrence).

2. For the argument that the Warren Court specifically chose habeas to accomplish these goals, see Lucas A. Powe, *The Warren Court and American Politics* (Cambridge, Mass.: Harvard University Press, 2000).

3. *Fay v. Noia*, 372 U.S. 391, 409 (1963). See also William J. Brennan, "Federal Habeas Corpus and State Prisoners: An Exercise in Federalism," *Utah L. Rev.* 7 (1960); William J. Brennan Jr., "The Bill of Rights and the States: The Revival of State Constitutions as Guardians of Individual Rights," *N.Y.U. L. Rev.* 61 (1986).

4. See Keith E. Whittington, "'Interpose Your Friendly Hand': Political Supports for the Exercise of Judicial Review by the United States Supreme Court," *American Political Science Review* 99, no. 4 (2005). Michael J. Klarman, "Majoritarian Judicial Review: The Entrenchment Problem," *Geo. L. J.* 85 (1996).

5. Modern habeas jurisprudence can almost be completely divided between contending interpretations of the Habeas Corpus Act of 1867 and its immediate post-Reconstruction development. See, for example, Lewis Mayers, "The Habeas Corpus Act of 1867: The Supreme Court as Legal Historian," *U. Chi. L. Rev.* 33 (1965); Paul M. Bator, "Finality in Criminal Law and Federal Habeas Corpus for State Prisoners," *Harv. L. Rev.* 76 (1962); Alan Clarke, "Habeas Corpus: The Historical Debate," *N.Y.L. Sch. J. Hum. Rts.* 14 (1997); Larry W. Yackle, "Explaining Habeas Corpus," *N.Y.U. L. Rev.* 60 (1985).

6. Pamela Brandwein, *Reconstructing Reconstruction: The Supreme Court and the Production of Historical Truth* (Durham, N.C.: Duke University Press, 1999), 1–3. Accordingly, Brandwein explains her historiographical account as providing "a rhetorical tool (an account of the production of 'credible' Reconstruction history) that would be useful to Warren Court defenders" (3).

7. For arguments that federalism was little changed during Reconstruction, see Michael Les Benedict, "Preserving the Constitution: The Conservative Basis of Radical Reconstruction," *Journal of American History* 61, no. 1 (1974); Phillip Shaw Paludan, *A Covenant with Death: The Constitution, Law, and Equality in the Civil War Era* (Urbana: University of Illinois Press, 1975); William E. Nelson, *The Fourteenth Amendment: From Political Principle to Judicial Doctrine* (Cambridge, Mass.: Harvard University Press, 1988). For Nelson, as for Harold Hyman, there were multiple and ultimately conflicting intentions on the part of Reconstruction's congresses that advocated broad rhetorical commitments to individual liberty and racial egalitarianism while maintaining fairly traditional conceptions of federalism. It was only when more and more challenges appeared in later decades that significant problems emerged. Harold M. Hyman, *A More Perfect Union: The Impact of the Civil War and Reconstruction on the Constitution* (New York: Knopf, 1973).

8. The use of courts to aid in enforcing national policy commitments in the federal system is a role that courts have played in a fairly efficient way throughout American constitutional history. See, for example, Klarman, "Majoritarian Judicial Review"; Michael J. Klarman, "Race and the Court in the Progressive Era: Rethinking *Buchanan v.*

Warley," *Vand. L. Rev.* 51 (1998); Michael J. Klarman, "The Racial Origins of Modern Criminal Procedure," *Mich. L. Rev.* 99, no. 1 (2000); J. Mitchell Pickerill and Cornell W. Clayton, "The Rehnquist Court and the Political Dynamics of Federalism," *Perspectives on Politics* 2, no. 2 (2004); Whittington, "Interpose Your Friendly Hand."

9. This dynamic is developed at length in Cornell W. Clayton and J. Mitchell Pickerill, "The Politics of Criminal Justice: How the New Right Regime Shaped the Rehnquist Court's Criminal Justice Jurisprudence," *Geo. L. J.* 94 (2005): 1420–1423.

10. Michael Klarman makes a related point in discussing the majoritarian influences on Japanese internment and in the Court's decision in *Korematsu.* Michael J. Klarman, "Rethinking the Civil Rights and Civil Liberties Revolutions," *Va. L. Rev.* 82, no. 1 (1996): 28–29.

11. For an overview and critique of Reconstruction historiography that makes these pre- and post-Appomattox distinctions, see the introduction to Harold Melvin Hyman, *The Radical Republicans and Reconstruction, 1861–1870* (Indianapolis: Bobbs-Merrill, 1967). See also Brandwein, *Reconstructing Reconstruction,* 4–5.

12. *Ex parte Merryman,* 17 F. Cas. 144 (1861); *Ex parte Milligan,* 71 U.S. 2 (1866); *Ex parte McCardle,* 74 U.S. 506 (1869).

13. Mark E. Neely, *The Fate of Liberty: Abraham Lincoln and Civil Liberties* (New York: Oxford University Press, 1991), xvi.

14. Arthur Bestor, "The American Civil War as a Constitutional Crisis," *American Historical Review* 69, no. 2 (1964): 329.

15. Edward S. Corwin, *The President: Office and Powers, 1787–1957: History and Analysis of Practice and Opinion* (New York: New York University Press, 1957).

16. Charles Warren, *The Supreme Court in United States History* (Washington, D.C.: Beard Books, 1999), 3:83–84.

17. *New York Tribune,* 26 March 1859, quoted in Warren, *Supreme Court in United States History,* 3:81.

18. 65 U.S. 66 (1860).

19. 65 U.S. 450 (1860).

20. 62 U.S. 506 (1859).

21. The most thorough account of the extraterritorial issues involved is Arthur Bestor, "State Sovereignty and Slavery: A Reinterpretation of Proslavery Constitutional Doctrine," *Journal of the Illinois State Historical Society* (1961).

22. Stanley I. Kutler, *Judicial Power and Reconstruction Politics* (Chicago: University of Chicago Press, 1968), chap. 1.

23. See Hyman, *A More Perfect Union,* 260.

24. Kutler, *Judicial Power,* 11–12. Abraham Lincoln's first inaugural address, 4 March 1861, in Herman Belz, *A New Birth of Freedom: The Republican Party and Freedmen's Rights, 1861 to 1866* (New York: Fordham University Press, 2000), 653–654.

25. Lincoln's first inaugural speech in part sought to assuage Southern fears about their property, assuring them, "There has never been any reasonable cause for such apprehension." As for fugitive slave laws, Lincoln proclaimed that it was incumbent upon the government "to conform and abide by all those acts which stand unrepealed." Belz, *New Birth of Freedom,* 647, 649. The so-called Corwin amendment was the original version of the Thirteenth Amendment, passed by Congress and signed by President

Buchanan, but not ratified. It provided that Congress could not act "to abolish or interfere, within any State, with the domestic institutions thereof, including that of persons held to labor or service." See Philip A. Klinkner with Rogers M. Smith, *The Unsteady March: The Rise and Decline of Racial Equality in America* (Chicago: University of Chicago Press, 1999), 48–51.

26. Works making this point differently include Carl Swisher, *History of the Supreme Court of the United States: The Taney Period, 1836–64* (New York: Macmillan, 1974), 844–849; Hyman, *A More Perfect Union,* 83; Robert G. Scigliano, *The Supreme Court and the Presidency* (New York: Free Press, 1971), 40.

27. Hyman, *A More Perfect Union,* 82–83; Swisher, *History of the Supreme Court,* 845. Maryland also served as the state where the first habeas writ was refused during the Civil War. On 2 May 1861, federal judge William F. Giles issued a writ of habeas corpus to Major W. W. Morris of the Union army for a minor who enlisted in the army without the consent of his parents. Major Morris disregarded the writ. Giles and Morris instead fought their battle through newspaper editorials. Interestingly, Giles, who sat on the federal circuit court of Baltimore with Taney, excused himself for Merryman's habeas hearing, most likely to give Taney the added effect of a single justice administering the habeas hearing. See Swisher, *History of the Supreme Court,* 842–844.

28. Swisher, *History of the Supreme Court,* 846; Hyman, *A More Perfect Union,* 84. See also John H. Hatcher, "Martial Law and Habeas Corpus," *W. Va. L. Q.* 46 (1939).

29. 17 F. Cas. 148. Others were presumably unaware of the order suspending habeas. District Judge William Giles attempted to issue the writ for a minor who enlisted in the army without parental consent. When the order was issued to the general in command of Fort McHenry, where the soldier was stationed, the officers at the garrison refused to accept it, simply stating in the return that they had orders to disregard habeas writs. See Swisher, *History of the Supreme Court,* 843–844; Neely, *Fate of Liberty,* 9.

30. For a thorough review of English and early colonial notions of suspension, see Paul Halliday and G. Edward White, "The Suspension Clause: English Text, Imperial Contexts, and American Implications," *Va. L. Rev.* 94 (2008).

31. 17 F. Cas. 153.

32. Ibid., 149.

33. Ibid. Taney even worried that he would be arrested as well. See Swisher, *History of the Supreme Court,* 846.

34. Taney specifically requested that a copy of his orders, attachments, and opinion be delivered to Lincoln. See Swisher, *History of the Supreme Court,* 847.

35. Abraham Lincoln, *The Collected Works of Abraham Lincoln,* ed. Roy Basler (New Brunswick: Rutgers University Press, 1953), 430.

36. See, for example, Benjamin A. Kleinerman, *The Discretionary President: The Promise and Peril of Executive Power* (Lawrence: University Press of Kansas, 2009), 178–179.

37. Belz, *New Birth of Freedom,* 418.

38. On departmentalism more generally, see Walter F. Murphy, "Who Shall Interpret? The Quest for the Ultimate Constitutional Interpreter," *Review of Politics* 48, no. 3 (1986); Walter F. Murphy, James Fleming, Sotirios Barber, and Stephen Macedo,

American Constitutional Interpretation, 4th ed. (New York: Foundation Press, 2008); Keith E. Whittington, *Constitutional Construction: Divided Powers and Constitutional Meaning* (Cambridge, Mass.: Harvard University Press, 1999); Keith E. Whittington, *Political Foundations of Judicial Supremacy: The Presidency, the Supreme Court, and Constitutional Leadership in U.S. History* (Princeton: Princeton University Press, 2007); Michael Stokes Paulsen, "The Most Dangerous Branch: Executive Power to Say What the Law Is," *Geo. L. J.* 83 (1994); William F. Harris, *The Interpretable Constitution* (Baltimore: Johns Hopkins University Press, 1993).

39. See Whittington, *Political Foundations of Judicial Supremacy,* 33.

40. My point is that *Merryman* cannot be treated out of context, especially when it is held up, by some, as the preeminent case of departmentalism. See Michael Stokes Paulsen, "The Merryman Power and the Dilemma of Autonomous Executive Branch Interpretation," *Cardozo L. Rev.* 15 (1993).

41. 10 Op. Atty. Gen. 74 (1861), "Suspension of the Privilege of the Writ of Habeas Corpus."

42. Ibid.

43. After the first suspension on 27 April 1861, the commander of United States forces on the Florida coast was authorized to suspend habeas in that state on 10 May 1861. Then, on 20 June 1861, habeas was suspended again for the arrest of William Henry Chase, a rogue general in the army's corps of engineers who, according to Lincoln and Seward, was guilty of "treasonable practices against his government." See Neely, *Fate of Liberty,* chap. 1.

44. For an account of congressional responses to the suspension of habeas corpus, see Charles Warren, "Lincoln's 'Despotism' as Critics Saw It in 1861," *New York Times,* 12 May 1918. See also Swisher, *History of the Supreme Court,* 851–852.

45. Quoted in Warren, *Supreme Court in United States History,* 3:96.

46. Ibid.

47. For a more general discussion of the limits of emancipation measures within the Republican Party, see Louis S. Gerteis, "Salmon P. Chase, Radicalism, and the Politics of Emancipation, 1861–1864," *Journal of American History* 60, no. 1 (1973).

48. Belz, *New Birth of Freedom,* 6.

49. *Congressional Globe,* 37th Cong., 2nd sess., App. 295 (4 June 1862), speech of Albert Porter.

50. Ibid., App. 297.

51. 37th Cong., 2nd sess., Report 120 (17 June 1862).

52. Ibid.

53. 12 Stat. 755 (1863).

54. James S. Liebman, *Federal Habeas Corpus Practice and Procedure* (Charlottesville, Va.: Michie, 1994), 40.

55. See Gerteis, "Salmon P. Chase."

56. Eric Foner, *Reconstruction: America's Unfinished Revolution, 1863–1877* (New York: Harper & Row, 1989), chap. 2.

57. Hyman, *A More Perfect Union,* 250.

58. Ibid., 257.

59. 67 U.S. 635 (1863).

60. See James G. Randall, "The Indemnity Act of 1863: A Study in War-Time Immunity of Governmental Officers," *Mich. L. Rev.* 20 (1921): 596.

61. 12 Stat. 755, 755–756 (1863). Alternatively, prisoners could be released to bail.

62. Hyman, *A More Perfect Union*, 253–254.

63. *Ex parte Vallandigham*, 68 U.S. 243 (1864). The War Department thus exhibited a significant amount of discretion in determining the lists of prisoners whose names would be provided to federal courts. Importantly, Lincoln's administration had already begun to release prisoners whose "offences were slight" as they set up internal commissions to make these determinations. See Hyman, *A More Perfect Union*, 254–255. See Alfred Kelly, Winfred Harbison, and Herman Belz, *The American Constitution: Its Origins and Development*, 7th ed. (New York: Norton, 1991), 305–307.

64. See Anthony G. Amsterdam, "Criminal Prosecutions Affecting Federally Guaranteed Civil Rights: Federal Removal and Habeas Corpus Jurisdiction to Abort State Court Trial," *U. Pa. L. Rev.* 113 (1964): 808–809.

65. 12 Stat. 755, 756 (1863).

66. 14 Stat. 46 (1866).

67. Randall, "Indemnity Act of 1863," 613. On removal legislation more generally during the Civil War and Reconstruction, see William M. Wiecek, "The Reconstruction of Federal Judicial Power, 1863–1875," *Am. J. Legal Hist.* 13 (1969).

68. Stanley Kutler makes this point more broadly in his work that resuscitates a more active and independent role for the federal judiciary during Reconstruction. Kutler, *Judicial Power.*

69. Courts will have more opportunity and more leeway to protect their power when a majority party is divided. In part this is because parties often defer or seek to transfer some legislative priorities to courts. See Mark A. Graber, "The Nonmajoritarian Difficulty: Legislative Deference to the Judiciary," *Studies in American Political Development* 7, no. 1 (1993); Clayton and Pickerill, "The Politics of Criminal Justice"; Cornell Clayton and David A. May, "A Political Regimes Approach to the Analysis of Legal Decisions," *Polity* 32, no. 2 (1999); George I. Lovell, *Legislative Deferrals: Statutory Ambiguity, Judicial Power, and American Democracy* (New York: Cambridge University Press, 2003).

70. 71 U.S. 2 (1866).

71. Warren, *Supreme Court in United States History*, 3:96.

72. See especially William Lasser, "The Supreme Court in Periods of Critical Realignment," *Journal of Politics* 47, no. 4 (1985): chap. 3; Kutler, *Judicial Power*, 89–95.

73. On the Republican guarantee clause, which was the asserted constitutional basis for the Wade-Davis bill and other congressional Reconstruction legislation during this period, see William M. Wiecek, *The Guarantee Clause of the U.S. Constitution* (Ithaca, N.Y.: Cornell University Press, 1972).

74. Quoted in Belz, *New Birth of Freedom*, 52.

75. Speech of Henry Winter Davis, 38th Cong., 1 sess., App. 44 (25 February 1864). See also 38th Cong., 1st sess., App. 82–85 (22 March 1864).

76. Belz, *New Birth of Freedom*, 58–60. See also William Lasser, *The Limits of Judicial Power: The Supreme Court in American Politics* (Chapel Hill: University of North Carolina Press, 1988), 60–63.

77. Quoted in Eric L. McKitrick, *Andrew Johnson and Reconstruction* (Chicago: University of Chicago Press, 1964), 49. See also Foner, *Reconstruction*, 198–216. Kelly, Harbison, and Belz, *American Constitution*, 324–325.

78. Every Southern state adopted black codes by 1866. See Charles Fairman, *Reconstruction and Reunion, 1864–88*, vol. 7, *History of the Supreme Court of the United States, Part Two* (New York: Macmillan, 1987), 7:110–117; Michael Vorenberg, *Final Freedom: The Civil War, the Abolition of Slavery, and the Thirteenth Amendment* (Cambridge: Cambridge University Press, 2001), 230–231.

79. Fairman, *Reconstruction and Reunion, Part Two*, 7:117–118.

80. Ibid., 7:118–121.

81. 14 Stat. 27 (9 April 1866).

82. At the time of the Freedman's Bureau veto, however, Congress did not believe its hand was completely forced toward military reconstruction. Only after future proclamations by Johnson that hostilities had ended did this position ripen. See Lasser, *Limits of Judicial Power*, 76–77. But see also McKitrick, *Andrew Johnson and Reconstruction*, 473–474.

83. Congress promptly passed another version of the Freedman's Bureau Bill. See Lasser, *Limits of Judicial Power*, 82.

84. Andrew Johnson, "Proclamation 153: Declaring the Insurrection in Certain Southern States to Be at an End," 2 April 1866, available at the American Presidency Project, University of California, Santa Barbara, http://www.presidency.ucsb.edu/ws/?pid=71987. See also Lasser, *Limits of Judicial Power*, 77.

85. Eric McKitrick argues, "The critical period of President Johnson's relations with Congress may be said to have terminated on April 6, 1866, with the successful repassage of the Civil Rights Bill over the President's veto." McKitrick, *Andrew Johnson and Reconstruction*, 274.

86. Lasser, *Limits of Judicial Power*, 85n87. Both Charles Warren and Charles Fairman, for example, cite only negative criticism of the Court *after* the individual opinions were released.

87. Lasser, *Limits of Judicial Power*, 79.

88. This point should not be overstated. As Kutler argued, "In December, 1866, as Congress assembled, there was, as yet, no definite, agreed-upon Republican program for reconstruction and certainly no general intention to institute military commissions and control in the South." Kutler, *Judicial Power*, 94. For criticisms of the Court's opinion, almost all of which are leveled after the decisions were released in December, see Warren, *Supreme Court in United States History*, 3:148–159.

89. 71 U.S. 2, 118–119 (1866).

90. 71 U.S. 2, 109 (1866).

91. *Ex parte Vallandigham*, 68 U.S. 243 (1864). Stanley Kutler suggests that the case "demonstrated solid support for presidential and legislative wartime policies." Kutler, *Judicial Power*, 52.

92. 71 U.S. 2, 121.

93. Ibid.

94. Davis to Julius Rockwell, 24 February 1867, quoted in Kutler, *Judicial Power*, 67.

95. 71 U.S. 2, 122.

96. Ibid., 125.

97. Ibid., 136.

98. Ibid., 140–141.

99. For a discussion of the case, see Warren, *Supreme Court in United States History,* 3:165–166.

100. Ibid., 3:164. For a discussion of the division among Republicans concerning alternate Reconstruction policies at the beginning of 1867, see McKitrick, *Andrew Johnson and Reconstruction,* 474–476.

101. 14 Stat. 385 (5 February 1867).

102. In characterizing the bevy of failed bills put forward to restructure the Supreme Court in December 1866 and January 1867, Charles Warren argues that "the radical attitude of the majority portended trouble for the future." Warren, *Supreme Court in United States History,* 3:176.

103. The most thorough historical accounts of the 1867 act agree on this point. See, for example, William M. Wiecek, "The Great Writ and Reconstruction: The Habeas Corpus Act of 1867," *Journal of Southern History* 36, no. 4 (1970): 538. Mayers, "Habeas Corpus Act of 1867," 32. William F. Duker, *A Constitutional History of Habeas Corpus* (Westport, Conn.: Greenwood Press, 1980), 193–194.

104. Act of 5 February 1867, chap. 28, *Statutes at Large of the United States,* 14 (1868) 385.

105. *Congressional Globe,* 39th Cong., 1st sess. (19 December 1865), 87.

106. 13 Stat. 571 (1865).

107. *Congressional Globe,* 39th Cong., 1st sess. (8 January 1866), 135.

108. The original handwritten bill is located in the National Archives and is quoted in Mayers, "Habeas Corpus Act of 1867," 34.

109. 14 Stat. 385.

110. This portion of the bill is as follows: "This act shall not apply to the case of any person who is or may be in the custody of the military authorities of the United States, charged with any military offense, or with having aided or abetted rebellion against the Government of the United States prior to the passage of this act." William McCardle did not fall under this category. See Fairman, *Reconstruction and Reunion, Part Two,* 7:448n458.

111. *Congressional Globe,* 39th Cong., 1st sess. (25 July 1866), 4151.

112. Ibid., 4229.

113. Mayers characterized the bill as "a measure drafted in vague terms . . . reported only orally, explained in one way in the house in which it originated and in an entirely different way in the other house, and passed without debate and with only the most casual attention in either chamber." Mayers, "Habeas Corpus Act of 1867," 32. Wiecek describes the bill as "enacted . . . inadvertently." Wiecek, "The Great Writ and Reconstruction," 538.

114. *Congressional Globe,* 39th Cong., 2nd sess. (31 January 1867), 889.

115. Wiecek, "The Great Writ and Reconstruction," 539; Liebman, *Federal Habeas Corpus Practice and Procedure,* 41.

116. 8 U.S. 75 (1807).

117. 24 F. Cas. 337 (1867).

118. The most thorough account of *Turner* is Harold Melvin Hyman, *The Reconstruction Justice of Salmon P. Chase:* In re Turner *and* Texas v. White (Lawrence: University Press of Kansas, 1997).

119. 24 F. Cas. 337, 339.

120. For an excellent overview of *McCardle*, which presents a more nuanced view of Congress' jurisdiction-stripping ability, see William W. Van Alstyne, "A Critical Guide to *Ex Parte McCardle*," *Ariz. L. Rev.* 15 (1973). See also Mark Graber, "Legal, Strategic, or Legal Strategy: Deciding to Decide during the Civil War and Reconstruction," in *The Supreme Court and American Political Development*, ed. Ronald Kahn and Kenneth Kersch (Lawrence: University Press of Kansas, 2006), 33–66.

121. Fairman, *Reconstruction and Reunion, Part Two*, 7:448.

122. Lasser, *Limits of Judicial Power*, 99. The charges against McCardle included disturbance of the peace, inciting insurrection, libel, and impeding Reconstruction. See Fairman, *Reconstruction and Reunion, Part Two*, 7:437–438.

123. See Whittington, *Constitutional Construction*, 20–71.

124. 73 U.S. 318, 324 (1868).

125. *Congressional Globe*, 40th Cong., 2nd sess. (12 March 1868), 1860. See Lasser, *Limits of Judicial Power*, 101–102.

126. Rep. Robert Schenk (R-Pa.) explicitly acknowledged that the repealer was designed to prevent the Surpeme Court from ruling on McCardle's case and congressional Reconstruction in general. For an overview of editorial accounts, see Warren, *Supreme Court in United States History*, 3:197–199.

127. *Congressional Globe*, 40th Cong., 2nd sess. (25 March 1868), 2094.

128. See Warren, *Supreme Court in United States History*, 3:200–202, Kutler, *Judicial Power*, 102, Fairman, *Reconstruction and Reunion, Part Two*, 7:469.

129. Kutler, *Judicial Power*, 102.

130. 15 Stat. 44 (1868).

131. Warren, *Supreme Court in United States History*, 3:203.

132. 74 U.S. 506, 514 (1869).

133. Ibid., 513.

134. Ibid., 515.

135. See Graber, "Legal, Strategic, or Legal Strategy," and Van Alstyne, "Critical Guide to *Ex Parte McCardle*."

136. I do not mean to suggest, as some do, that the 1867 act only contemplated freedmen. The point is simply that distrust of recalcitrant states was the most salient impetus for changes to habeas's jurisdiction during Reconstruction. See Mayers, "Habeas Corpus Act of 1867."

137. See Lasser, *Limits of Judicial Power*.

138. See Fairman, *Reconstruction and Reunion, Part Two*, 7:498–501.

139. See generally Wiecek, "Reconstruction of Federal Judicial Power."

140. Representative of the former argument is Warren, *Supreme Court in United States History*. For the latter argument, see Kutler, *Judicial Power*.

141. Benedict, "Preserving the Constitution."

142. Clayton and May, "A Political Regimes Approach to the Analysis of Legal Decisions"; Clayton and Pickerill, "The Politics of Criminal Justice." That habeas helps us

identify the conditions under which regime-affiliated Courts might stand their ground helps answer larger criticisms levied against the regime literature. See, for example, Thomas M. Keck, "Party Politics or Judicial Independence? The Regime Politics Literature Hits the Law Schools," *Law and Social Inquiry* 32, no. 2 (2007).

143. 17 Stat. 13 (1871).

144. See generally Charles Fairman, *Reconstruction and Reunion, 1864–88, Part One* (New York: Macmillan, 1971), 199–220.

145. Robert J. Kaczorowski, "Federal Enforcement of Civil Rights during the First Reconstruction Essay," *Fordham Urb. L. J.* 23 (1995); Kermit L. Hall, "Political Power and Constitutional Legitimacy: The South Carolina Ku Klux Klan Trials, 1871–1872," *Emory L. J.* 33 (1984). See also Duker, *Constitutional History of Habeas Corpus*, 149, n.190.

146. The alternative positions were that either the Republicans as a whole were never as radical as the Radicals (i.e., they were "conservative") or, despite the increase in national power to enforce national rights through the Reconstruction amendments, Republicans saw no contradiction in maintaining the notion that most rights would best be protected by state governments. According to this position, for example, Republicans were divided between an understanding of the Fourteenth Amendment as guaranteeing absolute rights and simply requiring equal application of rights. For the former argument, see Benedict, "Preserving the Constitution." For the latter argument, see Nelson, *Fourteenth Amendment*, 148–151.

147. William Gillette, *Retreat from Reconstruction, 1869–1879* (Baton Rouge: Louisiana State University Press, 1979); Klinkner with Smith, *Unsteady March.*

148. When Congress crafted the 1874 revised statutes, they disseminated the 1866 act's provisions into obscure places across the code. See Harold Melvin Hyman and William M. Wiecek, *Equal Justice under Law: Constitutional Development, 1835–1875* (New York: Harper & Row, 1982), 488.

149. Foner, *Reconstruction*, 499 511.

150. 11 F. Cas. 71 (1869).

151. Ibid. at 22.

152. Ibid. at 25.

153. Foner, *Reconstruction*, 582–583.

154. See Howard Gillman, "How Political Parties Can Use the Courts to Advance Their Agendas: Federal Courts in the United States, 1875–1891," *American Political Science Review* 96, no. 3 (2002): 516–517.

155. The Burlingame treaty, in part, guaranteed Chinese "the same privileges, immunities, and exemptions in respect to travel or residence as may there be enjoyed by the citizens or subjects of the most favored nation." 16 Stat. 739 (1868). The most thorough account of these cases is Christian G. Fritz, "A Nineteenth Century Habeas Corpus Mill: The Chinese before the Federal Courts in California," *Am. J. Legal Hist.* 32 (1988). See also Lucy Salyer, *Laws Harsh as Tigers: Chinese Immigrants and the Shaping of Modern Immigration Law* (Chapel Hill: University of North Carolina Press, 1995).

156. 1 F. Cas. 213, 217.

157. Ibid. For similar cases, see *Baker v. City of Portland*, 2 F. Cas. 472 (1879); *In re*

Parrot, 1 F. 481 (1880); *In re Wong Yung Quy,* 2 F. 624 (1880); *In re Quong Woo,* 13 F. 229 (1882). See also Fritz, "Nineteenth Century Habeas Corpus Mill," 351–353.

158. 4 F. Cas. 98 (1875).

159. 4 F. Cas. 98, 105.

160. Ibid. at 106.

161. 4 F. Cas. 98, 106.

162. 83 U.S. 36 (1873).

163. Ibid., 78. Although some argue that *Slaughterhouse* should best be understood primarily in terms of its nonracial economic aspects instead of as an early step away from meaningful national protection for freedmen, the fact remains that it became the basis on which other cases soon relied for more significant rollbacks of Reconstruction policy. See especially Ronald M. Labbe and Jonathan Lurie, *The Slaughterhouse Cases: Regulation, Reconstruction, and the Fourteenth Amendment* (Lawrence: University Press of Kansas, 2003). Michael Les Benedict, "Preserving Federalism: Reconstruction and the Waite Court," *Sup. Ct. Rev.* 1978 (1978), makes a similar point concerning the possibility of a purely economic reading of the case and emphasizes the need to distinguish among Chase, Waite, and Fuller Court readings of the Reconstruction amendments. For arguments that *Slaughterhouse* did, in fact, drain the privileges and immunities clause of its intended meaning and scope, see Robert J. Kaczorowski, "The Chase Court and Fundamental Rights: A Watershed in American Constitutionalism," *N. Ky. L. Rev.* 21 (1993); Foner, *Reconstruction,* 529–530; Rogers M. Smith, *Civic Ideals: Conflicting Visions of Citizenship in U.S. History* (New Haven, Conn.: Yale University Press, 1997), 331–335; Michael Kent Curtis, "Resurrecting the Privileges or Immunities Clause and Revising the *Slaughter-House* Cases without Exhuming Lochner: Individual Rights and the Fourteenth Amendment," *B.C. L. Rev.* 38 (1996); Sanford Levinson, "Some Reflections on the Rehabilitation of the Privileges or Immunities Clause of the Fourteenth Amendment," *Harv. J. L. & Pub. Pol'y* 12 (1989).

164. 92 U.S. 214 (1876); 92 U.S. 542 (1876). But see Pamela Brandwein, "The *Civil Rights Cases* and the Lost Language of State Neglect," in *The Supreme Court and American Political Development,* ed. Ronald Kahn and Ken Kersch (Lawrence: University Press of Kansas, 2006).

165. For a thorough discussion of the case and the problems in the Enforcement Acts' statutory construction, which in part guided the Court's decision, see Fairman, *Reconstruction and Reunion, Part Two,* 7:225–260. Hyman and Wiecek, *Equal Justice under Law,* 488–489, Smith, *Civic Ideals,* 334–337.

166. Fairman, *Reconstruction and Reunion, Part Two,* 7:263–276. See also Leslie Friedman Goldstein, "The Specter of the Second Amendment: Rereading *Slaughterhouse* and *Cruikshank,*" *Studies in American Political Development* 21, no. 2 (2007).

167. 109 U.S. 3 (1883).

168. Smith, *Civic Ideals,* 325–326, Foner, *Reconstruction,* 532–533.

169. 109 U.S. 3, 13–14.

170. Ibid., 17.

171. It should be noted that Bradley, like many others, distinguished between the rights guaranteed in the Civil Rights Act of 1866 and the rights that the 1875 Civil Rights Act sought to protect. Soon after the 1875 act passed, Bradley stated, "There are cer-

tain essential rights of citizenship which cannot be refused to the colored man. . . . The civil rights bill (of 1866) illustrates some, if not all, of these. . . . But whether the freedom of all hotels, railroad cars, theatres and places of amusement, is one of those essential rights, may be a question." See Fairman, *Reconstruction and Reunion, Part Two*, 7:288–289.

172. Smith, for example, divides Reconstruction into four parts: a preliminary phase that lasted from 1862 to 1865; an obstructed or presidential phase, lasting from 1865 to 1867; a congressional phase, which lasted from 1867 to 1876; and a remnant phase that effectively ended with Henry Cabot Lodge's failed elections bill in the early 1890s. Smith, *Civic Ideals*, 289–290.

173. See, for example, Benedict, "Preserving Federalism." Brandwein, "*Civil Rights Cases.*"

174. This is consistent with Michael Nelson's argument that there were at least two understandings of the Fourteenth Amendment, one absolutist and one that only prohibited the unequal application by states of certain rights. Nelson, *Fourteenth Amendment*.

175. Gilded Age "judges thus avoided the distractions and diffusion of energy that might have hampered them, if they had chosen to defend both the businessman and the negro at the same time." Robert G. McCloskey, *The American Supreme Court* (Chicago: University of Chicago Press, 2005), 80–81.

176. This pattern was part of Congress' larger project of entrenching its Gilded Age economic interests in the Court beginning with the removal and federal question legislation of 1875. See Gillman, "How Political Parties Can Use the Courts to Advance Their Agendas."

177. See Felix Frankfurter and James M. Landis, *The Business of the Supreme Court: A Study in the Federal Judicial System* (New Brunswick, N.J.: Transaction Publishers, 2007), 86–93; Fritz, "Nineteenth Century Habeas Corpus Mill."

178. Frankfurter and Landis, *The Business of the Supreme Court*, 88.

179. See, for example, "Annual Report of the American Bar Association," vol. 6 (1883), 243–267.

180. Seymour D. Thompson, "Abuses of the Writ of Habeas Corpus," *Am. L. Rev.* 18 (1884).

181. H.R. 730, 48th Cong., 1st sess. (8 March 1884).

182. H.R. 730, 48th Cong., 1st sess. (1884), 3.

183. Ibid., 4.

184. Ibid., 6.

185. 23 Stat. 437 (1885). In 1874, Congress condensed all habeas statutes into one section. As a result, federal prisoners could technically bring habeas challenges under the 1867 act before the Supreme Court. See Liebman, *Federal Habeas Corpus Practice and Procedure*, 43.

186. 117 U.S. 241 (1886).

187. The Court said it believed its decision was "in harmony with what we suppose was the intention of Congress in the enactments in question." Ibid., 252.

188. Ibid., 251.

189. Ibid. See also Liebman, *Federal Habeas Corpus Practice and Procedure*, 47–48.

190. For a discussion of cases that arguably fell into the category of exceptional circumstances of "national importance," see Liebman, *Federal Habeas Corpus Practice and Procedure,* 43–47. See also Ann Woolhandler, "Demodeling Habeas," *Stan. L. Rev.* 45 (1992).

191. Federal court discretion in habeas cases, as developed in *Royall,* was mandated in *In re Frederich,* 149 U.S. 70 (1893); exhaustion of state remedies became mandatory in *New York v. Eno,* 155 U.S. 89 (1894). See Liebman, *Federal Habeas Corpus Practice and Procedure,* 48–49.

192. 140 U.S. 278 (1891).

193. See also *Neal v. Delaware,* 103 U.S. 370 (1880).

194. 140 U.S. 278 at 370.

CHAPTER 4. FROM THE EXTRAORDINARY TO
THE ORDINARY: 1915–1969

1. *Frank v. Mangum,* 237 U.S. 309, 346 (Holmes dissenting).

2. Kenneth Kersch makes a similar point about criminal process rights. See Kenneth Kersch, *Constructing Civil Liberties: Discontinuities in the Development of American Constitutional Law* (New York: Cambridge University Press, 2004), chap. 2.

3. For arguments that suggest that habeas was always available to vindicate the most expansive conceptions of due process rights, see Justice Brennan's majority opinion in *Fay v. Noia,* 372 U.S. 391 (1963), and Gary Peller, "In Defense of Federal Habeas Corpus Relitigation," *Harv. CR-CL L. Rev.* 16 (1982).

4. 304 U.S. 144 (1938).

5. 323 U.S. 283 (1944); 27 U.S. 304 (1946).

6. *Palko v. Connecticut,* 302 U.S. 319 (1937); *Rochin v. California,* 342 U.S. 165 (1952).

7. 344 U.S. 443 at 465.

8. See Robert G. McCloskey, *The American Supreme Court* (Chicago: University of Chicago Press, 2005), 150; Mark V. Tushnet, *The Warren Court in Historical and Political Perspective* (Charlottesville: University Press of Virginia, 1993), 4.

9. See generally Rick Perlstein, ed., *Nixonland: The Rise of a President and the Fracturing of America* (New York: Scribner, 2008); Lucas A. Powe, *The Warren Court and American Politics* (Cambridge, Mass.: Harvard University Press, 2000); Thomas Byrne Edsall and Mary D. Edsall, *Chain Reaction: The Impact of Race, Rights, and Taxes on American Politics* (New York: Norton, 1991).

10. Richard Nixon, *Richard Nixon: Speeches, Writings, Documents,* ed. Rick Perlstein (Princeton: Princeton University Press, 2008), 147. Powe, *Warren Court and American Politics,* 407–410.

11. Notions of finality and federalism as criticisms of expansive habeas access are developed in Paul M. Bator, "Finality in Criminal Law and Federal Habeas Corpus for State Prisoners," *Harv. L. Rev.* 76 (1962), and Henry J. Friendly, "Is Innocence Irrelevant? Collateral Attack on Criminal Judgments," *U. Chi. L. Rev.* 38, no. 1 (1970).

12. *Rochin v. California,* 342 U.S. 165 (1952).

13. McCloskey, *American Supreme Court,* 166.

14. Technically, the exhaustion rule announced in *Royall* was, in the words of James Liebman, a "discretionary rule of preference," and not a mandatory rule. It was not until *New York v. Eno,* 155 U.S. 89 (1894), that the Court mandated that state habeas petitioners exhaust state remedies. See James S. Liebman, *Federal Habeas Corpus Practice and Procedure* (Charlottesville, Va.: Michie, 1994), 48–49.

15. 118 U.S. 356 (1886). For the argument that *Yick Wo* was even more of an outlier than I suggest, see Gabriel J. Chin, "Unexplainable on Grounds of Race: Doubts about *Yick Wo,*" *U. Ill. L. Rev.* 2008 (2008), who argues that the case only vindicated property rights in general and that if the Court was not bound by the Burlingame treaty, Chinese residents would not have been heard.

16. 118 U.S. 356, 374.

17. See Liebman, *Federal Habeas Corpus Practice and Procedure,* 50–51, for a detailed list of Fifth, Sixth, Eighth, and Fourteenth Amendment claims raised—and ultimately rejected—through habeas.

18. For a similar argument concerning fundamental versus nonfundamental criteria for habeas cases in the late nineteenth century, see Liebman, *Federal Habeas Corpus Practice and Procedure,* and Ann Woolhandler, "Demodeling Habeas," *Stan. L. Rev.* 45 (1992).

19. 201 U.S. 123, 129.

20. 118 U.S. 356, 370. For an account of the Court's shift from protecting liberties residually by banning class legislation to its modern mode of protecting discrete liberties, see Howard Gillman, "Preferred Freedoms: The Progressive Expansion of State Power and the Rise of Modern Civil Liberties Jurisprudence," *Political Research Quarterly* 47, no. 3 (1994).

21. *Neal v. Delaware,* 103 U.S. 370 (1880); *Ex parte Virginia,* 100 U.S. 339 (1880); *Strauder v. Virginia,* 100 U.S. 303 (1880). But see *In re Wood,* 140 U.S. 278 (1891). See generally Michael J. Klarman, *From Jim Crow to Civil Rights: The Supreme Court and the Struggle for Racial Equality* (New York: Oxford University Press, 2004).

22. The contrast here is between individual-level models of judicial decision making that are based on the policy preferences of the individual justice and purely contextual explanations for judicial decision making that might forsake the potential role of law to influence behavior. For the former, see Jeffrey A. Segal and Harold J. Spaeth, *The Supreme Court and the Attitudinal Model Revisited* (New York: Cambridge University Press, 2002). For the latter, see generally Robert A. Dahl, "Decision-Making in a Democracy: The Supreme Court as a National Policy-Maker," *J. Pub. L.* 6 (1957). See also Michael J. Klarman, "Rethinking the Civil Rights and Civil Liberties Revolutions," *Va. L. Rev.* 82, no. 1 (1996).

23. Smith, "Political Jurisprudence," 95.

24. Michael J. Klarman, "Race and the Court in the Progressive Era: Rethinking *Buchanan v. Warley,*" *Vand. L. Rev.* 51 (1998). See also Kersch, *Constructing Civil Liberties,* 70–71.

25. Klarman goes to similar lengths to highlight the extralegal influences on the Court's decision making, especially in his explanation of the different outcomes in *Frank* and *Moore.* My point here is that the extralegal forces were not nearly as important as the Court's institution-regarding conceptions of judicial duty and minimum

levels of fairness that were implicated by the larger Jim Crow order. Thus the extralegal factors did not influence the Court's behavior directly as much as they simply highlighted the ongoing threat to judicial integrity that these due process violations represented. See Michael J. Klarman, "The Racial Origins of Modern Criminal Procedure," *Mich. L. Rev.* 99, no. 1 (2000): 60–61.

26. See Benno C. Schmidt Jr., "Principle and Prejudice: The Supreme Court and Race in the Progressive Era, Part 1: The Heyday of Jim Crow," *Colum. L. Rev.* 82 (1982). See also Robert C. Post, "Defending the Lifeworld: Substantive Due Process in the Taft Court Era," *B. U. L. Rev.* 78 (1998). For a related argument interpreting the outcome in *Yick Wo v. Hopkins* as upholding mainly property rights, not racial equality, see Chin, "Unexplainable on Grounds of Race."

27. Schmidt, "Principle and Prejudice, Part 1," 456.

28. 237 U.S. 309 (1915).

29. See, for example, the discussion of *Frank* and *Moore* in Liebman, *Federal Habeas Corpus Practice and Procedure,* 52–59; Eric M. Freedman, *Habeas Corpus: Rethinking the Great Writ of Liberty* (New York: New York University Press, 2001), 49–65; Klarman, *From Jim Crow to Civil Rights.*

30. Klarman, *From Jim Crow to Civil Rights,* 63.

31. C. Vann Woodward, *The Strange Career of Jim Crow* (New York: Oxford University Press, 1966), 68–69.

32. See generally Richard Brown, *Strain of Violence: Historical Studies of Violence and Vigilantism* (New York: Oxford University Press, 1975); Philip Dray, *At the Hands of Persons Unknown: The Lynching of Black America* (New York: Random House, 2003); Richard C. Cortner, *A Mob Intent on Death: The NAACP and the Arkansas Riot Cases* (Middletown, Conn.: Wesleyan University Press, 1988).

33. Quoted in Schmidt, "Principle and Prejudice, Part 1," 455. Roosevelt actively courted Southern Progressive votes at the expense of black Republicans during the Progressive Party's 1912 convention partly by criticizing a then-familiar bogeyman in the form of black Republican political corruption. See Gary Gerstle, *American Crucible: Race and Nation in the Twentieth Century* (Princeton: Princeton University Press, 2001), 74–79.

34. See generally Woodward, *The Strange Career of Jim Crow,* 72–74; Philip A. Klinkner with Rogers M. Smith, *The Unsteady March: The Rise and Decline of Racial Equality in America* (Chicago: University of Chicago Press, 1999), 99–103; Julian E. Zelizer, *Arsenal of Democracy: The Politics of National Security from World War II to the War on Terrorism* (New York: Basic Books, 2009), 13–18.

35. William A. Dunning, *Reconstruction, Political and Economic, 1865–1877* (New York: Harper & Bros., 1907); Woodward, *The Strange Career of Jim Crow,* 93–94. See also John William Burgess, *Reconstruction and the Constitution, 1866–1876* (New York: C. Scribner's Sons, 1902). Robert W. Shufeldt, *The Negro: A Menace to Civilization* (Boston: Richard G. Badger, 1907). On the Dunning school, see Eric Foner, *Reconstruction: America's Unfinished Revolution, 1863–1877* (New York: Harper & Row, 1989), xvii–xix; Klinkner with Smith, *Unsteady March,* 95; Woodward, *The Strange Career of Jim Crow,* 105.

36. Quoted in Klinkner with Smith, *Unsteady March,* 109. See also Benno C. Schmidt

Jr., "Principle and Prejudice: The Supreme Court and Race in the Progressive Era, Part 3: Black Disfranchisement from the KKK to the Grandfather Clause," *Colum. L. Rev.* 82 (1982): 851–856; Klarman, *From Jim Crow to Civil Rights,* 67. See also Rick Tepker, "The Dean Takes His Stand: Julian Monnet's 1912 *Harvard Law Review* Article Denouncing Oklahoma's Discriminatory Grandfather Clause," *Okla. L. Rev.* 62 (2010).

37. Woodward, *The Strange Career of Jim Crow,* 84–85.

38. 238 U.S. 347 (1915).

39. On the short-term effects of *Guinn* on voting rights, see Klarman, *From Jim Crow to Civil Rights.*

40. *Bailey v. Alabama,* 219 U.S. 219 (1911); *United States v. Reynolds,* 235 U.S. 133 (1914). See also Klarman, *From Jim Crow to Civil Rights,* 73–75. But see Mark V. Tushnet, "Progressive Era Race Relations Cases in Their Traditional Context," *Vand. L. Rev.* 51 (1998). Tushnet argues that cases like *Guinn* were not so obviously unconstitutional.

41. Woodward, *The Strange Career of Jim Crow,* 92. See also Desmond S. King, *Separate and Unequal: African Americans and the U.S. Federal Government* (Oxford: Oxford University Press, 2007).

42. Maurice S. Evans, *Black and White in the Southern States: A Study of the Race Problem in the United States from a South African Point of View* (London: Longmans Green, 1915), 158–159.

43. See generally Michael Rogin, *"Ronald Reagan," the Movie, and Other Episodes in Political Demonology* (Berkeley: University of California Press, 1987), 190–235; Dray, *At the Hands of Persons Unknown,* 190–214; Klinkner with Smith, *Unsteady March,* 110.

44. The most thorough accounts of the Frank case are Dray, *At the Hands of Persons Unknown,* and Leonard Dinnerstein, *The Leo Frank Case* (New York: Columbia University Press, 1968).

45. Dray, *At the Hands of Persons Unknown,* 209.

46. 237 U.S. 309, 327 (1915).

47. 237 U.S. 309, 331 (1915).

48. 237 U.S. 309, 330–331 (1915).

49. 237 U.S. 309, 334 (1915).

50. 237 U.S. 309, 347 (1915).

51. *Res judicata* means that a prior decision by a court of competent jurisdiction is binding. Holmes's argument here was simply that if res judicata is not binding in civil cases, it should not bind the federal court in criminal proceedings.

52. 237 U.S. 309, 346.

53. 237 U.S. 309, 350.

54. 237 U.S. 309, 347.

55. 237 U.S. 309, 348.

56. Dray, *At the Hands of Persons Unknown,* 213.

57. Ibid., 214.

58. 261 U.S. 86 (1923). For an excellent overview and history of the case, see Cortner, *A Mob Intent on Death,* and Christopher Capozzola, *Uncle Sam Wants You: World War I and the Making of the Modern American Citizen* (New York: Oxford University Press, 2008).

59. See Klarman, "Racial Origins of Modern Criminal Procedure," 51.

60. Neither Holmes's nor McReynolds's opinion in this case addressed the constitutionality of racial discrimination on juries. This question resurfaced in *Brown v. Allen,* 344 U.S. 443 (1953).

61. 261 U.S. 86, 90–91.

62. 261 U.S. 86, 91.

63. 261 U.S. 86, 91.

64. 261 U.S. 86, 101.

65. Ibid., 93.

66. Bator, "Finality in Criminal Law and Federal Habeas Corpus for State Prisoners," 483–490. Bator argued that *Frank*'s provisions for habeas review became the basis for "all the great and beneficent expansions of the writ we have witnessed over the past fifty years" (487).

67. For an overview of failed antilynching legislation during the interwar period, see Richard B. Sherman, *The Republican Party and Black America from McKinley to Hoover, 1896–1933* (Charlottesville: University Press of Virginia, 1973), chap. 7; Klarman, *From Jim Crow to Civil Rights.*

68. Michael Klarman attributes the change from *Frank* to *Moore* to the interwar period's changing political and racial environment even though he admits that the Court's personnel changes during this period did not lend themselves to more racial egalitarianism on the Court. See Klarman, *From Jim Crow to Civil Rights.* See also Freedman, *Habeas Corpus,* 65–67.

69. Roosevelt's declaration of a limited national emergency began in 1939, almost two years before Pearl Harbor. See Paul L. Murphy, ed., *The Constitution in Crisis Times, 1918–1969* (New York: Harper & Row, 1971), 219–233; Edward S. Corwin, *Total War and the Constitution* (New York: Knopf, 1947).

70. The same can be said of Roosevelt's Justice Department, led by Attorney General Francis Biddle. Murphy, *The Constitution in Crisis Times,* 224–225.

71. The literature on Japanese internment is extensive. My account is informed by Roger Daniels, *The Decision to Relocate the Japanese Americans* (Malabar, Fla.: R. E. Krieger, 1975); Roger Daniels, *The Politics of Prejudice: The Anti-Japanese Movement in California and the Struggle for Japanese Exclusion,* 2nd ed. (Berkeley: University of California Press, 1977); Roger Daniels, *Concentration Camps, North America: Japanese in the United States and Canada during World War II* (Malabar, Fla.: R. E. Krieger, 1981); Roger Daniels, *Prisoners without Trial: Japanese Americans in World War II* (New York: Hill and Wang, 2004); Peter H. Irons, *Justice at War* (New York: Oxford University Press, 1983); Peter H. Irons, *A People's History of the Supreme Court: The Men and Women Whose Cases and Decisions Have Shaped Our Constitution,* rev. ed. (New York: Penguin Books, 2006); Eugene V. Rostow, "The Japanese American Cases: A Disaster," *Yale L. J.* 54, no. 3 (1945); Corwin, *Total War and the Constitution;* Morton Grodzins, *Americans Betrayed: Politics and the Japanese Evacuation* (Chicago: University of Chicago Press, 1949); Walter F. Murphy, "Civil Liberties and the Japanese American Cases: A Study in the Uses of Stare Decisis," *Western Political Quarterly* 11, no. 1 (1958).

72. 320 U.S. 81, 85.

73. Ibid., 100.

74. 320 U.S. 81 at 100, quoting *McCulloch v. Maryland,* 17 U.S. 316 at 407 (1819).

75. Ibid., 93–94.

76. Ibid., 96n2.

77. Ibid., 98–97. Admittedly, Stone attributes their lack of assimilation to official congressional and state-level discrimination. See 98n4.

78. Ibid., 98.

79. Ibid., 102. Additional justification for the curfew consisted of the necessity for Japanese to remain in their homes at night when bombing raids would be more likely.

80. 320 U.S. 81, 114. Murphy also criticized Stone for ignoring the Fifth Amendment challenge. Stone argued that the Fifth Amendment contained no equal protection clause, and that it was constitutional during war or crisis to make racial classifications. Murphy argued that while there was no equal protection clause in the Fifth Amendment, patently racist distinctions in legislation would nevertheless violate the Fifth Amendment's due process clause. See 320 U.S. 81, 112n2.

81. 323 U.S. 214, 243.

82. Ibid., 216.

83. Ibid., 223.

84. Ibid., 219–220.

85. Ibid., 234–235.

86. Ibid., 236.

87. Ibid., 236n2. "House Naval Affairs to Investigate Congested Areas," 78th Cong., 1st sess. (13 April 1943).

88. 323 U.S. 283 (1944).

89. Ibid., 214.

90. Ibid., 296.

91. Ibid., 302.

92. Ibid., 302.

93. 323 U.S. 283, 307.

94. Ibid., 308.

95. Ibid., 308.

96. 327 U.S. 304 (1946).

97. 327 U.S. 304 at 313–314.

98. 327 U.S. 304 at 317. See also Louis Fisher, *Military Tribunals and Presidential Power: American Revolution to the War on Terrorism* (Lawrence: University Press of Kansas, 2005), 136–139.

99. 327 U.S. 304 at 334.

100. 327 U.S. 304 at 317.

101. Most recently, Barry Friedman suggests that the Court's Japanese internment cases, which seemed to reflect and track unsympathetic public opinion to the predicament of Japanese Americans and residents who were interned, raise serious questions about the ability of regime-affiliated Courts to protect rights: "What we ought to care deeply about, what we ought to be asking, is how much capacity the justices have to act independently of the public's views, how likely they are to do so, and in what situations." At least in terms of habeas corpus, these questions are partly answered by understanding the Court's assertion of independence in cases where its ability to participate in at least some form of minimal judicial review or oversight is threatened.

See Barry Friedman, *The Will of the People: How Public Opinion Has Influenced the Supreme Court and Shaped the Meaning of the Constitution* (New York: Farrar, Straus and Giroux, 2009), 372–374.

102. Here again, jurisdiction refers to the loss of any court's ability to have its decision recognized as final. If jurisdiction is lost because of a constitutional violation during the trial, then a higher court (here understood as a federal court) can review the case via habeas.

103. 344 U.S. 443 (1953). See, for example, Bator, "Finality in Criminal Law and Federal Habeas Corpus for State Prisoners"; Henry M. Hart Jr., "The Supreme Court 1958 Term—Foreword: The Time Chart of the Justices," *Harv. L. Rev.* 73 (1959). The most thorough legal rebuttal to this position is Liebman, *Federal Habeas Corpus Practice and Procedure*. See also Freedman, *Habeas Corpus*.

104. Liebman, *Federal Habeas Corpus Practice and Procedure*.

105. 344 U.S. 443 at 489.

106. It should be noted that Brown had been denied certiorari (not habeas) by the Supreme Court earlier. The lower district court then took this denial into consideration in denying habeas to Brown et al. Presumably this affected its decision. Much of the case thus turned on whether the denial of certiorari by the Supreme Court should affect its decisions. The court emphatically said it should not. See *Darr v. Burford* 339 U.S. 200 (1950). See also Liebman, *Federal Habeas Corpus Practice and Procedure*, 61–62; Freedman, *Habeas Corpus*, 95–143.

107. Liebman, *Federal Habeas Corpus Practice and Procedure*, 61.

108. 344 U.S. 443 at 508.

109. 344 U.S. 443, 498.

110. 344 U.S. 443, 499.

111. 4 F. Cas. 98, 106 (1875).

112. 344 U.S. 433, 501.

113. 117 U.S. 241 (1886).

114. 344 U.S. 443, 504.

115. 344 U.S. 443, 515.

116. 287 U.S. 45 (1932). See also Klarman, *From Jim Crow to Civil Rights*, 123–125.

117. See Klarman, "Racial Origins of Modern Criminal Procedure," 61–63.

118. 344 U.S. 443 at 508.

119. The limited nature of *Brown v. Allen* is further evident in the companion case, *Daniels v. Allen*, 344 U.S. 443 (1953), where the Court refused to allow habeas to issue for state-level procedural default issues because direct review was prevented due to the adequate and independent state grounds rule.

120. 344 U.S. 443 at 510.

121. 344 U.S. 443, 449.

122. See generally Klinkner with Smith, *Unsteady March*; Mary Dudziak, *Cold War Civil Rights: Race and the Image of American Democracy* (Princeton: Princeton University Press, 2002); Kersch, *Constructing Civil Liberties*.

123. 347 U.S. 483 (1954). See also Kevin J. McMahon, *Reconsidering Roosevelt on Race: How the Presidency Paved the Road to Brown* (Chicago: University of Chicago Press, 2004).

124. See generally Henry Abraham, *Freedom and the Court: Civil Rights and Liberties in the United States,* 5th ed. (New York: Oxford University Press, 1988).

125. This regime use of judicial review is detailed in Klarman, *From Jim Crow to Civil Rights;* Keith E. Whittington, "'Interpose Your Friendly Hand': Political Supports for the Exercise of Judicial Review by the United States Supreme Court," *American Political Science Review* 99, no. 4 (2005).

126. Bator, "Finality in Criminal Law and Federal Habeas Corpus for State Prisoners." Before *Brown,* dissent largely came from the Judicial Conference of Senior Circuit Court Judges, led by John J. Parker. Parker's committee was successful in securing in the judicial code in 1948 a codification of the exhaustion requirement. See Larry W. Yackle, "The Habeas Hagioscope," *S. Cal. L. Rev.* 66 (1992): 2341–2342. On John J. Parker more generally, see Peter G. Fish, "Guarding the Judicial Ramparts: John J. Parker and the Administration of Federal Justice Judges and Court Reform," *Just. Sys. J.* 3 (1977), and Klarman, *From Jim Crow to Civil Rights,* 101, 108, 116.

127. 344 U.S. 443 at 535–536.

128. 344 U.S. 443 at 537.

129. This memo was unearthed by Saul Brenner. Saul Brenner, "The Memos of Supreme Court Law Clerk William Rehnquist: Conservative Tracts, or Mirrors of His Justice's Mind," *Judicature* 76 (1992). See also Freedman, *Habeas Corpus,* 119–123. Rehnquist's memo was written in response to *McGee v. Ekberg,* 343 U.S. 970 (1952). See Yackle, "Habeas Hagioscope," 2343.

130. Quoted in Freedman, *Habeas Corpus,* 123. Rehnquist was referring to *West Coast Hotel v. Parrish,* 300 U.S. 379 (1937).

131. Larry Yackle estimates that versions of Parker's proposed changes to habeas, supported by groups such as the National Association of State Attorneys General (NASG), were introduced at least six times in the decade after *Brown v. Allen.* See Yackle, "Habeas Hagioscope," 2344n55.

132. Just a year before, Howard Fatzer was the attorney general for the state of Kansas and in that capacity had represented Kansas in *Brown v. Board of Education,* 347 U.S. 483 (1954).

133. Hearings before Subcommittee 3, 84th Cong., 1st sess., on H.R. 5649 (7 and 24 June 1955), 55.

134. Ibid., 56.

135. Ibid., 61.

136. Ibid., 87.

137. Ibid.

138. See generally Powe, *Warren Court and American Politics.*

139. 367 U.S. 643 (1961); 338 U.S. 25 (1949).

140. Quoted in Powe, *Warren Court and American Politics,* 195.

141. That Court critics spanned the political spectrum, even before the Warren Court's great leap forward after 1962, is evidenced by reactions to *Brown v. Board of Education.* See generally Alexander M. Bickel, *The Least Dangerous Branch: The Supreme Court at the Bar of Politics* (Indianapolis: Bobbs-Merrill, 1962); John Hart Ely, *Democracy and Distrust: A Theory of Judicial Review* (Cambridge: Harvard University Press, 1980); Laura Kalman, *The Strange Career of Legal Liberalism* (New Haven,

Conn.: Yale University Press, 1996); Thomas M. Keck, *The Most Activist Supreme Court in History: The Road to Modern Judicial Conservatism* (Chicago: University of Chicago Press, 2004).

142. 372 U.S. 335 (1963).

143. 377 U.S. 533 (1964).

144. See Robert M. Cover and Alexander Aleinikoff, "Dialectical Federalism: Habeas Corpus and the Court," *Yale L. J.* 86, no. 6 (1977); Owen M. Fiss, "Dombrowski," *Yale L. J.* 86, no. 6 (1977).

145. Cover and Aleinikoff cite *Lee v. Macon County Bd. of Education,* 221 F. Supp. 297 (1963), as the quintessential example. In a series of cases throughout the year after this desegregation order, lower courts enjoined a mayor, school board officials, and the state superintendent of schools to carry out the district court's plan. The injunctive penalties also had beneficial effects, according to Cover and Aleinikoff, including providing a forum in which both sides could work out manageable plans. Cover and Aleinikoff, "Dialectical Federalism," 1035.

146. See Anthony Lewis, *Gideon's Trumpet* (New York: Random House, 1964).

147. The independent and adequate state grounds rule suggests that the Supreme Court "will not hear a case if the decision of the state's highest court is supported by a state law rationale that is independent of federal law and adequate to sustain the result." See Erwin Chemerinsky, *Federal Jurisdiction,* 4th ed. (New York: Aspen, 2003), 704–730.

148. 372 U.S. 391 at 432.

149. 372 U.S. 391, 433.

150. 372 U.S. 293 (1963).

151. Ibid., 294. See also Neil D. McFeeley, "A Change of Direction: Habeas Corpus from Warren to Burger," *Western Political Quarterly* 32, no. 2 (1979): 181.

152. 373 U.S. 1 (1963).

153. See also Jordan Steiker, "Innocence and Federal Habeas," *UCLA L. Rev.* 41 (1993): 320, who argues that "advocates for broad or narrow habeas jurisdiction are peculiarly interested in reconstructing a habeas tradition rather than relying on more formal tools of statutory construction, such as reliance on the text or intent of the drafters."

154. 372 U.S. 391, 400.

155. Ibid.

156. Ibid., 400–401.

157. Ibid., 401.

158. Ibid., 402.

159. Ibid.

160. Ibid., 406.

161. 372 U.S. 391 (1963) at 410n19. The cases are *Ex parte McCready,* 1 Hughes 598 (1874); *Ex parte Bridges,* 2 Woods 428 (1875); *In re Wong,* 6 Sawyer 237 (1880); *In re Parrott,* 6 Sawyer 349 (1880); *In re Ah Lee,* 6 Sawyer 410 (1880); *In re Ah Chong,* 6 Sawyer 451 (1880); and *Ex parte Houghton,* 7 Fed. 657 (1881).

162. 4 F. Cas. 98.

163. On the Chinese habeas cases more generally, see Christian G. Fritz, "A Nine-

teenth Century Habeas Corpus Mill: The Chinese before the Federal Courts in California," *Am. J. Legal Hist.* 32 (1988).

164. 47 F. Cas. 717, 718.

165. See also Liebman, *Federal Habeas Corpus Practice and Procedure.*

166. 372 U.S. 391, 410.

167. Ibid., 410.

168. The literature on incorporation is vast. See generally Michael Kent Curtis, *No State Shall Abridge: The Fourteenth Amendment and the Bill of Rights* (Durham, N.C.: Duke University Press, 1986); William E. Nelson, *The Fourteenth Amendment: From Political Principle to Judicial Doctrine* (Cambridge, Mass.: Harvard University Press, 1988); Michael J. Perry, *We the People: The Fourteenth Amendment and the Supreme Court* (New York: Oxford University Press, 1999); Gary L. McDowell and Judith A. Bacr, "Fourteenth Amendment: Should the Bill of Rights Apply to the States?," *Utah L. Rev.* 1987 (1987); Akhil Reed Amar, *The Bill of Rights: Creation and Reconstruction* (New Haven, Conn.: Yale University Press, 1998); Abraham, *Freedom and the Court;* Horace Edgar Flack, *The Adoption of the Fourteenth Amendment* (Baltimore: Johns Hopkins Press, 1908); Stanley Morrison, "Does the Fourteenth Amendment Incorporate the Bill of Rights: The Judicial Interpretation," *Stan. L. Rev.* 2 (1949).

169. Reprinted as William J. Brennan, "Federal Habeas Corpus and State Prisoners: An Exercise in Federalism," *Utah L. Rev.* 7 (1960).

170. Ibid., 440.

171. Ibid., 441.

172. 372 U.S. 391, 411–412.

173. 378 U.S. 478 (1964); 384 U.S. 436 (1966). See also Perlstein, *Nixonland,* 110, 260.

174. For an excellent overview of *Escobedo,* see Powe, *Warren Court and American Politics,* 388–394. See also Friedman, *The Will of the People,* 270–279.

175. 378 U.S. 438 at 489.

176. 378 U.S. 478 at 496.

177. See, for example, "Use of Confession in Trial Is Curbed," *New York Times,* 23 June 1964.

178. Powe, *Warren Court and American Politics,* 391.

179. See, for example, Walter F. Murphy and Joseph Tanenhaus, "Public Opinion and Supreme Court: The Goldwater Campaign," *Public Opinion Quarterly* 32, no. 1 (1968); Edsall and Edsall, *Chain Reaction;* Rick Perlstein, *Before the Storm: Barry Goldwater and the Unmaking of the American Consensus* (New York: Hill and Wang, 2001); Kersch, *Constructing Civil Liberties,* chap. 2; Cornell W. Clayton and J. Mitchell Pickerill, "The Politics of Criminal Justice: How the New Right Regime Shaped the Rehnquist Court's Criminal Justice Jurisprudence," *Geo. L. J.* 94 (2005); Keck, *Most Activist Supreme Court,* chaps. 3 and 4.

180. Nan Robertson, "Ervin Protests Curbs on Police," *New York Times,* 23 July 1966.

181. Powe, *Warren Court and American Politics,* 393. Friedman, *The Will of the People,* 275.

182. Bator, "Finality in Criminal Law and Federal Habeas Corpus for State Prison-

ers." See also "Alabama Justice Hits High Court," *New York Times,* 11 August 1963, which details the 1963 annual meeting of the conference of state justices that excoriated the Court's habeas and other criminal procedure decisions during the 1963 term.

183. The merits of redundancy between state and federal courts through habeas are developed most fully in Cover and Aleinikoff, "Dialectical Federalism."

184. Friendly, "Is Innocence Irrelevant?," 1067.

185. 384 U.S. 436 (1966).

186. Powe, *Warren Court and American Politics,* 394. See also Donald Grier Stephenson, *Campaigns and the Court: The U.S. Supreme Court in Presidential Elections* (New York: Columbia University Press, 1999), 176–177; Kersch, *Constructing Civil Liberties,* 121–127.

187. 384 U.S. 436 at 446.

188. Ibid., 542–543. During the same term the Court also decided *Johnson v. New Jersey,* 384 U.S. 719 (1966), in which the Court announced that *Miranda* would apply to trials already begun instead of applying to interrogations from that point forward. Reaction was swift and negative, to say the least. See Stephenson, *Campaigns and the Court,* 178.

189. Edsall and Edsall, *Chain Reaction,* 110–111.

190. See Stephenson, *Campaigns and the Court,* 180n1, 94.

191. 82 Stat. 197 (1968).

192. Powe, *Warren Court and American Politics,* 410; Clayton and Pickerill, "Politics of Criminal Justice," 1399–1402; Friedman, *The Will of the People,* 276–277.

193. Quoted in Powe, *Warren Court and American Politics,* 410. See also Thomas J. Sugrue, *Sweet Land of Liberty: The Forgotten Struggle for Civil Rights in the North* (New York: Random House, 2008), 324–334.

194. The term "countermajoritarian hero" is from Corinna Barrett Lain, "Countermajoritarian Hero or Zero—Rethinking the Warren Court's Role in the Criminal Procedure Revolution," *U. Pa. L. Rev.* 152 (2003).

195. Richard M. Nixon, "What Has Happened to America?" *Reader's Digest,* October 1967, quoted in Nixon, *Richard Nixon,* 123.

CHAPTER 5. INNOCENCE AND GUILT: HABEAS FROM
BURGER TO REHNQUIST

1. See generally Rick Perlstein, ed., *Nixonland: The Rise of a President and the Fracturing of America* (New York: Scribner, 2008), 110, 260, 284, 474; Thomas M. Keck, *The Most Activist Supreme Court in History: The Road to Modern Judicial Conservatism* (Chicago: University of Chicago Press, 2004), 108, 113; Robert G. McCloskey, *The American Supreme Court* (Chicago: University of Chicago Press, 2005), 166; David A. Yalof, *Pursuit of Justices: Presidential Politics and the Selection of Supreme Court Nominees* (Chicago: University of Chicago Press, 1999), 97–98; Thomas Byrne Edsall and Mary D. Edsall, *Chain Reaction: The Impact of Race, Rights, and Taxes on American Politics* (New York: Norton, 1991), 69–70.

2. Richard Nixon, *Richard Nixon: Speeches, Writings, Documents,* ed. Rick Perlstein (Princeton: Princeton University Press, 2008), 147.

3. Louis Michael Seidman, "Factual Guilt and the Burger Court: An Examination of Continuity and Change in Criminal Procedure," *Colum. L. Rev.* 80 (1980). Walter F. Murphy and Joseph Tanenhaus, "Public Opinion and the United States Supreme Court—Mapping of Some Prerequisites for Court Legitimation of Regime Changes," *Law & Soc'y Rev.* 2 (1967). Public opinion polls measuring the public's perception of court leniency of criminals grew from 48 percent in 1956 to 63 percent in 1968. However, opinion would soon change in the opposite direction. See Lawrence Baum, "Explaining the Burger Court's Support for Civil Liberties," *PS* 20, no. 1 (1987): 25–26.

4. Paul M. Bator, "Finality in Criminal Law and Federal Habeas Corpus for State Prisoners," *Harv. L. Rev.* 76 (1962); Henry J. Friendly, "Is Innocence Irrelevant? Collateral Attack on Criminal Judgments," *U. Chi. L. Rev.* 38, no. 1 (1970).

5. William H. Rehnquist, statement to the Senate Subcommittee on Constitutional Rights, Speedy Trial Act (I), Hearing (14 July 1971), 94 121.

6. Ibid., 97.

7. Indeed, one of Rehnquist's other suggestions for the bill's modification was to modify *Mapp*'s exclusionary rule. Ibid.

8. Ibid., 115.

9. Ibid., 99, 103, 109, 112.

10. Ibid., 100–101.

11. Ibid., 114.

12. Ibid., 102,

13. 344 U.S. 443, 537.

14. For a discussion of Rehnquist's sometimes controversial role as Justice Jackson's law clerk, see Tinsley E. Yarbrough, *The Rehnquist Court and the Constitution* (Oxford: Oxford University Press, 2000), 1–11. See also Saul Brenner, "The Memos of Supreme Court Law Clerk William Rehnquist: Conservative Tracts, or Mirrors of His Justice's Mind," *Judicature* 76 (1992).

15. For an excellent overview of the many proposals for habeas reform during the Reagan administration, see Larry W. Yackle, "The Reagan Administration's Habeas Corpus Proposals," *Iowa L. Rev.* 68 (1982); Cary Federman, "Who Has the Body? The Paths to Habeas Corpus Reform," *Prison Journal* 84, no. 3 (2004).

16. Bator, "Finality in Criminal Law and Federal Habeas Corpus for State Prisoners." Both Paul Bator and Henry Friendly were also cited numerous times in the Reagan Justice Department's most important statement regarding federal habeas corpus. See Office of Legal Policy, U.S. Department of Justice, "Report to the Attorney General on Federal Habeas Corpus Review of State Judgments" (1988).

17. See Irene Rosenberg and Yale Rosenberg, "Guilt: Henry Friendly Meets the Maharal of Prague," *Mich. L. Rev.* 90 (1991).

18. Bator, "Finality in Criminal Law and Federal Habeas Corpus for State Prisoners," 442, 453n24.

19. Ibid., 455.

20. Friendly, "Is Innocence Irrelevant?"

21. Ibid., 160.

22. 394 U.S. 217 (1969); Black's dissent is at 242–232.

23. Ibid., 237.

24. 394 U.S. 217 at 240–241.

25. For an excellent overview of the Rehnquist Court's federalism jurisprudence, see Cornell W. Clayton and J. Mitchell Pickerill, "Guess What Happened on the Way to Revolution? Precursors to the Supreme Court's Federalism Revolution," *Publius* 34, no. 3 (2004); J. Mitchell Pickerill and Cornell W. Clayton, "The Rehnquist Court and the Political Dynamics of Federalism," *Perspectives on Politics* 2, no. 2 (2004).

26. 408 U.S. 238 (1972); 428 U.S. 153 (1976); 481 U.S. 279 (1987).

27. 372 U.S. 293 (1963), 315.

28. See James S. Liebman, *Federal Habeas Corpus Practice and Procedure* (Charlottesville, Va.: Michie, 1994), 62–64; Neil McFeeley, "Habeas Corpus and Due Process: From Warren to Burger," *Baylor L. Rev.* 28 (1976): 548.

29. 114 U.S. 564 (1885).

30. Ibid., 569.

31. 371 U.S. 236 (1963).

32. Ibid., 240. For an overview of the civil application of habeas, see Dallin H. Oaks, "Habeas Corpus in the States—1776–1865," *U. Chi. L. Rev.* 32 (1964), and Liebman, *Federal Habeas Corpus.*

33. Ibid., 243.

34. 411 U.S. 345 (1973).

35. Ibid., 352.

36. Ibid., 355.

37. 410 U.S. 690 (1973).

38. 410 U.S. 690, 697n1.

39. 117 U.S. 241 (1886).

40. 404 U.S. 270 (1971).

41. 404 U.S. 270, 275.

42. 404 U.S. 270, 275, 278.

43. 404 U.S. 270, 279.

44. 409 U.S. 41 (1972).

45. 409 U.S. 41, 46 (1972).

46. 411 U.S. 258 (1973).

47. 100 U.S. 303 (1880).

48. Ibid., 268.

49. Ibid., 266.

50. Ibid., 276.

51. Ibid., 277n10. Marshall went to great lengths (although to no avail) to convey the extent of discriminatory practices in Tennessee's selection of grand jurors in 1948. For example, although the county in which the jurors selected was 25 percent black, no blacks had served on the grand jury before 1948. Even when blacks appeared on the juror rolls, the state placed a "c" or "col" next to their names.

52. 412 U.S. 218 (1973); 394 U.S. 217 (1969).

53. 394 U.S. 217, 231–243.

54. 412 U.S. 218, 227, 224.

55. Ibid., 250, 254.

56. Ibid., 253.

57. 8 U.S. 75 (1807) at 202–203.

58. Bator, "Finality in Criminal Law and Federal Habeas Corpus for State Prisoners," 475.

59. 412 U.S. 218, 256. See Chapter 3 for a detailed discussion. It is important to note that Powell skipped the "repealer" period (1868–1885) of Supreme Court review of habeas corpus. During this time, as I have detailed, lower federal courts did in fact grant habeas in many cases to state prisoners. See also Liebman, *Federal Habeas Corpus Practice and Procedure.*

60. 412 U.S. 218, 256.

61. Ibid., 257.

62. Ibid., 257–258.

63. Ibid., 258.

64. Ibid., 263–264.

65. 428 U.S. 465 (1976).

66. McFeeley, "Habeas Corpus and Due Process," 556.

67. I am not suggesting that the Court's decision in *Stone* was purely the result of the larger institution-regarding concerns of the Court to protect its own ability to issue the writ. To be sure, the larger political regime of the mid-1970s was deeply divided for many reasons, not the least of which was the decreased power and legitimacy of the Republican Party in the wake of Watergate. That the Burger Court can rightly be characterized as the "counterrevolution that wasn't" is also partly explained by the comparatively less conservative predilections of Republican appointees (with the exception of Rehnquist), the accumulated precedential record of the Warren Court, the disintegrating New Deal/Great Society coalition, the collegial relationship between Justices Brennan and Powell, Chief Justice Burger's ineffective leadership, and the largely positive reception and approbation of the Warren Court's decisions by the 1970s. See Baum, "Explaining the Burger Court's Support for Civil Liberties"; Mark Tushnet, "The Burger Court in Historical Perspective: The Triumph of Country-Club Republicanism," in *The Burger Court: Counter-Revolution or Confirmation?*, ed. Bernard Schwartz (New York: Oxford University Press, 1998). Nevertheless, the Court's more institution-regarding concerns discussed in this section deserve to be placed among these other factors.

68. Powell's accomplices in the robbery also testified against him in trial, implicating him as the shooter.

69. The Nevada vagrancy and loitering ordinance defined a vagrant as someone who "1) Loiters or wanders upon the streets or from place to place without apparent reason or business and 2) refuses to identify himself and account for his presence when asked by a police officer to do so 3) if surrounding circumstances are such as to indicate to a reasonable man that public safety demands such identification."

70. 428 U.S. 465 (1974), 482.

71. 394 U.S. 217, 225.

72. 428 U.S. 465, 489.

73. Ibid.

74. Powell asserted, "We adhere to the view that these considerations support the

implementation of the exclusionary rule at trial and its enforcement on direct appeal of state-court convictions." At 428 U.S. 465, 493.

75. 428 U.S. 465, 493n35. The quoted section at the end of this excerpt is from Bator, "Finality in Criminal Law and Federal Habeas Corpus for State Prisoners," 509.

76. 428 U.S. 465, 525.

77. 433 U.S. 72 (1977).

78. This is known as the contemporaneous-objection rule.

79. For an overview of *Wainwright* from the perspective of the theoretical and practical difficulties in actually determining cause and prejudice, see Saul B. Goodman and Jonathan B. Sallet, "*Wainwright v. Sykes:* The Lower Federal Courts Respond," *Hastings L. J.* 30 (1978).

80. 433 U.S. 72, 88.

81. Ibid.

82. 442 U.S. 415 (1979).

83. 442 U.S. 415, 423.

84. 443 U.S. 545 (1979).

85. 443 U.S. 545, 575.

86. 455 U.S. 509 (1982).

87. *Sanders v. United States,* 373 U.S. 1, 18 (1963).

88. 455 U.S. 509, 521 (1982).

89. 456 U.S. 107 (1982).

90. 456 U.S. 107, 126–127.

91. 456 U.S. 107, 127n31. Friendly, "Is Innocence Irrelevant?," 145.

92. 456 U.S. 107, 128. See also Sandra D. O'Connor, "Trends in the Relationship between the Federal and State Courts from the Perspective of a State Court Judge Symposium: State Courts and Federalism in the 1980s," *Wm. & Mary L. Rev.* 22 (1980).

93. 477 U.S. 478 (1986).

94. To be sure, habeas reform was not the only way the Reagan coalition sought to create and then enforce regime principles. On the political and legal strategies adopted by conservatives more generally, see Steven M. Teles, *The Rise of the Conservative Legal Movement: The Battle for Control of the Law* (Princeton: Princeton University Press, 2008); Sean Wilentz, ed., *The Age of Reagan: A History, 1974–2008* (New York: Harper, 2008), chap. 7.

95. 676 F. 2d 261 (1982).

96. 676 F. 2d 261, 267.

97. 676 F. 2d 261, 268.

98. 676 F. 2d 261, 269.

99. Yackle, "The Reagan Administration's Habeas Corpus Proposals," 610n612.

100. Letter from Smith to the Senate, 3 March 1982, quoted in ibid., 614.

101. Ibid., 614.

102. Office of Legal Policy, "Report to the Attorney General on Federal Habeas Corpus Review of State Judgments," 27 May 1988. See also Dawn E. Johnsen, "Ronald Reagan and the Rehnquist Court on Congressional Power: Presidential Influences on Constitutional Change," *Ind. L. J.* 78 (2003): 363–364; Cornell W. Clayton and J. Mitch-

ell Pickerill, "The Politics of Criminal Justice: How the New Right Regime Shaped the Rehnquist Court's Criminal Justice Jurisprudence," *Geo. L. J.* 94 (2005): 1405–1406.

103. Ibid., 22. The report claimed that the Warren Court's habeas jurisprudence was derived "from remarkable misconceptions concerning the historical function of habeas corpus."

104. Ibid., ii.

105. Ibid., 22.

106. Ibid., 1, quoting *Berger v. United States,* 295 U.S. 78, 88 (1935).

107. Ibid, 62–65.

108. Ibid., 53.

109. "Ad Hoc Committee on Federal Habeas Corpus in Capital Cases Committee Report," also referred to as the Powell Committee Report, 135 Cong. Rec. 24694 (1989).

110. Lewis F. Powell Jr., "Capital Punishment," *Harv. L. Rev.* 102 (1988).

111. *Gregg v. Georgia,* 428 U.S. 153 (1976).

112. Powell, "Capital Punishment," 1038.

113. *Furman v. Georgia,* 408 U.S. 238 (1972).

114. Powell, "Capital Punishment," 1044. For a deeper appreciation of Powell's jurisprudential understanding of habeas as requiring more deference to state courts' determination of constitutional questions, consider his remarks to the ABA's Bill of Rights conference in 1992: "Federalism . . . is a two-way street. Though the Constitution sets a national floor, the states may extend protections further, giving their citizens protections not afforded by the federal charter." Lewis F. Powell Jr., "Our Bill of Rights," *Ind. L. Rev.* 25 (1991): 940–941.

115. See Larry W. Yackle, "A Primer on the New Habeas Corpus Statute," *Buff. L. Rev.* 44 (1996).

116. 499 U.S. 467 (1991).

117. 481 U.S. 279 (1987).

118. 481 U.S. 279, 292.

119. Ibid., 316.

120. *Gregg v. Georgia,* 428 U.S. 238, 186–187 (1972).

121. Ibid., 319.

122. 481 U.S. 279 at 314–318.

123. 489 U.S. 288 (1989).

124. 476 U.S. 79 (1986) at 86.

125. See Liebman, *Federal Habeas Corpus Practice and Procedure,* 70. *Teague* thus overruled *Linkletter v. Walker,* 381 U.S. 618 (1965).

126. 489 U.S. 288, 300.

127. See also Sharad Sushil Khandelwal, "The Path to Habeas Corpus Narrows: Interpreting 28 U.S.C. 2254(D)(1)," *Mich. L. Rev.* 96 (1997). *Teague* also provided for a second type of exception, specifically allowing for habeas to challenge convictions that involve different punishments.

128. 489 U.S. 288, 309.

129. 492 U.S. 195.

130. 492 U.S. 195, 203.

131. Ibid.

132. 497 U.S. 227 (1990).

133. 472 U.S. 320 (1985).

134. 497 U.S. 227, 229.

135. 497 U.S. 227; Friendly, "Is Innocence Irrelevant?," 150.

136. 372 U.S. 391, 411–412 (1963).

137. 499 U.S. 467 at 489.

138. Here the Court again relied on Paul Bator: "There comes a point where a procedural system which leaves matters perpetually open no longer reflects humane concern but merely anxiety and a desire for immobility." Bator, "Finality in Criminal Law and Federal Habeas Corpus for State Prisoners," 452–453. 499 U.S. 467, 492.

139. 506 U.S. 390 (1993).

140. 506 U.S. 390, 407.

141. 506 U.S. 390, 407–408, quoting *Patterson v. New York,* 432 U.S. 197, 202 (1977).

142. 110 Stat. 1214 (1996). The AEDPA literature is voluminous. See generally Stephen I. Vladeck, "AEDPA, Saucier, and the Stronger Case for Rights-First Constitutional Adjudication," *Seattle U. L. Rev.* 32 (2008); Lee Kovarsky, "AEDPA's Wrecks: Comity, Finality, and Federalism," *Tul. L. Rev.* 82 (2007); John H. Blume, "AEDPA: The Hype and the Bite," *Cornell L. Rev.* 91 (2005); James S. Liebman, "Effective Death Penalty: AEDPA and Error Detection in Capital Cases," *Brook. L. Rev.* 67 (2001); Adam N. Steinman, "Reconceptualizing Federal Habeas Corpus for State Prisoners: How Should AEDPA's Standard of Review Operate after *Williams v. Taylor?*," *Wis. L. Rev.* 2001 (2001); Evan Tsen Lee, "Section 2254(D) of the New Habeas Statute: An (Opinionated) User's Manual," *Vand. L. Rev.* 51 (1998); James S. Liebman and William F. Ryan, "Some Effectual Power: The Quantity and Quality of Decisionmaking Required of Article III Courts," *Colum. L. Rev.* 98 (1998); Mark Tushnet and Larry Yackle, "Symbolic Statutes and Real Laws: The Pathologies of the Antiterrorism and Effective Death Penalty Act and the Prison Litigation Reform Act," *Duke L. J.* 47 (1997); Yackle, "Primer on the New Habeas Corpus Statute."

143. Liebman, "Effective Death Penalty"; Tushnet and Yackle, "Symbolic Statutes and Real Laws"; Yackle, "Primer on the New Habeas Corpus Statute"; Justin J. Wert, "Nothing New under the Sun: Habeas Corpus and Executive Power during the Bush Administration," *American Review of Politics* 29 (2009).

144. AEDPA, sec. 104.

145. AEDPA, sec. 2254(d).

146. See Office of Legal Policy, "Report to the Attorney General on Federal Habeas Corpus Review of State Judgments," 27 May 1988, 56–65.

147. See Liebman, "Effective Death Penalty," 411–412.

148. Liebman, "Effective Death Penalty," 413. For an excellent discussion of the Clinton administration's more general rightward shift in the criminal justice arena, see Clayton and Pickerill, "Politics of Criminal Justice," 1406–1409.

149. Office of Legal Policy, "Report to the Attorney General on Federal Habeas Corpus Review of State Judgments," 27 May 1988, 59–61.

150. Liebman, "Effective Death Penalty," 414.

151. 428 U.S. 465 (1976).

152. See *Kimmelman v. Morrison,* 477 U.S. 365 (1986), and *Rose v. Mitchell,* 443 U.S. 545 (1979). See also *Jackson v. Virginia,* 443 U.S. 307 (1979), in which the Court refused to apply *Stone* to due process claims of insufficient evidence at trials.

153. Again, this dynamic suggests that the Court does not simply mirror societal or political forces, but rather makes decisions that at times evidence the degree to which the judicial role is autonomous from other institutions, especially those with which it is allied. See Rogers M. Smith, "Political Jurisprudence, the 'New Institutionalism,' and the Future of Public Law," *American Political Science Review* 82, no. 1 (1988): 95; Howard Gillman, "The Court as an Idea, Not a Building (or a Game): Interpretive Institutionalism and the Analysis of Supreme Court Decision-Making," in *Supreme Court Decision-Making: New Institutionalist Approaches,* ed. Cornell W. Clayton and Howard Gillman (Chicago: University of Chicago Press, 1999). At least for habeas cases, this institutionally protective phenomenon answers the important criticisms of the regime politics literature, specifically those critics who, although sympathetic to the regimes approach more generally, nevertheless argue that judicial independence still exists. See, for example, Thomas M. Keck, "Party Politics or Judicial Independence? The Regime Politics Literature Hits the Law Schools," *Law and Social Inquiry* 32, no. 2 (2007).

154. See also McCloskey, *American Supreme Court,* 166, 168.

CONCLUSION: THE NOT-SO-GREAT WRIT OF LIBERTY

1. See, for example, Jack M. Balkin and Sanford Levinson, "Understanding the Constitutional Revolution," *Va. L. Rev.* 87, no. 6 (2001).

2. This means that the arguments put forth by both the proponents *and* opponents of increased federal habeas for state prisoners are too rigid. Compare, for example, Gary Peller, "In Defense of Federal Habeas Corpus Relitigation," *Harv. CR-CL L. Rev.* 16 (1982). Paul M. Bator, "Finality in Criminal Law and Federal Habeas Corpus for State Prisoners," *Harv. L. Rev.* 76 (1962).

3. Recent works that replicate this dichotomy include Clement Fatovic, *Outside the Law: Emergency and Executive Power* (Baltimore: Johns Hopkins University Press, 2009); Benjamin A. Kleinerman, *The Discretionary President: The Promise and Peril of Executive Power* (Lawrence: University Press of Kansas, 2009); William H. Rehnquist, ed., *All the Laws but One: Civil Liberties in Wartime* (New York: Vintage Books, 2000); Clinton Rossiter, *Constitutional Dictatorship: Crisis Government in the Modern Democracies* (Princeton: Princeton University Press, 1948); John Yoo, *The Powers of War and Peace: The Constitution and Foreign Affairs after 9/11* (Chicago: University of Chicago Press, 2005); John Yoo, *War by Other Means: An Insider's Account of the War on Terror* (New York: Atlantic Monthly Press, 2006); Lee Epstein, Daniel E. Ho, Gary King, and Jeffrey A. Segal, "The Supreme Court during Crisis: How War Affects Only Non-War Cases," *N.Y.U. L. Rev.* 80 (2005). Some do not make such a sharp distinction and recognize that peacetime political development can influence wartime constitutional development. See, for example, Mary Dudziak, "Law, War, and the History of Time," *Cal. L. Rev.* 98 (2010); Mark Tushnet, ed., *The Constitution in Wartime: Beyond Alarmism and Complacency* (Durham, N.C.: Duke University Press, 2005), introduction.

Others make a related argument that wartime has significant effects, both positive and negative, on the "normal" development of civil rights and liberties. See, for example, Philip A. Klinkner with Rogers M. Smith, *The Unsteady March: The Rise and Decline of Racial Equality in America* (Chicago: University of Chicago Press, 1999); Mark Graber, "Counter-Stories: Maintaining and Expanding Civil Liberties in Wartime," in Tushnet, *The Constitution in Wartime;* Mary Dudziak, *Cold War Civil Rights: Race and the Image of American Democracy* (Princeton: Princeton University Press, 2002).

4. 542 U.S. 507 (2004); 542 U.S. 466 (2004); 548 U.S. 557 (2006); 128 S. Ct. 2229 (2008).

5. 428 U.S. 465 (1976).

6. Bator, "Finality in Criminal Law and Federal Habeas Corpus for State Prisoners."

7. Henry J. Friendly, "Is Innocence Irrelevant? Collateral Attack on Criminal Judgments," *U. Chi. L. R.* 38, no. 1 (1970).

8. Office of Legal Policy, "Report to the Attorney General on Federal Habeas Corpus Review of State Judgments," 27 May 1988. See also Dawn E. Johnsen, "Ronald Reagan and the Rehnquist Court on Congressional Power: Presidential Influences on Constitutional Change," *Ind. L. J.* 78 (2003): 363–364; Cornell W. Clayton and J. Mitchell Pickerill, "The Politics of Criminal Justice: How the New Right Regime Shaped the Rehnquist Court's Criminal Justice Jurisprudence," *Geo. L. J.* 94 (2005): 1405–1406. On the Republican Party's larger electoral strategy that culminated in a successful realignment, see Earl Black and Merle Black, *The Rise of Southern Republicans* (Cambridge, Mass.: Harvard University Press, 2002), chap. 7.

9. 110 Stat. 1214 (1996).

10. 542 U.S. 507 (2004).

11. 119 Stat. 2739. The relevant provision provided that "no court, justice, or judge shall have jurisdiction to hear or consider . . . an application for a writ of habeas corpus filed by or on behalf of an alien detained by the Department of Defense at Guantánamo Bay, Cuba." 119 Stat. 2742.

12. 126 S. Ct. 2749 (2006); 120 Stat. 2600.

13. 2005 U.S. Briefs 184.

14. 128 S. Ct. 2229 (2008).

15. See, for example, Stephen I. Vladeck, "Boumediene's Quiet Theory: Access to Courts and the Separation of Powers," *Notre Dame L. Rev.* 84 (2008); Paul Halliday and G. Edward White, "The Suspension Clause: English Text, Imperial Contexts, and American Implications," *Va. L. Rev.* 94 (2008).

16. 2006 U.S. Briefs 1195, 12.

17. 339 U.S. 763 (1950).

18. The case is also only the second time that the Court overturned a congressional statute removing federal jurisdiction. See Vladeck, "Boumediene's Quiet Theory," 2108.

19. 128 S. Ct. 2229, 2259.

20. 128 S. Ct. 2229, 2259–2260.

21. 128 S. Ct. 2229, 2260.

22. 128 S. Ct. 2229, 2261.

23. 128 S. Ct. 2229, 2263.

24. See *Felker v. Turpin*, 518 U.S. 65 (1996).

25. 128 S. Ct. 2229, 2264.

26. See 128 S. Ct. 2229, 2266.

27. Ibid., 2267.

28. Ibid., 2269.

29. Ibid., 2276.

30. Ibid., 2277.

References

Abraham, Henry Julian. *Freedom and the Court: Civil Rights and Liberties in the United States.* 5th ed. New York: Oxford University Press, 1988.

Ackerman, Bruce A. *We the People.* Cambridge, Mass.: Belknap Press of Harvard University Press, 1991.

Aldrich, John Herbert. *Why Parties? The Origin and Transformation of Political Parties in America.* Chicago: University of Chicago Press, 1995.

Amar, Akhil Reed. *The Bill of Rights: Creation and Reconstruction.* New Haven, Conn.: Yale University Press, 1998.

Amsterdam, Anthony G. "Criminal Prosecutions Affecting Federally Guaranteed Civil Rights: Federal Removal and Habeas Corpus Jurisdiction to Abort State Court Trial." *U. Pa. L. Rev.* 113 (1964): 793.

Baker, H. Robert. *The Rescue of Joshua Glover: A Fugitive Slave, the Constitution, and the Coming of the Civil War.* Athens: Ohio University Press, 2006.

Balkin, Jack M., and Sanford Levinson. "Understanding the Constitutional Revolution." *Va. L. Rev.* 87, no. 6 (2001): 1045–1109.

Barnum, David G. "The Supreme Court and Public Opinion: Judicial Decision Making in the Post–New Deal Period." *Journal of Politics* 47, no. 2 (1985): 652–666.

Bator, Paul M. "Finality in Criminal Law and Federal Habeas Corpus for State Prisoners." *Harv. L. Rev.* 76 (1962): 441.

Baum, Lawrence. "Explaining the Burger Court's Support for Civil Liberties." *PS* 20, no. 1 (1987).

Bederman, David J. "The Cautionary Tale of Alexander Mcleod: Superior Orders and the American Writ of Habeas Corpus." *Emory L. J.* 41 (1992): 515.

Belz, Herman. *A New Birth of Freedom: The Republican Party and Freedmen's Rights, 1861 to 1866.* New York: Fordham University Press, 2000.

Benedict, Michael Les. *A Compromise of Principle: Congressional Republicans and Reconstruction, 1863–1869.* New York: Norton, 1974.

———. "Preserving the Constitution: The Conservative Basis of Radical Reconstruction." *Journal of American History* 61, no. 1 (1974): 65–90.

———. *Preserving the Constitution: Essays on Politics and the Constitution in the Reconstruction Era.* New York: Fordham University Press, 2006.

———. "Preserving Federalism: Reconstruction and the Waite Court." *Sup. Ct. Rev.* 1978 (1978): 39.

Bestor, Arthur. "The American Civil War as a Constitutional Crisis." *American Historical Review* 69, no. 2 (1964): 327–352.

———. "State Sovereignty and Slavery: A Reinterpretation of Proslavery Constitutional Doctrine." *Journal of the Illinois State Historical Society* 54 (1961): 117.

Bickel, Alexander M. *The Least Dangerous Branch: The Supreme Court at the Bar of Politics.* Indianapolis: Bobbs-Merrill, 1962.

Black, Earl, and Merle Black. *The Rise of Southern Republicans*. Cambridge, Mass.: Harvard University Press, 2002.

Blasi, Vincent. *The Burger Court: The Counter-Revolution That Wasn't*. New Haven, Conn.: Yale University Press, 1983.

Bloch, Susan, and Maeva Marcus. "John Marshall's Selective Use of History in *Marbury v. Madison*." *Wis. L. Rev.* 1986 (1986): 301.

Blume, John H. "AEDPA: The Hype and the Bite." *Cornell L. Rev.* 91 (2005): 259.

Bork, Robert H. *The Tempting of America: The Political Seduction of the Law*. New York: Free Press, 1990.

Brandwein, Pamela. "The *Civil Rights Cases* and the Lost Language of State Neglect." In *The Supreme Court and American Political Development*, edited by Ronald Kahn and Ken Kersch, 275–325. Lawrence: University Press of Kansas, 2006.

———. *Reconstructing Reconstruction: The Supreme Court and the Production of Historical Truth*. Durham, N.C.: Duke University Press, 1999.

Brennan, William J. "Federal Habeas Corpus and State Prisoners: An Exercise in Federalism." *Utah L. Rev.* 7 (1960): 423.

Brennan, William J., Jr. "The Bill of Rights and the States: The Revival of State Constitutions as Guardians of Individual Rights." *N.Y.U. L. Rev.* 61 (1986): 535.

Brenner, Saul. "The Memos of Supreme Court Law Clerk William Rehnquist: Conservative Tracts, or Mirrors of His Justice's Mind." *Judicature* 76 (1992): 77.

Brown, Richard. *Strain of Violence: Historical Studies of Violence and Vigilantism*. New York: Oxford University Press, 1975.

Burger, Warren E. "The Need for Change in Prisons and the Correctional System." *Ark. L. Rev.* 38 (1984): 711.

———. "Post Conviction Remedies: Eliminating Federal–State Friction Criminal Law." *J. Crim. L. Criminology and Police Sci.* 61 (1970): 148.

———. "Report on the Federal Judicial Branch—1973 Report." *A.B.A. J.* 59 (1973): 1125.

Burgess, John William. *Reconstruction and the Constitution, 1866–1876*. New York: C. Scribner's Sons, 1902.

Burke, Edmund. *Edmund Burke: Selected Writings and Speeches*. Edited by Peter J. Stanlis. Washington, D.C.: Regnery 1997.

Burnham, Walter Dean. *Critical Elections and the Mainsprings of American Politics*. New York: Norton, 1970.

Butterfield, Herbert. *The Whig Interpretation of History*. London: G. Bell and Sons, 1931.

Campbell, Stanley W. *The Slave Catchers: Enforcement of the Fugitive Slave Law, 1850–1860*. Chapel Hill: University of North Carolina Press, 1970.

Capozzola, Christopher. *Uncle Sam Wants You: World War I and the Making of the Modern American Citizen*. New York: Oxford University Press, 2008.

Casper, Jonathan D. "The Supreme Court and National Policy Making." *American Political Science Review* 70, no. 1 (1976): 50–63.

Chafee, Zechariah. "The Most Important Human Right in the Constitution." *B.U. L. Rev.* 32 (1952): 143.

Chemerinsky, Erwin. *Federal Jurisdiction*. 4th ed. New York: Aspen, 2003.

————. "Thinking about Habeas Corpus." *Case W. Res. L. Rev.* 37 (1986): 748.

Chin, Gabriel J. "Unexplainable on Grounds of Race: Doubts about *Yick Wo.*" *U. Ill. L. Rev.* 2008 (2008): 1359.

Clarke, Alan. "Habeas Corpus: The Historical Debate." *N.Y.L. Sch. J. Hum. Rts.* 14 (1997): 375.

Clayton, Cornell, and David A. May. "A Political Regimes Approach to the Analysis of Legal Decisions." *Polity* 32, no. 2 (1999): 233–252.

Clayton, Cornell W., and J. Mitchell Pickerill. "Guess What Happened on the Way to Revolution? Precursors to the Supreme Court's Federalism Revolution." *Publius* 34, no. 3 (2004): 85–114.

————. "The Politics of Criminal Justice: How the New Right Regime Shaped the Rehnquist Court's Criminal Justice Jurisprudence." *Geo. L. J.* 94 (2005): 1385.

Clinton, Robert N. "A Mandatory View of Federal Court Jurisdiction: Early Implementation of and Departures from the Constitutional Plan." *Colum. L. Rev.* 86 (1986): 1515.

Cole, David, and James X. Dempsey. *Terrorism and the Constitution: Sacrificing Civil Liberties in the Name of National Security.* 3rd ed. New York: New Press, 2006.

Cortner, Richard C. *A Mob Intent on Death: The NAACP and the Arkansas Riot Cases.* Middletown, Conn.: Wesleyan University Press, 1988.

Corwin, Edward S. *The President: Office and Powers, 1787–1957: History and Analysis of Practice and Opinion.* New York: New York University Press, 1957.

————. *Total War and the Constitution.* New York: Knopf, 1947.

Cover, Robert M. *Justice Accused: Antislavery and the Judicial Process.* New Haven, Conn.: Yale University Press, 1975.

Cover, Robert M., and Alexander Aleinikoff. "Dialectical Federalism: Habeas Corpus and the Court." *Yale L. J.* 86, no. 6 (1977): 1035–1102.

Currie, David P. *The Constitution in the Supreme Court: The First Hundred Years, 1789–1888.* Chicago: University of Chicago Press, 1985.

Curtis, Michael Kent. *No State Shall Abridge: The Fourteenth Amendment and the Bill of Rights.* Durham, N.C.: Duke University Press, 1986.

————. "Resurrecting the Privileges or Immunities Clause and Revising the *Slaughter-House* Cases without Exhuming Lochner: Individual Rights and the Fourteenth Amendment." *B.C. L. Rev.* 38 (1996): 1.

Dahl, Robert A. "Decision-Making in a Democracy: The Supreme Court as a National Policy-Maker." *J. Pub. L.* 6 (1957): 279.

Daniels, Roger. *Concentration Camps, North America: Japanese in the United States and Canada during World War II.* Malabar, Fla.: R. E. Krieger, 1981.

————. *The Decision to Relocate the Japanese Americans.* Malabar, Fla.: R. E. Krieger, 1975.

————. *The Politics of Prejudice: The Anti-Japanese Movement in California and the Struggle for Japanese Exclusion.* 2nd ed. Berkeley: University of California Press, 1977.

————. *Prisoners without Trial: Japanese Americans in World War II.* New York: Hill and Wang, 2004.

Dinan, John J. *The American State Constitutional Tradition.* Lawrence: University Press of Kansas, 2006.

Dinnerstein, Leonard. *The Leo Frank Case*. New York: Columbia University Press, 1968.

Dray, Philip. *At the Hands of Persons Unknown: The Lynching of Black America*. New York: Random House, 2003.

Dudziak, Mary. *Cold War Civil Rights: Race and the Image of American Democracy*. Princeton: Princeton University Press, 2002.

———. "Law, War, and the History of Time." *Cal. L. Rev.* 98 (2010).

Duff, John J. *A. Lincoln: Prairie Lawyer*. New York: Rinehart, 1960.

Duker, William F. *A Constitutional History of Habeas Corpus*. Westport, Conn.: Greenwood Press, 1980.

———. "The Right to Bail: A Historical Inquiry." *Albany L. Rev.* 42 (1977): 33.

Dunning, William A. *Reconstruction, Political and Economic, 1865–1877*. New York: Harper & Bros., 1907.

Dworkin, Ronald. *A Matter of Principle*. Cambridge, Mass.: Harvard University Press, 1985.

Edsall, Thomas Byrne, and Mary D. Edsall. *Chain Reaction: The Impact of Race, Rights, and Taxes on American Politics*. New York: Norton, 1991.

Eisgruber, Christopher L. "John Marshall's Judicial Rhetoric." *Sup. Ct. Rev.* (1996): 439.

———. "Justice Story, Slavery, and the Natural Law Foundations of American Constitutionalism." *U. Chi. L. Rev.* 55 (1988): 273.

Elkins, Stanley M., and Eric L. McKitrick. *The Age of Federalism*. New York: Oxford University Press, 1995.

Ellis, Joseph J. *Founding Brothers: The Revolutionary Generation*. New York: Knopf, 2000.

Ely, John Hart. *Democracy and Distrust: A Theory of Judicial Review*. Cambridge: Harvard University Press, 1980.

Epstein, Lee, Daniel E. Ho, Gary King, and Jeffrey A. Segal. "The Supreme Court during Crisis: How War Affects Only Non-War Cases." *N.Y.U. L. Rev.* 80 (2005): 1.

Ericson, David F. "The Nullification Crisis, American Republicanism, and the Force Bill Debate." *Journal of Southern History* 61, no. 2 (1995): 22.

Evans, Maurice S. *Black and White in the Southern States: A Study of the Race Problem in the United States from a South African Point of View*. London: Longmans Green, 1915.

Fairman, Charles. *Reconstruction and Reunion, 1864–88, Part One*. New York: Macmillan, 1971.

———. *Reconstruction and Reunion, 1864–88*. Vol. 7, *History of the Supreme Court of the United States, Part Two*. New York: Macmillan, 1987.

Fallon, Richard, and Daniel Meltzer. "Habeas Corpus Jurisdiction, Substantive Rights, and the War on Terror." *Harv. L. Rev.* 120 (2006): 2029.

Farrand, Max. *The Records of the Federal Convention of 1787*. New Haven, Conn.: Yale University Press, 1911.

Fatovic, Clement. *Outside the Law: Emergency and Executive Power*. Baltimore: Johns Hopkins University Press, 2009.

Faulkner, Robert K. "John Marshall and the Burr Trial." *Journal of American History* 53, no. 2 (1966): 247–258.

Federman, Cary. *The Body and the State: Habeas Corpus and American Jurisprudence.* Albany: State University of New York Press, 2006.

———. "Who Has the Body? The Paths to Habeas Corpus Reform." *Prison Journal* 84, no. 3 (2004): 317–339.

Feldman, Stephen M. "The Rule of Law or the Rule of Politics? Harmonizing the Internal and External Views of Supreme Court Decision Making." *Law and Social Inquiry* 30, no. 1 (2005): 89–135.

Finkelman, Paul. "The Kidnapping of John Davis and the Adoption of the Fugitive Slave Law of 1793." *Journal of Southern History* 56, no. 3 (1990): 397–422.

——— —. "Story Telling on the Supreme Court: *Prigg v. Pennsylvania* and Justice Joseph Story's Judicial Nationalism." *Sup. Ct. Rev.* 1994 (1994): 247.

Fish, Peter G. "Guarding the Judicial Ramparts: John J. Parker and the Administration of Federal Justice Judges and Court Reform." *Just. Sys. J.* 3 (1977): 105.

Fisher, Louis. *Military Tribunals and Presidential Power: American Revolution to the War on Terrorism.* Lawrence: University Press of Kansas, 2005.

Fiss, Owen M. "Dombrowski." *Yale L. J.* 86, no. 6 (1977): 1103–1164.

Flack, Horace Edgar. *The Adoption of the Fourteenth Amendment.* Baltimore: Johns Hopkins Press, 1908.

Foner, Eric. *Free Soil, Free Labor, Free Men: The Ideology of the Republican Party before the Civil War.* New York: Oxford University Press, 1970.

———. *Reconstruction: America's Unfinished Revolution, 1863–1877.* New York: Harper & Row, 1989.

Frankfurter, Felix, and James M. Landis. *The Business of the Supreme Court: A Study in the Federal Judicial System.* New Brunswick, N.J.: Transaction Publishers, 2007.

Freedman, Eric M. *Habeas Corpus: Rethinking the Great Writ of Liberty.* New York: New York University Press, 2001.

Freehling, William W. *The Road to Disunion.* New York: Oxford University Press, 1990.

Friedman, Barry. "The History of the Countermajoritarian Difficulty, Part One: The Road to Judicial Supremacy." *N.Y.U. L. Rev.* 73 (1998): 333.

——— —. "Pas de Deux: The Supreme Court and the Habeas Courts. The Future of Habeas Corpus: Reflections on *Teague v. Lane* and Beyond." *S. Cal. L. Rev.* 66 (1992): 2467.

——— —. "The Politics of Judicial Review." *Tex. L. Rev.* 84 (2005): 257.

———. "A Tale of Two Habeas." *Minn. L. Rev.* 73 (1988): 247.

———. *The Will of the People: How Public Opinion Has Influenced the Supreme Court and Shaped the Meaning of the Constitution.* New York: Farrar, Straus and Giroux, 2009.

Friendly, Henry J. "Is Innocence Irrelevant? Collateral Attack on Criminal Judgments." *University of Chicago Law Review* 38, no. 1 (1970): 142–172.

Fritz, Christian G. "A Nineteenth Century Habeas Corpus Mill: The Chinese before the Federal Courts in California." *Am. J. Legal Hist.* 32 (1988): 347.

Frymer, Paul. "Law and American Political Development." *Law and Social Inquiry* 33, no. 3 (2008): 779–803.

Funston, Richard. "The Supreme Court and Critical Elections." *American Political Science Review* 69, no. 3 (1975): 795–811.

Gates, John B. "Supreme Court Voting and Realigning Issues: A Microlevel Analysis of Supreme Court Policy Making and Electoral Realignment." *Social Science History* 13, no. 3 (1989): 255–283.

Gerstle, Gary. *American Crucible: Race and Nation in the Twentieth Century.* Princeton: Princeton University Press, 2001.

Gerteis, Louis S. "Salmon P. Chase, Radicalism, and the Politics of Emancipation, 1861–1864." *Journal of American History* 60, no. 1 (1973).

Gillette, William. *Retreat from Reconstruction, 1869–1879.* Baton Rouge: Louisiana State University Press, 1979.

Gillman, Howard. "The Court as an Idea, Not a Building (or a Game): Interpretive Institutionalism and the Analysis of Supreme Court Decision-Making." In *Supreme Court Decision-Making: New Institutionalist Approaches*, edited by Cornell W. Clayton and Howard Gillman, 65–87. Chicago: University of Chicago Press, 1999.

———. "Courts and the Politics of Partisan Coalitions." In *The Oxford Handbook of Law and Politics,* edited by Keith E. Whittington, R. Daniel Kelemen, and Gregory A. Caldeira, 644–662. Oxford: Oxford University Press, 2008.

———. "How Political Parties Can Use the Courts to Advance Their Agendas: Federal Courts in the United States, 1875–1891." *American Political Science Review* 96, no. 3 (2002): 511–524.

———. "Martin Shapiro and the Movement from 'Old' to 'New' Institutionalist Studies in Public Law Scholarship." *Annual Review of Political Science* 7 (2004): 363–382.

———. "Preferred Freedoms: The Progressive Expansion of State Power and the Rise of Modern Civil Liberties Jurisprudence." *Political Research Quarterly* 47, no. 3 (1994): 623–653.

Goldstein, Leslie Friedman. "The Specter of the Second Amendment: Rereading *Slaughterhouse* and *Cruikshank.*" *Studies in American Political Development* 21, no. 2 (2007): 131–148.

Goodman, Saul B., and Jonathan B. Sallet. "*Wainwright v. Sykes:* The Lower Federal Courts Respond." *Hastings L. J.* 30 (1978): 1683.

Gordon, Robert W. "Historicism in Legal Scholarship Symposium on Legal Scholarship: Its Nature and Purposes." *Yale L. J.* 90 (1980): 1017.

Graber, Mark. "Counter-Stories: Maintaining and Expanding Civil Liberties in Wartime." In *The Constitution in Wartime: Beyond Alarmism and Complacency,* edited by Mark Tushnet, 95–123. Durham, N.C.: Duke University Press, 2005.

———. "Federalist or Friends of Adams: The Marshall Court and Party Politics." *Studies in American Political Development* 12, no. 2 (1998): 229–266.

———. "Legal, Strategic, or Legal Strategy: Deciding to Decide during the Civil War and Reconstruction." In *The Supreme Court and American Political Development,* edited by Ronald Kahn and Kenneth Kersch, 33–66. Lawrence: University Press of Kansas, 2006.

Graber, Mark A. "Constructing Judicial Review." *Annual Review of Political Science* 8, no. 1 (2005): 425–451.

———. *Dred Scott and the Problem of Constitutional Evil.* Cambridge: Cambridge University Press, 2006.

———. "Establishing Judicial Review? Schooner Peggy and the Early Marshall Court." *Political Research Quarterly* 51, no. 1 (1998): 221–239.

———. "The Nonmajoritarian Difficulty: Legislative Deference to the Judiciary." *Studies in American Political Development* 7, no. 1 (1993): 35–73.

Grodzins, Morton. *Americans Betrayed: Politics and the Japanese Evacuation.* Chicago: University of Chicago Press, 1949.

Hall, Kermit L. "Political Power and Constitutional Legitimacy: The South Carolina Ku Klux Klan Trials, 1871–1872." *Emory L. J.* 33 (1984): 921.

Halliday, Paul D. *Habeas Corpus: From England to Empire.* Cambridge: Harvard University Press, 2010.

Halliday, Paul, and G. Edward White. "The Suspension Clause: English Text, Imperial Contexts, and American Implications." *Va. L. Rev.* 94 (2008): 575.

Hamilton, Alexander, James Madison, and John Jay. *The Federalist Papers.* New York: Bantam, 2003.

Harris, William F. *The Interpretable Constitution.* Baltimore: Johns Hopkins University Press, 1993.

Hart, Henry M., Jr. "The Power of Congress to Limit the Jurisdiction of Federal Courts: An Exercise in Dialectic." *Harv. L. Rev.* 66 (1952): 1362.

———. "The Supreme Court 1958 Term—Foreword: The Time Chart of the Justices." *Harv. L. Rev.* 73 (1959): 84.

Hatcher, John H. "Martial Law and Habeas Corpus." *W. Va. L. Q.* 46 (1939): 187.

Hirschl, Ran. *Towards Juristocracy: The Origins and Consequences of the New Constitutionalism.* Cambridge: Harvard University Press, 2004.

Hoffmann, Joseph L., and William J. Stuntz. "Habeas after the Revolution." *Sup. Ct. Rev.* 1993 (1993): 65.

Holt, Michael F. *The Rise and Fall of the American Whig Party: Jacksonian Politics and the Onset of the Civil War.* New York: Oxford University Press, 1999.

Holt, Wythe. "To Establish Justice: Politics, the Judiciary Act of 1789, and the Invention of the Federal Courts." *Duke L. J.* 1989 (1989): 1421.

Hurd, Rollin C. *A Treatise on the Right of Personal Liberty: And on the Writ of Habeas Corpus and the Practice Connected with It: With a View of the Law of Extradition of Fugitives.* Albany: W. C. Little, 1858.

Hyman, Harold M. *A More Perfect Union: The Impact of the Civil War and Reconstruction on the Constitution.* New York: Knopf, 1973.

Hyman, Harold Melvin. *The Radical Republicans and Reconstruction, 1861–1870.* Indianapolis: Bobbs-Merrill, 1967.

———. *The Reconstruction Justice of Salmon P. Chase: In re Turner and Texas v. White.* Landmark Law Cases and American Society. Lawrence: University Press of Kansas, 1997.

Hyman, Harold Melvin, and William M. Wiecek. *Equal Justice under Law: Constitutional Development, 1835–1875.* New American Nation Series. New York: Harper & Row, 1982.

Irons, Peter H. *Justice at War.* New York: Oxford University Press, 1983.

———. *A People's History of the Supreme Court: The Men and Women Whose Cases and Decisions Have Shaped Our Constitution.* Rev. ed. New York: Penguin Books, 2006.

Jenks, Edward. "The Myth of Magna Carta." *Independent Review* 4 (1904): 260.

Johnsen, Dawn E. "Ronald Reagan and the Rehnquist Court on Congressional Power: Presidential Influences on Constitutional Change." *Ind. L. J.* 78 (2003): 363.

Kaczorowski, Robert J. "The Chase Court and Fundamental Rights: A Watershed in American Constitutionalism." *N. Ky. L. Rev.* 21 (1993): 151.

———. "Federal Enforcement of Civil Rights during the First Reconstruction Essay." *Fordham Urb. L. J.* 23 (1995): 155.

Kahn, Ronald H. *The Supreme Court and Constitutional Theory, 1953–1993.* Lawrence: University Press of Kansas, 1994.

Kahn, Ronald, and Kenneth Kersch, eds. *The Supreme Court and American Political Development.* Lawrence: University Press of Kansas, 2006.

Kalman, Laura. "Border Patrol: Reflections on the Turn to History in Legal Scholarship." *Fordham L. Rev.* 66 (1997): 87.

———. *The Strange Career of Legal Liberalism.* New Haven, Conn.: Yale University Press, 1996.

Keck, Thomas M. *The Most Activist Supreme Court in History: The Road to Modern Judicial Conservatism.* Chicago: University of Chicago Press, 2004.

———. "Party, Policy, or Duty: Why Does the Supreme Court Invalidate Federal Statutes?" *American Political Science Review* 101, no. 2 (2007): 321–338.

———. "Party Politics or Judicial Independence? The Regime Politics Literature Hits the Law Schools." *Law and Social Inquiry* 32, no. 2 (2007): 511–544.

Keller, Morton. *America's Three Regimes: A New Political History.* New York: Oxford University Press, 2007.

Kelly, Alfred H. "Clio and the Court: An Illicit Love Affair." *Sup. Ct. Rev.* 1965 (1965): 119.

Kelly, Alfred Hinsey, Winfred Audif Harbison, and Herman Belz. *The American Constitution: Its Origins and Development.* 7th ed. New York: Norton, 1991.

Kersch, Kenneth. *Constructing Civil Liberties: Discontinuities in the Development of American Constitutional Law.* New York: Cambridge University Press, 2004.

Ketcham, Ralph. *The Anti-Federalist Papers and the Constitutional Convention Debates.* New York: New American Library, 1986.

Key, V. O., Jr. "A Theory of Critical Elections." *Journal of Politics* 17, no. 1 (1955): 3–18.

Khandelwal, Sharad Sushil. "The Path to Habeas Corpus Narrows: Interpreting 28 U.S.C. 2254(D) (1)." *Mich. L. Rev.* 96 (1997): 434.

King, Desmond S. *Separate and Unequal: African Americans and the U.S. Federal Government.* Oxford: Oxford University Press, 2007.

King, Gary, Robert O. Keohane, and Sidney Verba. *Designing Social Inquiry: Scientific Inference in Qualitative Research.* Princeton: Princeton University Press, 1994.

Klarman, Michael J. *From Jim Crow to Civil Rights: The Supreme Court and the Struggle for Racial Equality.* New York: Oxford University Press, 2004.

———. "Majoritarian Judicial Review: The Entrenchment Problem." *Geo. L. J.* 85 (1996): 491.

———. "Race and the Court in the Progressive Era: Rethinking *Buchanan v. Warley.*" *Vand. L. Rev.* 51 (1998): 881.

———. "The Racial Origins of Modern Criminal Procedure." *Mich. L. Rev.* 99, no. 1 (2000): 48–97.

―――. "Rethinking the Civil Rights and Civil Liberties Revolutions." *Va. L. Rev.* 82, no. 1 (1996): 1–67.

Kleinerman, Benjamin A. *The Discretionary President: The Promise and Peril of Executive Power.* Lawrence: University Press of Kansas, 2009.

Klinkner, Philip A., with Rogers M. Smith. *The Unsteady March: The Rise and Decline of Racial Equality in America.* Chicago: University of Chicago Press, 1999.

Kovarsky, Lee. "AEDPA's Wrecks: Comity, Finality, and Federalism." *Tul. L. Rev.* 82 (2007): 443.

Kramer, Larry D. "When Lawyers Do History, Marbury and Its Legacy: A Symposium to Mark the 200th Anniversary of *Marbury v. Madison*: The Constitutional Origins of Judicial Review." *Geo. Wash. L. Rev.* 72 (2003): 387.

Kutler, Stanley I. *Judicial Power and Reconstruction Politics.* Chicago: University of Chicago Press, 1968.

Labbe, Ronald M., and Jonathan Luric. *The Slaughterhouse Cases: Regulation, Reconstruction, and the Fourteenth Amendment.* Lawrence: University Press of Kansas, 2003.

Lain, Corinna Barrett. "Countermajoritarian Hero or Zero—Rethinking the Warren Court's Role in the Criminal Procedure Revolution." *U. Pa. L. Rev.* 152 (2003): 1361.

Lamb, Stephen C., and Charles M. Halpern. "The Supreme Court and New Constitutional Eras." *Brook. L. Rev.* 64 (1998): 1183.

Lasser, William. *The Limits of Judicial Power: The Supreme Court in American Politics.* Chapel Hill: University of North Carolina Press, 1988.

―――. "The Supreme Court in Periods of Critical Realignment." *Journal of Politics* 47, no. 4 (1985): 1174–1187.

Latner, Richard B. "The Nullification Crisis and Republican Subversion." *Journal of Southern History* 43, no. 1 (1977): 19–38.

Lee, Evan Tsen. "Section 2254(D) of the New Habeas Statute: An (Opinionated) User's Manual." *Vand. L. Rev.* 51 (1998): 101.

―――. "The Theories of Federal Habeas Corpus." *Wash. U. L. Q.* 72 (1994).

Leslie, William R. "The Pennsylvania Fugitive Slave Act of 1826." *Journal of Southern History* 18, no. 4 (1952): 429–445.

Levinson, Sanford. "Some Reflections on the Rehabilitation of the Privileges or Immunities Clause of the Fourteenth Amendment." *Harv. J. L. & Pub. Pol'y* 12 (1989): 71.

Levy, Leonard W. "Sims' Case: The Fugitive Slave Law in Boston in 1851." *Journal of Negro History* 35, no. 1 (1950): 39–74.

Lewis, Anthony. *Gideon's Trumpet.* New York: Random House, 1964.

Liebman, James S. "Apocalypse Next Time? The Anachronistic Attack on Habeas Corpus/Direct Review Parity." *Colum. L. Rev.* 92, no. 8 (1992): 1997–2097.

―――. "Effective Death Penalty: AEDPA and Error Detection in Capital Cases." *Brook. L. Rev.* 67 (2001): 411.

―――. *Federal Habeas Corpus Practice and Procedure.* Charlottesville, Va.: Michie, 1994.

Liebman, James S., and William F. Ryan. "Some Effectual Power: The Quantity and Quality of Decisionmaking Required of Article III Courts." *Colum. L. Rev.* 98 (1998): 696.

Lincoln, Abraham. *The Collected Works of Abraham Lincoln.* Edited by Roy Basler. New Brunswick: Rutgers University Press, 1953.

Litwack, Leon F. *North of Slavery: The Negro in the Free States, 1790–1860.* Chicago: University of Chicago Press, 1961.

Lovell, George I. *Legislative Deferrals: Statutory Ambiguity, Judicial Power, and American Democracy.* New York: Cambridge University Press, 2003.

Madison, James. *Notes of Debates in the Federal Convention of 1787.* New York: Norton, 1987.

Magliocca, Gerard N. *Andrew Jackson and the Constitution: The Rise and Fall of Generational Regimes.* Lawrence: University Press of Kansas, 2007.

Maltz, Earl M. *Slavery and the Supreme Court, 1825–1861.* Lawrence: University Press of Kansas, 2009.

Mayers, Lewis. "The Habeas Corpus Act of 1867: The Supreme Court as Legal Historian." *U. Chi. L. Rev.* 33 (1965): 31.

Mayhew, David R. *Electoral Realignments: A Critique of an American Genre.* New Haven, Conn.: Yale University Press, 2002.

McCloskey, Robert G. *The American Supreme Court.* Chicago: University of Chicago Press, 2005.

McDowell, Gary L., and Judith A. Baer. "Fourteenth Amendment: Should the Bill of Rights Apply to the States?" *Utah L. Rev.* 1987 (1987): 951.

McFeeley, Neil. "Habeas Corpus and Due Process: From Warren to Burger." *Baylor L. Rev.* 28 (1976): 533.

McFeeley, Neil D. "A Change of Direction: Habeas Corpus from Warren to Burger." *Western Political Quarterly* 32, no. 2 (1979): 174–188.

McFeeley, Neil Douglas. "The Historical Development of Habeas Corpus." *Sw. L. J.* 30 (1976): 585.

McIlwain, C. H. "Due Process of Law in Magna Carta." *Colum. L. Rev.* 14 (1914).

McKitrick, Eric L. *Andrew Johnson and Reconstruction.* Chicago: University of Chicago Press, 1964.

McMahon, Kevin J. *Reconsidering Roosevelt on Race: How the Presidency Paved the Road to Brown.* Chicago: University of Chicago Press, 2004.

Meador, Daniel John. *Habeas Corpus and Magna Carta: Dualism of Power and Liberty.* Charlottesville: University Press of Virginia, 1966.

Meese, Edwin, III, and Rhett DeHart. "Reining in the Federal Judiciary." *Judicature* 80 (1996): 178.

Meltzer, Daniel J. "Habeas Corpus Jurisdiction: The Limits of Models. The Future of Habeas Corpus: Reflections on *Teague v. Lane* and Beyond." *S. Cal. L. Rev.* 66 (1992): 2507.

Miller, Charles A. *The Supreme Court and the Uses of History.* Cambridge, Mass.: Belknap Press of Harvard University Press, 1969.

Miller, Geoffrey P. "The President's Power of Interpretation: Implications of a Unified Theory of Constitutional Law." *Law and Contemporary Problems* 56, no. 4 (1993): 35–61.

Mishler, William, and Reginald S. Sheehan. "The Supreme Court as a Countermajoritarian Institution? The Impact of Public Opinion on Supreme Court Decisions." *American Political Science Review* 87, no. 1 (1993): 87–101.

Morris, Thomas D. *Free Men All: The Personal Liberty Laws of the North, 1780–1861.* Baltimore: Johns Hopkins University Press, 1974.

Morrison, Stanley. "Does the Fourteenth Amendment Incorporate the Bill of Rights? The Judicial Interpretation." *Stan. L. Rev.* 2 (1949): 140.

Murphy, Paul L., ed. *The Constitution in Crisis Times, 1918–1969.* New York: Harper & Row, 1971.

——. "Time to Reclaim: The Current Challenge of American Constitutional History." *American Historical Review* 69, no. 1 (1963): 64–79.

Murphy, Walter F. "Civil Liberties and the Japanese American Cases: A Study in the Uses of *Stare Decisis.*" *Western Political Quarterly* 11, no. 1 (1958): 3–13.

——. "Who Shall Interpret? The Quest for the Ultimate Constitutional Interpreter." *Review of Politics* 48, no. 3 (1986): 401–423.

Murphy, Walter F., James Fleming, Sotirios Barber, and Stephen Macedo. *American Constitutional Interpretation.* 4th ed. New York: Foundation Press, 2008.

Murphy, Walter F., and Joseph Tanenhaus. "Public Opinion and Supreme Court: The Goldwater Campaign." *Public Opinion Quarterly* 32, no. 1 (1968): 31–50.

——. "Public Opinion and the United States Supreme Court—Mapping of Some Prerequisites for Court Legitimation of Regime Changes." *Law & Soc'y Rev.* 2 (1967): 357.

Nardulli, Peter F. "The Concept of a Critical Realignment, Electoral Behavior, and Political Change." *American Political Science Review* 89, no. 1 (1995): 10–22.

Neely, Mark E. *The Fate of Liberty: Abraham Lincoln and Civil Liberties.* New York: Oxford University Press, 1991.

Nelson, William E. "The Eighteenth-Century Background of John Marshall's Constitutional Jurisprudence." *Mich. L. Rev.* 76 (1977): 893.

——. *The Fourteenth Amendment: From Political Principle to Judicial Doctrine.* Cambridge, Mass.: Harvard University Press, 1988.

Nixon, Richard. *Richard Nixon: Speeches, Writings, Documents.* Edited by Rick Perlstein. Princeton: Princeton University Press, 2008.

O'Connor, Sandra D. "Trends in the Relationship between the Federal and State Courts from the Perspective of a State Court Judge Symposium: State Courts and Federalism in the 1980s." *Wm. & Mary L. Rev.* 22 (1980): 801.

Oaks, Dallin H. "Habeas Corpus in the States—1776–1865." *U. Chi. L. Rev.* 32 (1964): 243.

——. "Legal History in the High Court—Habeas Corpus." *Mich. L. Rev.* 64 (1965): 451.

——. "The Original Writ of Habeas Corpus in the Supreme Court." *Sup. Ct. Rev.* 1962 (1962): 153.

Oates, Stephen B. *With Malice toward None: The Life of Abraham Lincoln.* New York: Harper & Row, 1977.

Orren, Karen, and Stephen Skowronek. "Regimes and Regime Building in American Government: A Review of Literature on the 1940s." *Political Science Quarterly* 113, no. 4 (1998): 689–702.

——. *The Search for American Political Development.* New York: Cambridge University Press, 2004.

Paludan, Phillip Shaw. *A Covenant with Death: The Constitution, Law, and Equality in the Civil War Era.* Urbana: University of Illinois Press, 1975.

Paschal, Francis. "The Constitution and Habeas Corpus." *Duke L. J.* 1970 (1970): 605.

Paulsen, Michael Stokes. "The Merryman Power and the Dilemma of Autonomous Executive Branch Interpretation." *Cardozo L. Rev.* 15 (1993): 81.

————. "The Most Dangerous Branch: Executive Power to Say What the Law Is." *Geo. L. J.* 83 (1994): 217.

Peller, Gary. "In Defense of Federal Habeas Corpus Relitigation." *Harv. CR-CL L. Rev.* 16 (1982): 579.

Perlstein, Rick. *Before the Storm: Barry Goldwater and the Unmaking of the American Consensus.* New York: Hill and Wang, 2001.

Perlstein, Rick, ed. *Nixonland: The Rise of a President and the Fracturing of America.* New York: Scribner, 2008.

Perry, Michael J. *We the People: The Fourteenth Amendment and the Supreme Court.* New York: Oxford University Press, 1999.

Pickerill, J. Mitchell, and Cornell W. Clayton. "The Rehnquist Court and the Political Dynamics of Federalism." *Perspectives on Politics* 2, no. 2 (2004): 233–248.

Post, Robert C. "Defending the Lifeworld: Substantive Due Process in the Taft Court Era." *B. U. L. Rev.* 78 (1998): 1489.

Potter, David Morris. *The Impending Crisis, 1848–1861.* New York: Harper & Row, 1976.

Powe, Lucas A. "The Politics of American Judicial Review: Reflections on the Marshall, Warren, and Rehnquist Courts." *Wake Forest L. Rev.* 38 (2003): 697.

————. *The Warren Court and American Politics.* Cambridge, Mass.: Harvard University Press, 2000.

Powell, Lewis F., Jr. "Capital Punishment." *Harv. L. Rev.* 102 (1988): 1035.

————. "Our Bill of Rights." *Ind. L. Rev.* 25 (1991): 937.

Primus, Richard A. *The American Language of Rights.* New York: Cambridge University Press, 1999.

Radin, Max. "The Myth of Magna Carta." *Harv. L. Rev.* 60 (1946): 1060.

Randall, James G. "The Indemnity Act of 1863: A Study in War-Time Immunity of Governmental Officers." *Mich. L. Rev.* 20 (1921): 596.

Rehnquist, William H., ed. *All the Laws but One: Civil Liberties in Wartime.* New York: Vintage Books, 2000.

Reid, John Phillip. *The Ancient Constitution and the Origins of Anglo-American Liberty.* DeKalb: Northern Illinois University Press, 2005.

Rogin, Michael. *"Ronald Reagan," the Movie, and Other Episodes in Political Demonology.* Berkeley: University of California Press, 1987.

Rosen, Jeffrey. *The Most Democratic Branch: How the Courts Serve America.* New York: Oxford University Press, 2006.

Rosenberg, Irene, and Yale Rosenberg. "Guilt: Henry Friendly Meets the Maharal of Prague." *Mich. L. Rev.* 90 (1991): 604.

Rossiter, Clinton. *Constitutional Dictatorship: Crisis Government in the Modern Democracies.* Princeton: Princeton University Press, 1948.

Rostow, Eugene V. "The Japanese American Cases: A Disaster." *Yale L. J.* 54, no. 3 (1945): 489–533.

Salyer, Lucy. *Laws Harsh as Tigers: Chinese Immigrants and the Shaping of Modern Immigration Law*. Chapel Hill: University of North Carolina Press, 1995.

Schmidt, Benno C., Jr. "Principle and Prejudice: The Supreme Court and Race in the Progressive Era, Part 1: The Heyday of Jim Crow." *Colum. L. Rev.* 82 (1982): 444.

———. "Principle and Prejudice: The Supreme Court and Race in the Progressive Era, Part 3: Black Disfranchisement from the KKK to the Grandfather Clause." *Colum. L. Rev.* 82 (1982): 835 [i].

Scigliano, Robert G. *The Supreme Court and the Presidency*. New York: Free Press, 1971.

Segal, Jeffrey Allan, and Harold J. Spaeth. *The Supreme Court and the Attitudinal Model Revisited*. New York: Cambridge University Press, 2002.

Seidman, Louis Michael. "Factual Guilt and the Burger Court: An Examination of Continuity and Change in Criminal Procedure." *Colum. L. Rev.* 80 (1980): 436.

Semeraro, Steven. "Two Theories of Habeas Corpus." *Brook. L. Rev.* 71 (2005): 1233.

Shapiro, Martin. "Judicial Modesty: Down with the Old—Up with the New." *UCLA L. Rev.* 10 (1962): 533.

Sherman, Richard B. *The Republican Party and Black America from McKinley to Hoover, 1896–1933*. Charlottesville: University Press of Virginia, 1973.

Shufeldt, Robert W. *The Negro: A Menace to Civilization*. Boston: Richard G. Badger, 1907.

Silbey, Joel H. *The American Political Nation, 1838–1893*. Stanford, Calif.: Stanford University Press, 1991.

Skinner, Quentin. "Meaning and Understanding in the History of Ideas." *History and Theory* 8, no. 1 (1969): 3–53.

Skowronek, Stephen. *The Politics Presidents Make: Leadership from John Adams to Bill Clinton*. Cambridge, Mass.: The Belknap Press of Harvard University Press, 1997.

Smith, Jean Edward, ed. *John Marshall: Definer of a Nation*. New York: Holt, 1996.

Smith, Rogers M. *Civic Ideals: Conflicting Visions of Citizenship in U.S. History*. New Haven, Conn.: Yale University Press, 1997.

———. "Political Jurisprudence, the 'New Institutionalism,' and the Future of Public Law." *American Political Science Review* 82, no. 1 (1988): 89–108.

Steiker, Jordan. "Innocence and Federal Habeas." *UCLA L. Rev.* 41 (1993): 303.

Steinman, Adam N. "Reconceptualizing Federal Habeas Corpus for State Prisoners: How Should AEDPA's Standard of Review Operate after *Williams v. Taylor*?" *Wis. L. Rev.* 2001 (2001): 1493.

Stephenson, Donald Grier. *Campaigns and the Court: The U.S. Supreme Court in Presidential Elections*. New York: Columbia University Press, 1999.

Sugrue, Thomas J. *Sweet Land of Liberty: The Forgotten Struggle for Civil Rights in the North*. New York: Random House, 2008.

Sundquist, James L. *Dynamics of the Party System: Alignment and Realignment of Political Parties in the United States*. Washington: The Brookings Institution, 1973.

Sunstein, Cass R. "The Idea of a Useable Past." *Colum. L. Rev.* 95 (1995): 601.

Swisher, Carl. *History of the Supreme Court of the United States: The Taney Period, 1836–64*. New York: Macmillan, 1974.

Tamanaha, Brian Z. *Beyond the Formalist–Realist Divide: The Role of Politics in Judging.* Princeton: Princeton University Press, 2010.

Teles, Steven M. *The Rise of the Conservative Legal Movement: The Battle for Control of the Law.* Princeton: Princeton University Press, 2008.

Tepker, Rick. "The Dean Takes His Stand: Julian Monnet's 1912 *Harvard Law Review* Article Denouncing Oklahoma's Discriminatory Grandfather Clause." *Okla. L. Rev.* 62 (2010): 427.

Thomas, George. *The Madisonian Constitution.* Baltimore: Johns Hopkins University Press, 2008.

Thompson, Seymour D. "Abuses of the Writ of Habeas Corpus." *Am. L. Rev.* 18 (1884): 1.

Tucker, St. George. *Blackstone's Commentaries: With Notes of Reference, to the Constitution and Laws, of the Federal Government of the United States; and of the Commonwealth of Virginia.* Vol. 4. 1803.

Tushnet, Mark. "The Burger Court in Historical Perspective: The Triumph of Country-Club Republicanism." In *The Burger Court: Counter-Revolution or Confirmation?,* edited by Bernard Schwartz, 203–215. New York: Oxford University Press, 1998.

Tushnet, Mark, ed. *The Constitution in Wartime: Beyond Alarmism and Complacency.* Durham, N.C.: Duke University Press, 2005.

Tushnet, Mark, and Larry Yackle. "Symbolic Statutes and Real Laws: The Pathologies of the Antiterrorism and Effective Death Penalty Act and the Prison Litigation Reform Act." *Duke L. J.* 47 (1997): 1.

Tushnet, Mark V. *The New Constitutional Order.* Princeton: Princeton University Press, 2003.

———. "Progressive Era Race Relations Cases in Their Traditional Context." *Vand. L. Rev.* 51 (1998): 993.

———. *The Warren Court in Historical and Political Perspective.* Constitutionalism and Democracy. Charlottesville: University Press of Virginia, 1993.

Van Alstyne, William W. "A Critical Guide to *Ex Parte McCardle.*" *Ariz. L. Rev.* 15 (1973): 229.

Vladeck, Stephen I. "AEDPA, Saucier, and the Stronger Case for Rights-First Constitutional Adjudication." *Seattle U. L. Rev.* 32 (2008): 595.

———. "Boumediene's Quiet Theory: Access to Courts and the Separation of Powers." *Notre Dame L. Rev.* 84 (2008): 2107.

Vorenberg, Michael. *Final Freedom: The Civil War, the Abolition of Slavery, and the Thirteenth Amendment.* Cambridge: Cambridge University Press, 2001.

Warren, Charles. "Federal and State Court Interference." *Harv. L. Rev.* 43 (1929): 345.

———. "New Light on the History of the Federal Judiciary Act of 1789." *Harv. L. Rev.* 37 (1923): 49.

———. *The Supreme Court in United States History.* Washington, D.C.: Beard Books, 1999.

Wechsler, Herbert. "The Political Safeguards of Federalism: The Role of the States in the Composition and Selection of the National Government." *Colum. L. Rev.* 54 (1954): 543.

Wert, Justin J. "Nothing New under the Sun: Habeas Corpus and Executive Power during the Bush Administration." *American Review of Politics* 29 (2009): 273–289.

———. "With a Little Help from a Friend: Habeas Corpus and Magna Carta after Runnymede." *PS: Political Science and Politics* 43, no. 3 (2010).

White, G. Edward. "The Arrival of History in Constitutional Scholarship." *Va. L. Rev.* 88 (2002): 485.

White, G. Edward, and Gerald Gunther. *The Marshall Court and Cultural Change, 1815–35.* History of the Supreme Court of the United States. New York: Macmillan, 1988.

Whittington, Keith E. *Constitutional Construction: Divided Powers and Constitutional Meaning.* Cambridge, Mass.: Harvard University Press, 1999.

———. "'Interpose Your Friendly Hand': Political Supports for the Exercise of Judicial Review by the United States Supreme Court." *American Political Science Review* 99, no. 4 (2005): 583–596.

———. "Once More unto the Breach: Postbehavioralist Approaches to Judicial Politics." *Law & Soc. Inquiry* 25 (2000): 601.

———. *Political Foundations of Judicial Supremacy: The Presidency, the Supreme Court, and Constitutional Leadership in U.S. History.* Princeton: Princeton University Press, 2007.

———. "Presidential Challenges to Judicial Supremacy and the Politics of Constitutional Meaning." *Polity* 33, no. 3 (2001): 365–395.

Wiecek, William M. "Clio as Hostage: The United States Supreme Court and the Uses of History Bicentennial Constitutional and Legal History Symposium." *Cal. W. L. Rev.* 24 (1987): 227.

———. "The Great Writ and Reconstruction: The Habeas Corpus Act of 1867." *Journal of Southern History* 36, no. 4 (1970): 530–548.

———. *The Guarantee Clause of the U.S. Constitution.* Ithaca, N.Y.: Cornell University Press, 1972.

———. *Liberty under Law: The Supreme Court in American Life.* Baltimore: Johns Hopkins University Press, 1988.

———. "The Reconstruction of Federal Judicial Power, 1863–1875." *Am. J. Legal Hist.* 13 (1969): 333.

Wilentz, Sean, ed. *The Age of Reagan: A History, 1974–2008.* New York: Harper, 2008.

Wood, Gordon S. *Empire of Liberty: A History of the Early Republic, 1789–1815.* New York: Oxford University Press, 2009.

Woodward, C. Vann. *The Strange Career of Jim Crow.* New York: Oxford University Press, 1966.

Woolhandler, Ann. "Demodeling Habeas." *Stan. L. Rev.* 45 (1992): 575.

Yackle, Larry. *Federal Courts: Habeas Corpus.* New York: Foundation Press, 2003.

———. "Federal Habeas Corpus in a Nutshell." *Hum. Rts.* 28 (2001): 7.

Yackle, Larry W. "Explaining Habeas Corpus." *N.Y.U. L. Rev.* 60 (1985): 991.

———. "The Habeas Hagioscope." *S. Cal. L. Rev.* 66 (1992): 2331.

———. "A Primer on the New Habeas Corpus Statute." *Buff. L. Rev.* 44 (1996): 381.

———. "The Reagan Administration's Habeas Corpus Proposals." *Iowa L. Rev.* 68 (1982): 609.

Yalof, David A. *Pursuit of Justices: Presidential Politics and the Selection of Supreme Court Nominees.* Chicago: University of Chicago Press, 1999.

Yarbrough, Tinsley E. *The Rehnquist Court and the Constitution.* Oxford: Oxford University Press, 2000.

Yoo, John. *The Powers of War and Peace: The Constitution and Foreign Affairs after 9/11.* Chicago: University of Chicago Press, 2005.

————. *War by Other Means: An Insider's Account of the War on Terror.* New York: Atlantic Monthly Press, 2006.

Zelizer, Julian E. *Arsenal of Democracy: The Politics of National Security from World War II to the War on Terrorism.* New York: Basic Books, 2009.

Index